Interindustry

economics

*NEW YORK · JOHN WILEY & SONS, INC.*_____

London · Sydney

Hollis B. Chenery

Professor of Economics
Stanford University

Interindustry

economics

Paul G. Clark

Economist
The Rand Corporation

Associate Professor of Economics
Williams College

SIXTH PRINTING, FEBRUARY, 1967

Library of Congress Catalog Card Number: 59-11806

Printed in the United States of America

Preface

Although a formal analysis of the interdependence of economic units has been available since the time of Walras, the corresponding field of applied economics has developed only in the last twenty years. Its origin is in the pioneering work of Leontief, who first applied his input-output model to empirical studies in the 1930's. Since then, the input-output approach has developed greatly, and alternative models have been suggested. The resulting field of quantitative analysis, which we refer to as interindustry economics, is the subject of this book.

Postwar developments in interindustry economics have been stimulated by the interest of economists in a variety of problems that cannot be easily handled by either partial or aggregative analysis. Such problems arise when patterns of production undergo substantial changes, as in periods of reconstruction, balance of payments disequilibrium, defense mobilization, or accelerated economic development. The prevalence of such conditions in recent years has led a number of governmental and private research groups to undertake empirical studies based on Leontief's input-output model. At the same time, concern with allocation problems involving specific resource limitations has also stimulated the development of activity analysis and linear programming by Dantzig, Koopmans, and others. These methods add elements of choice to interindustry models and promise to improve their usefulness for analysis of economic policy.

Despite wide interest in the problems with which interindustry economics is concerned, it has remained a field for the specialist. Although the basic assumptions employed are as simple as those of Keynesian models, the large number of functional relations required for a realistic interindustry study makes the model more complex and its implications less obvious. The theoretical aspects of the field have therefore appealed mainly to mathematical economists, who have concentrated on elucidating the formal properties of the models employed. On the other hand, statistical implementation of the interindustry approach has fallen primarily to government agencies having the necessary substantial research resources at their disposal. There have been intrinsic difficulties in making such detailed and specialized data accessible to general economists.

The purpose of this book is to present a unified discussion of interindustry techniques and their empirical applications. Our main concern is with the substantive conclusions about the structure and performance of an economy that can be derived using the interindustry approach. We therefore stress theoretical models that appear best suited to the analysis of policy problems and that use existing statistical materials. We also investigate concrete examples of interindustry studies in some detail and try to evaluate the usefulness of their results. Our discussion is aimed primarily at general economists interested in a broad survey of the field, but we hope that it contains matters of interest to specialists as well.

The first part of the book gives an introduction to interindustry theory, starting with the simplest input-output model and developing more complicated systems by successive extensions. The range of possible formulations is illustrated by eight models, four in input-output form and four using linear programming, each of which is presented in verbal and algebraic form and in numerical examples. Since we are concerned with empirical studies, the data requirements of alternative models and the realism of underlying assumptions are considered in separate chapters on statistical implementation and empirical testing. The choice between the input-output and linear-programming formulations is shown to depend on the problem and the available data; various combinations of the two approaches are suggested.

The second part of the book discusses the main types of application for which interindustry analysis seems appropriate, illustrating each application with actual instances taken from interindustry experience in one or more countries. Here we have drawn heavily on studies made in the United States and Italy, the countries with which we are most familiar. Interindustry results for Japan, Norway, Denmark, Argentina, and Colombia are also discussed, and research under way in other countries is indicated wherever possible. The application given the greatest attention is the study of structural changes accompanying economic growth, a problem to which we feel input-output analysis and linear programming can make a unique contribution.

To a considerable extent, this approach to interindustry economics reflects our own experience in the field. We first worked with input-output as a tool of academic research at Harvard and then had occasion to make an extensive input-output study of the Italian economy directed at answering specific policy questions. We have since worked (separately) with interindustry research groups in the United States, Japan, and South America. An earlier version of Part I was used by Chenery in teaching interindustry analysis to graduate students and government economists at Stanford University, the University of Tokyo, and the United Nations Training Program in Economic Development in Santiago, Chile; we have tried to make the improvements suggested by this experience. Primary responsibility for the various chapters may be indicated as follows. Chenery: Chapters 1, 2, 3, 4, 8 (with the assistance of T. Watanabe), 11, 12. Clark: Chapters 5, 6, 7, 9, 10. However, the book is as completely a joint product as could be achieved in two extensive revisions, after innumerable discussions over the last twelve years.

Stanford, California Hollis B. Chenery
Santa Monica, California Paul G. Clark
March, 1959

Acknowledgments

Our greatest debt is to Wassily Leontief, who established the empirical field of interindustry analysis and who has been a valued teacher and critic of our efforts in this area.

Our study of the Italian economy, of which this book is a lineal descendant, was made possible by the support of the Directors of the U.S. Mutual Security Agency in Rome, Leon Dayton and Vincent Barnett, and by the dedicated work of the Italian staff of the Program Division, under Dr. Vera Cao-Pinna.

The evaluation of interindustry results in Part II of our book benefited greatly from discussions and correspondence with research workers in a number of countries: S. Shishido and T. Watanabe of Japan; V. Cao-Pinna, C. Righi, and C. Napoleoni of Italy; M. Balboa and P. Vuscovic of the Economic Commission for Latin America; P. Sevaldsen of Norway; B. Cameron of Australia; P. Mahalanobis of India; I. Stewart of Great Britain; and W. D. Evans, M. Hoffenberg, H. Barnett, F. Moore, R. Grosse, and the staff of the Harvard Economic Research Project in the United States. In many cases, they provided us with valuable unpublished materials.

In revising the manuscript for publication, we have been helped by the comments of K. Arrow, H. Houthakker, J. Hooper, J. Haldi, C. Howe, D. Bear, and G. Bickel of Stanford; and R. Boti and T. Vietorisz of the Economic Commission for Latin America. A special debt is

ix

owed Mathilda Holzman, who not only edited the entire manuscript but also managed to reconcile most of the authors' differences, stylistic and other. Mary Baird supervised the typing and assembling of successive drafts with great competence.

Studies of the application of interindustry techniques to problems of economic development, which form the basis for Chapters 4, 8, and 11, were done as part of the program of the Stanford Project for Quantitative Research in Economic Development under a grant from the Ford Foundation.

H. B. C.
P. G. C.

Contents

Summary of Notation

1 Introduction   1

    A. HISTORICAL DEVELOPMENT OF INTERINDUSTRY ECONOMICS   2
    B. PARTIAL, INTERINDUSTRY, AND AGGREGATE ANALYSES   4
    C. USES OF INTERINDUSTRY ECONOMICS   6
    D. OUTLINE OF THE BOOK   7

part I **Models of Structural Interdependence**

2 Basic Input-Output Theory   13

    A. THE INTERINDUSTRY ACCOUNTING SYSTEM   14
    B. BASIC INPUT-OUTPUT MODELS   22
    C. INTRODUCTION TO METHODS OF SOLUTION   25
    D. THE ASSUMPTIONS OF INPUT-OUTPUT ANALYSIS   33
    APPENDIX: INPUT-OUTPUT SOLUTIONS   43

3 Extensions of the Basic Model   55

    A. FINAL DEMAND AND PRIMARY INPUTS   56

xi

B. INDUCED CONSUMPTION AND INCOME GENERATION   63
C. INTERREGIONAL ANALYSIS   65
D. DYNAMIC MODELS OF CAPITAL FORMATION   71

4 Choice in Interindustry Models   81

A. INPUT-OUTPUT ANALYSIS AND LINEAR PROGRAMMING   82
B. CHOICE ON THE DEMAND SIDE   92
C. CHOICE ON THE SUPPLY SIDE   100
D. SOLUTION BY THE SIMPLEX METHOD USING PRICES   116
E. THE VALUATION OF PRIMARY FACTORS   123
F. ALTERNATIVE INTERINDUSTRY MODELS   126
   APPENDIX: SOLUTIONS TO INTERINDUSTRY PROGRAMMING
   MODELS   130

5 Empirical Bases for Interindustry Models   137

A. SIGNIFICANCE OF EMPIRICAL IMPLEMENTATION   137
B. BASIC INPUT-OUTPUT TABLES   138
C. SUPPLEMENTARY RELATIONSHIPS FOR INTERINDUSTRY
   MODELS   146

6 Testing the Validity of Input-Output Assumptions   157

A. THE CONSTANCY OF INPUT RATIOS   157
B. DIRECT TESTS OF INPUT RATIOS   158
C. OVERALL TESTS OF INPUT-OUTPUT PROJECTIONS   164

part II Applications of Interindustry
         Analysis

7 A Survey of Interindustry Research   183
A. RESEARCH IN SELECTED COUNTRIES   186
B. CHARACTERISTIC FEATURES OF INTERINDUSTRY RESEARCH   195

8 An International Comparison of the Structure of Production   201

A. BASIS FOR THE COMPARISON   202
B. THE NATURE OF INTERDEPENDENCE IN PRODUCTION   205
C. SIMILARITIES IN INPUT COEFFICIENTS   211
   APPENDIX   213

9   Structural Analysis   **232**

    A. NATURE OF STRUCTURAL ANALYSIS   232
    B. INDIVIDUAL INDUSTRIES   233
    C. INTERNATIONAL TRADE   241
    D. FINAL DEMANDS, PRIMARY FACTORS AND PRICES   246

10   Projection of the Economic Structure   **249**

    A. NATURE OF INTERINDUSTRY PROJECTION   249
    B. THE ITALIAN FIVE-YEAR EXPANSION GOALS   251
    C. EVALUATION OF THE ITALIAN PROJECTION   255
    D. PROJECTIONS FOR COLOMBIA AND ARGENTINA   267
    E. THE U.S. EMERGENCY MODEL   271

11   Resource Allocation in Development Programs   **278**

    A. STRUCTURAL DISEQUILIBRIUM IN UNDERDEVELOPED
       ECONOMIES   279
    B. DEVELOPMENT PROGRAMS IN PRACTICE   281
    C. THE USE OF LINEAR PROGRAMMING CONCEPTS   283
    D. A PILOT STUDY OF SOUTHERN ITALY   290
    E. PRACTICAL USE OF PROGRAMMING METHODS   298
       APPENDIX: DATA FOR THE PROGRAMMING MODEL OF
       SOUTHERN ITALY   301

12   Interregional Analysis   **308**

    A. COMPARISON OF INTERREGIONAL STUDIES   308
    B. REGIONAL INPUT-OUTPUT STUDIES   311
    C. INTERREGIONAL PROGRAMMING MODELS   323
    D. USES OF INTERREGIONAL ANALYSIS   329

13   The Future of Interindustry Analysis   **333**

    INDEX   337

Summary of notation

The symbols which are used with some frequency are listed below with the page on which they are defined. They represent a compromise among the various systems of notation used in input-output analysis and linear programming.

Variables[1, 2]		Defined on Page
Y_i	Autonomous or final demand for commodity i	15, 18
W_i	Intermediate use of commodity i	15, 18
Z_i	Total supply of commodity i	18
X_j	Gross production of commodity j (also activity level of activity j)	18, 85
M_j	Imports of commodity j (also level of import activity j)	18

[1] Subscripts are used for commodities and activities:

    (a) for produced commodities: $i = 1 \cdots m$
    (b) for primary inputs: $h = m + 1 \cdots m + l$
    (c) for activities and activity levels: $j = 1 \cdots n$

In general, h and i refer to rows or equations, j to columns. Variables without subscripts are totals (L, K, C, etc.)

[2] Superscripts are used for time and place:
    (a) Period: t
    (b) Region: α, β

E_j	Exports of commodity j (also level of export activity j)	16
U_j	Value of commodities purchased by sector j	18
X_{ij}	Use of commodity i in sector (activity) j	18
V_j	Value of primary factors (value added) used in sector j	18
P_i, P_h	Equilibrium (shadow) price of commodity or factor	61, 117
F_h	Use of factor h	60
L	Use of labor	58
K	Use of capital	58
B_i	Constant term in equation i (includes $Y_i, \bar{F}_h$)	86
C	Criterion or objective	86
D_i, D_h	Disposal of commodity i or non-use of factor h	87
Π_j	Profitability of activity j	118
Z_j	Gross value of activity j	118

Parameters (constants)[3]

a_{ij}	Input coefficient: direct use of commodity i by sector (activity) j	22
m_i	Import coefficient $\left(\dfrac{M_i}{X_i}\right)$	23
r_{ij}	Total direct and indirect use of commodity i by sector j (element in inverse matrix)	25
f_{hj}	Direct use of primary factor h by sector j	58, 87
r_{hj}	Total direct and indirect use of primary factor h by sector j	60
c_j	Direct effect of activity j on the criterion C	86

Vectors and Matrices

$\mathbf{A}_j$	Activity j (or column of input coefficients in sector j)	84
$\mathbf{A}$	Technology matrix of input coefficients $[a_{ij}]$ (in linear programming, matrix of input and output coefficients)	47, 84
$(\mathbf{I} - \mathbf{A})$	Leontief matrix	49
$\mathbf{Y}$	Vector of final demands	47
$\mathbf{X}$	Vector of activity levels (program)	47, 85
$\mathbf{R}$	Inverse matrix of input-output system	50
$\mathbf{B}$	Vector of restrictions	85
$\boldsymbol{\alpha}_j$	Equivalent combination vector of activity j	132

[3] Variables which are held constant in a given problem are sometimes indicated by a bar, as $\bar{Y}, \bar{F}$.

chapter 1

Introduction

Interindustry economics is concerned with quantitative analysis of the interdependence of producing and consuming units in a modern economy. In particular, it studies the interrelations among producers as buyers of each others' outputs, as users of scarce resources, and as sellers to final consumers.

Interindustry analysis is needed in a range of empirical problems for which the techniques of national income analysis and of partial equilibrium analysis are inadequate. For example, an increase in demand for automobiles will have quite a different effect on specific sectors of an economy from an increase in demand for housing or for clothing, but these differences are not distinguished in an aggregate analysis. Similarly, an estimate of the future demand for electric power cannot be made very adequately from a partial-equilibrium study of the existing power market alone but must also take into account the probable changes in output of the power-using industries. In both of these examples, some kind of analysis of interindustry relations is needed.

The theoretical background for interindustry economics is provided by the general equilibrium models of Walras and Pareto. These very comprehensive theories must be restricted in scope and simplified in form to enable the functional relations to be statistically determined, just as Keynesian theory is simplified in national-income analysis or Marshallian theory is simplified in studies of individual markets. In each case, the theoretical concepts have to be reformulated to some extent to facilitate measurement, and the resulting model takes on a character of its own. Since there are alternative simplifications which can be made, each must be tested against the available data to determine its usefulness. Such systems should therefore be regarded as working hypotheses which are used to guide empirical research and which are subject to revision as a result of it.

The first empirical interindustry model was formulated by Professor Wassily Leontief, whose system has come to be known as "input-output analysis." Recent theoretical developments, particularly the discovery of mathematical techniques of linear and nonlinear programming, have suggested alternative interindustry models. We shall therefore use the term "interindustry economics" in a broad sense to refer to any empirical analysis of economic phenomena which explicitly takes into account the interdependence among the productive units of an economy. Input-output analysis is probably only the first of several quantitative methods for handling such problems.

A. Historical Development of Interindustry Economics

Although intersectoral models in economics are customarily traced back to the *Tableau Economique* of Quesnay, published in 1758, the inspiration for modern work in this field comes from Leon Walras (1877). The Walrasian system states the interdependence among productive sectors of the economy in terms of the competing demands of each industry for factors of production and the substitutability among their outputs in consumption. Walras' model contains sets of equations for consumer income and expenditure, production cost in each sector, and total demand and supply of commodities and factors of production.[1]

The main use of this type of mathematical formulation has been to demonstrate the existence of determinate solutions for the quantities and prices in the system under assumptions of maximizing behavior. The Walrasian model has also been held up as an example of the emptiness of economic theory at this level of abstraction, since few

---

[1] The Walrasian system was perfected by Pareto and Cassel, and a more precise statement of the mathematical properties of its solution was given by Wald. The relationship of the Walrasian system to modern interindustry models is discussed in Balderston (1954), Kuenne (1954), and Dorfman, Samuelson and Solow (1958), Ch. 13.

interesting conclusions about economic reality can be drawn from the formal properties of the model, and the system as formulated does not lend itself to empirical verification.

Interindustry analysis as a form of applied economics begins with the work of Leontief. He started to do research on an empirical model of the American economy in 1931 and published his first results in 1936 and 1941. Leontief's approach was to simplify the Walrasian system to the extent necessary to derive a set of parameters for his model from a single observation of each of the interindustry transactions in the economy. He therefore omitted the effects of limited factor supplies from the system. He also used the original Walrasian assumption of fixed "coefficients of production" instead of allowing for substitution among inputs. In thus eliminating all effects of price on the composition of consumer demand, on the purchase of intermediate goods, and on the supply of labor and other factors, the Leontief model precludes many of the adjustments characterizing the Walrasian concept of general equilibrium.

One of the most valuable results of the first Leontief study was to stimulate empirical work on interindustry relations in a number of countries.[2] Input-output tables have now been compiled for more than twenty countries, the most elaborate being the U.S. Government study for 1947. The principal research will be discussed in Chapter 7. As in the case of national income research, the accumulation of statistical material has suggested alternative techniques of analysis, and there is now a considerable variety of input-output models in use. To distinguish them from the original, we shall use the term "Leontief model" for the analytical system developed by Professor Leontief, as given in the second edition of *The Structure of the American Economy* (1951).

The latest contribution to the field of interindustry economics is the mathematical technique of activity analysis or linear programming, developed first by Dantzig and Koopmans (see Koopmans, 1951). Although most of the applications of this technique have been to problems of single plants or firms, which will not concern us here, the method itself is also useful for industry-wide and interindustry analysis. Linear programming offers a way of getting around the restrictive assumption of constant input coefficients in each sector, while retaining a formulation which permits statistical measurement. This type of interindustry model will be discussed in Chapter 4.

[2] In a few countries, such as Denmark and the Netherlands, work on interindustry statistics antedated the formulation of econometric models for their use.

B. Partial, Interindustry, and Aggregative Analyses

A convenient introduction to the methodology of interindustry economics is provided by a comparison to the more familiar methods of partial and aggregative analysis. We are particularly interested in contrasting their purposes, basic assumptions, and limitations in empirical work.

The partial equilibrium system of Marshall and its derivatives may be regarded as one type of simplification of general equilibrium theory and the Leontief system as an opposite type. The main purpose of partial equilibrium analysis is to explain the reactions of producers and consumers of a given commodity to each other's behavior and thereby to determine price and output levels in a given market. Partial equilibrium analysis thus concentrates on one of the Walrasian sectors. It specifies the relations between this industry and its suppliers and consumers through sets of supply and demand functions. Each of these functions assumes no significant change in the other sectors. Variations in the levels of output of using industries or in the income of households appear as (unexplained) shifts in demand functions. Similarly, changes in other uses of inputs may cause shifts in the supply functions to the given sector.

The Leontief system is primarily concerned with this variation in elements that are taken as fixed in partial analysis. On the other hand, Leontief takes the equilibrium adjustment of input proportions in production as given and invariant throughout the analysis. Supply and demand in each market are equated, not through changes in price and resulting movements along supply and demand curves, but through a horizontal shift in the demand function of each industry resulting from changes in production levels in other sectors. The assumption of maximizing behavior, which is central to partial equilibrium analysis, plays no explicit role in the Leontief system. It is assumed that producers have little or no choice as to factor proportions in the short run and react to demand changes by changing output rather than price. (The assumptions under which this type of reaction is consistent with profit maximization are taken up in the next chapter.)

A *priori*, both these models seem to be drastic simplifications of the general equilibrium system. As such, they have explanatory value in isolating the effects of a particular set of variables and working out their interactions under *ceteris paribus* conditions. Whether or not they also have practical value in explaining observed phenomena or predicting future events depends in large part on the analyst's skill in either identifying cases in which the violations of the assumptions are relatively unimportant or in compensating for them where they are not negligible. It should be obvious, however, that in general a combination of both types of analysis will produce better results than will either of them alone.

Econometric studies designed to estimate the parameters in the functions used in partial analysis have been disappointing for the most part. Neither the supply nor the demand curve has proved subject to reliable statistical measurement. The most promising work on the supply side has been done for single plants by first estimating the underlying technologically determined production and cost functions. The derivation of production functions for a whole industry, however, presents obstacles which have not yet been satisfactorily overcome in many cases. It is this empirical difficulty rather than theoretical necessity which has been mainly responsible for the continued use of Leontief's original assumption of fixed input coefficients in most interindustry analysis.

Aggregative income analysis is closer methodologically to the input-output system than is partial analysis. Both income and input-output analyses rely more heavily on statistically determined uniformities in aggregate behavior than on deductions from theoretical propositions concerning the rational actions of representative units. Income analysis determines the level of total production or income from assumptions about its "autonomous" elements and the induced responses of the remaining components. Similarly, interindustry analysis determines levels of production in each sector from estimates of "final" uses of output and the assumed structure of production. In the next chapter, it is shown that these two types of model are very similar in their mathematical structure. For each type of Keynesian model—i.e., induced consumption, induced investment, etc.—there is a corresponding input-output model in which the Keynesian variables are disaggregated.

The basic difference between interindustry systems and more aggregative models is the explicit recognition in interindustry analysis of specific commodities having different production requirements and uses. The interindustry system is therefore able to show the differing effects on the rest of the economy of an increase in the demand for individual commodities, which in a Keynesian model would be indistinguishable parts of production and consumption. The choice between the two approaches for different types of problem will be considered in later chapters. Here it may be pointed out that the two techniques are entirely complementary. Their use together does not require a revision of the conceptual framework of the interindustry analysis, which would be needed if Marshallian analysis were to be combined with it.

C. Uses of Interindustry Economics

Applications of economic analysis fall into several categories according to their purpose and the nature of the assumptions that are made. For interindustry studies, it is useful to distinguish three types:

(1) Analysis of the economic structure;
(2) Formulation of programs of action;
(3) Prediction of future events.

The first—structural analysis—is designed to reveal the properties of a given model or economic principle in a particular context. For this purpose, it is desirable to abstract from factors which are not necessarily related to the mechanism being studied; hence the familiar *ceteris paribus* assumption. In models of any complexity, importance attaches to the interaction among the parameters. The investigation of such interaction for various hypothesized values of the autonomous variables may be called a structural analysis. An excellent example is Samuelson's study of the multiplier-accelerator interaction, in which the stability of the system is shown to depend on the values taken by both parameters. In input-output, a typical structural analysis would be the effect of an increase in exports on a given industry or factor of production.

The formulation of programs for government or business requires an analysis of the effects of a given type of action on certain economic variables. In general a model covering at least part of the economic system must be analyzed in quantitative terms. For example, policies of restricting imports or of expanding production of steel must take into account the needs of the steel-using sectors. Ideally, the analysis should be formulated in a way that will assist the choice among alternative policies and that will guide the execution of the policy agreed on. The type of economic model needed therefore depends both on the nature of the problem and the means available for achieving a solution.

The main distinction between program formulation and prediction is that for the latter some analysis must be made of *all* factors affecting a given outcome. Program formulation may therefore be thought of as conditional prediction; the two become identical only in the event that the conditions assumed in the program are actually fulfilled.

Interindustry techniques are useful for both structural analysis and policy guidance. So far, they have demonstrated only limited value for prediction. The main test of their contribution in a particular case is the extent to which the structure of interindustry transactions may be expected to be an important factor. The demand for steel, for example, is likely to be more dependent on the level of output in using industries than on its price. The simplifications of the input-output model (i.e., neglecting price effects) will therefore have less effect on the result in this case than will those of the partial equilibrium model (i.e., assuming all other demands constant). The contrary would be true of an analysis of the respective demands for butter and margarine, however. Similarly, income analysis has serious deficiencies as a basis for a program of industrialization or mobilization, because it does not take account of the bottlenecks which may occur as the result of rapid changes in the composition of demand or supply. On the other hand, aggregate models may be quite adequate (and much easier to apply) for the analysis of cyclical events in which change in the composition of production is not a significant factor.

Most academic research in this field has been designed to reveal the quantitative significance of various types of interdependence. This kind of study is invaluable for the validation and improvement of these techniques, but it is not directly concerned with economic policy. Other work in the interindustry field, both in the U.S. and abroad, has been stimulated primarily by the prospects for developing a technique which would have practical value in guiding decisions in government and business. The U.S. government research program of 1950–1954 was designed to analyze problems of mobilization. A principal aim of government-sponsored interindustry research in Denmark, Norway, Italy, the Netherlands, and Japan has been to determine the relation of imports and exports to domestic production and to guide policy affecting them. In the less developed countries—Argentina, Colombia, Mexico, Peru, Puerto Rico, India, Yugoslavia, and others—work on input-output analysis has been undertaken as an aid to planning economic development.

D. Outline of the Book

The use of any analytical tool requires an understanding of both its theoretical form and its empirical content. These will be covered in Part I of our study. Interindustry theory is presented in three chapters, going from simple models to more complicated ones. Methods of solution are introduced at an early stage so that the reader can work out numerical examples as he goes along. Chapters 2 and 3 discuss input-output theory deriving from the Leontief system, and Chapter 4 develops linear programming techniques for use within an empirical interindustry framework. Chapter 5 discusses the principal statistical problems involved in constructing input-output models and the merits of the solutions adopted in various countries. Finally, in Chapter 6 we try to evaluate the tests that have been made of the validity of input-output assumptions and the possibility of devising more useful tests.

Part II is concerned with various types of application that have been made of interindustry techniques. Research in ten leading countries is surveyed in Chapter 7, which indicates the diversity in purpose and statistical approach that now exists. In Chapter 8 we use the statistical data from four countries—the United States, Japan, Norway, and Italy —as a basis for a comparison of their economic structures. Our purpose is to ascertain similarities and differences in interindustry relations and to give the reader some feel for interindustry data.

The remainder of Part II illustrates specific types of problems for which interindustry analysis seems particularly promising. Each chapter outlines the methods used for a given type of study and then discusses two or three examples in some detail. Most of the examples are chosen from the countries for which the greatest variety of applications has been published—the United States and Italy. Chapters 9 and 12 cover several types of structural analysis; 10 and 11 are concerned with the formulation of economic programs.

Since wide-scale experimentation with interindustry techniques is only about ten years old, the main efforts have been devoted to input-output statistics and less has been done with applications. The work currently under way in Japan, the United Kingdom, Norway, Australia, Latin America, India, and other areas suggests that this balance is being righted, however, and that a much greater variety of applications will be forthcoming in the near future.

BIBLIOGRAPHY [3]

Balderston, J., "Models of General Economic Equilibrium," in *Economic Activity Analysis* (O. Morgenstern, ed.), John Wiley and Sons, New York, 1954.

[3] Selected bibliographies will be given at the end of each chapter, the complete reference being given the first time an item is mentioned. In Part I, selections

*Barna, T., "Introduction," in *The Structural Interdependence of the Economy* (T. Barna, ed.), John Wiley and Sons, New York, 1956.

Dorfman, R., P. Samuelson, and R. Solow, *Linear Programming and Economic Analysis*, McGraw-Hill Book Company, New York, 1958.

Koopmans, T. C. (ed.), *Activity Analysis of Production and Allocation*, Cowles Commission Monograph No. 13, John Wiley and Sons, New York, 1951.

*Kuenne, R., "Walras, Leontief, and the Interdependence of Economic Activities," *Quarterly Journal of Economics*, LXVIII, No. 3, 323–354 (August 1954).

Leontief, W. (1936), "Quantitative Input-Output Relations in the Economic System of the United States," *Review of Economics and Statistics*, XVIII, No. 3, 105–125 (August 1936).

*———. (1951), *The Structure of the American Economy, 1919–1939*, Oxford University Press, New York, second edition, 1951.

(The first three parts of this book reproduce the text of the 1941 edition without change; Part IV comprises four chapters which originally appeared in articles on the application of the input-output system.)

Phillips, A., "The Tableau Economique as a Simple Leontief Model," *Quarterly Journal of Economics*, LXIX, No. 1, 137–144 (February 1955).

Walras, L., *Elements of Pure Economics* (W. Jaffe, tr.), Richard D. Irwin, Homewood, Illinois, 1954.

---

particularly recommended for supplementary reading on interindustry theory are starred. A more complete bibliography will be found in V. Riley and R. L. Allen, *Interindustry Economic Studies*, Operations Research Office, Johns Hopkins University, 1955.

part I

Models of structural interdependence

chapter **2**

Basic input-output theory

This chapter covers the basic theoretical elements of the simplest
kind of interindustry analysis—Leontief's input-output model. The
possibilities for more complex formulations to increase the realism of
the system are very wide, but most of them can be treated as generalizations of this simple model. We first present the most elementary—
and therefore least realistic—form of the input-output model. Like
the simplest Keynesian model, it is based on a single type of structural
relationship and serves mainly as an introduction to a body of theory.
A variety of elaborations will be taken up in the two following chapters.

Like all formal economic models, the input-output system is derived
from assumptions about economic behavior and definitions of the variables used in the analysis. It will be convenient to start with the conceptual basis of the input-output accounting system, which simply
provides a framework for measuring the flows of current inputs and
outputs between the various sectors of the economy. A comparison
of this accounting system to the national income formulation of the
same set of data should make clear the complementary relation between the two kinds of analysis. We then consider Leontief's assumptions about the input-output relations within the several sectors. The
combination of these assumptions with the accounting definitions,

13

when reduced to algebraic form, constitutes the input-output model.
After a brief introduction to methods of solving the equations in such
a model, we proceed to examine the economic justification for simplifying reality in this particular way.

A. The Interindustry Accounting System[1]

Since interindustry analysis is concerned with interrelations arising
from production, the main function of interindustry accounts is to
trace the flow of goods and services from one productive sector to another. The principal features of interindustry accounts are shown by
the example in Table 2.1. This table, which is called a transactions

TABLE 2.1. EXAMPLE OF INTERINDUSTRY ACCOUNTS*

Producing Sectors	S	A	B	F	Total Intermediate Use (W_i)	Final Use (Y_i)	Total Use (Z_i)
Services	20	25	15	80	140	60	200
Agriculture	0	25	0	120	145	105	250
Basic industry	0	25	45	40	110	40	150
Finished goods	0	0	0	80	80	320	400
Total purchases (U_j)	20	75	60	320	475		
Primary inputs (V_j)	180	175	90	80		525	
Total output (X_j)	200	250	150	400			1000

(Column group header over S A B F: "Using Sectors")

* Based on the Italian input-output data shown in Table 8.12, below.
Imports are omitted for simplicity. Arbitrary value units are assumed.

matrix, covers all the goods and services produced in an economy. It
is distinguished by the fact that production activities are grouped together into a number of sectors, of which four are shown here (services, agriculture, basic industry, finished goods). Tables in actual use
range in size from 20 to 200 productive sectors.[2]

Each sector appears in the accounting system twice, as a producer
of output and as a user of inputs. The elements in each row of the
table show the disposition made of the output of that sector during

[1] Although the input-output accounting system has considerable interest apart
from its use in an economic model, it is only the latter aspect which concerns us
here. The system is discussed from a statistical point of view in Chapter 5.

[2] The reader should refer to the four actual input-output tables in Chapter 8.

the given accounting period. For example, of the total available products of basic industry (150 units) 25 are used by agriculture, 45 by
establishments in the basic industry sector itself, and 40 by producers
of finished goods. The total intermediate use—i.e., use for further production—is therefore 110. The remaining uses—for investment, private consumption, government consumption, or exports—are lumped
together here as "final use." The units employed may be either values
(e.g., a million dollars' worth) or physical quantities, but we shall
follow Leontief in using value units (measured in constant prices).

The role of basic industry as a purchaser of inputs is shown by
column B. The total purchased from all industries is 60; the remainder of 90 units consists of "primary" or unproduced inputs. In
an accounting sense, this direct payment for primary factors—land,
labor, and capital—comprises the value added in the sector. Since
imports have been omitted from this example, the total value of output of each commodity is equal to its total use.[3]

The relative importance of intermediate and final use and the order
of magnitude of the sales from one sector to another in an industrial
economy are also illustrated by Table 2.1, which is based on the
actual input-output table for Italy given in Chapter 8. The average
ratio of intermediate to total use, shown here as 475 out of 1000, varies
between 40% and 50% in the four cases studied below. There is, however, a considerable variation in this ratio for individual sectors, represented here by the range from 20% for finished goods to 73% for products of basic industry.

The basic design of these interindustry accounts is derived from the
division of uses into two categories—intermediate and final—and the
corresponding division of inputs into "produced" and "primary." The
first distinction is logically similar to that which is made in Keynesian
income analysis between "induced" and "autonomous" elements. In

[3] The following accounting conventions, which are discussed in Chapter 5, are
listed here to give a better understanding of the input-output examples in these
first chapters:

(1) Transactions are usually recorded at the producer's price rather than at
the purchaser's cost, which means that trade and transport margins are ascribed
to the using sectors.

(2) In principle, the flows should correspond to the use of inputs for current
production rather than to the time when they are purchased. The differences
between purchase and use are reflected in stock changes, which are part of final
use.

(3) Purchases on capital account are normally charged entirely to final use,
and depreciation allowances are therefore included with primary inputs.

both models, there is some choice as to the uses which will be considered autonomous (or "final," in input-output terminology), which must be determined from both theoretical and empirical considerations.[4] For the present, we shall be concerned with the Leontief "open" model, in which total final use has approximately the same meaning as the gross national product.

TABLE 2.2. INTERINDUSTRY ACCOUNTING SYSTEM

		Purchasing Sectors									
		Intermediate Use		Final Use					Total Use = Total Supply	Supply	
		Sector $1 \cdots j \cdots n$	Total Inter-mediate Use	Investment	Consumption	Government	Exports	Total Final Use		Imports	Production
Producing sector	1 2 · · · i · · · n	$X_{11} \cdots X_{1j} \cdots X_{1n}$ $\quad$ (Quadrant II) $X_{i1} \quad X_{ij} \quad X_{in}$ $X_{n1} \cdots X_{nj} \cdots X_{nn}$	W_1 W_i W_n	I_1 I_i I_n	C_1 C_i C_n	G_1 (Quadrant I) G_i G_n	E_1 E_i E_n	Y_1 Y_i Y_n	Z_1 Z_i Z_n	M_1 M_i M_n	X_1 X_i X_n
Total produced inputs		$U_1 \quad U_j \quad U_n$									
Primary inputs (Value added)		$V_1 \quad V_j \quad V_n$ (Quadrant III)		V_I	V_C	V_G (Quadrant IV)	V_E		V		V
Total production		$X_1 \quad X_j \quad X_n$		I	C	G	E	Y	Z	M	X

The formal properties of the accounting system are shown in Table 2.2, which introduces a notation that will be followed hereafter. The

[4] The focus of the corresponding accounting systems is quite different, however. The aim of input-output analysis is to determine levels of total production for each sector of the economy, and the choice of autonomous elements is primarily a matter of convenience. In national income accounting, importance attaches to the gross national product as a measure of the performance of the economy and as a predictor of the behavior of its components. It is statistically convenient to have final use defined in the same way in input-output analysis, however, as a step toward a unified national accounting system. In our discussion, we shall use the term "autonomous" rather than "final" demand whenever there is a wide departure from the national accounts concept.

separation between intermediate and final use of output and between produced and primary inputs leads to four types of transactions, which are shown in the four quadrants of the table.

Quadrant I contains the final use of produced commodities and services, broken down by major types of use. (More than ninety per cent of the gross national product would appear in this category.)

Quadrant II comprises the main part of the interindustry accounts. Each entry, X_{ij}, indicates the amount of commodity i used by sector j, measured in constant prices. The total intermediate use of any commodity is identified as W_i, and the total purchases from other sectors by a given industry as U_j.

Quadrant III contains the use of inputs which are "primary" in the sense of not being produced within the system. In a static model, the use of existing capital stock is a primary input, as is the use of the customary primary factors, labor and land. (When output is valued at market prices, indirect taxes must also be treated as a primary input to make the accounts balance.) The total payment for primary inputs by each sector therefore corresponds approximately to the value added in production, being the difference between the value of output and cost of inputs produced outside the given establishment. Except when measurements of the separate inputs are needed (as in Chapters 3 and 4), we shall use the term value added (V_j) for the total use of primary inputs by a given sector.

Quadrant IV contains the direct input of primary factors to final use, of which the main examples are government employment and domestic service. These transactions do not enter into most interindustry models, but they should be recorded to make the totals consistent with national aggregates.

The last two columns of Table 2.2 break down total supply of each commodity between imports and domestic production.[5] If each commodity is only produced by one sector and there are no joint products, as is assumed in the preceding example, total supply of commodity i is equal to production in sector i plus imports of i. These assumptions will be made in the remainder of this chapter.[6]

[5] Alternatively, imports may be treated as a deduction from final use (as in national income accounting) or may be added to primary inputs. In the latter case, each column total represents total supply rather than domestic production.

[6] These are the assumptions of the input-output model, as explained in the next section. When they are not made, it is necessary to have a separate notation for commodities and sectors because a given commodity such as steel may be produced by several sectors. In a more general interindustry accounting system, outputs of each commodity by each sector are distinguished.

The formal structure of input-output accounts can best be expressed in symbols. The basic elements are defined as follows:[7]

Z_i = total supply of commodity i
X_i = total production of commodity i
M_i = imports of commodity i
X_{ij} = amount of commodity i used in sector j
Y_i = final demand for commodity i
W_i = total intermediate use of commodity i $\left(\sum_j X_{ij}\right)$[8]

U_j = total use by sector j of inputs purchased from other industries $\left(\sum_i X_{ij}\right)$

V_j = total use of primary inputs (value added) in sector j.

These concepts lead to two balance equations. The first applies to rows in Table 2.2. It states that for each commodity total supply is equal to total demand, which is composed of intermediate demand plus final demand:

$$\overset{\textit{Supply}}{} \qquad \overset{\textit{Demand}}{}$$
$$Z_i = M_i + X_i = \sum_j X_{ij} + Y_i = W_i + Y_i \qquad (i = 1 \cdots n) \quad (2.1)$$

The second equation applies to columns in Table 2.2. It states that the total production in each sector is equal to the value of inputs purchased from other sectors plus value added in that sector:[9]

$$X_j = \sum_i X_{ij} + V_j = U_j + V_j \quad (j = 1 \cdots n) \qquad (2.2)$$

[7] Our notation is similar to that of Leontief (1951) except that he does not distinguish between primary and produced inputs and equates total supply and total production. The usefulness of these distinctions will appear later.

[8] $\sum_j X_{ij}$ indicates a summation for all values of j, i.e., the row sum, $X_{i1} + X_{i2} + \cdots + X_{in}$. Similarly, $\sum_i X_{ij}$ is the column sum, $X_{1j} + X_{2j} + X_{3j} + \cdots + X_{nj}$.

[9] The discussion assumes that production and use are measured in value units. It is often convenient to think of input-output relations in physical terms, however, and of the values as representing $1,000,000 worth of each commodity at base-year prices. It is also possible to construct input-output tables directly in physical units for many commodities. In this case, we can use Eqs. (2.1) and (2.4) below but not (2.2).

These two equations may be taken as definitions of final demand (Y_i) and the value of primary inputs (V_j), respectively. Final demand (or final use) is the difference between the total supply of a commodity available and the amount used up in production and hence includes changes in stocks. The value of primary inputs (value added) is defined as the difference between the value of production in a sector and payments for inputs purchased from other productive sectors. These definitions correspond closely to the concepts of final output and value added used in national income analysis.

From these definitions, it is easy to demonstrate the relationship between input-output accounts and the national income aggregates. Adding up the balance Eqs. (2.1) for each row and treating imports as a deduction from final demand gives:

$$\sum_i X_i = \sum_i \sum_j X_{ij} + \sum_i Y_i - \sum_i M_i$$

(In Table 2.1, $1000 = 475 + 525$.)

Adding similarly across all the columns gives:

$$\sum_j X_j = \sum_j \sum_i X_{ij} + \sum_j V_j$$

Since $\sum_i X_i = \sum_j X_j$, these equations are equal to each other. Combining them and eliminating the total of all interindustry transactions from both sides gives the basic national accounts identity:

$$\sum_i Y_i - \sum_i M_i = \sum_j V_j \qquad (2.3)$$

In Table 2.1, the total of factor payments (525) corresponds to gross national income, whereas total final demand (525) less imports (0) corresponds to the gross national product by use.

It is important to note that there is no necessary correspondence between totals of the individual columns of final demand and the total use of any single primary input. From the accounting point of view, the significant difference between the two types of sector is that the productive sectors must have balanced budgets (total input equal to total output), but the values of primary inputs and final uses must only balance in the aggregate.

An empirical comparison of the two accounting systems can be made by consolidating the same set of data, first in interindustry form and

TABLE 2.3. ALTERNATIVE CONSOLIDATIONS OF U.S. INTERINDUSTRY DATA,
1947* (IN BILLIONS OF DOLLARS)
(a) *Input-Output Form*

Producing Sector \ Purchasing Sector	Agriculture	Industry	Services	Final Use	Total Use
Agriculture	11	19	1	10	41
Industry	5	89	40	106	240
Services	5	37	37	106	185
Primary Inputs	20	95	107	21 (50)	243 (293)
Total Output	41	240	185	243 (293)	709 (759)

(b) *National Accounts Form*

Producing Sector \ Purchasing Sector	Business	Government	Foreign Trade (Exports)	Households (Consumption)	Gross Investment	Total Receipts
Business	244	16	16	157	33	466
Government	28	(4)	(1)	(31)		28 (64)
Foreign Trade (Imports)	7	1		1		9
Households	187	16 (14)	1	2		206 (220)
Total Payments	466	33 (51)	17 (18)	160 (191)	33	709 (759)

* *Source:* Liebling (1955), Tables 6 and 7. Inventory changes have been treated on a net basis here and included in gross investment. National accounts data have been used for the breakdown of quadrant IV, in which the items not included in the GNP are given in parenthesis. Liebling shows that there are substantial differences in Table (b) from the Department of Commerce concepts although the total GNP is approximately the same.

then in national accounts form. Liebling (1955) has provided such a comparison using the U.S. input-output table for 1947, the results of which are reproduced in Tables 2.3(a) and 2.3(b).

Table 2.3(a) is similar to the previous example of Table 2.1, but in addition to the entries in quadrants I, II, and III it gives total transactions in quadrant IV of $71 billion. The components of this total are shown in Table 2.3(b). The latter is composed of the five sector accounts used in national income accounting, of which one (business) includes all the productive sectors and the others give breakdowns of final use and primary inputs.

In both tables, the gross national product can be computed in two ways by means of Eq. (2.3). In either case, the total final demand for produced commodities and services is the sum of the items in quadrant I ($222). To this we must add the direct use of primary inputs of $21 in quadrant IV ($19 from households and $2 from imports) to get a total final use of $243 billion. The gross national product is equal to this figure less imports ($9) or $234. (The remaining items in parenthesis in quadrant IV are taxes and transfers which do not enter the GNP.) The same total can be gotten from Table 2.3(b) by adding up value added net of imports ($215 in quadrant III plus $19 in quadrant IV).

This example shows that the final demand which is relevant for the input-output system—total demand for goods and services less intermediate use—accounts for about 90% of the gross national product in the United States. The remainder is direct employment of primary factors, mainly by government.[10] This use should be included in the interindustry accounting system for completeness, but it will have no effect on the solution to the input-output model.

The complementary nature of the two accounting systems is also illustrated in these tables. The commodity classification used in the interindustry accounts gives a detailed breakdown of quadrant II, whereas the functional breakdown of final use and primary inputs gives more detail in the other three quadrants.[11]

[10] Where the government produces a marketable output, such as electric power, this activity is included with the productive sectors.

[11] When either accounting system is modified to improve the stability of relations in a given model, the correspondence between the two may be lost, but there are obvious advantages in preserving a consistent over-all framework for the initial compilation of data. A discussion of the theoretical and statistical differences between the two systems is given in Sigel (1955), Liebling (1955), and Stone (1956).

B. Basic Input-Output Models

The main purpose of the input-output model is to explain the magnitudes of the interindustry flows in terms of the levels of production in each sector. Several assumptions are necessary for such a procedure to be theoretically meaningful.[12] First, it must be possible to form the *productive sectors* in such a way that a single production function can be assumed for each one. This assumption is made in all general equilibrium models as well as in Marshallian partial-equilibrium analysis. In empirical applications, it involves identifying all productive activities as belonging to a specified sector.

The Leontief input-output model also makes several special assumptions which are not necessarily made in other interindustry models. The most important of these are (i) that a given product is only supplied by one sector; (ii) that there are no joint products; and (iii) that the quantity of each input used in production by any sector is determined entirely by the level of output of that sector.

These assumptions make possible important simplifications in the Walrasian equations of general equilibrium. All of the productive activities having a given output such as steel are consolidated into a single steel-producing sector. It is therefore possible to speak of steel as an *industry* as well as steel as a commodity. Whereas the Walrasian model deals with relations among individual productive units (plants), the Leontief model is concerned only with relations among groups of productive units or industries.[13]

These assumptions of the input-output model make it possible to write an equation for the demand (X_{ij}) of each industry (j) for each commodity (i) as a function of its own level of output (X_j). For statistical and computational convenience, these input functions are assumed to be linear over a given range of outputs and hence to be of the following form:[14]

$$X_{ij} = \bar{X}_{ij} + a_{ij}X_j \qquad (2.4)$$

The parameter a_{ij} is called the *marginal input coefficient*. The con-

[12] Leontief (1951), pp. 35–38. The assumptions are discussed in Section D, below.

[13] When the special assumptions of the input-output model are not made, it is still useful for empirical work to aggregate productive activities into industries, but a given commodity may then be produced by several industries.

[14] W. D. Evans (1956) has analyzed the properties of the corresponding nonlinear system and shown that it would be computationally manageable.

stant $\bar{X}_{ij}$ includes any fixed-cost elements which do not vary with the level of output. When it is zero, the input function becomes:

$$X_{ij} = a_{ij}X_j \qquad (2.4a)$$

The original Leontief model is derived by combining the accounting relations given in Eq. (2.1) for each commodity with the input functions of Eq. (2.4a).[15] In the simplest form of the model, imports are determined outside the system. Substituting the value of X_{ij} from Eq. (2.4a) into Eq. (2.1) and rearranging terms gives a balance equation for each commodity or sector:

$$X_i - \sum_j a_{ij}X_j = Y_i - M_i \qquad (i = 1 \cdot \cdot \cdot n) \qquad (2.5)$$

In this system of n equations, there are n unknown production levels (X_j), n^2 parameters (a_{ij}) describing the input functions, and two sets of n autonomous variables $(Y_i$ and $M_i)$ whose values are specified for a given problem.[16] (Similar equations can be written for each primary input, but they have no effect on the solution.)

When trade is important, it is often desirable to make imports dependent variables. As a first approximation, it can be assumed that the level of imports (M_i) is a function of the total supply of that commodity (Z_i) and hence is related to the level of domestic production (X_i). Assuming a linear function over a certain range gives:

$$M_i = \bar{M}_i + m_iX_i \qquad (2.6)$$

In this formulation, the parameter m_i is called the *import coefficient*, which is closely related to the marginal propensity to import a given

---

[15] Leontief (1951), pp. 36–37, and (1953a), pp. 17–20.

[16] Equation (2.5) can be stated in a more general form by retaining the constant term in (2.4). The basic equation then becomes:

$$X_i - \sum_j a_{ij}X_j = \tilde{Y}_i - M_i \qquad (i = 1 \cdot \cdot \cdot n) \qquad (2.5a)$$

where

$$\tilde{Y}_i = \sum_j \bar{X}_{ij} + Y_i$$

Here $\tilde{Y}_i$ includes autonomous elements of intermediate use as well as final uses. In input-output practice to date, the parameters $\bar{X}_{ij}$ have only been estimated for a few commodities (see Chapters 7 and 8).

commodity.[17] Substituting this import function in Eq. (2.5a) and collecting terms gives the following set of relations:

$$(1 + m_i)X_i - \sum_j a_{ij}X_j = \bar{Y}_i \qquad (i = 1 \cdots n) \qquad (2.7)$$

where

$$\bar{Y}_i = Y_i + \sum_j \bar{X}_{ij} - \bar{M}_i$$

The variable $\bar{Y}_i$ is the total autonomous demand, which is equal to final demand (Y_i) when the other two terms are zero.[18]

Equations (2.7) are the basic equations of the input-output system in the general case.[19] They are based on a division of variables between those which vary with the level of output in each sector (X_{ij} and M_i) and those which do not. The former are eliminated by means of the input functions and the import functions. This formulation is usually thought of as merely a way of determining the levels of production in each sector corresponding to any given set of autonomous demands. In a more general sense, however, Eqs. (2.7) constitute a simplified production function for the whole economy. When we add the equations for the use of capital and labor, which have been omitted so far, this input-output model can translate any final "bill of goods" into requirements for capital and labor, or alternatively can be used to specify the outputs achievable with given amounts of primary factors.

Although the most usual problems to which the input-output system is applied involve specifying the $\bar{Y}$'s and determining the X's, it

---

[17] The marginal propensity to import is usually defined as a ratio to total production.

[18] Except where it is explicitly stated, no distinction will be made between the terms "autonomous" and "final" demand from now on.

[19] Leontief prefers to work with Z as the dependent variable in this equation instead of X. When there are no autonomous imports, the two are related by the equation: $Z_i = (1 + m_i)X_i$. If the import coefficients are taken as fixed for all applications, Z_i is to be preferred to X_i as the dependent variable on computational grounds because it is easier to find the general solution given in Eqs. (2.8) below. In countries where imports are a significant fraction of total supply in a number of sectors, it may be convenient to assume different values of m in different problems. The form given in Eqs. (2.7) is then more useful because a change in m_i does not affect the corresponding column of input coefficients. X_i is usually taken as the dependent variable in countries other than the United States for this reason.

is equally feasible to assume any consistent set of n values for some X's and some $\bar{Y}$'s and to determine the remaining n. In all cases it is necessary to solve a system of n simultaneous equations in n unknowns. The solution to this problem may be written in the form:

$$X_i = r_{i1}\bar{Y}_1 + r_{i2}\bar{Y}_2 + \cdots + r_{in}\bar{Y}_n \qquad (i = 1 \cdots n) \quad (2.8)$$

These equations represent a transformation of the original Eqs. (2.7) in which a new set of constants (r_{ij}) is derived from the original parameters $(a_{ij}$ and $m_i)$. This form, which is discussed in the Appendix, is known as the *general solution*. It is also possible to solve for particular values of X and $\bar{Y}$ without finding the general solution, however, as will be shown in the next section.

We have so far avoided making any economic interpretation of the crucial parameters in the input-output model, the a_{ij}'s, in order to make clear first the logical structure of the system. Leontief interprets these parameters as fixed coefficients of production which are technologically determined. This reasoning is the most compelling argument for adopting the model in this simple form, but it is not the only basis for assuming some relation between inputs purchased by a sector and its level of output. Any stable relation between input and output, because of institutional factors such as tax rates or behavioral factors such as a constant structure of demand, can be equally well incorporated into this type of model.

C. Introduction to Methods of Solution

One of the drawbacks of interindustry, as compared to national-income, models has been that the former seem to require much more formidable computations. There has been correspondingly less of the illustrative use of the Leontief system which has proven so fruitful in the case of Keynesian models. There is, however, much to be learned from input-output systems which are small enough to be handled by simple numerical methods. Once these have been mastered, the interpretation of the results of larger and more realistic models becomes easier and one is better able to evaluate the underlying assumptions. In this section we therefore present one of the simplest methods of solving input-output systems and work out some examples; a more complete treatment will be given in the Appendix.

Although they appear cumbersome at first sight, methods of successive approximation or "iteration" are actually quite efficient for solving input-output models of moderate size.[20] Economists are already familiar with such methods in working out the effects of autonomous investment in a Keynesian multiplier process. In addition to providing a solution to the level of income finally attained in equilibrium, the multiplier chain gives some insight into the way increases in income are transmitted through the economy. The simplest income-determination model can be thought of as a one-sector input-output model, as follows:

$$X_t = cX_{t-1} + I_t \tag{2.9}$$

Investment I is the autonomous part of the system, corresponding to final demand, and the marginal propensity to consume c is analogous to an input coefficient. In both systems, it is necessary to produce in excess of the "outside" demands on the system to satisfy the induced requirements—those related to the level of production—which in this case consist of consumption. Equation (2.9) has been written as a difference equation by making consumption depend on total production or income of the previous period (X_{t-1}), and the iterative solution can be thought of as a sequence in time.

A solution to this equation is a value of X which will maintain itself: $X_t = X_{t-1}$. We can find such a value for a particular value of I, given c, or for all possible values. One common way of finding a particular solution is to trace out the successive increments in income resulting from a single investment until they dwindle to zero. If the marginal propensity to consume is 0.5 and $I_o = 100$, this series is:

$$X_1 = 100,$$
$$X_2 = 0.5(100) = 50,$$
$$X_3 = 0.5(50) = 25$$
$$X_n = 0.5X_{n-1} = (0.5)^{n-1}100$$
$$\sum_{t=1}^{t=\infty} X_t = 100 + 50 + 25 + \cdots = 200 \tag{2.10}$$

In addition to representing the total effects of a single investment over time, the sum of this series indicates the level of total production required to sustain a continuing level of investment of 100 with consumption at 50 per cent of income.[21] This second interpretation provides an analogy to the static input-output system.

[20] An admirable treatment of the whole subject of input-output solutions is given in Evans (1956).

[21] An alternative way of reaching the equilibrium solution to the latter problem is to assume that I_t equals 100 in each period and trace out the production levels

A second method of solution is to obtain a general formula for the equilibrium value of X_t, which in this case is very simple:

$$X_t = X_{t-1} = \frac{I_t}{1-c} = \frac{100}{0.5} = 200 \qquad (2.11)$$

When we turn to input-output systems of more than three sectors, however, the general solution becomes more difficult to calculate than the iterative approximation. We shall therefore take up the iterative methods for finding particular solutions first.

To construct an illustrative input-output system, we take the accounting data of Table 2.1 and assume that input functions are computed from Eq. (2.4a). The input coefficients are therefore derived by dividing each interindustry purchase by the total output of the sector. The resulting matrix of input coefficients is shown in Table 2.4.

TABLE 2.4.   INPUT-OUTPUT COEFFICIENTS (MODEL I)*

Producing Sector	S	Using Sector A	B	F
Services	0.1	0.1	0.1	0.2
Agriculture	0	0.1	0	0.3
Basic Industries	0	0.1	0.3	0.1
Finished Goods	0	0	0	0.2
Value Added	0.9	0.7	0.6	0.2

* The coefficients agree closely with those that can be derived from Table 8.12, below, for Italy.

Let us now assume that we know the final demands of Table 2.1 but not the levels of production. Our problem is then to solve the fol-

given by equation (2.9) until an equilibrium position is reached as indicated by $X_t = X_{t-1}$:

t	I_t	$0.5X_{t-1}$	X_t
1	100	0	100
2	100	50	150
3	100	75	175
4	100	87.5	187.5
5	100	93.75	193.75
...	...	...	...
∞	100	100	200

The difference between these two versions of the iterative method is that in the first case only the increments are computed period by period, whereas in the second case the total level of output in each period is determined.

lowing set of equations obtained from (2.5), which constitute Model I, for the total outputs:

$$X_s = (0.1X_s + 0.1X_A + 0.1X_B + 0.2X_F) + 60$$

$$X_A = (0.1X_A + 0.3X_F) + 105$$

$$X_B = (0.1X_A + 0.3X_B + 0.1X_F) + 40$$

$$X_F = (0.2X_F) + 320$$

(2.12)

To reach a solution, we can follow the approach used in (2.10) to solve the single-equation national income model. We assume that the first increment in production $(\Delta X_i{}^1)$ is equal to the autonomous element (final demand) and determine the increase in output from other sectors needed to produce this amount. These interindustry demands ("first round effects") are then summed up for each sector and become the second increment in output $(\Delta X_i{}^2)$.[22] These derived demands are again multiplied by the input coefficients to determine further increases in output.

A systematic way of carrying out this iterative procedure is shown in Table 2.5. In the first round of the solution, the final demand of 320 in sector F, for example, is multiplied by each of the input coefficients in column F to give 64, 96, 32, and 64 for the inputs required from each of the four sectors. (The value added in each sector has no effect on the solution, but is included to show how final demand is successively translated into a requirement for primary inputs and as a check on the computation.) After similar multiplications have been performed for the other columns, the rows are summed to give the second increment to production, $\Delta X_i{}^{(2)}$. In sector S, for example, this increment is $(6 + 10.5 + 4 + 64)$ equal to 84.5. This value is entered at the bottom of column S along with the second increments for the other sectors, 106.5, 54.5, and 64.0. The calculation is then repeated using these increments as production levels and again calculating the increase in output from each sector needed to support them. The total demand generated after each round in the calculation is shown in the next to last column. After three iterations, for example, demand has reached 194.5 in sector S as compared to the true value of 200.

This method can be used to give solutions of any desired degree of accuracy. In the present case, the largest error is 1.6% in sector B after four iterations, and the average error is 0.45%. The error can be

[22] Since the input-output model represents a static equilibrium position rather than a dynamic system, the iterative sequence refers only to "computational time" rather than to a chronological sequence.

TABLE 2.5. INCREMENTAL SOLUTION TO MODEL I

Producing Sectors	Using Sectors				Inter-Industry Use (ΔX_i^t)	Final Demand ($Y_i = \Delta X_i^1$)	Estimate of Total Demand (X_i^t)	Actual Total Demand (i)
	S	A	B	F				
S	**0.1**	**0.1**	**0.1**	**0.2**				
	6.0	10.5	4.0	64.0	84.5	60	144.5	
	8.5	10.6	5.4	12.8	37.3		181.8	200
	3.7	3.0	3.4	2.6	12.7		194.5	
	1.3	0.7	1.4	0.5	3.9		198.4	
A	**0**	**0.1**	**0**	**0.3**				
	...	10.5	...	96.0	106.5	105	211.5	
	...	10.6	...	19.2	29.8		241.3	250
	...	3.0	...	3.8	6.8		248.1	
	...	0.7	...	0.8	1.5		249.6	
B	**0**	**0.1**	**0.3**	**0.1**				
	...	10.5	12.0	32.0	54.5	40	94.5	
	...	10.7	16.4	6.4	33.5		128.0	150
	...	3.0	10.0	1.3	14.3		142.3	
	...	0.7	4.3	0.3	5.3		147.6	
F	**0**	**0**	**0**	**0.2**				
	...	...	...	64.0	64.0	320	384.0	
	...	...	...	12.8	12.8		396.8	400
	...	...	...	2.6	2.6		399.4	
	...	...	...	0.5	0.5		399.9	
Value added	**0.9**	**0.7**	**0.6**	**0.2**				
	54.0	73.5	24.0	64.0	215.5	525		
	76.0	74.6	32.7	12.8	196.1			
	33.6	20.8	20.1	2.6	77.1			
	11.4	4.7	8.6	0.5	25.2			
ΔX_i^t	60.0	105.0	40.0	320.0	525.0			
	84.5	106.5	54.5	64.0	309.5			
	37.3	29.8	33.5	12.8	113.4			
	12.7	6.8	14.3	2.6	36.4			

reduced by extrapolating from the last iteration according to the formula given in the footnote.[23]

An algebraic statement of the method we have been following is as follows:

$$\Delta X_i^{(1)} = Y_i$$

$$\Delta X_i^{(2)} = \sum_j a_{ij} \Delta X_j^{(1)}$$

$$\Delta X_i^{(3)} = \sum_j a_{ij} \Delta X_j^{(2)} \qquad (2.13)$$

$$\Delta X_i^{(n)} = \sum_j a_{ij} \Delta X_j^{(n-1)}$$

$$X_i^n = \sum_{t=1}^{t=n} \Delta X_i^{(t)}$$

[23] Evans (p. 73) gives the following method of extrapolation for the remaining terms in the solution. First, form the ratios of the last two increments in production for each sector:

$$r_S = \frac{3.9}{12.7} = 0.307$$

$$r_A = \frac{1.5}{6.8} = 0.220$$

$$r_B = \frac{5.3}{14.3} = 0.371$$

$$r_F = \frac{0.5}{2.6} = 0.192$$

The average of these ratios, 0.273, is then used in the following expression to determine the remainder in each sector:

$$\left(\frac{r}{1 - r} \right) \Delta X^n$$

where ΔX^n is the last increment. Application of this method to our example gives the following result for each sector:

$$r/(1 - r) = 0.273/0.727 = 0.376$$
$$X_S = 198.4 + 0.376(3.9) = 199.9$$
$$X_A = 249.6 + 0.376(1.5) = 250.2$$
$$X_B = 147.6 + 0.376(5.3) = 149.6$$
$$X_F = 399.9 + 0.376(0.5) = 400.1$$

Evans shows that this procedure can be justified theoretically and that the ratios converge toward a common value (the dominant characteristic root of the matrix) as the iteration is continued.

When there is only one sector, this set of equations reduces to (2.10) for the Keynesian model. (Equations (2.13) are given in matrix form in the appendix.)

As in Keynesian analysis, there is some economic interest in tracing the process by which the indirect effects of an increase in autonomous demand spread through the economy. The iterative solution should not be interpreted as a dynamic model, however, because the increases in production induced in other sectors must take place *before* a given final demand can be satisfied.

The existence of a solution in the Leontief system is assured by the same condition as in the Keynesian system: expenditures induced within the system must be less than the income which generates them. In the Keynesian system this means a marginal propensity to consume of less than unity. In the Leontief system it is sufficient for the sum of the input coefficients (apart from payments to primary factors) to be less than unity in at least one sector.[24] This condition is always satisfied in the Leontief open model which we have been considering, since only purchases from other industries for current production are induced. The smaller the fraction of interindustry purchases by each sector, the more rapidly the rounds of the iterative procedure converge to the solution, just as in the Keynesian case.

The "leakages" in the Keynesian model are savings, taxes, and imports, whereas the leakages in the Leontief model are all factor payments, taxes, and imports. In equilibrium, total leakages equal autonomous expenditure. The convergence of the leakages (value added) toward the total of autonomous elements (final demand) is shown in Table 2.5. At the end of four iterations, value added totals 513.9, compared to final demand of 525. This is the best check on the extent to which the iterative process has worked itself out. This gap can be reduced to any desired size by successive rounds of the solution. As we shall see in the next chapter, the assumption of induced consumption can also be made in the Leontief system—as indeed it was in the original version—and the autonomous elements and leakages then become identical with those in the Keynesian model.

The methods for securing a general solution or inverse matrix of the form of Eq. (2.8) are more complicated than the iterative procedure for securing single solutions. The inversion of a matrix of any size will normally be done in a computing laboratory with an electronic computer. Since many inverse matrices have now been

[24] Necessary conditions for the existence of a solution to the Leontief system are discussed in Evans (1956), pp. 60–62, and Dorfman, Samuelson, and Solow (1958), pp. 213–215 and 254–260.

published, however, the analyst is mainly concerned with understanding their meaning and use.

Table 2.6 gives the coefficients r_{ij} in the general solution to model I. From this table, the value of any production level X_i can be determined as the sum of the coefficients in its row multiplied by the corresponding levels of final demand. For example:

$$X_S = 0.351(320) + 0.141(105) + 0.159(40) + 1.111(60) = 200.0$$

The Y's are recorded as a row along the bottom of the table, since each element in a column is multiplied by the same final demand. The method of determining a solution is merely to perform the $(n \times n)$ multiplications and add up the products for each row. This has been done in Table 2.6 for our example.

TABLE 2.6.   General Solution (Inverse Matrix) for Model I*

Sector	1 (F)	2 (A)	3 (B)	4 (S)	X_i
1 (F)	**1.250**	0	0	0	
	400.00				400.00
2 (A)	**0.417**	**1.111**	0	0	
	133.34	*116.66*			250.00
3 (B)	**0.238**	**0.159**	**1.429**	0	
	76.19	*16.66*	*57.14*		149.99
4 (S)	**0.351**	**0.141**	**0.159**	**1.111**	
	112.16	*14.82*	*6.35*	*66.67*	200.00
Y_j	320	105	40	60	

* The order of sectors has been changed for reasons given in the Appendix. The numbers in italics are equal to the coefficients multiplied by the corresponding final demands (Y_j) at the foot of each column. The row sum of these numbers equals the level of production (X_i).

The added usefulness of the general solution is shown by the fact that either the Y's or the X's can be varied and a new solution for the remaining variables obtained by a simple calculation. Furthermore, the effect of each Y can be determined separately. The inverse matrix is therefore valuable in exploring the general properties of the system, in which many calculations must be made with the same set of data. Such uses will be illustrated in the next chapter. The disadvantage of the general solution is that a change in any one of the input coefficients or import functions may affect any or all of the elements of this

solution.   Since the cost of securing the inverse of a matrix increases
with the cube of the number of sectors while that of single solutions
increases only with the square, it is not economical to compute the
inverse for systems larger than 40–50 sectors unless wide use will be
made of the results.[25]

D. The Assumptions of Input-Output Analysis

Input-output analysis is essentially a simplified general theory of
production.   Studies of consumption, investment and other final demand elements must precede the input-output analysis, but these
elements are taken as given data in the model itself.   The essential
assumptions of input-output theory are concerned almost entirely with
the nature of production.

The input-output model is based on the premise that it is possible
to divide all productive activities in an economy into sectors whose
interrelations can be meaningfully expressed in a set of simple input
functions.   Although we shall examine separately the sector concept
and the suggested simplification of the production function, it should
be recognized that the validity of each one depends on that of the
other.   Input functions for one grouping of activities may show considerable stability, but for a different grouping they may be much
less constant.   The criteria for establishing sectors must be derived
from a knowledge of the characteristics of the productive activities
being aggregated as well as of the use of the outputs.

The Leontief model includes some types of interdependence among
economic units and excludes other types.   It specifically includes the
interdependence resulting from the sales of commodities from one
sector to another and from the use of the same primary factors.   It
specifically excludes substitution among the outputs of different sectors, either in final uses or as inputs to other sectors, and non-market
interdependence in the form of external economies and diseconomies.

The properties of Leontief models can be derived from three basic
assumptions, which it will be useful to state at the outset:

(1) *Each commodity (or group of commodities) is supplied by a
single industry or sector of production.*   Corollaries of this assumption are (*a*) that only one method is used for producing each group

---

[25] If a special solution requires four iterations, the number of special solutions
which is equivalent to one general solution (in number of multiplications required) is approximately $n/3$, where n is the size of the matrix (see Evans, p. 78).

of commodities; and (*b*) that each sector has only a single primary output.

(2) *The inputs purchased by each sector are a function only of the level of output of that sector.* (The stronger assumption is usually made that the input function is linear, but this is a matter of convenience.)

(3) *The total effect of carrying on several types of production is the sum of the separate effects.* This is known as the additivity assumption, which rules out external economies and diseconomies.

In Chapter 4 we shall take up the more general activity analysis model of production, which abandons the first assumption but retains the other two. The latter model does not exclude substitution, as does the Leontief system, since it assumes that there may be more than one way of producing a given commodity.

The validity of each of these assumptions depends both on the nature of production in single plants and on the way in which these units are aggregated into sectors. Some assumptions may be more valid for aggregates than for individual units, as for example the exclusion of joint products and external economies. Others may hold for single productive processes but not for sectors. We must therefore consider together the nature of the underlying production relationships and the effects of aggregation in evaluating the structure of the model.

It is not to be expected that such a simple system will prove useful for all kinds of problems. A given aggregation into sectors may be valid for one purpose but not for another. Substitution may be negligible under some circumstances but of dominant importance in others. A theoretical analysis of these assumptions is therefore necessary to establish criteria for aggregation and to ascertain the type of problem for which the model is likely to be useful. Empirical tests of the results, such as those reported in Chapter 6, can then be made and interpreted in the light of such analysis.

1. The Sector Concept[26]

All economic theory is based on the assumption of uniformity in the characteristics and behavior of certain basic units, whether they be single households, firms, industries, consumers as a whole, or na-

[26] The problem of aggregation into sectors is discussed from an empirical point of view by Barna (1956) Holzman (1953), and Fisher (1958), and more abstractly by Balderston and Whitin (1954), Dorfman, Samuelson and Solow (1958) and Thiel (1957).

tional economies. Such uniformity is sometimes predicated on the assumption of similar behavior by each of the units in the group, as in Marshall's representative firm; in other cases a predictable aggregate reaction is expected from widely different individual responses, as in the Keynesian consumption function. In the latter case, the relative importance of the different components must remain constant.

In its first theoretical formulation, the Leontief sector was, like the Marshallian or Walrasian industry, assumed to be composed of plants producing a single homogeneous product by similar techniques. In transforming this formal model into an empirical tool, the problem of aggregating all activities into sectors has assumed great importance. Two types of solution suggest themselves, depending on which type of aggregate we have in mind. An attempt to stick to the "pure" industry concept would involve grouping together only plants in which *both* the output and input structures were similar. Given the variety of products produced by the typical plant, a close approximation to this concept is impossible. Furthermore, even if input data were available for separate products and the resulting thousands of sectors could be handled computationally, the assumptions of additivity and nonsubstitutability among outputs would no longer be tenable. Such a narrow sector definition would in practice require the abandonment of the input-output model and the use of an activity analysis model of the type discussed in Chapter 4.

In empirical interindustry studies, a productive sector corresponds to the second type of aggregate—i.e., a grouping of both processes and products which differ in some respects. The behavior of such a group need only be uniform with respect to the characteristics used as a basis for aggregation if these correspond to the assumptions of the model. For example, an aggregation of production activities which is satisfactory for a Leontief model need not have stable inputs of primary factors, since these do not affect the solution for production levels.

For most types of input-output analysis, the best basis for aggregation is a similarity of input structure. Even though there is a considerable variation in the commodities produced by a sector, a change in composition of output will have no effect on the inputs required from other sectors if this criterion is satisfied. A second basis for aggregation is the use of outputs of several processes in fixed proportions. This condition is most likely to be met in successive stages of processing of the same material, as in spinning and weaving. If yarn is used only for the making of cloth, then inputs into both spinning and weaving processes will be proportional to cloth output. The correspondence is rarely perfect, however, because some other demands for the semi-finished product usually exist. The use of pig iron in foundries as well as in making steel is a typical example. In such cases, the relative importance of the nonproportional uses must be the determining factor in the decision to aggregate. Fixed proportions in consumption, as indicated by identical income elasticities, might be another case for the use of this principle where interindustry uses are relatively unimportant.

The formal justification for the rules just given can be derived by answering the following question. Under what conditions can sectors m and n be consolidated without affecting the production estimates for the other sectors in the model? The input coefficients of the consolidated sector may be stated as follows:

$$X_{(m+n)} = X_m + X_n$$

$$
\begin{aligned}
a_{i(m+n)} &= \frac{X_{i(m+n)}}{X_{(m+n)}} = \frac{X_{im} + X_{in}}{X_m + X_n} \\
&= \frac{a_{im}X_m + a_{in}X_n}{X_m + X_n} = a_{im}\left(\frac{X_m}{X_m + X_n}\right) + a_{in}\left(\frac{X_n}{X_m + X_n}\right) \\
&= w_m a_{im} + w_n a_{in}, \text{ where } w_m = \left(\frac{X_m}{X_m + X_n}\right)
\end{aligned}
\tag{2.14}
$$

If all the input coefficients $a_{i\,(m+n)}$ of the consolidated sector are unaffected by changes in the output levels, X_m and X_n, the demands of the consolidated sector for the output of other sectors will be equal to the sum of the demands of its components since the total output, $X_{(m+n)}$, is equal to the sum $X_m + X_n$. Equation (2.14) shows that there are two conditions under which this will be true:

(1) If a_{im} equals a_{in}, then no change in the weights resulting from changes in the proportions in which X_m and X_n are demanded will affect the aggregate coefficient. This is the first rule of similar input coefficients.

(2) If X_m and X_n are demanded in fixed proportions, the weighted average of the input coefficients will always be the same, regardless of differences in its components. This leads to the second rule of output proportionality.

Strictly speaking, the first rule is a criterion for aggregating productive activities and the second a rule for aggregating commodities.

In the first case, the proportions of commodities X_m and X_n in the combined total will not be known although they could easily be computed after the solution for the other sectors has been completed. In the second case, there is no loss of information at all since X_m and X_n are fixed fractions of $X_{(m+n)}$. (It can easily be shown that these rules apply to any number of sectors.)

The above tests, if rigidly met, would lead to *perfect* aggregation —i.e., no error would be introduced into the solution as a result of aggregation. In practice the choice is among combinations of sectors which satisfy these criteria to varying degrees. In this case, we must look beyond the relations involving the sectors directly concerned and consider the differences in their indirect effects as well.[27]

A third type of aggregate will inevitably occur in input-output tables because of the form in which production and consumption data are collected: the aggregation of substitutes. Sectors aggregated on this basis will have unstable input coefficients unless the productive processes also have similar inputs. It is sometimes argued that substitutes should be aggregated because errors due to substitution will thereby be reduced. This conclusion is incorrect. Aggregation of two sectors, such as coal and oil, has the effect of using a weighted average of their input coefficients, which would have the same effect on other industries as keeping the sectors separate. It is true that a better estimate of the combined demand for coal and oil would be gotten, in the event of substitution between the two, than for each component, but subsequently adding together the production totals for the two sectors gives the same answer. If substitutes such as coal and oil are not aggregated, on the other hand, it is often possible to analyze the probable extent of substitution separately and to introduce a change in their input proportions into the solution, as shown in Chapter 10. In this respect, the input-output method is considerably more flexible than a formal statement of the model would suggest.

The above principles are based on the assumption that the aim of aggregation is to produce the minimum average error for all the production totals of the solution. If accuracy in some estimates is more important than others, as is usually the case, we should give more weight to the effect of aggregation on these sectors. In some prob-

---

[27] If we could compile a larger input-output table first and then consolidate it to smaller size, we could use the inverse matrix as a guide and look for proportional columns or rows, which corresponds to the two rules given above (see Dorfman, Samuelson, and Solow, p. 243). This suggestion is of relatively little use in practice because the main problems arise in the original classification of data.

lems, measurement of the production of services or other outputs may be unimportant, and therefore only the demands of these sectors for other inputs will need to be considered. On the other hand, accurate measurement of the use of specific scarce materials or imported goods may be crucial. When the objectives of the analysis can thus be specified in advance, the importance of possible errors can be estimated better, and it becomes easier to find bases for aggregation. Strictly speaking, the validity of any actual aggregation can only be determined by reference to specific uses of the model, since perfect aggregation is never achieved.[28]

Decisions on classification are aided by taking cognizance of natural divisions of productive sequences which result from a combination of technological, economic, and locational factors. Both agricultural and mineral raw materials go first through a stage of purification and processing into uniform "finished" or "basic" materials, such as steel, cement, cloth, or flour. In this form they are most readily transported and typically receive further processing in different plants. The later stages of manufacture take the form of combining several basic materials into fabricated goods—automobiles, clothing, bread, etc. The first or processing stages are characterized by the performance of a series of operations on the same raw material, with by-products often used to produce secondary outputs. When these successive steps are performed in relatively fixed proportions, such as smelting and refining or spinning and weaving, it is often justifiable to combine them into a single sector. Alternatively, it may be possible to consolidate the performance of similar processing of a range of raw materials. These two types of aggregation may be called vertical and horizontal. The first is identified with the raw material and finished product, while the second is based on a similarity of process, which implies similar equipment and use of power, labor, etc.

In the later fabricating and finishing stages, it is less often possible to identify a sector by its principal material input, since a greater variety of materials is likely to be used. Industries are commonly identified by process and product. We distinguish clothing from household linens, for example, by the type of finishing rather than the nature of the raw material used.

---

[28] From a statistical point of view, the alternatives for forming sectors are severely limited by the nature of the data available. The aggregations corresponding to the several statistical bases of information—by product, process, or plant—will be taken up in Chapter 5. Some empirical tests of alternative aggregations are given in Fisher (1958).

Before leaving the subject of aggregation, we may note that both assumptions (1) and (3) on pp. 33–34 are more valid the larger the aggregates used, but assumption (2) is less valid. The finer the sector breakdown, the larger the proportion of secondary products and the more likely the existence of significant external effects on other sectors. If we should carry the breakdown of sectors to the extent of subdividing productive processes which are technologically interrelated, such as production of gasoline and fuel oil, the concept of an independent sector would break down. A partial solution of the process *versus* product problem in aggregation is given by an input-output model in which there are more rows (commodities) than columns (productive sectors). This model is discussed in Chapter 5.

2. The Input Function

Because of the no-substitution assumption (2), the general production function of the form

$$X_j = f(X_{1j}, X_{2j} \cdots X_{nj}) \tag{2.15}$$

takes the form of minimum requirements for each input:

$$X_j \leq X_{ij}/a_{ij}, \qquad (i = 1 \cdots n) \tag{2.16}$$

Equation (2.16) states that a minimum amount of each input is required for a given output.[29] The output is therefore fixed by whichever limit is reached first. In actuality, no more than the limitational amount of any input would be used, and the partial relation between each input and output reduces to the equality given in (2.4a).

The absence of substitution among inputs might be explained on one of two grounds: either (i) the technology is such that no substitution is possible; or (ii) relative prices do not change, so that it is not efficient to alter input proportions regardless of the shape of the production function. In his original formulation, Leontief (1951, pp. 38–40) relied primarily on the first assumption. He argued that a large proportion of what economists usually call substitution was due to the use of large aggregates, such as "consumption," in which a change in the proportion of automobiles and foodstuffs consumed, for example, would cause a change in the proportions of inputs of labor and capital used. This type of substitution is eliminated by the use of a finer sector breakdown. As for true substitution in a given productive process, Leontief suggested that there may be a high degree of

[29] See Dorfman, Samuelson, and Solow (1958), p. 231.

complementarity among inputs, so that changes in relative prices will affect their proportions only slightly.

The assumption of complementarity is much more likely to be true in the short run, when equipment cannot be varied to any great extent, than it is in the longer run.   A more rigorous statement of the Leontief

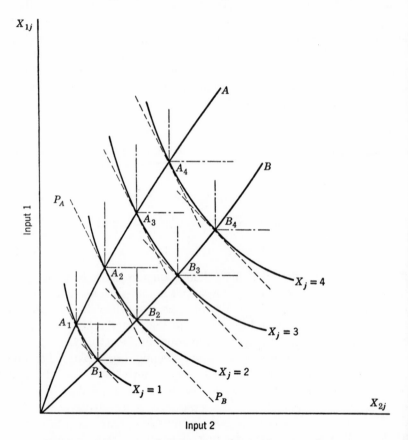

Fig. 2.1.   Long-run and short-run production functions for sector *j*.

hypothesis might run as follows.   Assume that substitution requires a change in the type of machinery, so that current input proportions are fixed by the existing equipment.   The long-run and short-run production functions for a given plant would then appear as in Fig. 2.1. The long-run production function is shown by solid lines, while the fixed-plant function is given by the L-shaped dashed lines.   If existing plants had been built with price ratios indicated by the set of price lines P_A, the proportions in which they use inputs 1 and 2 would be given by the corresponding expansion line A. The input coefficients for the whole industry would be a weighted average of the ratios (X_{ij}/X_j) for plants of different sizes (e.g., A_1, A_2, A_3). These ratios would be stable so long as the proportion of output coming from plants of different sizes did not change. If we assume a change in relative prices to P_B, the optimum input proportions would then lie along line B. New plants or replacements of old plants would embody these proportions, and gradually the weighted average would shift from say A_2 to B_2 (or to B_3 if the average plant size also increases).[30]

The hypothesis just outlined can best be tested by detailed engineering and statistical studies of individual plants rather than by using time series for whole sectors. The latter inevitably incorporate the effects of technological change as well as movements along the long-run isoquants, and the two cannot readily be distinguished. An evaluation of the available evidence on this point will be given in Chapter 6.

Turning to the second possible explanation of stable input functions, there are both theoretical and empirical grounds for expecting relative prices to be fairly stable apart from periods of wartime shortages and the like. Samuelson and others have shown that in a competitive system having only one scarce factor (or fixed relative prices of factors) and no joint production, relative commodity prices will be fixed and the choice of productive technique in each sector will not be affected by the composition of demand. Even though there is a range of possible techniques and input proportions in each sector, there will be no tendency to vary these proportions unless the relative prices of the primary inputs change. Although there are secular changes in the relative prices of the primary factors, the assumption of constant prices over fairly short periods is often a reasonable one. This "substitution theorem" will be considered in more detail in Chapter 4.

A further question arises as to whether the input coefficients in the Leontief system should be interpreted as physical constants, as Leontief does, or as value ratios which combine the effects of both changes in relative prices and in quantities. Klein (1953, pp. 205–210) has suggested that the latter interpretation is more in keeping with economic theory and that there may be greater stability in value ratios than in physical input-output ratios, reflecting an elasticity of sub-

[30] Of course the weighted average need not lie on the expansion line, unless we restrict the shape of the production function, although in the present case it would be close to it.

stitution between inputs close to unity. The merits of this suggestion can hardly be discussed in the absence of direct observation of inter-industry flows in both physical and value terms over a period of years. It may be noted, however, that an empirical model based on Klein's hypothesis would be more complicated to apply than Leontief's be-cause the quantity solution is dependent on the price solution.[31]

In summary, the degree of stability of input functions depends in part on the way the sectors are selected and in part on the underlying properties of the productive system. Observed changes in these re-lations come from three sources:

(1) Changes in the composition of demand (product mix),
(2) Changes in relative prices of inputs,
(3) Changes in the technological alternatives available.

Of these three, technological change seems to have been the most important source of variation in input functions in the American econ-omy, which is the only one which has been studied over any con-siderable period of time from this point of view. In the long run, technological change is also responsible for most of the changes in relative prices that take place, and it is therefore very difficult to dis-tinguish between the effects of the last two factors.

In the short run, it is probable that pure substitution phenomena in the manufacturing sectors are important for a fairly limited range of inputs, within groups in which substitution is planned for in the design of processing equipment. Leading examples are the fuels, metals, textile fibers, and building materials groups. Where such areas of potential substitution can be identified, "side analyses" of these inputs can be made and incorporated in the input-output solu-tion.[32]

The chief value of the simple Leontief input-output system is to provide a basis for the initial empirical explorations of the field of interindustry relations. The model gives a consistent framework for data collection in otherwise unrelated sectors, and a test of its assump-tions shows the areas where a more complicated theoretical formula-tion is needed. The data requirements for more complicated models are so much greater, however, that it is likely that the simple models presented in this chapter will continue to be used in interindustry analysis of most parts of the economy for some time to come.

[31] Under Leontief's assumption, the analysis is made in constant prices of the base year, and output levels are independent of price changes.
[32] See Chapter 10.

APPENDIX: Input-Output Solutions

The main need of the interindustry analyst is for insight into the effects of interdependence rather than for detailed instructions for solving large systems of simultaneous equations. Given the advantages of modern computing equipment, this job will almost certainly be turned over to a specialist. However, the solution of numerical examples by hand provides a feel for the working of interindustry models which is difficult to acquire otherwise. The methods illustrated below are chosen with this purpose in mind rather than for their efficiency with larger systems. The relative merits of various methods for large-scale computations are discussed in Evans (1956), to which the reader is referred.

We take up first an alternative iterative method for special solutions which is both efficient and instructive. We then restate the input-output system in matrix form and calculate the general solution to Model I in several ways that illustrate the economic significance of its elements.

A. Special Solutions

A special solution to a set of simultaneous equations applies only to a particular set of values for the constant terms—in our case, the final demands. The general solution, on the other hand, can be used with any set of final demands so long as the structural coefficients are kept constant. The most familiar method of solving simultaneous equations, that of substitution or elimination, can be applied in either case.

Although it becomes very cumbersome for large systems of equations, the method of substitution leads to a useful iterative procedure for special solutions when some of the coefficients are zero, as in the example we have been using. For illustration, we first write out Eqs. (2.5) corresponding to our assumed input coefficients and final demands (from Table 2.4):

$$0.9X_S - 0.1X_A - 0.1X_B - 0.2X_F = 60$$
$$+ 0.9X_A \qquad\qquad - 0.3X_F = 105$$
$$- 0.1X_A + 0.7X_B - 0.1X_F = 40$$
$$0.8X_F = 320$$
$$0.9X_S + 0.7X_A + 0.6X_B + 0.2X_F = V$$

Normally, we would eliminate one variable from each pair of equations and proceed in this way until a numerical value had been found for one variable. This would be substituted in one of the other equations to solve for a second variable, and so on, until all unknowns had been determined. In the present case, the procedure is simplified by the fact that the fourth equation has only one coefficient different from zero, and we can solve for X_F directly. This value can then be used in the second equation to solve for X_A, and X_F and X_A together for X_B, as follows:

(1) $\quad X_F = \dfrac{320}{0.8} = 400$

(2) $\quad X_A = \dfrac{1}{0.9}[105 + 0.3(400)] = 250$

(3) $\quad X_B = \dfrac{1}{0.7}[40 + 0.1(400) + 0.1(250)] = 150 \qquad\qquad (2.17)$

(4) $\quad X_S = \dfrac{1}{0.9}[60 + 0.2(400) + 0.1(250) + 0.1(150)] = 200$

(5) $\quad V = 0.2(400) + 0.7(250) + 0.6(150) + 0.9(200) = 525$

The order in which this system was solved suggests a rearrangement of the sectors, starting with F, which is dependent only on final demand. The others are ordered in such a way that each is only dependent on the output levels of preceding sectors. When this is possible, as in the present case, the resulting coefficient matrix is called *triangular* because it has all zeros above the diagonal (see Table 2.6 above).

The Gauss-Seidel method of iteration (Evans, pp. 72–77) follows closely the procedure which has just been used in (2.17). For a perfectly triangular matrix, the procedure corresponds exactly to the solution by substitution and would therefore require only a single iteration. If there are some nonzero coefficients above the diagonal, however, successive iterations must be used, each based on previously calculated output levels for the transactions above the diagonal. The total output for sector 2 in round t, for example, can be written as follows:

$$X_2^{(t)} = \frac{1}{(1 - a_{22})}[Y_2 + a_{21}X_1^{(t)} + a_{23}X_3^{(t-1)} + a_{24}X_4^{(t-1)}] \quad (2.18)$$

To illustrate the Gauss-Seidel iteration, we shall modify the data used in Eq. (2.17) by adding the above-diagonal elements that were

TABLE 2.7. ILLUSTRATION OF GAUSS-SEIDEL ITERATION

Producing Sector	Using Sector (1)	(2)	(3)	(4)	$\sum_{i\neq j} a_{ij}X_j$ (5)	Y_i (6)	(7) = (5) + (6)	$\dfrac{1}{(1-a_{ii})}$ (8)	X_i^t (9)
1 Finished goods	**0.2** ...		**0.01** 0.4		0.4	320	320.4	0.8	400.5
			1.5		1.5		321.5		401.9
2 Agriculture	**0.3** 120.2	**0.1** ...	**0.01** 0.4		120.6	105	225.6	0.9	250.7
	120.6		1.5		122.1		227.1		252.3
3 Basic industry	**0.1** 40.1	**0.1** 25.1	**0.3** ...	**0.02** 1.2	66.3	40	106.3	0.7	151.9
	40.2	25.2		4.0	69.4		109.4		156.3
4 Services	**0.2** 80.1	**0.1** 25.1	**0.1** 15.2	**0.1** ...	120.4	60	180.4	0.9	200.4
	80.4	25.2	15.6		121.2		181.2		201.4
X_i^t $t = 0$	320	105	40	60					
$t = 1$	400.5	250.7	151.9	200.4					
$t = 2$	401.9	252.3	156.3	201.4					

dropped originally in rounding off the coefficients in Table 2.4. The
revised coefficients and the calculation are shown in Table 2.7. The
first round is much the same as that shown in (2.17) with the addition
of the above-diagonal elements. In the second round (2.18) is applied again, using production levels from round 1 for above-diagonal
elements. In the present example, the second iteration provides a
close approximation to the correct answer.

Two differences between the Gauss-Seidel method and the iterative
procedure given earlier in Table 2.5 should be noted. In the first
place, the column of coefficients is multiplied each time by the estimate of *total* production, not by the increment.[33] Secondly, values
for sectors already estimated in the *current* round are used instead of
estimates from the previous round. Only sectors which follow X_i in
the sequence have values from the previous round.

The practical value of this method depends on the extent to which
actual input-output systems can be arranged in triangular form. The
experiments with the American, Italian, Norwegian, and Japanese
matrices described in Chapter 8 show that in these cases from 4 to
13% of interindustry transactions (or less than 6% of total demands)
lie above the diagonal in the optimum arrangement of sectors. For
hand calculation, the triangular iterative procedure frequently offers a
considerable saving in time, particularly if accuracy within 1 to 2% is
adequate. Even a single round of the Gauss-Seidel method provides
an approximation to the answer which is accurate to within 5% in most
sectors. As Evans points out, however, the choice of method for
machine computation depends largely on the equipment used.

B. Matrix Notation and the General Solution

Although we make use of only the most elementary matrix operations in this book, it is helpful in discussing the general solution to
first state the input-output system in matrix form. The definitions
given will also facilitate the presentation of linear programming in
Chapter 4. Good introductions to matrix algebra as applied to economics are given in a number of places, such as Klein (1953), Kemeny,
Snell, and Thompson (1957), and Dorfman, Samuelson, and Solow
(1958), so we present only the concepts needed to discuss interindustry systems.

(1) A *matrix* is a rectangular array of numbers. The size of the
matrix is indicated by the number of rows (m) and columns (n),
written as $m \times n$. The collection of input coefficients in the Leon-

[33] This can also be done with the first method as a way of controlling errors.

tief system forms a *square matrix*, since there are equal numbers of rows and columns. This is usually called the "technological" matrix. For a 3×3 system, it may be written as follows:

$$\mathbf{A} = \begin{bmatrix} a_{11} & a_{12} & a_{13} \\ a_{21} & a_{22} & a_{23} \\ a_{31} & a_{32} & a_{33} \end{bmatrix}$$

A matrix will be identified here by a capital letter in bold-face type.

(2) The numbers comprising a matrix are called *elements*. The subscripts already used for the input-output system correspond to the usual matrix notation, in which a_{ij} indicates the element in the *i*th row and *j*th column. Elements of the $\mathbf{A}$ matrix are identified by small *a*'s.

(3) A *column vector* is a matrix having a single column of *m* elements. A *row vector* is similarly a matrix having a single row. In the Leontief system, the input coefficients of each industry constitute a column vector which describes its technology. This concept provides the basis for activity analysis, which is discussed in Chapter 4.

A matrix can be defined as a group of column vectors:

$$\mathbf{A} = [\mathbf{A}_1 \quad \mathbf{A}_2 \quad \mathbf{A}_3]$$

Here the vector components of the $\mathbf{A}$ matrix are indicated by $\mathbf{A}_j$. Each of them represents a column of coefficients a_{ij} $(i = 1 \cdots m)$.

The production levels and final demands in the Leontief system may be written as column vectors:

$$\mathbf{X} = \begin{bmatrix} X_1 \\ X_2 \\ X_3 \end{bmatrix} \qquad \mathbf{Y} = \begin{bmatrix} Y_1 \\ Y_2 \\ Y_3 \end{bmatrix}$$

The sets of capital and labor coefficients, or of coefficients for any commodity input, constitute row vectors.

(4) A *diagonal matrix* is a square matrix which has at least one non-zero element on its diagonal and zeros elsewhere. Two diagonal matrices are needed to express the input-output model of equation (2.7):

(*a*) The *identity matrix*:

$$\mathbf{I} = \begin{bmatrix} 1 & 0 & 0 \\ 0 & 1 & 0 \\ 0 & 0 & 1 \end{bmatrix}$$

(*b*) The matrix of *import coefficients* (some of which are zero):

$$\mathbf{M} = \begin{bmatrix} m_1 & 0 & 0 \\ 0 & m_2 & 0 \\ 0 & 0 & m_3 \end{bmatrix}$$

(5) *Matrix addition* consists of adding corresponding terms—those having the same subscripts. This can only be done if the two matrices have the same number of rows and columns. For example:

$$\mathbf{A} + \mathbf{B} = \begin{bmatrix} a_{11} & a_{12} \\ a_{21} & a_{22} \end{bmatrix} + \begin{bmatrix} b_{11} & b_{12} \\ b_{21} & b_{22} \end{bmatrix} = \begin{bmatrix} (a_{11} + b_{11}) & (a_{12} + b_{12}) \\ (a_{21} + b_{21}) & (a_{22} + b_{22}) \end{bmatrix}$$

Matrix subtraction is performed in a similar way.

(6) *Matrix multiplication* consists of multiplying each element of a row (*i*) in the first matrix by the corresponding element in a column (*j*) of the second matrix. The products are summed to give the *ij*th element in the product matrix. This operation can only be carried out if the number of columns in the first matrix is equal to the number of rows in the second. The product of an $m \times n$ matrix and an $n \times p$ matrix is therefore $m \times p$. Matrix multiplication is not commutative. Even if both matrices are square and of the same size, the result of matrix multiplication will in general depend on the order in which it is performed.

In input-output analysis, we frequently have occasion to multiply a matrix by a column vector. By the above rule, this can only be done if the column vector is the second term. In this case we *premultiply* the vector by the matrix, meaning that each row in the matrix is multiplied by the elements of the column. The result is also a column vector, since $n \times n$ by $n \times 1$ gives a product matrix which is $n \times 1$.[34] For example, the product of the technology matrix and the vector of production levels is the vector of intermediate demands:

$$\mathbf{AX} = \begin{bmatrix} a_{11} & a_{12} & a_{13} \\ a_{21} & a_{22} & a_{23} \\ a_{31} & a_{32} & a_{33} \end{bmatrix} \begin{bmatrix} X_1 \\ X_2 \\ X_3 \end{bmatrix}$$

$$= \begin{bmatrix} (a_{11}X_1 + a_{12}X_2 + a_{13}X_3) \\ (a_{21}X_1 + a_{22}X_2 + a_{23}X_3) \\ (a_{31}X_1 + a_{32}X_2 + a_{33}X_3) \end{bmatrix} = \begin{bmatrix} W_1 \\ W_2 \\ W_3 \end{bmatrix} = \mathbf{W}$$

[34] A row vector is *postmultiplied* by a matrix for the same reason, and the product is also a row vector.

We can now express the input-output models in matrix terms.   The simpler version is written:

$$X_1 - (a_{11}X_1 + a_{12}X_2 + a_{13}X_3) = Y_1$$
$$X_2 - (a_{21}X_1 + a_{22}X_2 + a_{23}X_3) = Y_2 \qquad (2.5)$$
$$X_3 - (a_{31}X_1 + a_{32}X_2 + a_{33}X_3) = Y_3$$

In matrix form, this becomes:

$$\mathbf{X} - \mathbf{AX} = \mathbf{Y}$$

In order to carry out the indicated substraction, we can multiply $\mathbf{X}$ by the identity matrix, since $\mathbf{IX} = \mathbf{X}$.   This gives:

$$\mathbf{IX} - \mathbf{AX} = (\mathbf{I} - \mathbf{A})\mathbf{X} = \mathbf{Y} \qquad (2.5m)$$

which is equivalent to:

$$
\begin{bmatrix}
(1 - a_{11}) & -a_{12} & -a_{13} \\
-a_{21} & (1 - a_{22}) & -a_{23} \\
-a_{31} & -a_{32} & (1 - a_{33})
\end{bmatrix}
\begin{bmatrix}
X_1 \\
X_2 \\
X_3
\end{bmatrix}
=
\begin{bmatrix}
Y_1 \\
Y_2 \\
Y_3
\end{bmatrix}
$$

The matrix $(\mathbf{I} - \mathbf{A})$ if often called the *Leontief matrix*.   It has the properties that all the elements on the diagonal are positive, while those off the diagonal are negative or zero.

When imports are added to the system, we have:

$$(1 + m_i)X_i - \sum_j a_{ij}X_j = Y_i \qquad (i = 1 \cdots n) \qquad (2.7)$$

In matrix form, this version is written:

$$(\mathbf{I} + \mathbf{M} - \mathbf{A})\mathbf{X} = \mathbf{Y} \qquad (2.7m)$$

(7) *Matrix Inversion*

To find the general solution, Eq. (2.8), we need an operation corresponding to division in elementary algebra.   To solve for X in the single equation $aX = Y$, we divide through by a, which is equivalent to multiplying by its reciprocal: $X = (1/a) Y = a^{-1}Y$.   The matrix operation corresponding to finding $1/a$ is called *matrix inversion,* and the result is the reciprocal or *inverse matrix,* $\mathbf{A}^{-1}$.   The inverse of $\mathbf{A}$ is defined as that matrix which when multiplied by $\mathbf{A}$ gives the identity matrix, $\mathbf{I}$.   Therefore, $\mathbf{AA}^{-1} = \mathbf{I}$.   In this case, the order of multiplication does not matter.   The inverse is only defined for square matrices.

With this definition of the inverse, the general solution of the input-output system of (2.5) may be stated as:

$$\mathbf{X} = (\mathbf{I} - \mathbf{A})^{-1}\mathbf{Y} \text{ or } \begin{bmatrix} X_1 \\ X_2 \\ X_3 \end{bmatrix} = \begin{bmatrix} r_{11} & r_{12} & r_{13} \\ r_{21} & r_{22} & r_{23} \\ r_{31} & r_{32} & r_{33} \end{bmatrix} \begin{bmatrix} Y_1 \\ Y_2 \\ Y_3 \end{bmatrix} \qquad (2.8m)$$

In order to avoid confusion, we call the elements in the inverse (reciprocal) matrix r_{ij} and the inverse itself $\mathbf{R}$. In the more general system $(2.7m)$, which includes induced imports,

$$\mathbf{R} = (\mathbf{I} + \mathbf{M} - \mathbf{A})^{-1}$$

Equation $(2.8m)$ states in matrix form the general solution already given in (2.8). To solve for the vector $\mathbf{X}$, each column of coefficients in the inverse is multiplied by the corresponding element of the final demand vector $\mathbf{Y}$ and the products are added for each row, as in Table 2.6.

C. Evaluating the Inverse Matrix[35]

An excellent discussion of methods for computing the inverse matrix and their relative merits is given in Dwyer (1951). Here we shall calculate the inverse to a 2×2 Leontief matrix in three different ways which give some insight into the economic meaning of the results. We assume

$$\mathbf{A} = \begin{bmatrix} 0 & 0.5 \\ 0.25 & 0 \end{bmatrix} \quad \text{and} \quad \mathbf{I} - \mathbf{A} = \begin{bmatrix} 1 & -0.5 \\ -0.25 & 1 \end{bmatrix}$$

From the definition of the inverse, $(\mathbf{I} - \mathbf{A})\,\mathbf{R} = \mathbf{I}$, or

$$\begin{bmatrix} 1 & -0.5 \\ -0.25 & 1 \end{bmatrix} \begin{bmatrix} r_{11} & r_{12} \\ r_{21} & r_{22} \end{bmatrix} = \begin{bmatrix} 1 & 0 \\ 0 & 1 \end{bmatrix}$$

(a) For a small matrix such as this, we can write out the equations involving the elements in each column of $\mathbf{R}$ and then solve by substitution.

Column 1	Column 2
$r_{11} - 0.5r_{21} = 1$	$r_{12} - 0.5r_{22} = 0$
$-0.25r_{11} + r_{21} = 0$	$-0.25r_{12} + r_{22} = 1$
$r_{11} = 1.143$	$r_{12} = 0.571$
$r_{21} = 0.286$	$r_{22} = 1.143$

[35] 29-order inverse matrices for three countries are given in the appendix to Chapter 8.

This procedure has the effect of calculating each column in the inverse separately and is useful when only one or a few columns are required. In economic terms, each element r_{ij} indicates the amount of commodity i that must be produced to sustain a final demand of 1.0 in sector j. Another method of carrying out the calculation of a single column in the inverse, therefore, is to assume a final demand of 1.0 in one sector and apply either of the iterative procedures that have already been described.

(b) The derivation of the inverse matrix is commonly explained by means of determinants (see Dwyer, Ch. 13). The determinant Δ of a 2 $\times$ 2 matrix is $(a_{11}a_{22} - a_{21}a_{12})$. Each element in the inverse, r_{ij}, is equal to the cofactor of the element a_{ji}[36] (in which the subscripts are reversed) divided by the determinant of the matrix. If A_{ij} is defined as the cofactor of a_{ji}, then:

$$r_{ij} = \mathbf{A}_{ij}/\Delta \qquad (2.19)$$

For our example, the value of the determinant is:

$$\Delta = 1 - 0.125 = 0.875$$

Equation (2.19) gives:

$$r_{11} = \frac{1.0}{0.875} = 1.143$$

$$r_{21} = \frac{0.25}{0.875} = 0.286$$

$$r_{12} = \frac{0.50}{0.875} = 0.571$$

$$r_{22} = \frac{1.0}{0.875} = 1.143$$

This method of computing the inverse shows that the latter will only exist if the determinant of the original matrix is different from zero. If the determinant is zero, the columns of the matrix are linearly de-

---

[36] The notation follows Dwyer. The cofactor of a_{ji} is the value of the determinant obtained by omitting row j and column i from the original matrix. The sign $(-1)^{i+j}$ is attached, with the result that all the cofactors of a Leontief matrix are positive. In a 2 x 2 matrix:

$$A_{11} = a_{22} \qquad A_{12} = a_{12}$$
$$A_{21} = a_{21} \qquad A_{22} = a_{11}$$

pendent—i.e., one can be expressed as a linear combination of the others—and the matrix is said to be singular.

(c) Finally, we can use the iterative procedure of (2.13) to derive an approximate expression for the inverse matrix R. Equation (2.13) can be restated in matrix form as:

$$X = Y + AY + A^2Y + A^3Y + \cdots \cdot \tag{2.13m}$$

This equation shows that each round in the iteration consists of raising the matrix to a successively higher power, which gives the method the name of *expansion in powers*.[37] A comparison of equations (2.8m) and (2.13m) shows that:

$$X = (I - A)^{-1}Y = RY = (I + A + A^2 + A^3 + \cdots)Y$$

or

$$R = I + A + A^2 + A^3 + \cdots \cdot \tag{2.20}$$

Equation (2.20) indicates that (a) each element in the inverse is nonnegative since I and A contain only nonnegative elements; (b) each element in the inverse depends in general on all of the elements in the technology matrix unless certain ones of these are zero.

Use of Eq. (2.20) gives an approximation to the inverse which would converge to the true value if carried out further:

$$R = \begin{bmatrix} 1 & 0 \\ 0 & 1 \end{bmatrix} + \begin{bmatrix} 0 & 0.5 \\ 0.25 & 0 \end{bmatrix} + \begin{bmatrix} 0.125 & 0 \\ 0 & 0.125 \end{bmatrix}$$

$$+ \begin{bmatrix} 0 & 0.063 \\ 0.031 & 0 \end{bmatrix} = \begin{bmatrix} 1.125 & 0.563 \\ 0.281 & 1.125 \end{bmatrix}$$

Each element in the inverse can thus be thought of as the sum of a series of which the first term is the coefficient in the Leontief matrix with positive sign. This notion is useful in breaking down the total effect of a given final demand into a direct effect $(I + A)Y$ and a series of indirect effects $(A^2 + A^3 + \cdots)Y$. For any element off the diagonal, the sum of the indirect effects is represented by $(r_{ij} - a_{ij})$. To facilitate comparisons between the direct coefficients a_{ij} and the total coefficients r_{ij}, we shall follow the practice of bring-

---

[37] This form is analogous to the expression for the Keynesian multiplier as the sum of $(1 + c + c^2 + c^3 + \cdots)$ which would be obtained from Eq. (2.9). Convergence of the series is assured, as in the Keynesian case, by the property of the Leontief matrix noted previously—that the sum of the coefficients a_{ij} in each column is less than or equal to one and at least one column total is less than one.

ing the $(I - A)$ matrix and its inverse together as we have done in Table 2.6.

Problems

1. Recompute the solution to model I given in Table 2.5 (p. 29) if agricultural capacity is limited to 150 and additional requirements for agricultural products must be imported.

2. Compute each colume of the inverse matrix given in Table 2.6 (p. 32) by Gauss-Seidel iteration.

3. In the example of section C of the Appendix (p. 50), assume import coefficients of $m_1 = 0.2$, $m_2 = 0.3$. (a) Compute the inverse matrix by two different methods. (b) Write an expression for the total imports required as a function of final demands.

4. Using the tables in the appendix to Chapter 8, compare the direct effects on other sectors of $100 million of final demand for machinery in the United States (p. 222, Table 8.9) to the total effects (p. 228, Table 8.12). Trace out the origins of the indirect requirements shown for machinery, iron and steel, iron ore, and electric power.

BIBLIOGRAPHY

Balderston, J. B., and T. M. Whitin, "Aggregation in the Input-Output Model," in *Economic Activity Analysis*, 1954.

Barna, T., "Classification and Aggregation in Input-Output Analysis," in *The Structural Interdependence of the Economy*, 1956.

°Dorfman, R., P. Samuelson, and R. Solow, *Linear Programming and Economic Analysis*, McGraw-Hill Book Company, New York, 1958, Chapters 9 and 10.

Dwyer, P. S., *Linear Computations*, John Wiley and Sons, New York, 1951.

°Evans, W. D., "Input-Output Computations," in *The Structural Interdependence of the Economy*, 1956.

°Evans, W. D., and M. Hoffenberg, "The Nature and Uses of Interindustry-Relations Data and Methods," in National Bureau of Economic Research, *Input-Output Analysis: An Appraisal*, Princeton University Press, Princeton, 1955.

Fisher, W. D., "Criteria for Aggregation in Input-Output Analysis," *Review of Economics and Statistics*, XL, No. 3, 250–260 (August 1958).

Holzman, M., "Problems of Classification and Aggregation," in Leontief and others, *Studies in the Structure of the American Economy*, Oxford University Press, New York, 1953.

Kemeny, J. G., J. L. Snell, and G. L. Thompson, *Introduction to Finite Mathematics*, Prentice-Hall, Englewood Cliffs, New Jersey, 1957.

Klein, L. R., *A Textbook of Econometrics*, Row, Peterson and Company, Evanston, Illinois, 1953.

Leontief, W. (1953a), "Structural Change," in *Studies in the Structure of the American Economy*, 1953.

°———. (1951), *The Structure of the American Economy, 1919–1939*, 1951, Parts I and II.

Liebling, H. I., "Interindustry Economics and National Income Theory," in *Input-Output Analysis: An Appraisal*, 1955.

°Sigel, S. J., "A Comparison of the Structures of Three Social Accounting Systems," in *Input-Output Analysis: An Appraisal*, 1955.

Stone, R., "Input-Output and the Social Accounts," in *The Structural Interdependence of the Economy*, 1956.

Theil, H., "Linear Aggregation in Input-Output Analysis," *Econometrica*, XXV, No. 1, 111–122 (January 1957).

3

Extensions of the basic model

The basic input-output model determines the relations between autonomous demands[1] Y_i and levels of production X_i. The range of applications of this model can be extended in two different ways. One is to examine the relations among economic variables which are "outside the model" but which are indirectly related by way of the interindustry system. An example of this type of extension is given by the relation between imports and national income. A solution to an input-output problem of the kind we have discussed starts with a given level of total income and determines imports as a by-product in solving for production levels. Any variation in the composition of final demand may affect imports, however, without a change in the level of income. We could, for example, determine the separate effects of investment, consumption, and exports on imports and hence the effect of varying their proportions in gross national product. Similar analyses could be made for skilled labor, indirect taxes, or any other variable which is determined in part by the levels of production in each sector. The characteristic feature of such extensions of the original model is that we are not primarily interested in the levels of production but in aggregates that can be derived from them.

[1] Henceforth we shall use Y_i (rather than $\bar{Y}_i$) to denote autonomous demand, however defined.

A second type of extension is to "close the model" by assuming that one or more of the previously autonomous elements is determined in some way by the levels of production. In this chapter we take up three such possibilities. The first consists of adding behavioral equations which will "explain" those elements in final demand, such as consumption, that depend in part on the level of income generated. These relations resemble a disaggregated Keynesian consumption function, but they may contain other variables which are specified in advance. The second example involves the subdivision of the economy into several regions, each having its own structural characteristics. In such a model, exports are explained as imports into another region. In the third case, we use a period analysis to explain investment in one period as a function of demands and production in later periods, using a form of the acceleration principle. These three modifications of the open static model can be combined in various ways, but here only the simplest forms will be illustrated. For each case, we have tried to select a model suited to empirical work.

A. Final Demand and Primary Inputs

The components of final demand and the use of primary inputs are related through the input functions. We now wish to eliminate the production levels from the system so that any component of final demand can be translated directly into demands for primary factors, or alternatively the demand for any primary input can be determined as a function of each component of Y.

The problem can be illustrated in concrete terms by giving a breakdown of the final demand in our previous example and assuming input coefficients for three primary factors. These additional specifications are shown in Table 3.1. For convenience, the Leontief matrix and the elements in the inverse matrix r_{ij} are also repeated from Chapter 2. Given this information, we should like to answer the following questions: (i) What is the effect of each component in final demand (investment, consumption, and exports) on the level of production in each sector? (ii) What are the requirements of primary factors for each of these components of the national income? (iii) What is the factor requirement per unit of final demand in each sector?

The answer to the first question may be found by making separate solutions for each of the final demand components in the same way as we have solved for total production. Since we have already computed the inverse matrix, the easiest method of solution is to multiply

TABLE 3.1. DATA FOR EXTENDED MODEL I

Sector	1	2	3	4	Y_C	Y_1	Y_E	Y
			Input Coefficients*				Final Demand†	
Produced Inputs								
1	**0.8** *1.250*				215	70	35	320
2	**-0.3** *0.417*	**0.9** *1.111*			100	0	5	105
3	**-0.1** *0.238*	**-0.1** *0.159*	**0.7** *1.429*		35	0	5	40
4	**-0.2** *0.351*	**-0.1** *0.141*	**-0.1** *0.159*	**0.9** *1.111*	60	0	0	60
Primary Inputs								
†Capital (K)	**-0.70** *2.33*	**-2.00** *2.59*	**-1.80** *2.66*	**-0.55** *0.61*				
†Labor (L)	**-0.06** *0.469*	**-0.20** *0.356*	**-0.14** *0.325*	**-0.79** *0.878*				
†Natural resources (N)	**0** *0.655*	**-1.0** *1.270*	**-1.0** *1.429*	**0** *0*				
Total Final Demands					410	70	45	525

* The elements in the inverse matrix are given in italics from Table 2.5 and Table 3.3, below. The direct coefficients in the Leontief matrix are in bold face.

† Exports have been included in final demand by way of illustration; to be consistent with Eq. (2.5), they should be considered as net of imports.

‡ The units in which primary inputs are measured are arbitrary.

the elements in each column in the inverse by the corresponding element of final demand and to sum these products horizontally, as in Table 2.6.[2] The results of this calculation are shown in Table 3.2. Except for rounding errors, they add up to the production levels previously computed from the total final demand.

Once the production levels in each sector corresponding to each component of demand are known, the corresponding factor requirements are easily determined from the factor input coefficients. The labor used in producing the consumption component, for example, is:

$$L_C = 0.06(268.8) + 0.20(200.7) + 0.14(117.1) + 0.79(161.7) = 200.4$$

A similar expression can be written for each factor:[3]

$$L = \sum_j l_j X_j$$

$$K = \sum_j k_j X_j \tag{3.1}$$

or in general,
$$F_h = \sum_j f_{hj} X_j$$

One use for this type of calculation is to compare the factor proportions in each component of final demand. This can be done by computing "factor intensities," defined as the amount of each factor required to produce one unit of final demand. (For example the labor intensity of consumption is determined by dividing $200.4/410 = 0.489$.) In our example, exports are less labor intensive, more resource intensive and more capital intensive than the other components. Comparisons of this sort are of considerable interest for the study of international trade, economic development, and other problems of resource allocation, which will be discussed in Chapters 9 and 11.

The calculations made so far have utilized rows in the inverse matrix. The factor requirements to produce a given commodity can be determined in the same way from a single column in the inverse. The elements of the first column, for example, tell us the output required in each sector per unit of final demand for commodity 1. If

[2] An actual calculation of this kind for the American economy is given by Evans and Hoffenberg (1952), p. 124.
[3] Since we shall frequently refer to the use of labor and capital, we use the symbols L and K for the demand for these factors. When the argument refers to any primary factor, we use the symbol F_h.

TABLE 3.2. EFFECTS OF COMPONENTS OF FINAL DEMAND ON OUTPUTS AND PRIMARY INPUTS

Effects on:	Components of Final Demand			Total Final Demand
	Consumption	Investment	Exports	
Production levels				
X_1	268.8	87.5	43.7	400.0
X_2	200.7	29.2	20.1	250.0
X_3	117.1	16.7	16.3	150.1
X_4	161.7	24.5	13.8	200.0
Factor use				
Labor (L)	200.4	32.8	19.8	253.0
Capital (K)	889.2	163.1	107.7	1160.0
Natural Resources (N)	317.8	45.9	36.4	400.1
Factor intensity				
Labor intensity	0.489	0.469	0.440	0.482
Capital intensity	2.17	2.33	2.39	2.21
Resource intensity	0.775	0.656	0.809	0.762

we want to know the labor required to produce this output, we multiply each of these elements by the corresponding labor input coefficients:

$$L_1 = 0.06(1.25) + 0.20(0.417) + 0.14(0.238) + 0.79(0.351)$$

$$= 0.469$$

The results of similar calculations for each sector are shown in the first column of Table 3.3. These totals are analogous to the elements in the inverse matrix itself because they measure the total effect of any element in final demand Y_j on any factor F_h in the same way that

TABLE 3.3. TOTAL USE OF PRIMARY FACTORS PER UNIT OF FINAL DEMAND (r_{hj})

Commodity (j)	Labor	Capital	Natural Resources
1	0.469	2.33	0.655
2	0.356	2.59	1.270
3	0.325	2.66	1.429
4	0.878	0.61	0

the inverse measures the effect of Y_j on X_i.[4] It will therefore be convenient to give them the same symbol and define

$$r_{hj} = \sum_i f_{hi} r_{ij} \qquad (3.2)$$

for any factor h.

Having now determined the factor requirements per unit of each commodity in final demand, we have an alternative way of computing the total of each primary factor required to produce any category of final demand. The labor required for consumption, for example, could be computed as the sum of each commodity in the consumption column multiplied by its labor requirement:

$$L_C = 0.469(215) + 0.356(100) + 0.325(35) + 0.878(60) = 200.5$$

Or in general

$$F_h = \sum_j r_{hj} Y_j \qquad (3.3)$$

The total factor requirement can be computed either from equation (3.1) or (3.3).[5] (The reader may satisfy himself on this point by computing the factor requirements in Table 3.2 in both ways.) Similarly, the factor intensities given in Table 3.2 for each column of final demand are the weighted averages of the factor intensities of each commodity in the column, as shown by the calculation just made for L_C.

The analysis of the use of each primary factor leads to a theory of price determination in the input-output system. Under rather restrictive assumptions, the resulting prices can be thought of as market prices, as in the work of Leontief. Even without making these assumptions, we can define a measure of total resource use which corresponds to the "shadow price" or opportunity cost of linear programming.

Consider first a system in which there is only one homogeneous primary factor, F. We could then define the cost of a given commodity as the total amount of F required to produce it. If no profits are assumed, the price of each commodity would equal its total cost.

[4] See Dorfman, Samuelson, and Solow (1958), pp. 230–237, for a more extended discussion of this relationship.

[5] The equality between the two is easily shown:

$$F_h = \sum_i f_{hi} X_i = \sum_i \sum_j f_{hi} r_{ij} Y_j = \sum_j r_{hj} Y_j$$

Under this one-factor theory of value, there is only one set of prices which will result in equal remuneration to F in all its uses. They may be defined as:

$$P_j = f_j P_f + \sum_i a_{ij} P_i \qquad (j = 1 \cdots n) \qquad (3.4)$$

If we take the price of F as as a unity, Eq. (3.4) states that the price of any commodity is equal to the amount of F used directly per unit of output f_j plus the amount of each input times its price.

Equations (3.4) are similar in form to Eqs. 2.5, with prices as variables instead of outputs and with f_j as the autonomous element instead of Y_j, except that they pertain to single columns of inputs instead of to rows. The solution to this set of equations is therefore the same as Eq. (2.8) with the appropriate change in subscripts to indicate the jth column in the inverse:[6]

$$P_j = r_{1j} f_1 + r_{2j} f_2 + \cdots + r_{nj} f_n \qquad (j = 1 \cdots n) \qquad (3.5)$$

This equation is identical with (3.2), by which we have already computed the total use of any factor per unit of Y_j, with P_j instead of r_{hj}. If labor were the only factor in the system, therefore, the prices (measured in labor units) would be given by the first column of Table 3.3:

$$P_1 = 0.469$$
$$P_2 = 0.356$$
$$P_3 = 0.325$$
$$P_4 = 0.878$$

Leontief has extended this method of computing prices by adding an autonomous element of profit in each sector, π_j. With this addition, and with labor as the primary factor, equations (3.4) become:

$$P_j = \pi_j + l_j P_l + \sum_i a_{ij} P_i \qquad (j = 1 \cdots n) \qquad (3.4a)$$

[6] In matrix form, we can write (3.4) as:

$$\mathbf{P}' = \mathbf{F}' + \mathbf{P}'\mathbf{A} \qquad (3.4m)$$

where $\mathbf{P}'$ is the row vector of prices and $\mathbf{F}'$ is the row vector of factor inputs. The derivation of (3.5) then follows the same form as the derivation of (2.8m) above:

$$\mathbf{P}'(\mathbf{I} - \mathbf{A}) = \mathbf{F}'$$
$$\mathbf{P}' = \mathbf{F}'(\mathbf{I} - \mathbf{A})^{-1} = \mathbf{F}'\mathbf{R} \qquad (3.5m)$$

The solution to Eq. (3.4a) corresponding to Eq. (3.5) is:

$$P_j = \sum_i r_{ij} l_i P_l + \sum_i r_{ij} \pi_i \tag{3.6}$$

Leontief (1951, pp. 188–201) uses these equations to determine the effect on prices of varying either profits or wages (or some elements of each).

This type of solution can be illustrated in our example by defining profits as the return to factors other than labor; we compute them as a residual from Table 3.1 on the assumption that the units of measurement have been defined so as to make the market price of labor and of each commodity equal to 1.0. The implied profit rates per dollar of output are: $\pi_1 = 0.14$, $\pi_2 = 0.50$, $\pi_3 = 0.46$, $\pi_4 = 0.11$. Substituting these values in Eq. (3.6) for commodity 1 gives:

$$\sum_i r_{i1} \pi_i = 0.14(1.25) + 0.50(.417) + 0.46(.238) + 0.11(.351) = 0.5316$$

$$P_1 = 0.469 P_l + 0.5316 = 1.0006 \text{ for } P_l = 1.0$$

(The prices of other commodities can similarly be shown to be 1.0, since the profit rates were defined from this assumption.)

This analysis has the effect of breaking down the price of each commodity into two components, one representing total labor use and the other depreciation, profits, taxes, etc. If coefficients and profit rates remained unchanged, our analysis would imply that a 10% rise in labor cost would produce a 4.69% rise in price in sector 1 and one of 8.78% in sector 4, for example. The assumption of constant input coefficients becomes quite tenuous if we try to apply Eq. (3.6) when there are large changes in the price structure, however, because most of the arguments for constant input coefficients depend on the absence of variation in relative prices. This type of analysis is likely to be empirically valid only when applied to the smaller components, such as imports and taxes, which do not produce great changes in relative prices.

This discussion of price changes applies to an empirically derived input-output system in which the units of measurement for each input and output are the amounts purchasable for a given sum in the base year. Under input-output assumptions, in which there is only one way of producing each commodity, price analysis is limited to determining the differential changes in commodity prices which would result from given variations in the cost of primary inputs. Under the more general assumptions taken up in the next chapter, however, we shall be able to go further and use equations of the type of (3.4) to determine the opportunity costs of the primary inputs themselves. The equilibrium or shadow prices will then acquire a new significance as measures of resource use which take into account the possible adjustments in technology and trade to relative factor scarcity.

B. Induced Consumption and Income Generation

In the models used thus far, there has been no analysis of the level of income. It has been assumed that final demand is studied outside the interindustry framework and taken as given. This procedure is justified if the level of income and its use do not depend on the composition of production, since in this case a breakdown of income generated by sector will add nothing to an analysis in more aggregated terms. Under less rigid assumptions, the level of income does depend on the composition of production, however, and the procedure is no longer valid. In this case, the autonomous elements should not include all of final demand, and the level of income should be determined within the model itself.

TABLE 3.4. MODEL II: INCOME GENERATION MODEL*
$(I - A)$

Sector	1	2	3	Autonomous Demand†	X_i
1. Primary Production	**1.0**	**−0.5**	**−0.3**	20	382.8
	4.286	*3.714*	*3.143*		
2. Secondary Production	**−0.25**	**1.0**	**−0.5**	80	425.7
	3.571	*4.429*	*3.286*		
3. Household Income	**−0.75**	**−0.5**	**1.0**	0	500.0
	5.000	*5.000*	*5.000*		
4. Primary Inputs (Saving plus taxes)	**0**	**0**	**−0.2**	100	

* The inverse matrix $(I - A)^{-1}$ is shown in italics.
† Government expenditure, investment, and net exports.

The simplest way of closing the model is to treat some elements of final demand as dependent on the level of income. The general procedure is shown in model II, Table 3.4, in which the payments to households appear inside the matrix as row 3 and the use of this income is shown in the corresponding column. Since X_3 in this case represents household or personal income, the first two input coefficients in column 3 (0.3 and 0.5) indicate the marginal propensity of households to consume commodity 1 and commodity 2. The coefficient in row 4 (0.2) represents private savings and direct taxes. The primary inputs in sectors 1 and 2 represent the amounts not paid out to households (mainly gross business savings and business taxes), here assumed to be zero. The equality between autonomous demands (government expenditures, investment, and exports) and primary inputs (savings, taxes, and induced imports) is therefore preserved.

To illustrate first the case in which the result is unaffected by the composition of production, we have assumed in model II that all factor payments go directly to households and that the only entries in the row for savings and taxes are in the household column. We should therefore expect the level of income to be the same as we would compute from a simple multiplier formula, using an autonomous demand of 100 and a propensity to save of 0.2, that is, 500. The general solution to model II, which is also shown in Table 3.4, shows that this is indeed the case. Each element in the household row of the inverse matrix is 5.00, so that any element of autonomous demand will have a multiplier effect of 5. Since the solution for the level of production in each sector is also given, the income generated can be checked by multiplying these production levels by the coefficients in the household sector: 382.8 (0.75) + 425.7 (0.5) = 500.0. Similarly savings and taxes can be shown to equal autonomous demand of 100.

The form of model II also indicates that if corporate savings and business taxes are not zero and are different in each sector, the result will no longer be independent of the composition of final demand as it was in this case. The aggregate propensity to save will then be a weighted average of the propensities of the various sectors, as shown by Goodwin (1949) and Chipman (1950). If the open model is used in this case, it will usually be necessary to make several trial solutions before a level of income is found that is consistent with the savings-investment equality.[7]

[7] Models in which consumption is included within the matrix have a significant disadvantage from a computational point of view in that they converge much more slowly in an iterative solution than those in which only production is determined in the analysis. The speed of convergence varies inversely with the sum of the input coefficients in each column. In model II, $\sum_i a_{ij}$ for inputs 1–3 totals 1.0 except for sector 3, whereas in general the average is less than 0.5 for an open model. Since the open model gives the same result when income can be estimated in advance, it will only be convenient to determine income within the system when several saving sectors are distinguished or when it is necessary to trace the levels of production and consumption over time.

The procedure followed here would apply equally to any other component of final demand which could be assumed to be equal to a certain portion of factor payments and to require inputs in given proportions. If we wish to assume balanced foreign trade and a given export composition, for example, we can construct a foreign trade sector with a row for imports and a column for exports in the same way. Another possibility is to make government expenditure equal to tax receipts. It is less plausible to make investment depend on the level of savings, however. A more defensible treatment, in which investment expenditures are derived from needed increases in capacity, is given in section D below.

C. Interregional Analysis

Comprehensive economic models are almost all deficient in that they ignore the effects of geographical factors. Interindustry analysis offers one possibility for integrating locational theory with a general analysis of production. The input-output model is only a first step in this direction, however, because it does not include any elements of choice. It can explain locational phenomena only on the assumption that there is a certain stability in the geographical distribution of production. In this section we shall present one simple interregional model, but we shall return to the problem again in Chapter 12 after we have taken up the linear programming approach.

An interregional system may be the result of breaking down a national economy into separate regions or of combining several national models into a larger economic unit. Conceptually, the problems are similar in both cases although only the first approach has been tried empirically. From one point of view, a regional division of sectors may be thought of as merely an extension of the rules of classification. Production or consumption of the same commodity in different areas should be treated as separate sectors when such a subdivision has a significant effect on the total solution. Apart from such considerations, however, we may be interested in regional totals of income, employment, and production for their own sake. In this case, it is necessary to select a geographical definition of regions which is the same for all sectors.

A regional interindustry analysis may distinguish the effects of geographical differences in the location of final demand, in sources of supply, and in production techniques. To fit into the input-output model, such differences must be assumed to be fixed over some period

of time.   On *a priori* grounds, there is less reason to expect stability
in trade patterns than in input coefficients, however, so the usual input-
output assumption of constancy should be considered as merely a first
step toward a more realistic analysis.

Our approach to interregional analysis is similar to the national-income models used to analyze international trade.[8]   Our model explains the levels of exports of each commodity in terms of the demand
for imports in other regions or countries.   The basis for this analysis
of imports has already been given in Eqs. (2.7), and it only remains
to extend the model to include several regions simultaneously.

For simplicity, we shall consider a two-region model, although the
analysis can be extended to any number of regions without modifica-
tion.   As compared to the single-region models discussed thus far, the
exports of one region to another become flows which are to be explained within the system rather than being assumed to be autonomous.   For each sector, therefore, we have a set of accounting relations such as those shown in Table 3.5.   The rows in this table show

TABLE 3.5.   INTERREGIONAL ACCOUNTS FOR SECTOR i

From: \ To:	Consuming Region α	β	Production in Region
Producing Region			
α	$X_i^{\alpha\alpha}$	$X_i^{\alpha\beta}$	X_i^{α}
β	$X_i^{\beta\alpha}$	$X_i^{\beta\beta}$	X_i^{β}
Supply in region	Z_i^{α}	Z_i^{β}	

the distribution of production by areas of use, and the columns show
the distribution of supplies to each region.   The element $X_i^{\alpha\beta}$ indicates
the amount of commodity produced in region α for use in region β—
i.e. the first superscript refers to the source and the second refers to
the region of use.

In this notation, we can redefine the variables of the single-region
model as follows:

Production in α:

$$X_i^{\alpha} = X_i^{\alpha\alpha} + X_i^{\alpha\beta}$$

[8] Metzler (1950) gives a multi-region model of international trade and income
determination based on a single sector of production in each country.   Our model
extends this approach to many sectors.   The relation of this model to those of
Leontief (1953a, Ch. 4) and Isard (1951) is discussed in Chapter 12.

Supply in α:

$$Z_i{}^\alpha = X_i{}^{\alpha\alpha} + X_i{}^{\beta\alpha}$$

Imports into α:

$$M_i{}^\alpha = X_i{}^{\beta\alpha} = Z_i{}^\alpha - X_i{}^{\alpha\alpha}$$

Exports from α:

$$E_i{}^\alpha = X_i{}^{\alpha\beta} = X_i{}^\alpha - X_i{}^{\alpha\alpha} \qquad (3.7)$$

The balance Eqs. (2.5) are similarly rewritten, deducting exports from autonomous demand and also from domestic production:

$$Total\ Demand\ in\ \alpha \quad Supply\ in\ \alpha$$

$$Z_i{}^\alpha = \sum_j a_{ij}{}^\alpha X_j{}^\alpha + Y_i{}^\alpha = X_i{}^{\alpha\alpha} + X_i{}^{\beta\alpha} \qquad (i = 1 \cdots n) \quad (3.8)$$

There is one equation of the form of (3.8) for each commodity and region, or $2n$ equations in our case, but there are $6n$ variables: $2n$ autonomous demands, $2n$ production levels, and $2n$ import levels (the exports of one region are equal to the imports of the other). In order to solve these equations for given final demands, therefore, we must make an assumption about supply sources. Here, we make the same assumption as we have previously: that imports are a fixed fraction of the total supply of each commodity. In order to provide for the general case of more than two regions, we shall call these proportions "supply coefficients." They are defined for each source of supply (including the region itself) from the following equation:

$$X_i{}^{\alpha\beta} = s_i{}^{\alpha\beta} Z_i{}^\beta \qquad (3.9)$$

The supply coefficient therefore extends the idea of a given marginal propensity to import each commodity to any number of regions. We can make the same correction for differences between marginal and average ratios as we have for imports in (2.6) if we wish. Whether we use marginal or average ratios, the sum of the supply coefficients for a given commodity must equal 1.0 if we include the intra-regional supply.

This assumption enables us to express the total production of a given commodity in one region as a function of the total demands in all regions:

$$X_i{}^\alpha = s_i{}^{\alpha\alpha} Z_i{}^\alpha + s_i{}^{\alpha\beta} Z_i{}^\beta \qquad (i = 1 \cdots n) \qquad (3.10)$$

We can now solve for the production levels corresponding to given final demands in all regions by substituting from equations (3.8) into (3.10) and collecting terms:

$$X_i{}^\alpha = \left[\sum_j s_i{}^{\alpha\alpha} a_{ij}{}^\alpha X_j{}^\alpha + \sum_j s_i{}^{\alpha\beta} a_{ij}{}^\beta X_j{}^\beta \right] + [s_i{}^{\alpha\alpha} Y_i{}^\alpha + s_i{}^{\alpha\beta} Y_i{}^\beta] \quad (3.11)$$

These equations state that total production is equal to the amounts used for further production in both regions plus the shipments to both regions for final demand. The extension to more than two regions is straightforward.

It is necessary here to include household consumption within the model in the manner indicated in the preceding section because the location of production depends on the location of consumption, and the latter cannot be determined separately from the calculation of the income generated in each sector and region. The autonomous demands Y_i therefore include only investment and government expenditure.

An example of an interregional model is given in Tables 3.6 and

TABLE 3.6. DATA FOR REGIONAL MODEL (III)

| Sector | Supply Coefficients | | | |
	$S^{\alpha\alpha}$	$S^{\beta\alpha}$	$S^{\alpha\beta}$	$S^{\beta\beta}$
1	0.5	0.5	0.1	0.9
2	0.8	0.2	0.4	0.6
3	1.0	0	0	1.0

| | Consumption Coefficients (Column 3) | |
	α	β
1	0.3	0.4
2	0.4	0.4
3	0	0
S	0.3	0.2

3.7. We have assumed the same technological coefficients as in model II for both regions but have taken different propensities to consume for households in the two regions. The supply coefficients imply that region α specializes in commodity 2 and region β in commodity 1. The consolidated model III in Table 3.7 is formed by carrying out

TABLE 3.7. Model III: Interregional Model*

Producing Sectors†	1α	2α	3α	1β	2β	3β	Autonomous Elements‡ Demands Y_i	Shipments $s_i Y_i$	Total Production X_i
1α	**1.00** / 1.817	**-0.25** / 1.018	**-0.15** / 0.767	**0** / 0.723	**-0.05** / 0.755	**-0.04** / 0.677	20	10	102.6
2α	**-0.20** / 1.512	**1.0** / 2.369	**-0.32** / 1.296	**-0.10** / 1.372	**0** / 1.317	**-0.16** / 1.249	80	64	201.5
3α	**-0.75** / 2.118	**-0.50** / 1.948	**1.0** / 2.223	**0** / 1.228	**0** / 1.225	**0** / 1.132	0	0	177.7
1β	**0** / 1.786	**-0.25** / 2.091	**-0.15** / 1.645	**1.0** / 3.288	**-0.45** / 2.686	**-0.36** / 2.239	0	10	307.5
2β	**-0.05** / 0.966	**0** / 1.019	**-0.08** / 0.863	**-0.15** / 1.386	**1.0** / 2.298	**-0.24** / 1.252	0	16	125.5
3β	**0** / 1.823	**0** / 2.078	**0** / 1.665	**-0.75** / 3.158	**-0.50** / 3.163	**1.0** / 3.302	0	0	233.4
Sα	**0** / 0.636	**0** / 0.584	**-0.30** / 0.667	**0** / 0.368	**0** / 0.367	**0** / 0.340			53.3
Sβ	**0** / 0.365	**0** / 0.416	**0** / 0.333	**0** / 0.632	**0** / 0.633	**-0.20** / 0.660			46.7
							100	100	

(Purchasing Sectors: 1α, 2α, 3α, 1β, 2β, 3β)

* The direct coefficients shown in boldface are equal to $-s_i a_{ij}$. The elements in the inverse matrix are shown in italics.
† Sector 3 is regional income.
‡ Autonomous elements are government plus investment.

the multiplication of supply coefficients and input coefficients indicated in Eqs. (3.11). The consolidated coefficient for the flow from sector 1β to 2α, for example, is determined from: $s_1^{\beta a} a_{12}^{a} = (0.5)(0.5) = 0.25$.

When the interregional model is put in the consolidated form of Table 3.7, its properties are the same as those of an ordinary Leontief $(I-A)$ matrix and it can be solved by any of the methods of the last chapter. Here we give the general solution as in model II.[9] To illustrate its use, we take the autonomous demands for model II and assume that they are localized entirely in region α. The demands must first be translated into shipments for final use by multiplying by the proper supply coefficients. These shipments are then multiplied by the corresponding columns in the inverse matrix and the results summed by row to give the solution for production levels shown in the last column. A check is given by the equality of total saving $(53.3 + 46.7 = 100)$ and total autonomous demands.

One interesting feature of this solution is the fact that the total amount of income generated depends on the distribution of production between the two regions, since the marginal propensity to save differs between the two. The propensity for the combined system is a weighted average of the regional propensities, 0.2 and 0.3, which turns out to be 0.24. Even though autonomous demand was concentrated in α, there is more income generated in β (233.4 compared to 177.7), because of the trade pattern. More realistic examples of this kind of solution will be given in Chapter 12.

The validity of interregional input-output models depends on the stability of trade patterns, expressed in our model by the supply coefficients. For some commodities, this assumption is quite reasonable. The best cases are the strongly market-oriented industries such as services, retail distribution, bakeries, and the like, for which imports are not a feasible alternative. Stable supply patterns are also likely to result from strong product differentiation, especially that based on differences in natural resources, as for example Scotch whiskey, Swedish iron ore, or Egyptian cotton. At the other extreme are homogeneous commodities available from several sources with small transport differentials. In these cases the supply pattern depends more heavily on the distribution of demand and relative costs of production. The extent to which supply coefficients have been stable in the United States is indicated in Chapter 12.

[9] An iterative method of solution which keeps the two regional matrices separate is given in Chenery (1956).

D. Dynamic Models of Capital Formation[10]

The construction of a general dynamic interindustry model would require the addition of three sets of factors to the static open model:

(1) Income generation
(2) Alternative production techniques
(3) Capital formation

Of these, we have already considered the inclusion of income generation in a static model, and the same formulation can be used in a period analysis. The problem of alternative techniques takes us beyond the basic Leontief assumption of fixed coefficients, and it will be deferred to the next chapter. Here we shall discuss the simplest methods of analyzing capital formation within the interindustry system.

In the input-output framework, investment can only be explained in terms of the levels of output and capacity in each sector over time. The actual relationship between capital stock and output is subject to considerable variation, depending on whether we assume some building ahead of demand by industry, operation at some level of "economic capacity," or forced-draft operation near the maximum technological capacity. Moreover, there is a variety of ways of overcoming production bottlenecks—varying final demand, using substitute materials, working overtime, expanding existing plants, building new plants, etc. It is obvious that forecasting and planning models would usually require quite different assumptions, therefore, and that a long-run relationship may not hold for short-run variations in output.

The linear programming approach of the next chapter is able to handle this type of problem much better in a formal sense, but the advance specification of each alternative in precise terms may not be possible. The use of the simpler input-output system to explore various alternatives may be the more practical for many planning purposes. This approach will be illustrated after existing models have been discussed.

Dynamic input-output models have been proposed by Hawkins (1948), by Leontief (1953a), and by members of the U.S. Air Force planning staff, as reported in Holley (1953). Each of these models employs a crude acceleration principle to explain investment in each sector. Empirical tests of the acceleration principle have shown that it does not predict the timing of investment very well, particularly for

[10] This section involves a somewhat more complicated model and may be omitted without loss of continuity or deferred until after Chapter 4.

short periods, and that alternative formulations which allow for a variable relation of output to capital stock give significantly better results.[11]   Nevertheless, the simpler accelerator models give some insight into the nature of dynamic sequences and provide a starting point for more realistic analyses.[12]

The stocks which can be analyzed in dynamic interindustry models consist of materials and fixed capital which are used in production. Not all investment can be explained as a function of output levels, since a large fraction is composed of public works, inventories held for speculative purposes, and other items not directly related to production.   This part of investment must be kept in final demand.

The inventories of current inputs can be incorporated into the model in one of two ways.   Either a given stock-flow relation is assumed, or it is specified that production of the material must take place ahead of its consumption.   This "lead time" is defined as the period of turnover of the inventory (the stock divided by its rate of use), and its introduction has the effect of maintaining a given stock proportional to output.   The stock-flow relations fit better into the Leontief model, while lead times are used in the discrete Holley model and in the simplified version given here.

To analyze the accumulation of fixed capital, it is convenient to define K_j as the productive capacity in each sector, measured in the same units as X_j.   Further, we shall assume a capital-building activity in each sector, whose output is the change in capacity.   All of the inputs on capital account (excluding maintenance) are charged to this activity instead of being included in final demand, as in the static model. The same assumption will be made for stocks of these inputs as for inputs for current production—namely, that they vary linearly (but not necessarily proportionately) with the level of capacity.   We can therefore define an input coefficient (b_{ij}) for capital goods from the relationship:

$$S_{ij} = \bar{S}_{ij} + b_{ij}K_j \tag{3.12}$$

[11] See, for example, J. Meyer and E. Kuh, "Acceleration and Related Theories of Investment," *Review of Economics and Statistics,* Aug. 1955, pp. 217–31; H. Chenery, "Overcapacity and the Acceleration Principle," *Econometrica,* Feb. 1952, pp. 1–28.

[12] The models of Leontief and Holley are conceptually quite similar although the mathematical formulation and computational techniques used are different. Leontief's model is formulated as a set of differential equations with no time lags.   The Air Force has tested a similar continuous model and has also used a period analysis.   Since the latter formulation is more suitable for most empirical work, a simplified version of this model will be used here.

In this equation S_{ij} is the stock of commodity i needed to produce a level of capacity K in sector j.

The added amount of commodity i required in a period t will be equal to the change in the stock, $\Delta S_{ij}{}^t$, which is related to *future* increases in capacity:

$$\Delta S_{ij}{}^t = (S_{ij}{}^t - S_{ij}{}^{t-1})$$
$$= b_{ij}(K_j{}^{t'} - K_j{}^{t'-1}) = b_{ij}\Delta K_j{}^{t'} \qquad (3.13)$$

where $\Delta K_j{}^{t'}$ is the increase in capacity in period t'. Here it will be noted that the constant term in Eq. (3.12) drops out; b_{ij} may be called the marginal stock-capacity ratio for commodity i in sector j. An interval between the use of inputs and the availability of capacity has also been introduced. It is defined as the lead time, λ.[13] The input must precede the increase in capacity by this interval, and hence $t' = t + \lambda$.

The accounting equations of the static system (2.1) can now be restated by defining autonomous demand so as to exclude induced investment and by showing inputs for this purpose as going into increased stocks:

$$M_i{}^t + X_i{}^t = \sum_j X_{ij}{}^t + \sum_j \Delta S_{ij}{}^t + Y_i{}^t \qquad (i = 1 \cdots n) \quad (3.14)$$

(Imports) + (domestic production) = (intermediate demand) + (induced investment demand) + (final demand)

Using (3.13), we can state the corresponding balance equations for a dynamic system as:

$$(1 + m_i)X_i{}^t = \sum_j a_{ij}X_j{}^t + \sum_j b_{ij}\Delta K_j{}^{t'} + Y_i{}^t \quad (i = 1 \cdots n) \quad (3.15)$$

In actuality the amount of capacity building in each period, $\Delta K_j{}^t$, is composed of two parts. In addition to the amount necessary to permit the increase in production, $(X_j{}^t - X_j{}^{t-1})$, there may be a change in excess capacity. In simple accelerator models, such as Leontief's, the latter term is assumed to be zero so long as capacity is increasing, but in general it is desirable to provide for the possibility of building

[13] In actuality this lead time may be distributed over several periods of the analysis, but we shall follow the Air Force model in assuming a single lead time for each input. In the numerical example of Table 3.8, the lead time is one period for each type of input. Lead times also apply to current inputs, but we assume them equal to zero.

ahead of demand. An equation for the change in capacity can be derived from the definition of unused capacity:

$$K_i{}^t - X_i{}^t = U_i{}^t \qquad (3.16)$$

$$\Delta K_i{}^t - X_i{}^t + X_i{}^{t-1} = U_i{}^t - U_i{}^{t-1} = \Delta U_i{}^t \quad (i = 1 \cdots n) \quad (3.17)$$

where $U_i{}^t$ is the amount of unused capacity in period t.[14]

Equations (3.15) and (3.17) constitute a set of $2n$ equations in $4n$ unknowns $(X, Y, \Delta K, U)$ for each period. If we specify only the final demands, as in the static model, we still have a choice as to whether to build up excess capacity in earlier periods in order to reduce the amount of investment required later. It would also be possible to introduce a similar choice between supplying demands from current production or from previously accumulated stockpiles. If final demands fall as well as rise over time, which pattern of behavior will be either rational or probable is not obvious. In this case, linear programming methods can be used to determine the investment pattern that will minimize the total investment required or will satisfy some other criterion of optimality (see Dorfman, Samuelson, and Solow, 1958, Wagner, 1957). Alternatively, it is possible to specify in advance that excess capacity in each sector will be zero (or some given amount) in each period and then test the result to see whether this assumption was justified.[15] If we make this assumption, the model is similar to that of Leontief except for the time required to build capacity.

We can illustrate the working of a dynamic input-output model in its simplest form by taking two sectors and two time periods, which gives us a total of eight equations. In model IV, Table 3.8, the current output (balance) Eqs. (3.15) are shown as the first two equations in each period, numbers 1, 2, 5, and 6. The current input coefficients, a_{ij}, are taken from model III. The inputs into capacity building are assumed to come only from sector 2. The balance equa-

[14] In period one, we assume a given stock of capital from the previous period, $K_i{}^0$, and Eq. (3.17) becomes:

$$U_i{}' - K_i{}^0 = \Delta K_i{}' - X_i{}' \qquad (i = 1 \cdots n) \qquad (3.17a)$$

[15] An excellent discussion of dynamic interindustry models is given in Dorfman, Samuelson, and Solow, Chapters 11 and 12, in which the rigid assumptions of the Leontief model are criticized. Since their more general model does not seem very suitable for empirical work at the present stage of our knowledge of capital coefficients, we suggest that variations in excess capacity be included in the system but determined outside the model in empirical applications, as in model IV below.

TABLE 3.8. MODEL IV: CAPACITY BUILDING*

| | Output Period 1 | | | | Output Period 2 | | | | Restrictions |
| | Production | | Capacity Building | | Production | | Capacity Building | | |
Equations	X_1'	X_2'	$\Delta K_1'$	$\Delta K_2'$	X_1''	X_2''	$\Delta K_1''$	$\Delta K_2''$	
Input Period 1 — Current Output — Commodity 1 (1)	**1.0** *0.753*	**−0.5** *0.198*			*0.390*	*0.373*	*0.297*	*0.178*	$Y_1' = 75$
Input Period 1 — Current Output — Commodity 2 (2)	**−0.25** *−0.495*	**1.0** *0.396*			*0.781*	*0.747*	**−1.5** *0.594*	**−0.9** *0.356*	$Y_2' = 50$
Input Period 1 — Capacity — Commodity 1 (3)	**−1.0** *0.753*	*0.198*	**1.0** *1.00*		*0.390*	*0.373*	*0.297*	*0.178*	$-K_1^0 = -120$
Input Period 1 — Capacity — Commodity 2 (4)	*−0.495*	**−1.0** *0.896*		**1.0** *1.00*	*0.781*	*0.747*	*0.594*	*0.356*	$-K_2^0 = -110$
Input Period 2 — Current Output — Commodity 1 (5)					**1.0** *1.143*	**−0.5** *0.571*			$Y_1'' = 100$
Input Period 2 — Current Output — Commodity 2 (6)					**−0.25** *0.286*	**1.0** *1.143*			$Y_2'' = 100$
Input Period 2 — Capacity — Commodity 1 (7)					**−1.0** *0.753*	*0.198*	**1.0** *0.703*	*−0.178*	$\Delta U_1'' = 0$
Input Period 2 — Capacity — Commodity 2 (8)					*−0.495*	**−1.0** *0.896*	*−0.594*	**1.0** *0.644*	$\Delta U_2'' = 0$
Solution	142.7	135.4	22.7	25.4	171.4	142.9	28.7	7.4	

*The direct coefficients are given in boldface type and the coefficients of the inverse matrix in italics. Activities are dated by the timing of their outputs.

tion for commodity 2 in period 1 (line 2) therefore states that output of X_2' minus its use for current production $(-.25X_1')$ and minus the use for capacity building $(-1.5\Delta K_1'' - .9\Delta K_2'')$ is equal to the final demand in period 1 (50). In sector 1, the current output equation is the same as in the static model, since there is no use of commodity 1 for capacity building. The constant term in these equations is the final demand, as in the static model, and is shown in the last column.

To represent the capacity Eqs. (3.17 and 3.17a) in model IV, we follow the same procedure for writing the equations in matrix form by recording the coefficients in the column of the variable to which they apply and putting the constant term on the right. The coefficients in the capacity equations (3.17) are -1 for production in the current period (X_i^t) and $+1$ for production in the previous period and for ΔK_i^t. The right-hand term is $-K_i^0$ in the first period and zero thereafter, since we assume no excess capacity. For example, in period 1 the capacity equation for commodity 1 (line 3) means that the installation of additional capacity during the previous period for use in period 1 $(\Delta K_1')$ must be equal to production in period 1 (X_1') minus the capacity existing at the beginning of the period $(-K_1^0)$. In period 2, the same equation (line 7) indicates that capacity building must equal the difference in production levels between periods 1 and 2, on the assumption that excess capacity does not change.

The consolidated coefficient matrix which results from writing out the two sets of equations period by period is no longer of the same form as the Leontief static matrix. The first column in model IV shows that in addition to its current input and output, industry 1 requires an input (stock) of one unit of capacity in period 1 and results in 1 unit of capacity becoming available in period 2. (We assume that equipment is maintained from one period to the next.) The output coefficient in the capacity equation (line 7) results from our use of $(X_i + U_i)$ for K_i in Eq. (3.17), which avoids the necessity of treating K_i as a separate variable.

Each column (or column vector) in Table 3.8 belongs to the general category of "activities," to be discussed in the next chapter, of which the Leontief production activity is one example. An activity may be thought of as the transformation of inputs into outputs in fixed proportions. The production activities in model IV are Leontief activities augmented by capacity inputs and outputs. The capacity building activities have inputs from sector 2 in one period and an output of capacity ready for use one period later.

Since we have limited the number of activities to the number of equations in the model (by assuming no accumulation of excess capacity or stockpiling), we can solve model IV in any of the ways already used for the Leontief system, providing a solution exists. So long as total demand for output does not fall below the capacity already achieved in any period, our assumption of no excess capacity will be permissible; if this is not the case, the solution will contain negative levels of capacity building and we shall have to change some of the assumptions of the model.

A simple dynamic model of this sort would be useful for testing the overall feasibility of investment programs and for determining how investment should be allocated among sectors over time. Since we have eight equations in sixteen unknowns, we can in general fix any eight variables (so long as they are consistent) and solve for the remaining eight. To illustrate this procedure, we assume the following data as given:

Final demands:

$$Y_1' = 75 \qquad Y_1'' = 100$$
$$Y_2' = 50 \qquad Y_2'' = 100$$

Initial capacities:

$$K_1{}^0 = 120$$
$$K_2{}^0 = 110$$

Unused capacities:

$$U_1' = U_1'' = 0$$
$$U_2' = U_2'' = 0$$

These data provide the constant terms or restrictions at the right of Table 3.8. To solve for the remaining eight variables, we multiply elements in each row in the inverse matrix by the corresponding element in the restriction vector and add, as in previous solutions. To find X_1', for example, we compute:

$$X_1' = 75(0.753) + 50(0.198) + 100(0.390) + 100(0.373) = 142.7$$

The results are shown at the bottom of Table 3.8.

In a practical case, the feasibility of this program would depend on the amount of investment that would have to be started in period 0. This can be determined by multiplying the capacity building activities of period 1 by their capital coefficients: $I^0 = 1.5(22.7) + 0.9(25.4) = 56.9$. If this total does not exceed the amount of investment resources available (or the capacity of the investment goods industries), the program is feasible. Alternatively, we could take the initial allocation of investment in period 0 as given and let two of the restrictions, say Y_1'' and Y_2'', vary. This type of analysis determines the consistency, but not the optimality, of a set of consumption and investment targets or projections.

It is of some interest to examine the details of the general solution to see how one variable is related to another. Production in the last period, for example, depends only on final demand, which must include investment. In earlier periods, however, production depends on future demands as well as current ones because future demands affect the amount of capacity-building that must be started. The implications of the current output equations can be made clearer by rewriting the solutions to the first two as:

$$X_1' = 1.143Y_1' + 0.571Y_2' + 0.390(Y_1'' - Y_1')$$
$$+ 0.373(Y_2'' - Y_2')$$
$$X_2' = 0.286Y_1' + 1.143Y_2' + 0.781(Y_1'' - Y_1')$$
$$+ 0.747(Y_2'' - Y_2') \tag{3.18}$$

In this form, the coefficients applying to current final demand are the same as in period 2, and the additional terms in each equation reflect the operation of the acceleration principle. The accelerator terms apply to industry 1 (which produces no capital goods) as well as to industry 2 because of the indirect demands made by industry 2 on industry 1.

The capacity equations can also be rewritten in terms of the increments in final demand to make their significance clearer.

$$\Delta K_1'' = 0.753(Y_1'' - Y_1') + 0.198(Y_2'' - Y_2')$$
$$= 0.753(25) + 0.198(50) = 28.71$$
$$\Delta K_2'' = 0.396(Y_2'' - Y_2') - 0.495(Y_1'' - Y_1')$$
$$= 0.396(50) - 0.495(25) = 7.43 \tag{3.19}$$

The negative effect on $\Delta K_2''$ of an increase in Y_1'' arises from the fact that capacity to supply the increase must be built in the previous period. The effect on output (and capacity) in sector 2, from which capital goods come, is greater in period 1 than in period 2. Unless other demands on sector 2 are increasing, therefore, excess capacity will develop (which would produce a negative level of capacity building). This type of model thus extends to several sectors the mechanism of the acceleration principle.

When the analysis is continued over additional periods, the equations for output in the next to last period would have the form of (3.18). For earlier periods, there would be additional accelerator terms of similar form.[16]

Present work on dynamic interindustry models is aimed more at understanding the effects of structural interdependence than at developing a tool for use in prediction or planning. The problems involved in estimating capital inputs, to be discussed in Chapter 5, are much more difficult than those in determining current inputs. Experiments with the Holley model showed that it greatly overestimated investment requirements when predictions from it were compared to the actual performance of the economy. This upward bias is inherent in the simple accelerator assumption, which does not allow for variation in the rate of utilization of capacity and other factors discussed earlier. Thus the use of constant capital coefficients to determine investment is likely to be more valid in calculating the total requirement for normal operation, as in long-term planning, than it is in estimating the rate of investment year by year.

BIBLIOGRAPHY

Chenery, H. B., "Interregional and International Input-Output Analysis," in *The Structural Interdependence of the Economy*, 1956.

Chenery, H. B., P. G. Clark, and V. Cao-Pinna, *The Structure and Growth of the Italian Economy*, U.S. Mutual Security Agency, Rome, 1953, Chapter 5.

Chipman, J. S., "The Multi-Sector Multiplier," *Econometrica*, XVIII, No. 4, 355–374 (October 1950).

*Dorfman, R., P. Samuelson, and R. Solow, *Linear Programming and Economic Analysis*, 1958, Chapters 11 and 12.

*Evans, W. D., and M. Hoffenberg, "The Interindustry Relations Study for 1947," *Review of Economics and Statistics*, XXXIV, No. 2, 97–142 (May 1952).

Goodwin, R. M., "The Multiplier as Matrix," *Economic Journal*, LIX, No. 236, 237–555 (December 1949).

[16] In matrix form, the equation for output in period one for a three-period model becomes:

$$X' = L^{-1}Y' + (L^{-1} - H^{-1})(Y'' - Y') + H^{-1}B(L^{-1} - H^{-1})(Y''' - Y'') \quad (3.20)$$

where Y^t = the final demand vector for period t
$L = (I - A)$, the Leontief matrix
B = the matrix of capital coefficients
$H = (I - A + B)$

The first two terms in this expression are the matrix equivalent of (3.18). The H matrix represents the effect on output of both building capacity and operating it.

Hawkins, D., "Some Conditions of Macroeconomic Stability," *Econometrica*, XVI, No. 4, 309–322 (October 1948).

Holley, J., "A Dynamic Model," *Econometrica*, XX, No. 4, 616–642 (October 1952) and XXI, No. 2, 298–324 (April 1953).

Isard, W., "Interregional and Regional Input-Output Analysis, A Model of a Space-Economy," *Review of Economics and Statistics*, XXXIII, No. 4, 318–328 (November 1951).

°Leontief, W. (1953a), *Studies in the Structure of the American Economy*, 1953, Chapters 3 and 4.

———. (1951), *The Structure of the American Economy, 1919–1939*, 1951.

Metzler, L. A., "A Multiple-Region Theory of Income and Trade," *Econometrica*, XVIII, No. 4, 329–354 (October 1950).

°Moses, L., "The Stability of Interregional Trading Patterns and Input-Output Analysis," *American Economic Review*, XLV, No. 5, 803–832 (December 1955).

Wagner, H., "A Linear Programming Solution to Dynamic Leontief Type Models," *Management Science*, III, No. 3, 234–254 (April 1957).

4

Choice in interindustry models

Although the several models which we discussed in the last chapter differ in varying degrees from the original Leontief system, they are still recognizable members of the same family. All are based on the idea that the choice of technology, source of supply, and pattern of demand are independent of the outcome of the analysis. Use of the Leontief system does not preclude such choices, but it assumes that they are not dependent on the level of output in each sector and can therefore be fixed in advance.

In this chapter we take up interindustry models which embody quite a different view of the working of the economy. They take account of the fact that there are many different ways of producing goods and satisfying wants and that choices in one part of the economy may be dependent on choices in other parts. The mathematical techniques for handling these more general assumptions have been developed in recent years under the headings of linear programming and activity analysis.

In comparison to the Leontief system, the programming approach contains two innovations. In the first place, it includes alternative sources of supply as separate activities, and the level at which each is utilized becomes a variable in the model. The system therefore has more variables than equations and many possible solutions. The second innovation is the addition of a criterion for preferring one solution to another, which may be cost minimization, welfare maximization, or any other function of the activity levels.

Although this second feature has obvious value for normative or policy applications, its validity for description or prediction has yet to be demonstrated. In fact the assumption of maximizing behavior, which is central to so much of economic theory, usually plays a much smaller role in econometric attempts to apply these theories. The Leontief system is essentially a general equilibrium model in which the economizing assumption is omitted entirely. A programming model, on the other hand, can provide for an explicit choice among alternatives, such as imports and domestic production, whose relation must be predetermined in the Leontief system.

We shall develop interindustry programming models by starting from the input-output system and making more general assumptions.[1] In section A of this chapter, the concepts used in programming are defined and a comparison is made of its assumptions to those of input-output analysis. We then relax the input-output assumptions in several stages in order to show the effect of each on the nature of the programming solution. Section B maintains the given Leontief technology but allows a choice to be made among final demands; this programming model provides a systematic method of solving problems which are handled in input-output analysis by trial and error. Section C gives a more general programming formulation of interindustry analysis in which technological and other choices on the supply side are introduced. The remainder of the chapter outlines a version of the simplex method for solving programming problems which is particularly suited to interindustry analysis and discusses the economic interpretation of the results of such solutions. (The details of the simplex method are given in the Appendix.) Finally, we consider alternative forms of activity analysis for a whole economy.

A. Input-Output Analysis and Linear Programming

Activity analysis is a method of analyzing any economic transformation in terms of elementary units called activities. In abstract form, its use has led to a more general statement of the classical theory of production and of the relations between productive efficiency and

---

[1] Much more complete treatments of the general programming formulation are given in Dorfman, Samuelson, and Solow (1958) and Koopmans (1957).

prices.[2] In empirical work, it provides the conceptual framework for the mathematical technique of *linear programming*, which can be used to determine optimal solutions to various kinds of allocation problems.[3] We shall summarize first the concepts of activity analysis and then give an algebraic statement of the programming formulation which can be compared to the Leontief model.

1. Concepts of Activity Analysis

Since input-output analysis was developed before activity analysis and is derived from a more specialized set of assumptions, its concepts are both more concrete and more limited in their application. The logical framework of activity analysis is stated in very general terms without any necessary institutional connection. It can therefore be applied to varied units from single plants to whole economies, and to any type of transformation of inputs into outputs. When activity analysis is used for interindustry models, however, these concepts can be given a more specific meaning, and most of them can be thought of as generalizations of the input-output concepts with which we are already familiar. The principal change is the substitution of the more general notion of an *activity* (or set of activities) for the Leontief *industry*.

(i) A *commodity* in activity analysis has a meaning similar to that used in input-output theory.[4] Ideally, a commodity is homogeneous in all its uses, but in empirical applications it becomes an aggregate selected in such a way as to minimize the effect of aggregation on the solution. For interindustry analysis, we can usefully distinguish between primary and produced commodities and between intermediate and final uses as we have done in the input-output model. A *primary commodity* is any input not produced in the system, and hence its definition is based on the model selected. *Final uses* (more commonly called *requirements*) are those which are stipulated in advance, and they too depend on the model chosen, as in input-output analysis.

[2] An excellent statement of the theoretical conclusions of activity analysis is given in Koopmans (1957).

[3] Although the terms "activity analysis" and "linear programming" are often used as synonyms, the former properly refers to a set of concepts and their logical implications and the latter to methods of determining numerical solutions. We maintain this distinction because the concepts are useful even where the programming solution may not be applicable.

[4] Commodities in activity analysis can have several dimensions, with each described by a separate variable, but this refinement is not often feasible in an analysis of a whole economy.

(ii) An *activity* is any possible transformation of fixed proportions of commodity inputs into fixed proportions of commodity outputs. It includes the Leontief concept of an industry or sector of production as a special case. Transportation, storage, labor training, and selling can also be represented as activities, as can such less obvious input-output relations as meeting product specifications or providing goods to final users in fixed proportions.

An activity is represented mathematically by a column of coefficients, as in the Leontief system, with one coefficient for each input and each output. We shall write activity j as a column vector:

$$\mathbf{A}_j = \begin{bmatrix} a_{1j} \\ a_{2j} \\ \cdot \\ \cdot \\ \cdot \\ a_{mj} \end{bmatrix}$$

where a positive coefficient denotes an output and a negative coefficient an input.

(iii) We can write all possible activities together in matrix form as:

$$\mathbf{A} = (\mathbf{A}_1 \mathbf{A}_2 \cdots \mathbf{A}_n) = \overbrace{\begin{bmatrix} a_{11}a_{12} & \cdots & a_{1n} \\ \cdot & & \cdot \\ \cdot & & \cdot \\ \cdot & & \cdot \\ a_{m_1}a_{m_2} & \cdots & a_{mn} \end{bmatrix}}^{n \text{ activities}} \Big\} m \text{ commodities}$$

This matrix will be called the *technology matrix* although some of the relations may not be technological. It includes the Leontief $(\mathbf{I}\text{-}\mathbf{A})$ matrix as a special case in which the number of activities is equal to the number of commodities.[5] When there is some choice of activity, however, the number of activities n will be greater than the number of commodities m, and the matrix will no longer be square.

(iv) The extent to which an activity is utilized, which was defined by the gross output in the input-output system, becomes the *activity level* in activity analysis and linear programming. Any input or output may be selected as a unit of measurement. We may choose to define the unit level as that which produces a ton of steel or that which

---

[5] If the Leontief matrix is written in activity analysis form, the diagonal element $(1\text{-}a_{ii})$ becomes simply a_{ii}, with a positive sign.

uses 10 man-hours of labor, depending on the problem, but usually the output of the principal commodity will be most convenient. We shall use the same symbol for the level of activity j as we have used in the input-output system, X_j. The total of each input used or output produced by the activity is then $X_{ij} = a_{ij}X_j$, with outputs positive and inputs negative. A set of activity levels $(X_1 \cdot \cdot \cdot X_n)$ is called a *program*.

(v) The autonomous elements taken as given in activity analysis are called *restrictions* or *constraints*. They include not only the final demands of input-output but also the quantities of resources available and sometimes other limitations.[6] There will be a restriction for each type of commodity, positive for final (desired) outputs, negative for primary inputs, and zero for intermediate commodities.[7] The column of restriction may be written as

$$\mathbf{B} = \begin{bmatrix} B_1 \\ B_2 \\ \cdot \\ \cdot \\ \cdot \\ B_m \end{bmatrix}$$

2. The Programming Problem

Any choice among alternative uses of resources can be stated as a programming problem if: (i) it can be adequately represented by the concepts of activity analysis; and (ii) the objective of the policy maker can be described as a function of the activity levels. If the various functional relations satisfy the *linearity assumptions* given in the next section, the problem is one of *linear programming*. This technique has been applied to allocation problems as varied as the routing of tankers, the operation of petroleum refineries, the choice of crops, and the determination of an optimum exchange rate.

In the field of interindustry analysis, a typical programming problem is the choice of production techniques. Assume that there are produced commodities 1 and 2 and primary inputs L and K. Commodity 1 can be produced by activities $\mathbf{A}_1$, $\mathbf{A}_2$, or $\mathbf{A}_3$ and commodity 2 by

[6] *Qualities* of commodities, such as octane numbers, are often found as restrictions in industrial applications, but they are less likely to be used in an interindustry analysis.
[7] A "pure" intermediate commodity is one which is produced but for which there is no final demand (see Koopmans, 1957, p. 72). Final commodities may have intermediate uses as well.

A_4, A_5, A_6, or A_7. The input-output model can only answer questions of the type: Using A_1 and A_5, is it possible to produce given final outputs of 1 and 2 from the available L and K? The general programming problem is to discover the *best combination* of 1 and 2 that can be produced with the given L and K, which also involves determining the best choice of activities.[8]

The general linear programming problem may be stated algebraically in terms of the concepts just defined:

To maximize (or minimize) some linear function of the activity levels

$$C = \sum_j c_j X_j \tag{4.1}$$

Subject to

$$\sum_j a_{ij} X_j \geq B_i \qquad (i = 1 \cdots m) \tag{4.2}$$

and

$$X_j \geq 0. \qquad (i = 1 \cdots n) \tag{4.3}$$

We may note four differences between these equations and those which make up the Leontief system:

(i) We require some function of the activity levels (4.1) which enables us to choose one solution as better than another. This is called the *criterion* or *objective function*. In interindustry models the objective is usually to maximize total output (national product) or to minimize cost.[9]

(ii) There are alternative ways of producing the same output.

(iii) Unlike the open input-output system, the primary factors are as much a part of the model as the produced commodities, since any solution must satisfy resource limitations as well as requirements for final use.

(iv) The restraints consist of inequalities rather than of equalities. This formulation allows for the non-use of some resources.

To complete the statement of the programming problem, we need some further definitions. It is convenient to categorize *programs* by the extent to which they satisfy these equations. A set of activity levels which satisfies only Eqs. (4.2) is called a *solution*. If in addition it consists only of non-negative activity levels it is a *feasible solution*—i.e., it also satisfies (4.3). The feasible solution which maximizes (4.1) is called the *optimal program*.

[8] This example is discussed at length in section C below.

[9] Arrow (1957) gives an illuminating discussion of the nature of the objective function in various applications of programming.

The discovery of the optimal solution to a programming problem is facilitated if it is restated in terms of equations rather than inequalities. This can be done by adding new variables called *slack vectors* or *disposal activities* to represent the difference between the left-hand and right-hand terms in (4.2). In the equations for primary inputs, the disposal activity represents the non-use of resources—e.g., the existence of an excess supply of labor. In the final output equations, the disposal activity represents production of a given commodity in excess of minimum requirements. If additional amounts of particular commodities have some value, the latter type of disposal activity will have a positive coefficient in the objective function (as in model V of the next section). Non-use of primary resources is usually assumed to have neither value nor cost.

For interindustry programming, we have found it convenient to maintain the notation that we have used for input-output analysis, which distinguishes between two types of restrictions: final demands (Y_i) and available supplies of primary factors $(\bar{F}_n)$. Adding the levels of the corresponding disposal activities, D_i and D_h, we can write the inequalities of (4.2) as two sets of equations:

$$\sum_j a_{ij} X_j - D_i = Y_i \qquad (i = 1 \cdots m) \tag{4.4}$$

$$\sum_j f_{hj} X_j - D_h = \bar{F}_h \qquad (h = m + 1 \cdots m + l) \tag{4.5}$$

where all Y_i are positive or zero and $\bar{F}_h$ are negative.[10]

Equations (4.4) are the programming equivalent of the Leontief system. If there is only one activity for each produced commodity and no limitation of the type of (4.5), the Leontief model (2.5) appears as a special case of (4.4) in which $D_i = 0$.

3. A Comparison of Assumptions

We can now list the basic assumptions of linear programming[11] in a form in which they can be compared to those of input-output analysis (following the order of Chapter 2, section D).

---

[10] When there is no need to distinguish commodities and factors, these equations will be consolidated as:

$$\sum_j a_{ij} X_j - D_i = B_i \qquad (i = 1 \cdots m) \tag{4.4a}$$

[11] More general statements of the postulates of activity analysis are given in Koopmans (1957), pp. 72–77, and Dantzig (1951a).

(1) The input-output model assumes that each commodity is supplied by a single sector of production. In linear programming, this assumption is replaced by:

(*a*) A commodity can be produced by any number of activities.

(*b*) Each activity may have several outputs.

In interindustry analysis, joint products are usually of no great importance because they occur within the same commodity group. In this event, the sector concept of input-output can be retained. A sector or industry is then defined as the set of all activities producing a given commodity.

(2) Inputs used by an activity are a function only of the level of that activity.

(*a*) In linear programming, a linear homogeneous function ($X_{ij} = a_{ij}X_j$) is necessary; this is known as the *proportionality assumption*.

(*b*) In the input-output model, linearity is assumed but proportionality is not important.

(3) *Additivity* or lack of external economies and diseconomies is assumed in both models.

(4) *Non-negativity of activity levels* is necessary in both cases. In input-output, a separate assumption is not needed because non-negative outputs are a necessary property of all Leontief matrices, but in linear programming the condition must be imposed to prevent the appearance of negative activity levels in the solution. (Since a negative activity level implies reversing a productive process—producing coal and ore out of steel—it obviously must be ruled out.)

Apart from the formal differences, which are mainly in the first assumption, the linear programming model is more general in that it can be applied to choices which are outside the scope of input-output theory. An example of this type of model is discussed in section 4B.

4. A Note on Graphical Analysis[12]

The relation between activity analysis and traditional production theory is most easily seen in graphical terms. Since we shall make considerable use of graphs to show the parallels between the two approaches, it may be well to discuss some of the mechanics of graphical representation at the outset.

The analysis of the chapter is built around two examples, shown

[12] On graphical representations of linear programming, see also Vajda (1956, Chapter 5) and Dorfman (1953).

in Tables 4.1 and 4.2, below, which are designed to facilitate geo-metrical interpretation of various aspects of programming solutions. Here we illustrate several graphical representations of activities se-lected from these two models.

Assume first a simple Leontief model,[13] containing two activities, two produced commodities, and one primary input:

$$1.0X_1 - 0.5X_2 = Y_1$$

$$-0.25X_1 + 1.0X_2 = Y_2$$

$$-7.5X_1 - 5X_2 = -L$$

or

$$\mathbf{A}_1X_1 + \mathbf{A}_2X_2 = \begin{bmatrix} Y_1 \\ Y_2 \\ -L \end{bmatrix}$$

The most direct geometrical representation of this system is that which uses the activity (or production) levels as axes. Assuming $Y_1 = 10$, $Y_2 = 50$, the first two equations are shown as straight lines[14] in Figure 4.1(a). The solution is given by their intersection, point s, at which $X_1 = 40$, $X_2 = 60$. The third equation, which determines the use of labor, gives a family of straight lines for constant labor supplies, of which one is plotted. The line for $L = 600$, which in-cludes the solution for the given values of Y_1 and Y_2, also shows other combinations of the two activity levels which would use the same amount of labor.

The use of any other primary input can be shown in the same way as labor. For example, we shall add the following equation for capital use:

$$-1.25X_1 - 2.5X_2 = -K$$

The capital required by the given solution is 200, and other combina-tions of activity levels using this amount of capital are shown by the line $K = 200$. (This type of diagram is used in Figure 4.2 of the next section.)

Although activity axes illustrate the meaning of the restraints in linear programming, they do not show the alternative final outputs that can be produced from given amounts of resources. To do this, we need to take Y_1 and Y_2 as variables and eliminate the activity levels from the system. This transformation is accomplished by using the first two equations to solve for the X's in terms of the Y's, and

[13] Based on $\mathbf{A}_1\mathbf{A}_2$ of Table 4.1 and $\mathbf{A}_2\mathbf{A}_5$ of Table 4.2.

[14] The lines for $Y_1 = 0$ and $Y_2 = 0$ are also plotted for comparison with 4.1(b).

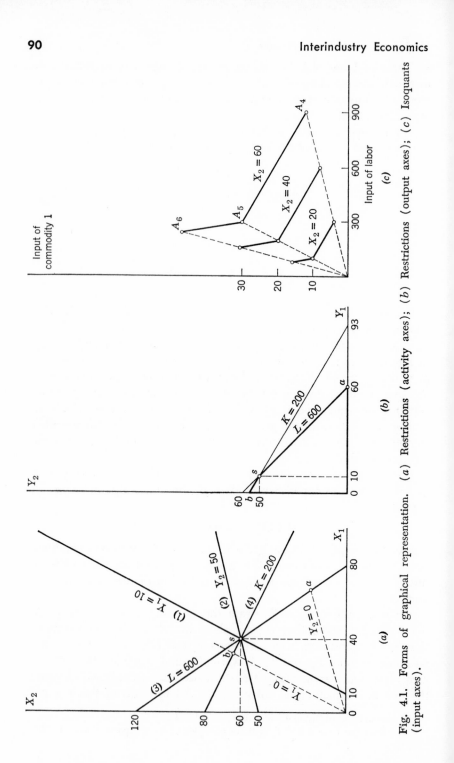

Fig. 4.1. Forms of graphical representation. (a) Restrictions (activity axes); (b) Restrictions (output axes); (c) Isoquants (input axes).

substituting these values in the last two equations.[15] The resulting equations express the demand for labor and capital in terms of final outputs instead of activity levels:

$$L = 10.0Y_1 + 10.0Y_2$$

$$K = 2.143Y_1 + 3.571Y_2$$

Figure 4.1(b) shows these labor and capital use equations plotted on the *final output axes*, Y_1 and Y_2, with the original solution ($Y_1 = 10$, $Y_2 = 50$) again shown at point s. The other combinations of Y_1 and Y_2 producible with the same amount of labor lie on the line $L = 600$, while those producible with the same amount of capital lie on $K = 200$.

We have now arrived at a concept familiar in economic theory, the *transformation function* or *production possibility curve*. If the economy has 600 units of labor and 200 units of capital, the maximum amounts of outputs that can be produced are determined by whichever factor is exhausted first. All feasible solutions must therefore lie inside of *both* curves and in the positive quadrant—i.e., in the closed area *oasbo*.[16] The line *asb* represents the transformation function for the economy—the locus of all points at which output of Y_1 is at a maximum for given outputs of Y_2. If we know the valuation given to each commodity we can find the *optimum* combination of Y_1 and Y_2 from this diagram by familiar methods. (This type of analysis is used below in Figs. 4.4, 4.5, and 4.6.)

Another graphical construction commonly used to represent production possibilities, either for a single commodity or for the total output of the economy, is the *isoquant* or *production function*. This type of curve describes alternative ways of producing the same output. We assume (from Table 4.2) three activities for producing commodity 2, with capital omitted in order to stay in two dimensions:[17]

$$\mathbf{A}_4 = \begin{bmatrix} -0.2 \\ 1.0 \\ -15.0 \end{bmatrix}, \qquad \mathbf{A}_5 = \begin{bmatrix} -0.5 \\ 1.0 \\ -5.0 \end{bmatrix}, \qquad \mathbf{A}_6 = \begin{bmatrix} -0.8 \\ 1.0 \\ -4.0 \end{bmatrix}$$

[15] In the present example, this transformation is easily done by substitution. The general form and an example of its use have been given in Eqs. (3.2) and (3.3). In general, such a reduction in the number of variables can always be accomplished if the non-negativity of activity levels is maintained.

[16] The points in this diagram are lettered to correspond to those of Fig. 4.1(a). The feasible area is also oasbo in Fig. 4.1(a). Individual activities lie in quadrants 2 and 4 when plotted on the Y_1Y_2 axes, as shown in Fig. 4.4.

[17] $\mathbf{A}_2$ has been renumbered $\mathbf{A}_5$ here to conform to Table 4.2.

To construct an isoquant for commodity 2, we use the *inputs* (Y_1 and L) as axes, and compute $X_{ij} = a_{ij}X_j$. Isoquants are shown in Fig. 4.1(c) for three levels of output of commodity 2, including that corresponding to the original solution ($X_2 = 60$). As will be shown in Figs. 4.3 and 4.7 below, the same procedure for cost minimization can be applied to the choice of technology in this form as in the case of smooth production functions.

The choice of axes for graphical analysis will be determined by the problem and the nature of the model. As we have shown, activity axes can be used to represent any number of restrictions in two variables.[18] Commodity axes (either inputs or outputs) are useful when there is a greater number of activities and the problem can be expressed in two or three restrictions. Models which do not meet either of these specifications cannot be represented in two dimensions, but often a part of the optimization problem (such as the choice of activity for a single output, as in Fig. 4.1(c)) can be analyzed graphically.

B. Choice on the Demand Side

Whenever we apply interindustry analysis to the formulation or testing of economic programs we are concerned with choices affecting the level and composition of the final output that can be produced. Since the input-output system contains no element of choice within the model, when it is used comparisons must be made among alternative solutions for different assumed demands. By means of the programming concepts just discussed, we can treat this choice systematically and make sure that the final result is indeed optimal for the given conditions. In solving this problem, we illustrate the logic of programming without greatly complicating the model or the method of solution.

1. An Illustration

To transform the input-output system into a programming model with alternative demands and resource limitations, we need the following additions:

(i) A set of equations for resource use corresponding to (4.5), with disposal activities to measure the amount of each resource not used;

(ii) Disposal activities to measure the final use of each commodity;

---

[18] Or in general for models in which the number of equations (after the introduction of slack variables) is two less than the number of variables, as in Model V below.

(iii) An objective function stating the value placed on the final use of each commodity.

An example of such a model is shown in the six equations of Table 4.1. Each column of coefficients represents an activity, the first two being Leontief-type production activities and the next five disposal activities for the resources and final products. The first two equations are a Leontief-like system except for the fact that the levels of final

TABLE 4.1. MODEL V: CHOICE AMONG FINAL USES

Equation	Commodities	Production Activities		Disposal Activities					Restrictions
				Unused Resource Activities			Final Use Activities		
		A_1	A_2	A_3	A_4	A_5	A_6	A_7	
(1)	Commodity 1	1.0	−0.5				−1		0
(2)	Commodity 2	−0.25	1.0					−1	0
(3)	Labor (L)	−7.5	−5	−1					−2000
(4)	Capital (K)	−1.25	−2.5		−1				− 600
(5)	Natural resources (N)	−1				−1			− 180
(6)	Objective function (C)	0	0	0	0	0	1.25	1.0	Maximum
	Activity level	X_1	X_2	X_3	X_4	X_5	X_6	X_7	

use are not fixed. Equations (3-5) for resource use correspond to Eq. (4.5) with each having an entry of (−1) from the appropriate disposal activity $(A_3 - A_5)$. Since we assume no minimum requirements of final output, the total output for final use is represented by the activity levels X_6 and X_7. The two equations of the input-output system are therefore changed as follows:

$$(1) \quad 1.0X_1 - 0.5X_2 - X_6 = 0$$

$$(2) \quad -0.25X_1 + 1.0X_2 - X_7 = 0$$

The three resource equations have restrictions representing the total amount of each resource available, measured in any convenient units; they are written:

$$(3) \quad -7.5X_1 - 5X_2 - X_3 = -2000 \text{ (labor)}$$

$$(4) \quad -1.25X_1 - 2.5X_2 - X_4 = - 600 \text{ (capital)}$$

$$(5) \quad -X_1 \qquad\qquad - X_5 = - 180 \text{ (natural resources)}$$

The objective of the economy is to maximize the total value of final output of commodities 1 and 2—i.e., of X_6 and X_7. We assume that commodity 1 is worth 1.25 and commodity 2 is worth 1.0. The objective function, which we may think of as the value of the national income, is then:

$$(6) \quad C = 1.25X_6 + 1.0X_7$$

Since activities $A_1 - A_5$ do not produce final output, they do not affect the objective directly.

The programming problem is thus to maximize C within the limitations provided by the available technology and supplies of resources. The system consists of five equations in seven variables and therefore has a large number of solutions.

2. The Nature of the Maximizing Problem

The input-output approach to this problem is to find a feasible program and then to consider alternative combinations of final output. Since activities A_1 and A_2, which form the input-output system, are the same as those used in section A.4, p. 89, we can start from the solution which we found there for final outputs of 10 (X_6) and 50 (X_7). With these values, equations (1) and (2) are written:

$$1.0X_1 - 0.5X_2 - 10 = 0$$
$$-0.25X_1 + 1.0X_2 - 50 = 0$$

for which the solution is:

$$X_1 = 40$$
$$X_2 = 60$$

The amounts of unused resources can be determined by substituting these values in the three remaining equations.

$$X_3 = 2000 - \quad 7.5X_1 - \quad 5X_2 = 1400 \text{ (unused labor)}$$
$$X_4 = \quad 600 - 1.25X_1 - 2.5X_2 = \quad 400 \text{ (unused capital)}$$
$$X_5 = \quad 180 - \qquad X_1 = 140 \text{ (unused natural resources)}$$

The program is feasible, since some of each resource is left unused.

The value of the program can be determined from Eq. (6) as:

$$C = 1.25(10) + 1.0(50) = 62.5$$

There are any number of feasible solutions of the type we have just found. The full range can be shown in the present example by plotting the equations on activity axes. As indicated above, activity levels X_1 and X_2 are the most convenient variables for this purpose,

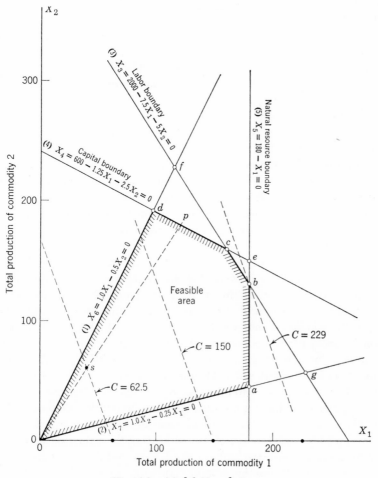

Fig. 4.2. Model V: solutions.

since they occur in all the equations. Each equation limits the values that the activity levels occurring in it may assume in a feasible solution because of the requirement that they all be non-negative. For example, Eq. (3), p. 93, limits the possibilities to combinations of X_1,

X_2, and X_3 which do not use more than 2000 units of labor. The largest value of X_1 for a given value of X_2 is found by setting X_3 (unused labor) equal to zero. In this way, we can construct a *boundary* separating feasible from infeasible solutions by plotting Eq. (3): $X_3 = 2000 - 7.5X_1 - 5X_2 = 0$. The result is shown in Fig. 4.2, with the direction of feasibility (i.e., $X_3 > 0$) indicated by the shading. The other two resource boundaries can be constructed in the same way from Eqs. (4) and (5) by setting X_4 and X_5 equal to zero. Equations (1) and (2) also limit the range of feasible solutions because no final output can be negative. We therefore set X_6 (final output of commodity 1) equal to zero and plot Eq. (1) and do the same thing for X_7 and Eq. (2).

Feasible solutions must lie below (toward the origin) the three resource limits; they must lie to the right of commodity boundary (1) and above commodity boundary (2). These five boundaries therefore outline a *feasible area OabcdO* within which are found all possible feasible solutions.[19] The trial input-output solution just found is shown as point s, which is well inside the feasible area.

It should be clear that no interior point like s can be an optimum solution because it is always possible to increase the output of both final products. Neither can the optimum be anywhere on the commodity boundaries (*Oa* or *Od*) short of the resource boundary because it is possible to increase the final output of one commodity by moving out from the origin along these lines. From these two observations, we conclude that the optimum solution must lie somewhere along the combined resource boundary *abcd*, which is the transformation function for the economy. We can easily reach a point on this boundary by a further input-output solution with X_6 or X_7 allowed to vary and one of the slack variables set at zero. To find the optimal point, however, we have to make use of the objective function.

Traditional production theory suggests a practicable method of finding the optimum. In the textbook case, if we know a transformation curve and also indifference curves indicating the valuation of possible output combinations, we look for the highest indifference curve which touches the transformation curve. Although in Fig. 4.2 the axes are levels of gross rather than final output, we can express the objective

---

[19] Solutions outside the boundaries would have one of the variables X_3 to X_7 negative and thus violate Eq. (4.3), $X_j \geq 0$. The further condition that X_1 and X_2 be non-negative is guaranteed by making final outputs (X_6 and X_7) non-negative. The feasible area therefore lies wholly in the first quadrant.

function in terms of these variables and follow the same procedure.[20]
The objective function can be transformed by eliminating the variables
X_6 and X_7 from Eq. (6) using equations (1) and (2),[21] which leaves
us with a new objective function containing only X_1 and X_2:

$$C = X_1 + 0.375X_2$$

(The coefficients now refer to the value added in producing each of
the two commodities.) This equation can be used to plot constant
values of the objective function, shown by dashed lines in Fig. 4.2.
We now see at a glance that the highest attainable value of the objective is reached at point b, at which $C = 229$, but for more complicated cases we shall need a systematic procedure for getting there.

3. Introduction to the Simplex Method of Solution[22]

The simplex method of solving linear programming problems makes
use of two fundamental properties of such systems. The first is
stated in the *basic theorem: The optimum solution to any linear programming problem will include no more activities than there are
restraints.* Any solution to m equations having exactly m activities
(some of which may be at zero level) is called a *basic solution.* In
our example, there are 5 equations, and therefore a basic solution
consists of five activities. The remaining two activities are said to be
"outside the basis"—i.e., to have activity levels equal to zero.

The absence of joint products in the present case simplifies the finding of basic solutions. Since some of each commodity is required by
any solution, the production activity for each commodity must appear in any basis (in models with alternative production activities, *at
least one* must appear for each commodity). In our model, a basic
solution will therefore contain activities 1 and 2 and three of the remaining five.

A basis can also be identified by the two activities that are left out.

[20] An alternative procedure would be to transform all of the other equations
into functions of final outputs, X_6 and X_7, and use these axes, but it is easier to
transform the objective function.

[21]
$$C = 1.25X_6 + X_7$$
$$= 1.25(X_1 - 0.5X_2) + (X_2 - 0.25X_1)$$
$$= X_1 + 0.375X_2$$

[22] The actual calculations involved in the solution to programming problems
are discussed in section D, pp. 116–123, and in the Appendix.

In Fig. 4.2, each of the five boundary lines was constructed by setting one disposal activity equal to zero. A *point of intersection* of two lines therefore implies that two such activities are equal to zero and represents a basis.

Not all bases can be *feasible* because some of them will lie outside one of the boundaries. The possibilities here are as follows:

Basis (Point)	Activities Excluded	Value of C	Feasible	Not Feasible
O	6,7	0	×	
a	5,7	196.9	×	
b	3,5	228.8	×	
c	3,4	220.0	×	
d	4,6	168.0	×	
e	4,5			×
(Not shown)	5,6			×
f	3,6			×
g	3,7			×
(Not shown)	4,7			×

The basic theorem assures us that we have to scrutinize at the most ten bases to see if they are feasible and at most five of these to see if they are optimal. In a larger system, however, the work required for this enumeration of all possible basic solutions would often be prohibitive, and further exclusion is necessary.

The second feature of the simplex method is a procedure for testing possible changes in a feasible basic solution, which is called the *simplex criterion*. It states that an activity should only be added to the basis (and an existing one deleted) if the net effect of the change is to raise the value of the objective function. If we start at O, for example, we might proceed to point a by adding A_6 and dropping A_5 and then to point b by adding A_7 and dropping A_3, since each of these changes increases the value of C. However, we should not proceed to point c, because this would cause a fall in the value of the objective function. The fact that the feasible region is *convex*[23] precludes the possibility that there are any higher values of the objective function beyond point c, so b is the optimum. However, the route by which we reach b will depend on where we start, and in larger systems there will be many such routes. In the present case

[23] A region is *convex* if it includes any linear combination of points on its boundaries. This property is a consequence of the assumptions of additivity and proportionality which are made in linear programming. The implications of convexity are explored further in section C.

there is only one other (consisting of $Odcb$) that would be followed in using the simplex method.

Consider now the economic significance of the transition from one basis to another, say from a to b. At point a, both labor and capital are surplus, and their disposal activities therefore appear in the basis. As we go from a to b, final output of commodity 2 (X_7) increases while final output of commodity 1 (X_6) declines. The value of total output increases because the value of the increased amount of commodity 2 available for final use is greater than the value of commodity 1 which is lost. In terms of the activity levels X_1 and X_2, a movement from a to b increases the value of C ($C = 1.0 \ X_1 + 0.375 \ X_2$), because X_2 increases while X_1 remains constant. Between b and c, there is an increase of 1.5 in X_2 for a decrease of 1 in X_1, but in the objective function a unit X_2 is only worth three-eighths as much as a unit of X_1. Any movement beyond b therefore results in a lower value of the objective. Geometrically this is apparent because the slope of bc is less than the slope of the objective function.[24] In effect, then, we are comparing the ratio of the marginal valuations of X_1 and X_2 to the marginal rates of substitution along the transformation function. Since both functions are straight lines, it will pay to go all the way from a to b if it is profitable to move from a at all.

Since the optimum solution depends on the values of the parameters assumed in the objective function, we can also calculate the ratios of these parameters (c_6/c_7) for which each point represents the optimum solution. The result is as follows:

c_6/c_7	Optimum Solution
0 –0.60	d
0.60–1.00	c
1.00–2.00	b
2.00– ∞	a

For example, if the two final commodities are valued equally, any point on the labor boundary between b and c will have the same value. In this event a nonbasic solution will produce as high a value of the objective function as the best basic solution. So long as all functions are linear, however, a nonbasic solution cannot be better than a basic solution.

Before leaving this example, we might see what the solution would

[24] For numerical calculations, the simplex criterion is based on an algebraic calculation of the effect of a unit change in the level of the activity being introduced, which will be explained in section D.

have been if the two commodities had been required in fixed proportions such as those at point s. In this case, the solution is at p, which is the point of intersection of a line from the origin through s with the resource boundary. In general, this type of solution would leave unused amounts of two resources instead of only one as before.[25] This assumption of constant proportions in the final demand vector is frequently made in input-output analysis, and the result is that expansion of the system is limited by whichever resource is exhausted first. Increasing the number of commodities does not affect this conclusion, since the number of activities will always be only one larger than the number of restraints.

C. Choice on the Supply Side

To introduce choices among possible supply activities, we need to go considerably further from the original Leontief model than we have done so far. In analyzing choices of final demands, we did not abandon any of the Leontief assumptions but merely added additional activities to describe possible combinations of demand and to ensure a feasible solution. Now, however, we shall make a more general assumption than that of the Leontief system: that there are alternative sources of supply, and that an efficient choice among them cannot be made in advance of the analysis.

In general, we may wish to introduce any or all of the following choices on the supply side:

(1) Choice of alternative production techniques in expanding productive capacity;

(2) Choice between imports and domestic production (which involves introducing exports into the model as well);

(3) Choice as to proportions of supplies from existing plants or regions;

(4) Choice between current production and depletion of inventory (which requires inventory accumulation in earlier periods).

It should be noted that each type of choice affects a particular set of parameters in the input-output model: (1) the input coefficients; (2) the import coefficients; (3) regional supply coefficients; (4) capital coefficients. Together with the choices on the demand side just dis-

---

[25] Since there would be only six activities in this case, five of them (including two slack vectors) would be required to form a basis.

TABLE 4.2. MODEL VI: CHOICE OF TECHNOLOGY

| | | Production Activities | | | | | | Disposal Activities | | | |
| | Industry 1 | | | Industry 2 | | | | Unused Resources | | Final Use | |
Commodities	A_1	A_2	A_3	A_4	A_5	A_6	A_7	A_8	A_9	A_{10}	Restrictions
(1) Commodity 1 (Y_1)	1.0	1.0	1.0	− 0.2	−0.5	−0.8	−0.75			−0.667	0
(2) Commodity 2 (Y_2)		−0.25	−0.50	1.0	1.0	1.0	1.0			−0.333	0
(3) Labor (L)	−12.5	−7.5	−6.0	−15.0	−5.0	−4.0	−4.5	−1			$\bar{L}$
(4) Capital (K)	− 1.10	−1.25	−0.30	− 1.00	−2.50	−0.60	−0.80		−1		$\bar{K}$
(5) Criterion (C)	0	0	0	0	0	0	0	0	0	1.0	Maximum

cussed, the addition of all of these types of choice would convert the input-output model into a general activity analysis. Both for theoretical discussion and for empirical application, however, it is more convenient to make these additions one at a time. Here we shall confine ourselves to the effect of alternative techniques of production on the interindustry system, which is the most serious omission of the Leontief model. The second and third types of choice will be illustrated in the examples discussed in Chapters 11 and 12.

An example which contains a choice among production activities is given by model VI (Table 4.2). The technology of the previous example has been expanded by adding two alternative production activities for commodity 1 and three for commodity 2; the third resource limitation has been dropped for convenience. As before, we take as our objective the maximization of national income, but we assume for simplicity that the two commodities are required in given proportions (two units of commodity 1 to one unit of commodity 2).

The analysis is conducted in three stages. We consider first the simplest case, in which there is only one primary factor (or in which relative prices of the two primary factors are unchanged). Since we have maintained Leontief's assumption of a single output per activity, we can first group the activities into industries and break down the maximizing problem into a choice of technique in each industry. In the second stage, we proceed from the efficient set of activities for an industry to the efficient set for the economy as a whole. The main purposes of this analysis are to show the conditions under which the simpler assumptions of input-output analysis are valid, and to trace the repercussions of technological change. Finally, we shall abandon the assumption of a single primary factor and investigate the production function for the whole economy in terms of the two primary inputs.

1. Efficiency within an Industry

The production alternatives within each industry can be conveniently analyzed by plotting the data of Table 4.2 in the form of production functions as indicated in Fig. 4.1(c). We ignore the capital inputs for the time being and use only the first three coefficients in each activity. In industry 2, for example, these state the amounts of inputs of commodity 1 and of labor required per unit of output of commodity 2 using the four different techniques, A_4 to A_7. These activities can be used to generate a whole set of isoquants because of the assumed properties of divisibility and additivity. To get the inputs required

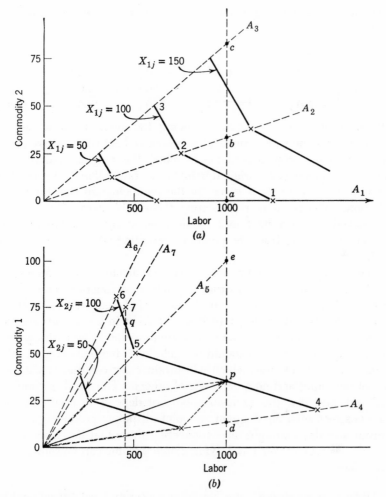

Fig. 4.3. Model VI: production functions.   (a) Industry 1; (b) Industry 2.
(Points lettered a–e correspond to Fig. 4.4.)

for 100 units of output from each activity, we multiply each coefficient
by 100.   Plotting these values for the input coordinates gives us the
numbered points 1 to 7 in Fig. 4.3, one for each activity.   To find
intermediate points, we use the assumption of additivity, which states
that the effect of operating two activities together is the sum of their
separate effects.   For example, if we wish to produce 50 units of
commodity 2 by activity 4 and 50 by activity 5 we multiply the coeffi-

cients in each activity by 50 and add the results to form a new *derived activity:*

$$50A_4 + 50A_5 =$$

$$50 \begin{bmatrix} -0.2 \\ 1.0 \\ -15.0 \end{bmatrix} + 50 \begin{bmatrix} -0.5 \\ 1.0 \\ -5.0 \end{bmatrix} = \begin{bmatrix} -10 \\ 50 \\ -750 \end{bmatrix} + \begin{bmatrix} -25 \\ 50 \\ -250 \end{bmatrix} = \begin{bmatrix} -35 \\ 100 \\ -1000 \end{bmatrix}$$

All other intermediate points producing 100 units of output can be found in the same way. Since all these derived activities are weighted averages of the original activities in which the weights total 100, the isoquant connecting the original points is a straight line. In geometric terms, this same result is given by the parallelogram rule for vector addition. The point *p*, representing the combination of A_4 and A_5 just calculated, can be found by drawing straight lines parallel to A_4 and A_5 starting from the points representing 50 units of output of each.

The concept of derived activities plus the definition of *technological efficiency* enable us to construct a production function for each industry. A production function should include only those combinations of inputs and outputs which would occur in a least-cost solution at some set of prices. An activity or combination of activities is *technologically inefficient* and should be excluded if there exists some other combination of activities which will produce a given output with less use of one input and no greater use of others. The word "technological" indicates that this exclusion does not depend on relative prices. To construct such an isoquant, we plot all points producing a given output and draw straight lines connecting those that lie closest to the origin. Any point, such as 7, lying above this line can be shown to be inefficient.[26]

---

[26] Point 7, representing A_7, uses 75 units of commodity 1 and 450 units of labor to produce 100 units of commodity 2. To compare this possibility to a combination of A_5 and A_6, we hold the labor input and output of commodity 2 constant and compute the amount of commodity 1 required. This is done by first calculating the activity levels of X_5 and X_6 which use 450 units of labor ($X_5 = 50$, $X_6 = 50$). We then determine the inputs into the derived activity having these weights as:

$$50A_5 + 50A_6 = 50 \begin{bmatrix} -0.5 \\ 1.0 \\ -5.0 \end{bmatrix} + 50 \begin{bmatrix} -0.8 \\ 1.0 \\ -4.0 \end{bmatrix} = \begin{bmatrix} -25 \\ 50 \\ -250 \end{bmatrix} + \begin{bmatrix} -40 \\ 50 \\ -200 \end{bmatrix} = \begin{bmatrix} -65 \\ 100 \\ -450 \end{bmatrix}$$

The derived activity (point *q*) therefore uses only 65 units of commodity 1 as compared to 75 units for A_7, showing that the latter is inefficient.

Although this concept of a production function for an industry is strictly applicable only if activities are divisible, it provides a useful approximation even when each activity represents a separate type of plant so long as no indivisible unit is too large in relation to total output.

2. Efficiency for the Economy[27]

Efficiency for the whole economy is defined in the same way as efficiency for a single industry, but now it is necessary to consider several outputs simultaneously. It is therefore more convenient to take combinations of activities having a constant input of the single primary factor rather than constant output combinations. We can do this by transforming the production activities of Table 4.2, setting the labor input at 1000 units and increasing the other coefficients proportionately. The result is shown in Table 4.3

TABLE 4.3. PRODUCTION ACTIVITIES IN LABOR INPUT UNITS

	Industry 1			Industry 2			
Inputs	A_1	A_2	A_3	A_4	A_5	A_6	A_7
(1) Commodity 1	+ 80	+ 133	+ 167	− 13	− 100	− 200	− 167
(2) Commodity 2	0	− 33	− 83	+ 67	+ 200	+ 250	+ 222
(3) Labor (L)	−1000	−1000	−1000	−1000	−1000	−1000	−1000

Since we are now holding the labor input constant, we can plot the activities for both industries on the commodity axes in the same diagram, Fig. 4.4. All activities in industry 1, which have positive coefficients for commodity 1 and negative ones for commodity 2, appear in the lower right-hand quadrant, and all activities in industry 2 appear in the upper left-hand quadrant. Since we rule out joint production, no activities can occur inside the first or positive quadrant (although A_1 is on the axis).

The line comprising efficient combinations in each industry can be found in the same way as in Fig. 4.2 except that now any movement upward or to the right represents an increase in efficiency (greater output or reduced input). A_7 is seen to be inefficient as before. In this case the locus of all efficient points in an industry comprises a cross

[27] The single-factor input-output system with substitution was defined as a "generalized Leontief model" by Georgescu-Roegen (1950). It is analyzed further by Chipman (1953), on which much of this section is based.

section of the production functions of Fig. 4.3 with labor held constant at 1000. The line *Odef* in Fig. 4.4 shows the effect of diminishing returns in industry 2 beyond point *d* as the input of commodity 1 is increased, as does *Oabc* in industry 1.[28]

We now turn to the question of efficiency for the economy as a whole. In the first place, the necessity of producing positive (or at

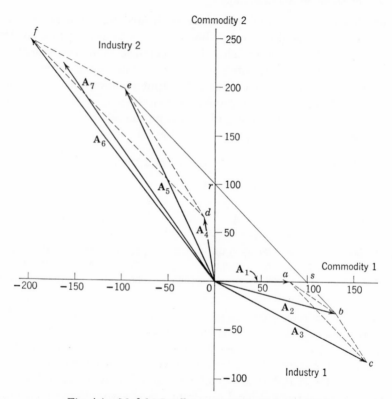

Fig. 4.4.   Model VI: efficient activities (labor units).

least non-negative) amounts of both commodities limits us to the first quadrant. Because we have ruled out joint products, we need at least two activities to satisfy this limitation. In our example, any combination of one of the three activities in industry 1 with one of the four in industry 2 will yield some positive output of both commodi-

---

[28] The points lettered *a* to *e* are also shown in Fig. 4.3. Further mathematical analysis and comparison to the general production function are given in Chipman (1953).

ties.[29]   The whole range of possibilities would be given by the portions of the nine possible lines (not drawn) *ad, ae, af, bd, be, bf, cd, ce, cf* lying in the first quadrant.   As in the case of a single industry, some of these combinations can be ruled out as inefficient.   Any movement away from the origin constitutes an improvement, since it represents an increase in the net availabilities of one or both final products with a given amount of labor input.   Using this test, it is clear that the line *be*, representing combinations of activities A_2 and A_5, is superior to any other combination.   It is easy to see that this result—i.e., one efficient activity per industry—is not limited to this particular example, but applies regardless of the number of activities available in each industry.   At most there is the possibility of several such production-possibility curves coinciding.   In our example, the segment *rs* in the first quadrant therefore contains all of the efficient combinations of Y_1 and Y_2 that can be produced with 1000 units of labor and the available technology.   The equation for this production-possibility curve can be derived by eliminating the activity levels from equation (3) in Table 4.3:

$$(1) \qquad 133X_2 - 100X_5 = Y_1$$

$$(2) \qquad -33X_2 + 200X_5 = Y_2$$

$$(3) \qquad -1000X_2 - 1000X_5 = -1000$$

which gives: $\qquad\qquad 10Y_1 + 10Y_2 = 1000.$

The transformation function just derived for the single-factor case has a rather remarkable property: the particular combination of final demands has no effect on the choice of activities.   The input coefficients are therefore fixed in this case despite the fact that other technological choices exist.   This is the *substitution theorem* which has been proved in varying degrees of generality by Samuelson, Koopmans, Arrow, and Georgescu–Roegen (Koopmans 1951*a*, Chapters VII–X).

The reason for this lack of substitution among inputs can be seen to lie in the dependence of prices in the Leontief system on total labor use alone.   Once an efficient set of activities for any combination of final demands has been found, the corresponding prices in terms of total labor use can be determined.   Because of the assumption of constant returns to scale, these prices do not depend on the levels of each activity but only on the input coefficients, as shown by Eqs. (3.4) and

[29] However, this would not be true if the angle *cOf* were greater than 180°.

(3.5) of the previous chapter. In our example, the prices corresponding to the system $A_2 - A_5$ are determined as follows from Table 4.2
and Eq. (3.4):

$$P_1 - 0.25P_2 - 7.5P_L = 0$$

$$-0.5P_1 + \quad P_2 - 5.0P_L = 0$$

Taking $P_L = 1.0$ gives:[30]

$$P_1 = 10.0$$

$$P_2 = 10.0$$

We can use the price of commodity 2 to determine the cost of production in industry 1 for each activity and then do the same thing for
industry 2. The result is as follows:

Industry 1		Industry 2	
Activity	Unit Cost	Activity	Unit Cost
A_1	12.5	A_4	17.0
A_2	10.0	A_5	10.0
A_3	11.0	A_6	12.0
		A_7	12.0

In each case the cost of production using any other activity would
be higher than that with the optimum combination already found
(A_2 and A_5). Since this calculation does not involve the levels of
output, it holds for all combinations of final demand.

The same type of result will obtain when capital is the only primary
factor. The reader may verify the fact that activities A_3 and A_4 are
then the most efficient combination and that commodity 2 becomes
more expensive relative to commodity 1.

TABLE 4.4. ACTIVITIES IN COMBINED UNITS

Inputs	A_1	A_2	A_3	A_4	A_5	A_6	A_7
Commodity 1	+ 59.2	+ 80	+138.9	− 10.5	− 33.3	−125.0	− 97.4
Commodity 2	0	− 20	− 69.4	+ 52.6	+ 66.7	+156.3	+129.9
(0.8K + 0.2L)	−200	−200	−200	−200	−200	−200	−200

Although the substitution theorem does not apply in general when
there are two or more primary factors, as will be illustrated below,
it is valid for the limiting case in which the relative prices of the two
factors do not change. Under these conditions, capital and labor can

[30] As shown earlier, prices in a one-factor system equal labor use per unit of
final output, given by the coefficients in the transformation function (p. 107).

be consolidated into a single factor with weights given by their relative prices. Assume, for example, that the cost of using a unit of capital is equal to the cost of four units of labor. So long as these relative costs are constant, we can form a consolidated unit of resource use composed of capital and labor coefficients with relative weights of

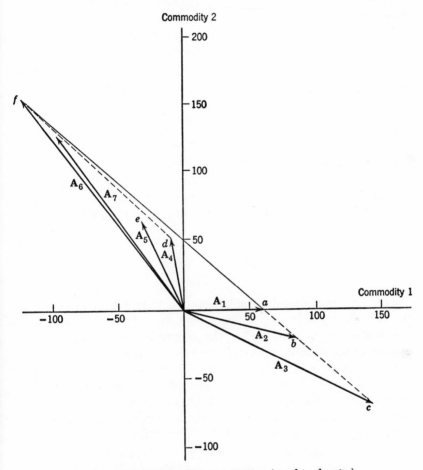

Fig. 4.5. Model VI: efficient activities (combined units).

4:1. This has been done in Table 4.4 where the input coefficient of the combined unit is taken as $(0.8k + 0.2l)$, and 200 such units define the activity level.[31]

On this basis, the system is again represented graphically in Fig.

[31] For example, activity 2 has an input of $0.8(1.25) + 0.2(7.5) = 2.5$ combined units. The output from 200 units is therefore $200/2.5 = 80$.

4.5. The differences in efficiency are now greatly reduced from Fig. 4.4, and there is little to choose among the three alternatives in industry 1 and between A_6 and A_7. The most efficient combination is in fact A_1A_6, which does not include any of the activities that comprised the most efficient sets in the previous two cases. This result illustrates the fallacy of single-factor measures of efficiency. The best choice does not come from minimizing the use of either capital or labor, nor even from combining the two separate results for these cases. Rather it is necessary to estimate simultaneously the total use of both capital and labor.

3. Technological Change

Even with labor as the only scarce factor, the substitution theorem does not mean that the choice of activity in an industry can be made independently of the choices in other industries. Prices in the Leontief system depend in general on the input coefficients of all other sectors, and a change in one sector may affect the cost comparison in any of the others. Consider, for example, the effect on the solution given in Fig. 4.4 of the discovery of a new technique, represented by the following activity A_8:

$$A_8 = \begin{bmatrix} -\ 30 \\ +\ 300 \\ -1000 \end{bmatrix}$$

Figure 4.6 shows that the combination of A_2 and A_8, represented by the line bh, would be more efficient than eb, and that A_8 would therefore replace A_5 in industry 2. The new technique results in a large change in the relative prices of the two commodities, however. At the lower price of Y_2 relative to Y_1, it is now cheaper to use activity A_3 instead of A_2 in industry 1. The efficient transformation curve becomes ch, which lies above bh (although ce lies below be). The unit cost comparison among the several activities is now as follows, using the prices of the system $A_3A_8(P_1 = 8.05, P_2 = 4.11)$:[32]

Industry 1		Industry 2	
Activity	Unit Cost	Activity	Unit Cost
A_1	12.50	A_4	16.61
A_2	8.53	A_5	9.03
A_3	8.05	A_6	10.44
		A_8	4.11

[32] In a programming solution, this result would be arrived at by proceeding from an initial basis of A_2A_5 to A_2A_8 and then to A_3A_8. The unit cost comparison is one way of applying the simplex criterion, as will be shown in section D.

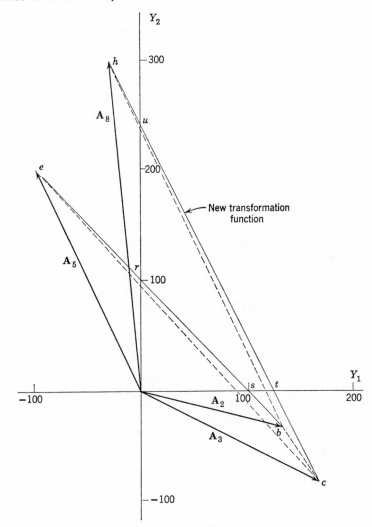

Fig. 4.6. Model VI: effect of technological change.

This calculation confirms algebraically the geometric result that A_3 is more efficient than A_2 when combined with A_8 because the unit cost of commodity 1 is shown to be lower by this method.

4. Production Functions with Two Primary Factors

We now wish to find a graphical representation of model VI which will show the efficient solutions for various amounts of labor and capital. Although two final outputs are produced, they are assumed to be required in the proportion indicated by activity A_{10}:0.667 units of commodity 1 to 0.333 units of commodity 2. The level of this final use activity is to be maximized.

Since no basic activity produces the required composite output, we must first transform model VI in such a way as to relate capital and labor inputs directly to feasible combinations of outputs. To do this, we take advantage of our previous analysis of the Leontief model. We have seen that any basic solution to the first two equations of model VI with a given level of final use (X_{10}) will consist of one activity from each industry. We shall call such a combination of activities an *elementary solution*. Since there are three efficient activities in each industry of model VI, there are 3x3 or nine possible elementary solutions.

We can use the elementary solutions to restate model VI in a reduced form in which the first two equations are eliminated. To do so, we determine the activity levels for each elementary solution which will satisfy the first two equations, taking X_{10} (final use) at unit level. For example, the combination of A_3 in industry 1 and A_4 in industry 2 gives the following pair of equations:

$$(1) \qquad 1.0X_3 - 0.2X_4 - 0.667X_{10} = 0$$

$$(2) \quad -0.5X_3 + 1.0X_4 - 0.333X_{10} = 0$$

for which $X_3 = 0.815$, $X_4 = 0.741$, $X_{10} = 1.0$ is a solution. We can now form a *combined activity* using these production levels as weights:

$$A_{34} = 0.815A_3 + 0.741A_4 + A_{10} = \begin{bmatrix} 0 \\ 0 \\ 16.0 \\ 0.985 \\ 1.0 \end{bmatrix}$$

All such combined activities have zero coefficients in the first two equations, which can therefore be eliminated. Furthermore, if we compute all possible elementary solutions in this way, we shall have included all the production possibilities from the original model and can replace it by a new version using only the combined activities.[33] The result of this calculation is shown in Table 4.5(a).

[33] A somewhat similar procedure is followed in the "complete description" method given by Dorfman, Samuelson, and Solow (1958), pp. 94–98.

TABLE 4.5.
(a) Model VI in Combined Activities

Equation	A_{34}	A_{36}	A_{35}	A_{14}	A_{16}	A_{15}	A_{24}	A_{26}	A_{25}	A_8	A_9	Restrictions
(3) Labor	16.0	13.78	10.0	14.17	13.0	12.08	13.69	11.25	10.0	−1	0	L
(4) Capital	0.985	1.133	2.555	1.140	1.227	1.783	1.491	1.167	2.619	0	−1	K
(5) Criterion (C)	1	1	1	1	1	1	1	1	1	0	0	

(b) Solutions for $C = 150$

Levels of Basic Activities

	A_{34}	A_{36}	A_{35}	A_{14}	A_{16}	A_{15}	A_{24}	A_{26}	A_{25}
Industry 1	122.2	233.3	166.7	110.0	140.0	125.0	115.8	175.0	142.9
Industry 2	111.1	166.7	133.3	50.0	50.0	50.0	79.0	93.8	85.7
Labor	2400	2067	1667	2125	1950	1813	2053	1688	1500
Capital	148	170	383	171	184	263	224	275	393
Efficient Points	X	X			X			X	X

* The subscripts indicate the basic production activities combined in each case.

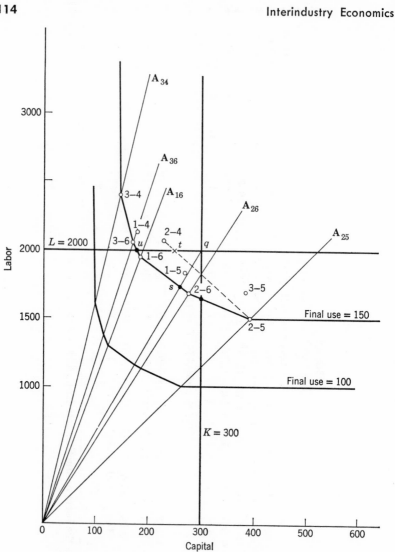

Fig. 4.7. Model VI: production function. (o indicates elementary solution. The numbers represent the activities included in the elementary solution.)

This transformed version of model VI contains the capital and labor inputs per unit of composite final output, which is the information we need to construct isoquants for the whole economy. As before, we find possible points by multiplying each input coefficient by a given activity level. The calculations for a final output of 150 are shown in Table 4.5(b) and plotted in Fig. 4.7. We can now proceed to construct the isoquant for $C = 150$ by connecting the points nearest the origin and eliminating the remaining inefficient solutions. Of the nine elementary solutions, five (3-4, 3-6, 1-6, 2-6, 2-5) are thus shown to be efficient for some price ratio of capital and labor.[34]

The line which we have just drawn is the isoquant for final use of 150. Since all activities are divisible, we can construct other isoquants, such as 100, by scaling off proportional distances from the origin along the rays A_{34}, A_{36}, A_{16}, A_{26}, A_{25} going through the elementary solutions or vertices. Adding the disposal activities for capital and labor,[35] we thus arrive at the complete production function illustrated in Fig. 4.7.

Finding optimum solutions to model VI is now a simple matter. We first assume 2000 units of labor and 300 of capital to be available and plot the corresponding boundaries. Their intersection at q is the highest output achievable and lies between the rays for activities 1-6 and 2-6, indicating that the solution will contain activities 1-2-6. The corresponding output can be estimated graphically to be about 175 by taking the ratio of oq to os. This solution can be verified algebraically by solving model VI for X_1, X_2, X_6, and X_{10} with the remaining activity levels set at zero. The result is:

$$X_1 = \quad 24.6$$

$$X_2 = 171.9$$

$$X_6 = 100.9$$

$$X_{10} = 173.7$$

The graphical analysis just completed is much more general than the determination of a single optimizing solution. The isoquants can be used in the same ways as the usual production function, making allowance for their kinks. For example, Fig. 4.7 illustrates the effect of varying either capital–labor proportions or relative prices on the choice of technology. If we wish to determine the efficient set of

---

[34] It should be noted that no *single* activity has been ruled out although this might have occurred. Furthermore, we see that it is unnecessary to consider any combination of more than three of the original activities because none is more efficient than a combination of exactly three. This follows from the basic theorem mentioned earlier, since a basis for the original model VI contains A_{10} (final use) plus three other activities.

[35] Adding the disposal activities A_8 and A_9 has the effect of extending the isoquants parallel to the axes.

activities corresponding to a price ratio of capital to labor of 4:1, which was the problem analyzed in Fig. 4.5, we construct isocost lines with this slope and find the lowest-cost point of contact with a given isoquant. The result is the point 1-6, the combination which we determined previously; any isoquant gives the same result. Further use will be made of this diagram in the next section.

D. Solution by the Simplex Method Using Prices

We now take up the simplex method of computing solutions to linear programming problems. Although other techniques have been proposed, the simplex method, which is due mainly to Dantzig, has proven to be most practical for a wide range of problems. We present here a revised version which is particularly suited to interindustry problems of the type of model VI, in which there may be many more possible activities than restrictions.

We start with the principles embodied in Dantzig's two basic theorems on linear programming:[36]

(1) If an optimum solution exists, it will be a *feasible basic solution.*[37]

(2) A basic solution can be improved by adding any activity which is *more efficient* (or more profitable) than the *equivalent combination* of activities in the basis.

(3) The optimal solution can be identified by the fact that no activities outside the basis are more profitable than those in the basis.

Although there are various algorithms for particular types of programming problems, there are two essential features in any procedure for applying these rules. The first is the calculation of only *feasible basic* solutions—i.e., those satisfying the restraints of Eqs. (4.2) and (4.3) above. The second is the comparison of outside activities to the basic set in terms of their net effect on the objective function. This comparison involves the notion of an *equivalent combination* of basic activities corresponding to any outside activity. Since a feasible basic solution satisfies all the equations in the model, an increase (from

---

[36] Dantzig's original article is published as Chap. XXI in Koopmans (1951a). Good discussions of the simplex method are given in Charnes, Cooper, and Henderson (1953), Pt. I, and Dorfman, Samuelson, and Solow (1958), Chapter 4.

[37] We do not take up the possibility of *degeneracy*, which exists when a solution has fewer positive activity levels than restrictions. It is unlikely to be a problem in interindustry models.

zero) in an additional activity level will require changes in the levels of some or all of the basic activities and a reduction in at least one of them in order to maintain a feasible solution. (Mathematically, this concept is expressed by Eqs. (4.11) in the Appendix.) Further increases in the new activity will eventually reduce one of the original activity levels to zero and a new basis will be obtained.

In the original version of the simplex method, it was necessary to calculate the equivalent combination corresponding to each excluded activity and then to evaluate its effect on the criterion function.[38] We shall now show that the *prices* of the basic solution can be used to make this comparison. They also provide a more direct economic interpretation of the simplex procedure.

When prices are used, it is convenient to state the simplex criterion in terms of profitability instead of efficiency. An activity is *profitable* if the value of its output is greater than the cost of its inputs when both are measured in terms of the equilibrium prices corresponding to the basis. This use of prices can be developed by starting with the prices in the simpler Leontief system, which we have already discussed.

In the input-output model, prices are defined as the total amount of the primary factor required per unit of net output of each commodity. These Leontief prices were defined by Eqs. (3.4) as those which would make the value of output equal to the cost of inputs in each sector. This system of equations has a determinate solution because the number of unknown prices $(m + l)$ is equal to the number of sector equations (n). Since this is also true of any basic solution, we can define *shadow prices* for all commodities and factors in an interindustry programming model in a similar way:[39]

$$c_j + \sum_i a_{ij}P_i + \sum_h f_{hj}P_h = 0 \qquad \begin{array}{l} (i = 1 \cdots m) \\[4pt] (h = m + 1 \cdots m + l) \\[4pt] (j = 1 \cdots n) \end{array} \qquad (4.6)$$

where $n = m + l$.

This set of equations is identical with (3.4) if there is only one primary factor. In the general interindustry model, however, there will

---

[38] This is the method outlined in Charnes, Cooper, and Henderson (1953), for example.

[39] The coefficients a_{ij} corresponding to the outputs of each activity j will be positive and the rest negative; the f_{hj} are negative.

be several such factors. The units in which shadow prices are measured are those of the criterion function, which in models V and VI is the national product. In other cases, such as model VII, below, the objective is to minimize the use of one factor. The choice of units is arbitrary because the system only determines relative prices. In general, there will be a different price solution for each basic set of $(m + l)$ activities.

The shadow prices just defined have the following meaning. The price P_i of each commodity Y_i in any solution measures the value of the resources required for its production with a given set of activities. The price of P_h of each primary factor F_h is also defined by means of Eqs. (4.6). In a minimizing problem, the factor price measures the increase in capital (or other factor being minimized) which would be required to offset a unit reduction in the amount of F_h available. In a maximizing problem, the factor price represents the value of output which would be foregone by the loss of one unit of the resource. The shadow price of a factor is therefore a measure of its *opportunity cost* or its *marginal product*.

Prices are used as follows in applying the simplex criterion. Assuming the problem has been stated as one of cost minimization, the *gross value* of an activity is defined as the excess of the value of its output over the cost of its purchased inputs, all valued at the shadow prices of a given basis:

$$Z_j = \sum_i a_{ij}P_i + \sum_h f_{hj}P_h \qquad (4.7)$$

The direct use of the factor being minimized constitutes the parameter c_j in the criterion function. The (net) "profitability" of any activity is then the difference between gross value and direct cost:[40]

(Unit profit)		(Gross value)		(Direct cost)
Π_j	$=$	Z_j	$-$	c_j

$$(4.8)$$

For the basic set of activities, profits are zero by definition, since this assumption was used in determining prices.

The procedure for reaching an optimum solution by Dantzig's "revised simplex method" can be stated in four steps:[41]

---

[40] In a maximizing problem, the criterion c_j would be value and the signs would be reversed.

[41] Based on G. B. Dantzig, "Computational Algorithm of the Revised Simplex Method," *Rand Corporation Memorandum 1266*, Oct. 1953.

(1) Find a feasible basis and compute the corresponding activity levels.

(2) Determine the shadow prices of the basis.

(3) Use these prices to evaluate the profitability of the activities not included in the basis, and select the most profitable one to introduce into the next basis.

(4) Determine the activity to be replaced in forming the new basis.

We shall now illustrate this procedure using the data of model VI. To simplify the calculation, we restate the problem as one of minimizing the use of capital, since there is then one less equation. We assume a given level of final output, 150, and set the corresponding activity level, X_{10}, equal to this value. The required amounts of 100 units of commodity 1 and 50 units of commodity 2 therefore become the restrictions B_1 and B_2 in the new version, model VII. The labor restriction, B_3, is 2000 units (with a negative sign) as in Fig. 4.7. The capital restriction is now dropped, and the capital coefficients instead become the coefficients of the objective function which is to be minimized. Activities A_7 (which was shown to be inefficient in all cases) and A_9 (the disposal activity for capital) are dropped. Model VII is shown in Table 4.6 in a form convenient for computing the shadow prices and profitability. In graphical form, it is illustrated by Fig. 4.7 without the capital boundary.

The four steps in the simplex procedure can be divided into two parts, the quantity solution (steps 4 and 1) and the price solution (steps 2 and 3). Both involve solutions to a set of $(m + l)$ simultaneous equations. Depending on the number of coefficients that are zero and the size of the system, it may be convenient to perform these solutions in various ways. The quantity solutions involve little more than the input-output calculations that we have already performed, however, so we leave them to the appendix and take up the price solution and its economic significance.

The simplex method can start from any feasible basic solution. In an interindustry model, we can always find a basis that is feasible in the commodity equations by selecting one activity per industry plus the disposal activities for the primary factors. If the activity levels of the disposal activities in the corresponding solution are positive, the basis is also feasible in the factor equations. We shall start from such a combination, $A_2 A_5 A_8$, which (as Fig. 4.7 shows) is the point farthest from the ultimate solution. The activity levels computed in step (1) for this basis are shown in section III of Table 4.6, row a.

TABLE 4.6. MODEL VII:* SUMMARY OF PRICE SOLUTION

Inputs	Basis no.	A₁	A₂	A₃	A₄	A₅	A₆	A₈	Restrictions Bᵢ	Prices Pᵢ	Total capital PᵢBᵢ
I. Price Analysis											
a_{1j}		**1.0**	**1.0**	**1.0**	**−0.2**	**−0.5**	**−0.8**		100		
(1) Commodity 1 ($a_{1j}P_1$)	a	2.14	2.14	2.14	−0.43	−1.07	−1.71			2.14	214
	b	5.20	5.20	5.20	−1.04	−2.60	−4.16			5.20	520
	c	3.24	3.24	3.24	−0.65	−1.62	−2.59			3.24	324
	d	2.03	2.03	2.03	−0.41	−1.02	−1.62			2.03	203
	e	2.60	2.60	2.60	−0.52	−1.30	−2.08			2.60	260
a_{2j}			**−0.25**	**−0.5**	**1.0**	**1.0**	**1.0**		50		
(2) Commodity 2 ($a_{2j}P_2$)	a		−0.89	−1.79	3.57	3.57	3.57			3.57	179
	b		−1.66	−3.32	6.63	6.63	6.63			6.63	332
	c		−0.94	−1.88	3.76	3.76	3.76			3.76	188
	d		−0.63	−1.26	2.52	2.52	2.52			2.52	126
	e		−0.79	−1.58	3.16	3.16	3.16			3.16	158
f_{3j}		**−12.5**	**−7.5**	**−6.0**	**−15.0**	**−5.0**	**−4.0**	**−1.0**	−2000		
(3) Labor ($f_{3j}P_3$)	a	0	0	0	0	0	0	0		0	0
	b	−3.83	−2.30	−1.84	−4.59	−1.53	−1.22	−0.31		0.306	−612
	c	−1.76	−1.06	−0.85	−2.12	−0.71	−0.56	−0.14		0.141	−281
	d	−0.93	−0.56	−0.45	−1.12	−0.37	−0.30	−0.07		0.074	−149
	e	−1.50	−0.90	−0.72	−1.80	−0.60	−0.48	−0.12		0.120	−240
(4) Capital (c_j)		**1.10**	**1.25**	**0.3**	**1.0**	**2.5**	**0.6**	**0**		0	0

TABLE 4.6. MODEL VII:* SUMMARY OF PRICE SOLUTION (Continued)

Inputs	Basis no.	A_1	A_2	A_3	A_4	A_5	A_6	A_8	Restrictions B_i	Prices P_i	Total capital P_iB_i
II. Profit† (Π_j)	a	1.04	0	0.06	2.14	0	1.26	0			
	b	0.28	0	−0.25	0	0	0.65	−0.31			
	c	0.38	0	0.22	0	−1.07	0	−0.14			
	d	0	−0.41	0.02	0	−1.37	0	−0.07			
	e	0	−0.34	0	−0.16	−1.24	0	−0.12			
III. Activity level (X_j)	a	0	142.9	0	0	85.7	0	500			
	b	0	118.3	0	71.4	8.2	0	0			
	c	0	124.3	0	67.6	0	13.5	0			
	d	131.4	0	0	14.3	0	35.7	0			
	e	80	0	100	0	0	100	0			
IV. Total capital (c_jX_j)	a		178.6			214.3					393
	b		148.0		71.4	20.4					240
	c		155.4		67.6		8.1				231
	d	144.6			14.3		21.4				180
	e	88.0		30.0			60.0				178

* Adapted from model VI by setting $X_{10} = 150$ and minimizing capital.
† Figures may not add because of rounding.

Step (2) consists of solving three simultaneous equations of the form of (4.6) coresponding to the three activities in the basis. They are:

$$
\begin{array}{ll}
(\text{From } \mathbf{A}_2) & P_1 - 0.25P_2 - 7.5P_3 = 1.25 \\
(\text{From } \mathbf{A}_5) & -0.5P_1 + \quad P_2 - 5\ P_3 = 2.5 \\
(\text{From } \mathbf{A}_8) & \quad\quad\quad\quad\quad - \quad P_3 = 0
\end{array}
$$

The solution is found by substitution to be: $P_1 = 2.14$, $P_2 = 3.57$, $P_3 = 0$. These values are recorded at the right of the first section in Table 4.6 in row a. The equations themselves are shown under $\mathbf{A}_2$, $\mathbf{A}_5$, $\mathbf{A}_8$, and the results can be checked by substituting the prices in these three equations and verifying that profit is zero.

Step (3) in this version of the simplex procedure is to compute the profitability of the remaining activities, $\mathbf{A}_1$, $\mathbf{A}_3$, $\mathbf{A}_4$, and $\mathbf{A}_6$, using the prices just determined from the basis. The profit on activity 3, for example, is calculated from Eqs. (4.7) and (4.8) as: $\Pi_3 = 1(2.14) - 0.5(3.57) - 6(0) - 0.3 = 0.06$. In Table 4.6, this calculation involves (i) multiplying the prices at the right by the corresponding input coefficients for activity 3, (ii) adding down the column, and (iii) subtracting c_3 from this total. The calculation is repeated for the remaining activities.

Step (3) is completed by selecting the most profitable activity, $\mathbf{A}_4$, for introduction into the next basis.[42] In order to add this activity, one of the old activities must drop out in order to retain a basic solution (number of activities equal to the number of equations). By the nature of the interindustry model, the activity that is replaced must be either another activity in the same industry ($\mathbf{A}_5$ in this case) or the activity representing unemployed labor ($\mathbf{A}_8$). The method for choosing between these possibilities utilizes the equivalent combination of $\mathbf{A}_4$, which is given in the Appendix. In essence, it consists of determining whether the addition of $\mathbf{A}_4$ will use up all the excess labor before it produces enough of commodity 2 to substitute completely for $\mathbf{A}_5$.[43] In our case, the unused labor is exhausted first and the second basis (b) becomes $\mathbf{A}_2\mathbf{A}_4\mathbf{A}_5$.

The next "round" in the analysis is computed in exactly the same

---

[42] This procedure does not ensure the greatest reduction in total cost, but it is an easy rule to follow and is normally used.

[43] In the interindustry model we can usually speak of one activity substituting for another since each has only one output, but more accurately the new activity replaces a combination of other activities.

way as the first. The quantity solution can be found by any of the methods given in Chapter 2—i.e., by substitution, by iteration, or by the use of the inverse. The same alternatives are available for the price solution. Using the prices shown for the second basis, we then reevaluate the excluded activities. In basis b, all of them are less profitable than before, but both A_6 and A_1 still show positive profits. The most profitable, A_6, is chosen for the next basis, and A_5 is found to be the activity replaced. The procedure continues in the same way until all of the excluded activities become unprofitable. The simplex criterion guarantees that this result represents the optimum solution, since at each stage the total capital used either declines or remains constant. In the present case the decline in capital cost is continuous although irregular.

It should be noted that this algebraic version of the simplex procedure gives the same results as would a graphical analysis using Fig. 4.7, but the route followed is different. The simplex method leads first to a point t on the labor boundary, combining 2-4 and 2-5, and then reaches point u by moving along that boundary. A production-function analysis would arrive at u by moving along the isoquant until it intersected the labor boundary.

The economic interpretation of this version of the simplex method is easier to follow than the original procedure because it simulates the working of the price mechanism in a competitive economy. In fact, Koopmans has shown that the results are identical with those that would be produced under perfect competition, given the same technological assumptions. The shadow prices may therefore be considered "efficiency prices," since they lead to an efficient allocation of resources.[44] From a computational point of view, this revised version is in general preferable to the original simplex method for interindustry systems, at least for hand calculation, since once prices are determined for a given basis it is easy to evaluate any number of alternative techniques of production.

E. The Valuation of Primary Factors

In the previous section, prices were utilized as an aid to finding the solution to the problem of resource allocation—i.e., the "quantity solu-

[44] A good nonmathematical discussion of this point is given in Koopmans (1951b). Shadow prices are also known as imputed, accounting, implicit, or intrinsic (Koopmans, 1957, p. 97).

tion." As an incident to this process, we observed that there was a different price solution corresponding to each basis and that a test of the optimality of the quantity solution could be made by using these prices. We now turn our attention more specifically to the nature of the price solution and to its practical value in interindustry analysis.

The objective of programming may be considered to be the proper valuation of the resources available to the economy just as well as the optimum allocation of these resources. Instead of trying to find the maximum value of output producible, we might look instead for the minimum valuation of the resources which will eliminate profits in each activity. It can be shown that the solution to one problem implies the solution to the other. This property of programming models is known as the duality of price determination and allocation.[45] It is not necessary to solve the dual problem separately because, as we have already seen, the price solution emerges as a byproduct of the quantity solution.

When the programming problem is formulated as one of minimizing capital (or any other input), prices can be shown to have the following properties, most of which have been illustrated in the preceding example:[46]

(1) The price of each final output is equal to the amount of capital required to produce an additional unit of it.

(2) The price of each primary factor is equal to its opportunity cost—i.e., the amount of capital which would be required to replace one unit of the resource.

(3) All prices are non-negative.

(4) Prices of resources not fully used are zero, since the disposal activity occurs in the solution.

(5) When inputs are valued by shadow prices, each activity used will produce an output worth exactly the cost of the inputs it absorbs —i.e., will have zero profits.

(6) In the optimum solution, no excluded activity will show positive profits.

The shadow prices provide an alternative way of calculating the total cost (or value) of a program. Instead of Eq. (4.1): $C =$

---

[45] The "dual theorem" is discussed in all of the references cited in the bibliography on linear programming. See especially Dorfman, Samuelson, and Solow (1959), Chapters 4 and 7.

[46] For a maximizing problem, the first two properties must be restated in terms of the value of final output.

$$\sum_j c_j X_j \qquad (j = 1 \cdot \cdot \cdot n) \text{ we can write,}$$

$$C = \sum_i P_i Y_i + \sum_h P_h \bar{F}_h \quad (i = 1 \cdot \cdot \cdot m) \quad (h = m + 1 \cdot \cdot \cdot m + l)$$

$$(4.9)$$

where the amounts of resources available $\bar{F}_h$ have a negative sign. The identity between Eqs. (4.1) and (4.9) as methods of determining total cost is shown in Table 4.6. In the last section of the table, capital is computed by (4.1) and in the last column it is computed by (4.9). This double calculation provides a useful check on the whole solution at each iteration. The equality between the two methods of computing the value of the objective function corresponds to the equality between the two ways of computing the total use of resources given in Eqs. (3.1) and (3.3) of the previous chapter.

Prices of final outputs in the programming model represent a significant improvement in realism over the prices in the one-factor Leontief system because they include the opportunity costs of using all other resources. Of perhaps more practical significance is the fact that they provide a way of determining the value of the resources themselves. In classical economic theory, the value of any resource and its compensation in a competitive economy are determined by its marginal productivity. The marginal productivity as usually defined is a partial equilibrium concept which implies that labor and output, for example, can be varied while other inputs are kept constant. In the programming model, on the other hand, variation in factor proportions is obtained by combining activities representing fixed bundles of inputs and outputs in different proportions. The latter model corresponds to a much wider range of actual technology than the former and therefore has much greater likelihood of empirical application.

For the economy as a whole, the advantages of the activity analysis model are particularly important. Although it may occasionally be possible to substitute capital for labor under *ceteris paribus* conditions in single productive processes, this technique of valuation is less plausible for the whole economy because alternative productive combinations are more complex. If information can be collected on available techniques in each industry, however, the programming model can determine possible substitutions among factors and outputs for the economy as a whole. One such possibility is shown in the production function of Fig. 4.7. The marginal rate of substitution of capital for labor varies from 0.12 when there are 2000 units of labor to 0.63 when there are only 1600 units, final output being kept constant at 150.

There are many actual situations in which market prices do not provide an efficient method of allocating resources, and rationing, taxes, subsidies, or other methods are adopted to remedy the resulting disequilibrium. Important cases involve structural unemployment of labor, balance of payments deficits, excess demand for capital, and similar phenomena. These types of disequilibrium are particularly important in the underdeveloped countries, where it is one of the main purposes of governmental development programs to offset them. In this context the resource valuation resulting from a programming model would be particularly useful. In fact, the use of such "accounting prices" may be one of the most effective ways of improving resource allocation without excessive centralization of investment planning and production control. These possibilities will be explored further in Chapter 11.

F. Alternative Interindustry Models

The programming models discussed in this chapter were derived by combining the sector assumptions of input-output analysis with the treatment of choice and computational methods of linear programming. Now that the principles of activity analysis and linear programming have been introduced in this way, we shall consider alternative formulations of a model in which there is a choice of technology. Two major possibilities have been suggested: activity analysis without optimization, and linear programming applied to single productive processes rather than to large aggregates.

One of the main deficiencies of input-output analysis in its current empirical form is that its parameters are derived almost entirely from statistical observations of aggregate industry behavior in past years. Since new techniques are continuously being introduced, any set of data on past relations is to some extent obsolete by the time it has been compiled. One way of extending the period over which such observations may be applicable is to treat the observed interindustry flows as an average of different processes. If it is possible to identify the most efficient techniques within each industry, it may be realistic to describe technological change for some time in the future as a process of replacing the least efficient methods, which are generally the oldest, by the best technology currently known in the industry.

A model based on this principle has been developed by Dr. Anne Carter, and is currently being tested by the Harvard Economic Research Project.[47] It does not require any optimization procedure for its solution because it is assumed that the "best practice" technique in each industry is not dependent upon choices in other industries and can therefore be specified for the model in advance. In linear programming terms, this amounts to assuming that one activity dominates all others in each industry over the range of price variation that is likely to occur. The set of activities in the optimum solution can therefore be specified in advance, and the only variables to be determined are the rates at which the new technology will be introduced in each industry. These rates are measured by the rate of investment in each sector.

This model of technological change represents a logical extension of the basic Leontief approach to interindustry analysis, which is to determine all choices from outside data and generate only the repercussions on activity levels from the interindustry system itself. As a framework for the study of past technological change this approach has obvious advantages because it can utilize information on observed production techniques and does not have to describe all of the alternatives required for a more general activity analysis model. However, it has not yet been determined whether the assumptions involved are sufficiently realistic to use such a model for predicting further technological change.

While the preceding model reduces the empirical difficulties of activity analysis, the other alternative of using industrial processes as the basic units would increase them enormously. This technique has developed from the application of linear programming to the study of production within a single plant or industry. A good example is the study by Manne (1958) of petroleum refining. In this formulation, the units considered are usually much less aggregated than those of interindustry analysis, being related to single types of productive equipment. Manne's model contains 105 equations in 205 variables, for example, while even the "simplified" version used by Marschak contains 44 equations (5 of which refer to equipment capacities, 3 to alternative types of raw material, 18 to intermediate products, 3 to exogenous inputs, and 15 to end products and their specifications).[48]

[47] Harvard Economic Research Project, *Report on Research for 1956–1957*, Cambridge, 1958 (mimeographed).
[48] The simplified model is given in Markowitz (1956).

Aside from its much greater detail, the method of process analysis is more general than input-output in that it can include a greater variety of activities and restrictions. In addition to equations for the three types of commodities of the input-output system—final products, intermediate products, and primary factors—process analysis may contain restrictions corresponding to the properties of final products, the location of supply and demand, and the capacity of individual types of equipment. In addition to the production activities of the input-output system, a process analysis model may include transportation, storage, investment, blending, sales, and other activities. This greater detail has been feasible because process analysis has so far been limited to the study of resource allocation in single plants, firms, and industries.

The extension of process analysis to cover the whole economy, which has been suggested by Markowitz (1956), Manne (1958), and others, would run into two serious difficulties not encountered at the industry level. There is first the limitation on data processing and computing capacity. At present, the largest-size programming model which can be handled by a general algorithm is about 250 equations. Larger systems are feasible if they possess special properties, but it is clear that an over-all model of the economy could not go into detail at all comparable to that which has already been used in the analysis of single sectors.

There are more serious theoretical objections to the substitution of processes for industries as basic units of analysis. Although the interindustry model introduces many artificial transactions in an effort to improve the stability of production relationships, the "industries" of the input-output system correspond in the main to identifiable groups of producers. Most of the flows which the model contains have their counterparts both in commercial transactions and in statistical series. Processes, on the other hand, are pure technological units, and the activity levels resulting from a process analysis are much harder to evaluate and utilize. This difficulty is not too serious at the industry level, but for the whole economy an elaborate system for identifying processes with industries would be necessary in order to make use of the results. Furthermore, the assumption that optimum use of all equipment in the economy could somehow be achieved either through the price system or through controls is a very strong one. If some concessions to immobility and inefficiency are to be made, it is much easier to make such modifications on an industry basis.

Our conclusion is that it is neither empirically feasible nor theoretically desirable to eliminate the industry concept from interindustry analysis and resort entirely to more basic units. Some type of compromise is required between the necessity of introducing more realistic descriptions of technological alternatives on the one hand and the need to maintain identifiable decision-making and operating units on the other. To retain the considerable advantages of process analyses, it would seem desirable to conduct them for single industries within an interindustry framework. This could be done by using prices from the interindustry model for scarce commodities instead of market prices and if necessary modifying these prices after the more detailed analyses of each sector are completed. As our solution to a programming model has shown, the effect of changes in other sectors on the optimal choices in any industry can be accounted for by changes in the shadow prices of inputs and outputs. Each price corresponds to a quantitative restriction on the model as a whole, so that if the prices of the interindustry model are consistent with those of the process analysis of a single sector, the results of the two can be combined to form a single integrated system.

Since all three of the approaches to the choice among technological alternatives discussed in this chapter are in an experimental stage, it is not possible to arrive at any very precise conclusions as to their validity or possible applications. In principle, however, all three are compatible and could be combined in a single interindustry model. The desirable form of such a model will depend mainly on its proposed uses. It is likely, however, that the simple assumptions of the input-output model will have to be used for large areas of the economy, and that more detailed analysis will be limited to relatively few important sectors.

The choice between a predetermined Leontief-type model of change and a programming formulation would seem to depend primarily on whether the purpose is prediction or planning. It is possible that a model which allocates resources in the most efficient manner will approximate the actual behavior of some sectors of the economy, but this has yet to be demonstrated. On the other hand, where the model is to be used as a guide to government policy, it is desirable to include those choices over which the government has some control whenever government action depends to some extent on the nature of the solution. The design of models for this purpose is considered in Chapters 10 and 11.

APPENDIX: Solutions to interindustry programming models[49]

1. The Revised Simplex Method

These notes are intended to facilitate hand calculation of illustrative programming models by Dantzig's revised simplex method. Any realistic interindustry model will probably require an electronic calculator, and the actual steps will depend on the characteristics of the particular machine. A tableau convenient for hand calculation is given by Tables 4.6 and 4.7.

Step 1: Find a Basic Solution

(a) *Select a feasible basic set of activities.* In interindustry systems this is usually possible by inspection if one activity is selected for each industry, having regard to the resource limits. The basic activities $(A_2 A_5 A_8)$ are recorded in column (1) of Table 4.7.

(b) *Determine the activity levels.* Unless the matrix can be made nearly triangular, it is worth while to find the inverse, as is done here. The inverse of the basis is recorded in columns (4) to (6). Since the disposal activity for labor is used, the first two rows are the same as the inverse to the corresponding input-output system $(A_2 A_5)$ with the third row indicating the total use of labor.

Step 2: Determine the Shadow Prices of the Basis

When an inverse is used, prices are determined from Eq. (3.5), which can be restated in the notation of this chapter as:

$$P_j = \sum_i c_i r_{ij}, \qquad (i = 1 \cdots m + l) \qquad (4.10)$$

[49] The following comparison of notations is given to facilitate reference to various expositions of programming theory (in all cases i applies to a row or restriction and j to a column or activity).

Authors	Input Coefficient a_{ij}	Activity Vector	Activity Level	Requirements Vector	Criterion Function	Profitability of Activity	Shadow Price	Equivalent Combination
Present Chapter	a_{ij}	A_j	X_j	B	$C = \Sigma c_j X_j$	$(Z_j - c_j)$	P_i	α_{ij}
Dantzig; Charnes, Cooper, and Henderson	a_{ij}	P_j	λ_j	P_o	$z = \Sigma \lambda_j c_j$	$(c_j - z_j)$		x_{ij}
Koopmans	a_{ij}	(a_j)	x_j	y		q_j	p_i	
Leontief	a_{ij}		X_j	Y			P_i	
Dorfman, Samuelson, and Solow	a_{ij}	A_j	x_j	s, C	$r = \Sigma v_j x_j$ $Z = \Sigma p_j x_j$	$(v_j - w_j)$ $(P_j - p_j)$	u_i	y_i

TABLE 4.7. MODEL VII: PRICE AND QUANTITY SOLUTIONS USING INVERSE

Basis	Row	(1) Basis Activities A_j	(2) c_i	(3) Price solution P_j	(4) 1	(5) Inverse of basis† 2	(6) 3	(7) Quantity solution Y_i	(8) Quantity solution X_j	(9) Entering activity A_k	(10) Entering activity α_k	(11) Activity replaced* $\theta_j = X_j/\alpha_j$
										$k=4$		
a	1	A_2	1.25	2.144	1.143	0.571	0	100	142.86	−0.2	0.344	416.8
	2	A_5	2.50	3.571	0.286	1.143	0	50	85.71	1.0	1.086	78.94
	3	A_8	0	0	−10.000	−10.000	−1.0	−2000	500	−15.0	7.000	71.43*
										$k=6$		
b	1	A_2	1.25	5.204	1.634	1.063	0.049		118.30	−0.8	−0.441	
	2	A_5	2.50	6.633	1.837	2.694	0.155		8.16	1.0	0.604	13.50*
	3	A_4	1.00	0.306	−1.429	−1.429	−0.143		71.43	−4.0	0.286	250.0
										$k=1$		
c	1	A_2	1.25	3.249	2.976	3.031	0.162		124.25	1.0	0.946	131.41*
	2	A_6	0.60	3.761	3.041	4.460	0.257		13.50	0	−0.169	
	3	A_4	1.00	0.141	−2.298	−2.703	−0.216		67.57	−12.5	0.405	166.67
										$k=3$		
d	1	A_1	1.10	2.033	3.148	3.205	0.172		131.41	1.0	0.514	255.7
	2	A_6	0.60	2.525	3.573	5.002	0.286		35.72	−0.5	−0.643	
	3	A_4	1.00	0.075	−3.574	−4.002	−0.286		14.30	−6.0	0.143	100.0*
e	1	A_1	1.10	2.596	16.005	17.606	1.200		80.00			
	2	A_6	0.60	3.156	−12.509	−13.009	−1.001		100.01			
	3	A_3	0.30	0.121	−25.015	−28.016	−2.001		100.0			

* The activity replaced is starred.
† The accuracy of the solution decreases in the later bases because of rounding errors.

where r_{ij} are the elements of column j of the inverse to the basis. The direct cost elements c_i are recorded in column (2) and the corresponding prices in column (3). This form is convenient because each cost (c_i) is multiplied by its own row in the inverse. For example,

$$P_1 = 1.25(1.143) + 2.5(0.286) = 2.144$$
$$P_2 = 1.25(0.571) + 2.5(1.143) = 3.571$$

Step 3: Determine the Profitability of Excluded Activities

As indicated in section D, this step utilizes the shadow prices just determined and the unmodified input coefficients of each activity. The most profitable activity (A_4) from Table 4.6 is selected for the next basis and entered in column (9). It is convenient to calculate profitability separately, as was done in Table 4.6, because the number of activities may greatly exceed the number in the basis. Only the current basis need be entered in Table 4.7.

Step 4: Determine the Activity to Be Replaced (A_r)

(a) *Determine the equivalent combination of the new activity* (A_k). The equivalent combination of basic activities corresponding to the activity being introduced (A_k) may be defined as the effect on each activity level of increasing X_k by one unit while maintaining a feasible solution. In our three-sector model, the equivalent combination $[\alpha_1\alpha_2\alpha_3]$ is defined as follows:[50]

$$\alpha_1 a_{11} + \alpha_2 a_{12} + \alpha_3 a_{13} - a_{1k} = 0$$
$$\alpha_1 a_{21} + \alpha_2 a_{22} + \alpha_3 a_{23} - a_{2k} = 0 \qquad (4.11)$$
$$\alpha_1 a_{31} + \alpha_2 a_{32} + \alpha_3 a_{33} - a_{3k} = 0$$

or

$$\alpha_1 A_1 + \alpha_2 A_2 + \alpha_3 A_3 - A_k = 0$$

The equivalent activity levels, which are sometimes called the "representation" of A_k, can be determined by solving these equations by means of the inverse:

$$\alpha_1 = r_{11}a_{1k} + r_{12}a_{2k} + r_{13}a_{3k}$$
$$\alpha_2 = r_{21}a_{1k} + r_{22}a_{2k} + r_{23}a_{3k} \qquad (4.12)$$
$$\alpha_3 = r_{31}a_{1k} + r_{32}a_{2k} + r_{33}a_{3k}$$

[50] The first three activities are the basic activities. The complete system of restrictions given by (4.2) reduces to this form because all of the other activity levels are zero.

The result of this operation is recorded in column (10) of Table 4.7.

(b) *Determine the X_j which first becomes zero.* The effect on each activity level in the old solution of increasing the level of the new activity is given by the corresponding value of α. The activity to be replaced (A_r) is the one which is first reduced to zero as X_k is increased. Algebraically,

$$X_j{}' = X_j{}^o - \alpha_j\theta, \qquad (4.13)$$

where θ is the level of the activity being introduced, and $X_j{}'$ is the new level of each activity. Setting this expression equal to zero and solving for θ will determine A_r as the basic activity with the minimum value of θ.

This calculation is shown in column (11) of Table 4.7. For the first basis, A_8 has the lowest value of θ, 71.43, and it drops out of the next basis.[51] The activity coming in, A_4, therefore replaces A_8 in the basis, and c_4 is inserted in place of c_8 in column (2) for the next calculation.

Step 1 in Succeeding Rounds

The determination of the new set of basic activities, $A_2A_5A_4$, completes one iteration of the simplex procedure, which is then repeated with A_4 inserted in place of A_8. It is not necessary to calculate the new basic solution from the beginning, however. Instead, the new inverse and its quantity solution can be computed by modifying the old inverse in the following three stages:[52]

(a) *Convert row r* by dividing through by the corresponding α_r. In the first basis, since A_8 is replaced, the third row in the new inverse is determined by dividing by $\alpha_8 = 7.0$. In general,

$$r_{kj}{}' = r_{rj}{}^o/\alpha_r, \qquad (4.14)$$

(b) *Convert the remaining rows* of the inverse from a similar formula:

$$r_{ij}{}' = r_{ij}{}^o - \alpha_i r_{kj}{}', \qquad (4.15)$$

where $r_{kj}{}'$ is the element in the same column of row k, as determined in (a). For example, $r_{12}{}' = 0.571 - (0.344)(-1.429) = 1.063.$

[51] If the supply of labor had been slightly larger, A_4 would have replaced A_5, and A_8 (the labor disposal activity) would have remained in the solution.

[52] Further details and justification of this procedure will be found in Dantzig (1951a) and Charnes, Cooper, and Henderson (1953) pp. 12–14, from which the notation used here is adapted. In the modified simplex method used here, their procedure is only applied to the basic activities rather than to all activities.

(c) *Determine the new activity levels* from Eq. (4.13). For example, $X_2' = 142.86 - 0.344(71.43) = 118.3$.

The only difference between the procedure just outlined and the original simplex method lies in the method of determining the profitability of excluded activities, Steps 2 and 3. In the original simplex method, this is done by calculating the representations of *all* the excluded activities and then evaluating the gross value from:

$$Z_j = \sum_i c_i \alpha_{ij} \tag{4.16}$$

It can readily be shown from the definition of the representation that this is equivalent to determining the gross value from $Z_j = \sum_i P_i a_{ij} + \sum_h P_h f_{hj}$, as indicated in Eq. (4.7). The "representation" has the same interpretation as a column in the inverse matrix, and the equivalence between $\sum_i c_i r_{ij}$ and $\sum_i P_i a_{ij}$ has already been demonstrated in Chapter 3, Eqs. (3.4) and (3.5).[53]

There are several advantages to the revised simplex procedure, particularly for hand calculation. The number of operations is substantially less because there is only one multiplication of each excluded activity by a column of coefficients instead of the two required by the original method. The number of zero elements is also greater, since the original activities have more zeros than their representations. Finally, easy checks on each step are available because the price solution for the basis can be substituted back into the original equations (as can the quantity solution in either version).

2. Solution to Nonlinear Interindustry Models

At the present time, there is no empirically tested algorithm available for nonlinear programming systems which is comparable to the simplex method for linear systems, but there are several methods for particular types of nonlinear system. Here we merely indicate the nature of one which has proven useful for interindustry models in which either the objective function or the restrictions are nonlinear.[54]

[53] The present case differs only in including equations for primary factors.

[54] Gradient methods of solution, which appear most promising, are discussed in Arrow, Hurwicz, and Uzawa (1958). The present method is given in Chenery and Uzawa, "Nonlinear Programming in Economic Development," in the same volume.

Examples of this type include demand for final goods as a function of price, supply of labor as a function of wages, and use of capital as an increasing function of output.

The essence of the method can be illustrated by reference to the example given in Chapter 11, section D, in which export demand is a function of price. The optimum solution is reached by solving a series of linear-programming problems for a reduced system in which the prices of labor and foreign exchange are taken as given. After each solution, factor prices are adjusted in accordance with excess demands and the level of exports in each sector is revised to make marginal revenue equal to marginal cost. It can be shown that the procedure will always converge to the optimum solution. This technique made it feasible to solve the nonlinear fourteen-equation system given in Chapter 11 quite readily by hand.

The solution to a general nonlinear programming system in which there are no increasing returns or other nonconvexities has been demonstrated by Kuhn and Tucker to have the following properties (see Dorfman, Samuelson, and Solow, Chapter 8): (i) Activities at positive levels must have zero profits—i.e., marginal revenue equal to marginal cost, as measured by shadow prices; (ii) unprofitable activities must appear at zero level; (iii) resources that are not fully used must have zero prices; and (iv) resources with positive prices must be fully used. These conditions, which are a generalization of the properties of the solution to the linear system, serve to identify the optimum solution to a nonlinear model.

BIBLIOGRAPHY

Allen, R. G. D., *Mathematical Economics,* The Macmillan Company, New York, 1956, Chapters 16, 17.

Arrow, K., "Decision Theory and Operations Research," *Operations Research,* V, No. 6, 765–774 (December 1957).

Arrow, K., L. Hurwicz, and H. Uzawa, *Studies in Linear and Nonlinear Programming,* Stanford University Press, 1958.

Charnes, A., W. W. Cooper, and A. Henderson, *An Introduction to Linear Programming,* John Wiley and Sons, New York, 1953.

*Chipman, J., "Linear Programming," *Review of Economics and Statistics,* XXXV, No. 2, 101–117 (May 1953).

Dantzig, G. (1951a), "The Programming of Interdependent Activities: Mathematical Model," in Koopmans (ed.), *Activity Analysis of Production and Allocation.*

* Selected Readings.

————. (1951*b*), "Maximization of a Linear Function of Variables Subject to Linear Inequalities," in Koopmans (ed.), *Activity Analysis of Production and Allocation*.

*Dorfman, R., "Mathematical or 'Linear' Programming: A Nonmathematical Exposition," *American Economic Review*, XLIII, No. 5, 797–825 (December 1953).

*Dorfman, R., P. Samuelson, and R. Solow, *Linear Programming and Economic Analysis*, 1958, Chapters 2–4.

Georgescu-Roegen, N., "Leontief's System in the Light of Recent Results," *Review of Economics and Statistics*, XXXII, No. 3, 214–222 (August 1950).

Koopmans, T. C. (ed.) (1951*a*), *Activity Analysis of Production and Allocation*, 1951.

————. (1951*b*), "Efficient Allocation of Resources," *Econometrica*, XIX, No. 4, 455–465 (October 1951).

*————. (1957), *Three Essays on the State of Economic Science*, McGraw-Hill Book Company, New York, 1957, Chapter 1.

Manne, A. S., "A Linear Programming Model of the U.S. Petroleum Refining Industry," *Econometrica*, XXVI, No. 1, 67–106 (January 1958).

*Markowitz, H., "Industry-Wide, Multi-Industry, and Economy-Wide Process Analysis," in *The Structural Interdependence of the Economy*, 1956.

Vajda, S., *The Theory of Games and Linear Programming*, Methuen and Company, London, 1956.

chapter **5**

Empirical bases
for interindustry models

A. Significance of Empirical Implementation

A notable feature of the theoretical models developed in the inter-industry approach is that they are consistently aimed at empirical implementation. The simple input-output model implies an input-output table, which experience has shown to be a practicable research objective. The more complex models are also formulated so as to be suitable for empirical work. Indeed, too much concern with statistical implementation, so that over-simplified theoretical formulations are accepted because they can be readily handled statistically, is probably a more serious danger in the approach than too little concern. Despite this danger, empirical applicability remains one of the strong points of the interindustry approach.

The central purpose of the empirical investigations described in this chapter is to derive appropriate parameters for interindustry models. A further result of these investigations may be a consider-able extension and integration of available statistical information about the operation of the economy. But from the standpoint of in-terindustry analysis, this result—however useful for other purposes—

137

is only of secondary importance. In particular, a danger to be avoided in these statistical investigations is elaboration and refinement beyond the point necessary for estimating parameters.

B. Basic Input-Output Tables

1. Design

The fundamental design of an input-output table is set by the accounting relationships of the input-output model, as discussed in Chapter 2. An essential step is to establish the classification of sectors. Each sector should have a homogeneous output, important enough to deserve separate study, and a homogeneous structure of inputs. To fit the intricate complexities of a modern industrial economy into this framework, however, requires a substantial amount of aggregation of more elementary economic activities. Even a table with 500 sectors, the largest number yet attempted, is a great simplification of reality. Certain theoretical principles of aggregation can be suggested, as discussed in Chapter 2, but they can only be expected to apply approximately.

In practice the most serious limitation on the system of classification is set by the availability of data—specifically, the classification used in a country's industrial census. Careful study of output distributions or input structures based on census data sometimes does reveal particular reclassifications which improve the homogeneity of input-output rows or columns. As a broad generalization, however, a striking result of experience in designing input-output tables is that industrial classifications in conventional use are with minor changes adequate for this purpose. Though the precise borders of an "industry" may be vague, its recognition as an entity both by business firms and by government statistical agencies is generally a sign that it should also be recognized in an input-output table. Moreover, the comparison of U.S., Italian, Japanese, and Norwegian tables in Chapter 8 indicates that the place of each industry in the structure of interindustry sales is much the same in various countries.

An important classification problem exists because typically the basic unit of industrial operation, and hence the basic unit of statistical data collection, is the establishment. An establishment may be a single plant building, with its capital equipment and associated labor force, but it often produces several kinds of products—a primary product (or set of products) of large value, plus certain less important secondary products. When a group of establishments is classified together to form a sector, the criterion used is that all should have the same primary product. However, the question of how to treat their several secondary products (which are primary to other groups of establishments combined into other sectors) remains. One method is simply to keep all of the secondary products in the output of the industry, of course adding them only in value units. This is the method used in reporting data in census publications, but it obviously conflicts with the homogeneity of product desired in an input-output row. Another method, the one actually used in constructing the 1947 U.S. table, is to allocate each secondary product as a fictitious input to the industry for which it is primary, and simultaneously to add it to that industry's output. Thus each input-output row at least contains all of the primary product, wherever produced, but it still counts the secondary products as well. A third method, followed to a considerable degree in Japan, is to shift completely to a product classification by subtracting each secondary product from the output of the original establishments and adding it to the industry for which it is primary. Correspondingly, an appropriate portion of the inputs of the original establishments must also be transferred to that industry's input structure. This transfer of inputs can be done only approximately by using the primary industry's input structure as a guide, since the basic input data collected from the establishments are not usually broken down on a product basis. But still this is probably the best of the three methods. Each input-output row is clearly more homogeneous, since it includes only the primary product, and for the purpose of estimating parameters each adjusted input-output column is likely to be quite as satisfactory as the original.

A somewhat related problem is that of treating multiple *primary* products, such as the various forms of rolled products of the steel industry. The simple input-output model is based on a square matrix, with the same number of rows and columns. Most input-output tables are therefore also of this form, which means that multiple primary products must be added together to form a single output row. There are some distinct advantages to designing a rectangular table, however, with a larger number of rows (products) than columns (industries). The most important advantage is that it permits at least a partial distinction between the effects on the rest of the economy of demands for the individual products, even though a complete separation (and hence a separate input-output column) is impracticable. If requirements of one product are met more largely by imports than requirements of another (for example, if a country imports some of its fuel oil but little of its gasoline), this difference can be recognized even though domestic production of both products is presumed to require the same structure of inputs. If one product requires specific inputs which are not required by the others (for example, tin plate produced in the steel industry), these specific inputs can be handled in a side calculation while retaining a single structure for the common inputs. Some lesser advantages of distinguishing multiple products are that greater product detail facilitates construction and checking of the table, that many of the most important products can be stated in physical units, and that it is convenient and understandable for the results of an analysis to emerge directly in terms of individual products. For these reasons, the original tables for Italy, Japan, and Australia all distinguish many more products than industries.

2. Construction

The only practicable source of sufficient statistical information to construct an input-output table is an industrial census which collects detailed information on inputs and outputs of individual industries. A considerable volume of output data is often available from other sources, but only a census can provide input data in sufficient generality and with sufficient detail. The year to which the table refers is therefore usually that of the census, though there are some possibilities of adjusting parts of the data from one year to another. This core of statistical information derived from the census must then be joined with an enormous variety of data from supplementary sources. Fortunately the accounting relationships of the input-output table provide both a means of locating specific gaps in the statistical data and a means of checking inconsistencies among difference sources.

The actual procedure for constructing a table usually starts with the setting of certain control totals for each industry. In particular, the estimate of total output of an industry is likely to be more reliable than the allocation of this output among the other sectors of the economy. The total supply of a commodity, derived from production plus imports, is therefore used as a control total. The total cost of materials as reported in the census can serve similarly as a control for part of an industry's column. The main work of constructing a table then consists in fitting the sets of figures in the rows and the columns into this framework of control totals, using the census plus all other information that the analyst can discover. Preferably this fitting process takes advantage of the double-entry character of the table, by separately allocating the outputs along the rows and distributing the inputs within the columns, and then accommodating the figures at each intersection of a row and column. Obviously this is a time-consuming process, but in the present state of economic statistics it is unavoidable. Only specifically designing the industrial census to collect information in a suitable input-output form could significantly facilitate it.[1]

3. Special Problems

A number of rather technical conceptual problems must also be faced in constructing an input-output table, and even the casual reader of any specific country's table may need to know how these problems were handled. (See table 7.1 for a tabulation of some of these special features.) One such question is whether the value figures in the table are stated in producers' prices or in purchasers' prices. The nature of the input-output model requires that transfers of goods from one sector to another should be portrayed as a direct transfer in the appropriate cell of the table, without regard to the variety of trading and transportation channels which may actually have been used. This means that the trade and transportation sectors must be treated as producing simply the value of their services, as measured by their gross margins. The two pricing systems are alternative methods of distributing these services among all the other sectors of the economy. In a producers' price system, each industry is treated as paying the transportation costs and trade margins on all its purchases of *inputs*, with the value of these services lumped together as purchases from the trade and transportation industries. Thus its output as well as its other inputs are stated at f.o.b. prices. Using this system means that the other inputs as stated in the census generally have to be corrected to eliminate these costs and margins. In a purchasers' price system, on the other hand, each industry is treated as paying the transportation costs and trade margins on all its sales of *output*, with the (presumably different) value of these services lumped together as purchases from the trade and transportation industries. Thus its output as well as its other inputs are stated at delivered prices. Of

[1] The recommendation of the National Accounts Review Committee that U.S. national accounts should include input-output data, flow-of-funds accounts, balance-of-payments statements, and national balance sheets in a conceptually integrated system is a hopeful development. This committee was appointed at government request and reported to the Joint Economic Committee of the Congress (National Bureau of Economic Research, 1958).

the two, the producers' price system is to be preferred in principle, in line with the underlying input-output assumption that the base-year pattern of inputs is more likely to be stable than the base-year pattern of output. This method requires data on the margins paid by each sector, however, so it is only followed by the countries having fairly complete statistics, as shown in Chapter 7.

Another conceptual problem is the treatment of competitive and noncompetitive imports. The distinction here is that competitive imports are similar to products produced in some domestic industry, while noncompetitive imports (such as coffee and bananas in the case of the U.S.) are not. Since separate information on use of imported and domestic materials in consuming industries is not usually available, it is convenient to allocate the competitive imports first as an addition to the supply of products from the appropriate domestic industry, and then to redistribute them along with domestic production in that industry's row. On the other hand, it is simpler to distribute noncompetitive imports directly to the consuming industries, and if there is no particular interest in individual commodities, they can even be lumped together in a single import row. (Note that we are discussing here simply the portrayal of import data in the input-output table. We shall discuss later in the chapter methods of using these data to derive parameters which determine the variation of imports with changes in demand.)

Still a third technical problem is what to do with unallocated inputs and outputs. Some unallocated figures are of course inevitable, both because of incomplete data and because of inconsistent data sources. The input-output accounting relationships insure that the total value of unallocated outputs in all industries will equal the total value of unallocated inputs, but there is no necessary balance for a single industry. What to do about these discrepancies? For an input-output table considered simply as a statistical document, the unallocated figures can be left in a special row and column (like the "errors and omissions" item in a balance of payments). For use in an input-output model, however, this arrangement is unsatisfactory. In a solution, an industry with a large unallocated input will generate a requirement, via the unallocated row and column, for additional production from those industries with large unallocated outputs. In applications, therefore, it is better to eliminate the unallocated figures completely. Undistributed outputs should be transferred to the most likely consuming industries and undistributed inputs to the most likely supplying industries—if necessary, using nothing more substantial than the analyst's judgment. A detailed commodity breakdown helps in this process.

4. Derivation of Input Coefficients

The essential purpose of constructing an input-output table is to derive parameters for use in an interindustry model. In particular, the table provides a basis for estimating the input coefficients, which describe the relationship between each input and the output of the industry in which it is used. Conceivably all input coefficients could be estimated directly from technological information about productive processes in the various industries, and indeed this approach offers great promise of improving statistical estimation procedures. A historical input-output table is still essential, however, for a number of reasons. Given the present availability of statistical as against technological information, only a historical table can be sufficiently comprehensive in covering the many industries in a complex modern economy. Moreover, many industries are made up of firms with different techniques of production, which markedly increases the difficulties of the technological approach. But since individual firms in the industry tend to expand and contract output together, the industry's average input coefficient is reasonably stable as well as easier to compute. (See Phillips, 1953, cited in Chapter 6.) Finally, the ultimate use of an interindustry matrix is to derive estimates of statistical variables such as total output, and the fact that a historical table uses these same statistical variables as control totals is a distinct advantage. An error in one coefficient in a row is likely to be offset by errors in other coefficients in the row, and this increases the stability and presumably the reliability of interindustry solutions (Evans, 1956).

The simplest method of estimating an input coefficient is to use the Walrasian assumption of proportionality—to assume that the ratio of an input to the using industry's output in the base year of the table will continue at other levels of output and in other years. This assumption, although used in almost all input-output work to date, is not appropriate in all parts of our economic structure, as the experience described in the next chapter indicates. Indeed, the greatest room for improvement of present interindustry models is to depart from the proportionality assumption for a considerable number of input coefficients important to the results of a solution. On the other hand, the proportionality assumption works pretty well for materials embodied in an industry's product, as distinguished from materials applied to the product during processing, and many of the important input coefficients do refer to this kind of input relationship. Moreover, proportionality is a useful simplifying assumption in parts of the matrix which have little effect on the solution, but which ought to be included for completeness.

Several more refined methods of estimating input coefficients are available. These represent attempts to distinguish the inputs which can reasonably be portrayed as proportional from other inputs which are substantially nonproportional. The source of the distinction can be either statistical observation of the input-output relationship over several years, using supplementary statistical sources, or technological study of the leading productive processes used in the industry. Once the distinction is drawn, the nonproportional inputs can be handled in a variety of ways. One possibility is to estimate the input directly without using an input coefficient, particularly if it seems to depend on economic variables other than current outputs (e.g., gasoline consumption in private automobiles, which appears to depend primarily on the number of autos already in use). Direct input estimates constitute an impurity in the interindustry approach, but they may help to obtain more reliable solutions in particular parts of the matrix. Another way is to date the input coefficients, keeping them proportional in any one solution, but altering their values according to the year to which the solution refers. This method is useful for inputs subject to notable time-trends (e.g., substitution of synthetics for natural fibers in the making of tires). Still a third device is to introduce a linear approximation to a curvilinear input relationship. One marginal input coefficient can be applied up to a certain level of output, another to an additional range of output on top of that, and so on. A variant here is to divide the base-year input into a fixed input to be treated autonomously and a variable input to be derived from a marginal input coefficient (e.g., electricity used both for general lighting and for processing power in a manufacturing industry). These linear approximations, of course, are only likely to be practicable after considerable study of an industry's production function.

Finally, an important improvement in estimates of input coefficients could be obtained by keeping the basic input-output table as nearly as possible up to date. It is an inherent limitation of the interindustry approach that the original construction of a basic table takes considerable time—though the time could be reduced by more adequate census information, and probably by adopting a less detailed industry classification designed with specific applications in mind. But once a basic table is completed, it can be brought up to date, at least in part, fairly readily. Individual important input coefficients can be adjusted on the basis of more recent information.   More recent control totals on total outputs in the various industries can be prepared, and a modified table can then be balanced out, allocating the undistributed inputs and outputs by the analyst's judgment.   A procedure similar to that formerly followed in the Netherlands for projecting an input-output table to a future plan-year (see Chapter 7) might be used. Industrial specialists for the producing and consuming industries could "bargain" on the basis of their qualitative knowledge of developments in their industries to arrive at reasonable and internally consistent estimates of particular inputs.   The procedure makes sense when we keep in mind that the main purpose of the up-dating is to derive more useful estimates of input coefficients.

5. Flexibility within the Matrix

There are a number of interesting possibilities for flexible treatment of particular parts of the economic structure, while staying within the general framework of input coefficients in an interindustry matrix. The treatment of variations in product-mix in multiproduct industries is an important case.   The most direct approach is to alter the census classification of industries so that input-output projections are less affected by product-mix variations (e.g., to include steel-reinforced aluminum cable in the aluminum industry rather than with copper wire in the wire products industry).   Beyond this, information on the product composition of an industry's output can be retained, for example, by breaking down the output of the steel industry among carbon, alloy, and stainless steel products.   It may then be possible to divide the industry for input-output purposes into separate parts, with some common input coefficients and some individual ones.   A further possibility is to construct a fictitious "process industry" selling its services to the conventionally defined industries.   Continuing the same example, a fictitious steel-processing industry might be established which used the common inputs and served separate carbon, alloy, and stainless steel industries, each with their distinctive inputs.

Another case of flexibility is the treatment of by-products.   If a by-product is distributed among consuming industries, and input coefficients are then estimated in the same way as for other products, some obviously incorrect results may appear in the solution.   For example, demand for hides by the leather industry may be portrayed as stimulating the livestock industry to increase its production of meat, rather than the other way around.   A much better way to handle a by-product is to treat it as a fictitious intra-industry sale (e.g., hides to the livestock industry) and to calculate a regular input coefficient related to the output of the industry itself. The supply determined in this way in the course of a solution can then be checked independently with the demand stemming from consuming industries, and implications for imports or for price changes may be inferred.

Finally, a number of different kinds of nonproportional sub-analyses can be readily related to the over-all interindustry analysis. The simplest kind is one which involves no feedback into the interindustry model, but simply calculates some further economic implications of the indicated pattern of industrial expansion. For example, employment effects are probably best estimated in this way, since they are nonproportional and vary from industry to industry because of such factors as nature of the work, productivity trends, and variation in hours. Sub-analyses which do involve feedback into the interindustry model are particulary useful in handling substitutions. For example, substitutions among fuel oil, diesel oil, bituminous coal, anthracite coal, natural gas, and manufactured gas are critical in determining the outputs of these industries. A sub-analysis of Btu requirements of consuming industries, in which demand for fuel is allocated among the fuels according to trends, prospective prices, and technical requirements, is a convenient way of estimating demands for individual fuels. These demands can then be fed back into the model so that it takes account of the inputs needed to produce the individual fuels. A linear programming sub-analysis has also been attempted to estimate requirements of certain critical materials, which again are peculiarly subject to substitution (Moore, 1953). This kind of subanalysis, given requirements for types of alloy steels and availabilities of the various critical materials, can in principle estimate the minimum requirements for the critical materials, taking account of all the substitutions which are economical in the light of their relative scarcities.

All of the possibilities for flexible empirical treatment of particular parts of the economy which are discussed here involve comparatively narrow modifications of the static Leontief model. They should be distinguished from the empirical work needed for more fundamental extensions of the model, which are discussed in the next section. Their purpose is simply to make the static general-equilibrium core of interindustry analysis more realistic and useful.

C. Supplementary Relationships for Interindustry Models

Many of the most interesting applications of interindustry analysis require knowledge of economic relationships in addition to the input-output relations in productive sectors. As indicated in Chapters 3 and 4, an interindustry model may call for consumption functions, for measures of capital requirements, for export and import demand elasticities, or for alternative production functions—to mention only the leading instances. Moreover, all of these supplementary relationships must be specified in adequate sector detail, and must be consistent with the conceptual features of the basic input-output matrix. Correspondingly there is need for a considerable amount of empirical research in addition to that concerned with the basic input-output table. The interindustry approach inevitably leads into many fields of econometrics.

1. Consumption Functions and Other Final Demands

Econometric research into the consumption behavior of households has been one of the most important developments of the last two decades, quite apart from any possible use in interindustry models. The interindustry approach itself, however, almost automatically generates a need for special research in this field. In an open model, consumption is much the largest of the final demands which must be specified in advance, and also it is often the element of demand least subject to policy determination. Inadequate procedures for projecting consumption are therefore an obvious source of substantial errors in existing applications of the open model. Moreover, in view of previous econometric research on consumption functions, it is natural to explore the possibility of closing interindustry models with respect to consumption—that is, to see whether consumption demands might be derived in a solution in ways analogous to the input demands of productive sectors.

Consumption can be analyzed statistically and incorporated in the interindustry framework in two main ways. One way is to calculate a separate consumption function for the products of each industry, using correlation techniques and time series data. The independent variables in these functions would include aggregate households' income (in virtually every case), and perhaps time, relative prices, and special influences (as seem appropriate). The only distinctive feature of the statistical research is the large number of separate functions which must be estimated, though if the procedure is not simply mechanical, it involves a considerable draft on our understanding of consumption behavior. In an open model—for which this approach seems best designed—these functions can be used to project consumption demands independently in advance of the solution, using estimates of households' income and any other independent variables. This was essentially the method actually used in the "emergency model" discussed in Chapter 10. It would also be possible to use these functions in a closed model, with the influence of households' income derived in the solution, but with the influence of the other independent variables still estimated in advance.

A way of analyzing consumption statistically which appears to be more consistent with the structural emphasis of the interindustry approach is to calculate consumption functions related to the incomes of different groups of households, using for the most part budgetary data. This is the approach now being explored by the Harvard Economic Research Project (Gilboy, 1956a and 1956b). On first examination of budgetary data this structural approach does not appear very promising, since the relationship of consumption to income is frequently nonproportional or even nonlinear, and since other factors than income have an influence. However, nonproportionality can be handled by calculating positive or negative constants in the functions, and treating them as autonomous demands. Nonlinearity can be taken care of by dividing the income scale into successive ranges, within each of which a linear approximation is satisfactory; with pre-war budget data, income ranges of $0–4000 and $4000-up seem adequate. Other factors influencing demand can be dealt with by grouping households in accordance with these factors; again using pre-war data, family size and city size seem relevant, but curiously not occupation. The ultimate results of this research at Harvard will only be known later; so far the budgetary data available have presented formidable difficulties. But if the research is successful, it would permit use of interindustry models which are closed with respect to consumption. That is, there would be a number of household sectors, each including families within a certain income range and with common family size and similar characteristics; and each household sector would have a complete set of demand functions, related to its income, for the products of all industries. The closed model must of course also generate the income of each household sector, presumably on the basis of employment in the various productive sectors of the economy. It would also be possible to use these several consumption functions in an open model by making estimates of the incomes of each of the household sectors in advance of the solution.

A similar research problem is presented by final demands other than consumption. Here we shall simply mention that in estimating the detailed demands of the government sector, which are needed for projecting final demands in an open model, substantial data difficulties are encountered. A modern economy really should have a census of government agencies containing information comparable to that in its census of industry! Empirical analysis of investment demands and export demands is discussed below.

2. Coefficients for Capital and Other Primary Inputs

Perhaps the most important statistical extension to increase the usefulness of the interindustry approach is in the field of capital requirements. In many important policy problems—particularly those of mobilization and economic development—the necessary investment programs of the various productive sectors constitute one of the main objectives of analysis. Existing methods of estimating these investment needs are crude and unsatisfactory, and the hope arises that at least the technological constraints on investment can be discovered within an interindustry framework. Moreover, the interindustry approach itself offers incentives to study capital requirements. In open models, investment is like consumption in being an important element of final demand which must be estimated in advance, though, unlike consumption, it is often subject to control. The possibility of closing the model, with investment programs generated in the solution itself, is also a natural line of study; the interdependence in a modern economy arising because some industries produce capital equipment for others is comparable in importance to the interdependence arising because some produce raw materials for others.

A substantial fraction of the interindustry research sponsored by the U.S. government from 1950 to 1954 was devoted to investigating capital requirements. The theoretical concept at the center of this work was the capital coefficient—the amount of capital needed for a unit expansion of an industry's capacity. Thus the concept had inherent in it a distinction between net investment and replacement investment (which had to be estimated by other methods), and focused exclusively on the desire to expand capacity as a cause for investment. Statistically, the main sources of data were studies of individual plant expansions, so there was a serious problem of getting representative estimates of capital requirements. Moreover, for each industry a complete set of capital coefficients was sought, one for each type of capital used, classified by the input-output producing sectors. Capital was typically measured in value at 1947 prices, and capacity in appropriate physical units. Within these general procedures, an extensive program of research in the capital structures of American industries was carried through.   Much of the information accumulated remains in government files today, but detailed sets of capital coefficients for approximately 200 input-output industries have been published (see Grosse, 1953).   Here we shall use this research experience to indicate what can be done to extend the statistical implementation of interindustry analysis into the field of capital requirements.

An important conceptual question in this kind of research is raised by the fact that existing plants commonly have excess capacity in certain facilities at the same time that bottlenecks in other facilities are limiting total output.   This is the question of balanced versus unbalanced expansions.   If a complete new plant is built from scratch, all types of facilities from power plant to loading dock must be included—a balanced expansion.   If a relatively small amount of capacity is added at an existing plant, on the other hand, only certain types of facilities may have to be added—an unbalanced expansion. Of course many kinds of unbalanced expansions are possible, depending on the initial patterns of excess capacity in particular facilities. There may also be unbalanced investments involving little or no expansion of capacity.

In the U.S. interindustry program it was decided to aim the research primarily at capital coefficients portraying balanced expansions. These balanced coefficients are most useful in analyzing relatively large increases in an industry's capacity extending over several years. If a smaller short-run expansion is desired, it is presumably rational first to undertake those unbalanced expansions with smaller capital requirements and possibly shorter construction time.

The statistical problems raised by the fact that many of the observations available for study described unbalanced expansions were met largely by analyzing separately the component facilities in a complete plant.   Capital equipment required for each facility was estimated from all the relevant observations, including some unbalanced expansions as well as balanced ones, and then the balanced coefficients were obtained by recombining the component facilities into a complete plant.   This approach demanded considerable technological investigation to carry it out.   It also at least raised the possibility of treating unbalanced expansions as well, provided adequate information on the initial status of all plants in an industry could be assembled.   Whereas the actual pattern of unbalanced expansions in some past period of time is not likely to be repeated, a future pattern might be built up from an appropriate combination of the capital requirements for component facilities.   There is also some possibility that unbalanced expansions in individual firms will average out in an industry-wide expansion program. Similarly, separate analysis of capital requirements for different products of an industry offered some scope for adjustment to changing product-mix in a future investment program.

Another important conceptual question in this kind of research is the choice between best-practice coefficients, describing the capital needed for new plants using modern techniques, and average-practice coefficients, describing the existing capital stock of many vintages and past techniques. In the U.S. research program best-practice coefficients were sought, primarily on the ground that the coefficients would be used in interindustry models analyzing changes from the existing industrial structure. In certain industries, however, alternative coefficients had to be estimated for alternative techniques; and in others, allowance had to be made for alternative scales of expansion in individual plants. In all industries, moreover, best-practice coefficients may be subject to radical changes if the technique commonly embodied in new plants is altered.

The actual statistical research procedure used in the U.S. program was as follows: The bulk of the data consisted of records of government plants constructed during World War II, and applications for government assistance in expanding private plants during World War II or the Korean War. The records or applications specified the expected increase in capacity, defined in whatever physical units were conventional in the industry, and provided a detailed list of the investment expenditures required to accomplish it. These expenditures were first grouped by component major facilities and classified according to supplying industries in the input-output classification. Price indexes were used to adjust the values to a common 1947 price level. The estimated increase in capacity was also checked where possible against subsequent production experience, and in some cases was adjusted accordingly. For each observation a set of first-draft capital coefficients was then calculated—the ratios between these specific investment expenditures and the expected increase in capacity. The first-draft coefficients calculated from the individual observations usually showed a wide range of variation, however, and further investigation of the individual plant expansions was required to explain or narrow the variation. The experience of the analysts was that much could be done by searching for ambiguous classifications, differences in products or techniques, differences in the nature of unbalanced expansions, etc. Ultimately, of course, some form of averaging of the observations, usually the median, had to be resorted to. Despite all these statistical difficulties, and many more, it remains true that the research in capital coefficients was one of the major statistical achievements of the U.S. program.

Because the U.S. research program was stopped in 1954 before capital coefficients were available for all industries, there is little actual experience with their use in interindustry applications. The simplest use, however, would be to combine them with an open model solved in two approximations. Considerable thought has also been given to the possibility of using capital coefficients in a closed model, as discussed in Chapter 3, though the assumptions about investment demands implied in such a model are extremely rigid. Perhaps the most promising use of capital coefficients in a closed model is in a linear programming formulation, discussed in Chapter 11 below.

Closely related to the capital coefficients themselves, two further sets of parameters are desirable in most interindustry models: existing industry capacities and normal replacement investment (Goldstein, Crosson, and Sonenblum, 1953; and Teitelbaum, 1953). Much less progress has been made in finding usable empirical measures of these parameters, however. The concept of capacity is fuzzy and difficult to measure statistically. In certain industries, characterized by high capital intensity with labor engaged mainly in tending the equipment, capacity is a reasonably definite concept. Here conventional capacity measures are likely to be used in business practice and hence can readily be assembled and incorporated in interindustry models. In other industries, in which labor is a principal limitational factor, capacity depends largely on conventional work patterns, and changes in these patterns depend on cost considerations. Here capacities can often be estimated only roughly from maximum levels of output recently attained under conditions of strong demand. In the U.S. research program, some experiments were also conducted with surveys of businessmen's estimates of maximum potential employment, separately for one-shift, two-shift, and three-shift work patterns, on the specified assumption that adequate supplies of labor are available at current wage rates. This approach appears to be promising at least for mobilization problems, in which labor allocation is subject to some degree of guidance.

The concept of replacement investment is equally imprecise and difficult to implement statistically. Quantitative estimates have usually been based on average useful lives of capital equipment as established by the Bureau of Internal Revenue for tax purposes, and on known or calculated gross investment in each type of equipment in appropriate past time periods. Since actual replacement needs are obviously not so rigid nor so bunched as mechanical use of average useful lives would imply, some form of moving average of past gross investment has to be used. In the U.S. interindustry program two variants of this approach were explored—one based on past production data for the capital-producing industries, and one based on estimated past gross construction of new capacity in the individual capital-using industries.

So much for capital requirements as an important extension of the basic input-output relationships. In certain applications it is also useful to extend the statistical research to requirements of other primary factors, notably labor. Labor inputs have been calculated in the United States, Japan, and Australia. Research is currently in progress at Harvard to study the occupational composition of the labor force employed in each input-output industry and to analyze changes in occupational composition over time. This research has focused particularly on the implications of occupational changes for the distribution of income. For use in conjunction with the consumption functions discussed above, of course, the labor force must be further classified into all of the household groups for which separate consumption functions are derived. Moreover, a fundamental problem which must be faced in any analysis of the labor force is that employment requirements are clearly not proportional to output.

3. Exports and Imports

The interrelationships between their domestic economies and their foreign trade are a major interest of many countries engaged in interindustry research. Progress in empirical analysis of foreign trade within the interindustry framework has been slight, however. Ultimately, adequate statistical methods for analyzing foreign trade are most likely to be developed in such countries as Norway, Japan, or Italy, because of the great policy significance of foreign trade problems there.

Exports enter nearly all interindustry models as an autonomous final demand, since the main factors influencing them stem from foreign countries rather than the domestic economy. Conventional techniques of analyzing export demands may well be satisfactory— classifying exports both by commodity group and by receiving country, and then estimating income-elasticities and price-elasticities from the time-series data. In an open model, exports can then be projected in advance using these elasticities and assumed values for foreign incomes and relative prices. In a development model, the estimated price elasticities also affect the necessary adjustment of the price of foreign exchange (see chapter 11).

Imports, on the other hand, are a derived demand in most inter-industry models, since they depend largely on domestic influences. There are several formal possibilities for handling competitive imports. (Noncompetitive imports can be handled like any other input, as mentioned earlier.) One extreme approach, used in most of the earlier input-output applications in this country, is to calculate a pro-portional input coefficient relating competitive imports to the total availability of domestic and imported products from the industry to which they are allocated, as in Eq. (2.7) above. Formally, this ap-proach uses the proportionality assumption, but of course the mean-ing is different, since these imports are allocated not to consuming industries, but to the competing domestic industry. Another extreme approach, corresponding to Eq. (2.5), is to estimate competitive im-ports autonomously, to enter them as negative items in final demand, and thus to avoid entirely the use of input coefficients for competitive imports. This method was used in the U.S. "emergency model" dis-cussed in Chapter 10. Neither of these approaches, it seems reason-ably clear, is likely to work well for many important imports of coun-tries more dependent on foreign trade than in the U.S. A more flexi-ble approach, favored by European input-output workers, is to intro-duce a variable import coefficient for each sector which faces com-petitive imports. The value adopted for this coefficient is an explicit estimate of the fraction of requirements for an industry's products which will be met from imports as opposed to domestic production.

In estimating the coefficient empirically, the analyst can allow for time-trends in substitution between the two sources of supply, ex-pected changes in comparative costs, limitations of domestic pro-ductive capacity (in which case the import coefficient can be raised as this capacity limit is reached), or limitations of foreign supply capacity (in which case the import coefficient can be lowered as this capacity is reached). Thus the analysis of import proportions is made a sep-arate research task outside the model itself, but the results of the out-side analysis can then be readily included within the matrix by the device of the import coefficient. Only further experimentation will show how complex an adequate analysis must be. Experience in Italy, however, suggests that simply using higher or lower marginal import coefficients, with base-year imports taken as unchanged, is an inadequate recognition of the substitution possibilities which exist.

The Japanese have also found import relationships a difficult analytical problem. The analysis of import needs clearly must deviate widely from the proportionality assumption.

4. Alternative Production Techniques

Interindustry models set up in the linear programming form can derive their most interesting results if alternative production techniques are recognized for a number of industries. Particularly in economic development problems, the choice between alternative techniques may be an important policy decision significantly affecting the total use of the economy's scarce capital and foreign exchange resources. Empirical methods of handling alternative techniques, however, are unfortunately only in the formative stage at present.

The most straightforward approach would doubtless be to go back to the underlying establishment reports in the industrial census upon which the input-output table is based. If distinct alternative production techniques are used in an industry, the establishments could be grouped according to technique and separate input structures developed for each group. The usual column of input coefficients in the Leontief model would then be simply a weighted combination of the separate coefficients for the different techniques. In the linear programming model, however, the alternative columns would be introduced explicitly, presumably with a constraint to represent the influence of existing capital equipment in preventing too large divergence from the base-year mixture of techniques.

A more difficult but quite promising approach is the direct investigation of engineering production functions (Chenery, 1953). From an engineering viewpoint, productive activity in an industry is accomplished by combining a set of more elementary industrial processes. The use of such processes in the framework of activity analysis was discussed in Chapter 4. The parameters in such an engineering production function may be derived from a combination of theoretical analysis and experimentation. In many cases, the function may permit calculating the effects of alternative sets of technological parameters within any one process. Moreover, if distinct production techniques are used in different plants in an industry, it may be possible to describe them as different combinations of the elementary industrial processes. Thus engineering analysis may permit alternative interindustry columns of input coefficients to be estimated directly from the basic engineering production functions.

Most hopefully of all, alternative techniques only on the verge of actual use might be described in this way, and the implications of their use then derived from an interindustry calculation. An approximate way of including new technology would be to derive input coefficients from the engineering designs of new plants. Particularly for the problem of planning economic development, this method can take advantage of information available to planning authorities in important sectors.

BIBLIOGRAPHY

Input-Output Tables

* Aukrust, O., and Secretariat of U.N. Economic Commission for Europe, "Input-Output Tables: Recent Experience in Western Europe," *Economic Bulletin for Europe,* VIII, No. 1, 36–53 (May 1956).

Evans, W. D., "Input-Output Computations," in T. Barna (ed.), *The Structural Interdependence of the Economy,* 1956.

*Evans, W. D., and M. Hoffenberg, "The Interindustry Relations Study for 1947," *Review of Economics and Statistics,* XXXIV, No. 2, 97–142 (May 1952).

*———, "The Nature and Uses of Interindustry-Relations Data and Methods," in *Input-Output Analysis: An Appraisal,* 1955.

National Bureau of Economic Research, *The National Economic Accounts of the United States,* New York, 1958.

Ritz, P. M. (ed.), *Input-Output Analysis: Technical Supplement,* National Bureau of Economic Research, New York, 1954.

Supplementary Relationships

Chenery, H. B., "Process and Production Functions from Engineering Data," in *Studies in the Structure of the American Economy,* 1953.

Gilboy, E. W. (1956a), "Consumption and Input-Output Analysis," in *The Structural Interdependence of the Economy,* 1956.

——— (1956b), "Elasticity, Consumption, and Economic Growth," *American Economic Review,* XLVI, No. 2, 119–133 (May 1956).

Goldstein, H., P. Crosson, and S. Sonenblum, "Capacity Estimates for 23 E-M Industries," Interindustry Item No. 36, U.S. Bureau of Mines, 1953.

Grosse, R. N., *Capital Requirements for the Expansion of Industrial Capacity,* U.S. Bureau of the Budget, Washington, D.C., 1953.

Moore, F. T., "Studies of Capital Coefficients in Mineral and Metal Industries," Interindustry Item No. 76, U.S. Bureau of Mines, 1953.

Teitelbaum, P., "Estimating Replacement Requirements for Producers' Durable Goods," Interindustry Item No. 30, U.S. Bureau of Mines, 1953.

chapter 6

Testing the validity
of input-output assumptions[1]

A. The Constancy of Input Ratios

Controversy about input-output analysis has raged most intensely over the original Leontief assumption of constant input ratios, or coefficients. This is hardly surprising, since the assumption that each industry has a production function in which all inputs vary proportionately with the industry's output is a radical simplification of traditional thinking about production functions. If held strictly, this assumption has at least four implications which appear to be contradicted by general observation. First, it implies that all inputs are uniformly affected by a change in the scale of production, thus ignoring the time-honored distinction between fixed and variable inputs and between short- and long-run. Second, it assumes that industries

---

[1] The principal summary evaluations of the input-output approach which have been made by economists not directly involved in such research are the papers by Christ (1955), Dorfman (1954), Hurwicz (1955), and Koopmans (1957, pp. 187–197) cited in the bibliography. The interested reader should examine these four major reviews.

can be classified sufficiently finely to eliminate multiproduct industries whose input structures would be affected by changes in the product-mix of their outputs.   Third, it means that economizing substitutions among inputs due to changes in relative prices or availabilities are of negligible importance.   Finally, it implies that technological changes in input structures are sufficiently rare and slow that they can be either disregarded or adjusted for in simple fashion.

Yet it should be clear—though input-output analysts may not always have made it so—that the assumption of constant input ratios can only be a first approximation to the more complex production functions of the real world.   Nonproportional inputs, changes in product-mix, input substitutions, and technological changes all do occur, beyond any question.   The really important question, therefore, is an empirical one: are the errors involved in using this simplifying assumption satisfactorily small?   Tests of this empirical question are the subject of this chapter.   The criteria for judging whether errors are or are not "satisfactorily small" are of course fundamental, and will be discussed as different tests are described.

If the errors should prove to be satisfactorily small, our concern might stop with this demonstration.   If they should prove to be unsatisfactorily large, however, our concern would extend to the possibility of reducing the errors by using more complex production functions in lieu of at least some of the constant input coefficients.   The previous chapter has already suggested that there are many possibilities for this kind of flexible treatment of particular parts of the economy within the general interindustry framework.

B. Direct Tests of Input Ratios

Two main kinds of tests of the empirical usefulness of the assumption of constant input coefficients have been attempted at various times.   One kind consists in direct comparisons of individual input ratios at different points in time; it is discussed in this section.   The other kind involves comparing the computed results of an input-output projection with the actual operation of the economy; it will be discussed in the next section.

Direct comparisons of individual input ratios from successive input-output tables would appear to be the simple and obvious way of testing the constancy assumption.   Serious statistical difficulties must first be faced, however.   Input-output tables for more than one year are not available in many countries, and when they do exist differences in concepts or simply in statistical procedures make satisfactory comparisons difficult. For the U.S. economy we have two highly aggregated tables for 1919 and 1929 compiled experimentally by Leontief, a middle-sized table for 1939 compiled by the Bureau of Labor Statistics under Leontief's direction, and a detailed table for 1947 compiled by the Bureau of Labor Statistics for the government's interindustry research program. Conceptual and statistical differences are particularly great between the 1939 and 1947 tables, and, though a reconciliation is being worked on at Harvard by Carter and others, no study of comparative input ratios between those years has yet been published.

A more fundamental problem is the criterion to be used in evaluating direct comparisons of input ratios. A test will certainly reveal a variety of changes in input ratios from one year to another, and these can be described by a frequency distribution and perhaps its average, but what then? A temptation is to leave it to the intuition of the reader to decide whether the changes are satisfactorily small, but this is obviously an undependable criterion. One possibility is to apply a test of statistical significance to the observed deviations from the hypothesis of no-change. But whether the hypothesis is rejected or not rejected at a conventional level of significance, this is not a test of the empirical usefulness of the simplifying constancy assumption. The most promising approach, as discussed below, is probably to base the criterion explicitly on the effect of a changed input ratio upon the results of an input-output calculation.

1. Tests in the U.S. and Japan

The first published test involving direct comparison of input ratios was prepared by Leontief from the three U.S. tables for 1919, 1929, and 1939, consolidated to a least-common-denominator of thirteen industries (see Leontief, 1953). His weighted results for the materials and services inputs, excluding labor (for which the assumption of constancy clearly does not apply), are summarized in Table 6.1. Though the only criterion here is the subjective judgment of the reader, these results scarcely suggest great stability of the input ratios. Between 1919 and 1929 only about a fifth of the coefficients (weighted by value) varied less than 20%, and between 1929 and 1939 only about a third. In the first decade about a sixth varied more than 50%, and in the second decade about a quarter.

TABLE 6.1. PERCENTAGE DISTRIBUTION OF WEIGHTS OF INPUT
COEFFICIENTS BY RELATIVE CHANGES*

	U.S. 1919–1929	U.S. 1929–1939
−2.1 to −1.0	0.3	0.4
−1.0 to −0.5	6.8	8.8
−0.5 to −0.2	24.4	26.0
−0.2 to 0	9.8	16.5
0 to +0.2	10.3	19.3
+0.2 to +0.5	39.8	13.6
+0.5 to +1.0	6.7	11.1
+1.0 to +2.0	1.9	4.5

* Relative changes are the differences between ratios divided by the mid-points between ratios. Weights are mean values of input flows. Percentages may not add exactly because of rounding.

Of course it should be realized that this was only a rough test of the assumption of constant input ratios. It had to be performed at a gross level of aggregation. The 1919 and 1929 tables were experimental, and the 1939 table had large undistributed outputs.

A similar test with Japanese input-output tables for 1951 and 1954, aggregated into 36 sectors, seems to lend more support to the assumption. (See Government of Japan, Ministry of International Trade and Industry, 1957.) As shown in the following table, more than three-fourths of the coefficients varied less than 20% in this period.

TABLE 6.2. PERCENTAGE DISTRIBUTION OF WEIGHTS OF INPUT
COEFFICIENTS BY RELATIVE CHANGES

Japan 1951–1954

−2.0 to −1.0	2.1
−1.0 to −0.5	3.3
−0.5 to −0.2	9.1
−0.2 to 0	26.3
0 to 0.2	50.6
0.2 to 0.5	7.2
0.5 to 1.0	0.7
1.0 to 2.0	0.6

The shorter interval of time is doubtless a major factor in the greater apparent stability of the coefficients, and it is also likely that the statistical quality of the Japanese tables is considerably better than that of the earlier U.S. tables. But neither of these tests, unfortunately, provides a criterion as to whether the observed changes are satisfactorily small.

2. Which Are the Important Input Coefficients?

One of the most interesting ventures in the U.S. government's interindustry research program of 1950–1954 was an attempt to narrow down the question of coefficient stability to the most important coefficients—important in affecting the results of applications to war mobilization problems (Berman, 1953). This study first established arbitrarily, for each of the 190 industries in the input-output model then in use, the maximum percentage error in calculated output which would be permissible in mobilization analyses. These allowable errors may be generalized as follows: 3% for key nonferrous metals and specialized defense products; 5% for steel, most metal-working, petroleum, electric power, and transportation; 7% for coal, nonmetallic minerals, and basic chemicals; 10% for other metal-working and building materials; 20–50% for food, textiles, and consumer goods; 100% for trade and services. The study then assumed, for each individual coefficient in the matrix, a hypothetical increase of 100%. Finally, the effect of each hypothetical change in an individual coefficient was calculated, and on this basis those coefficients whose instability would violate the standard of allowable errors in an input-output calculation were selected.

The results were striking. Out of about 10,000 nonzero coefficients in the 190 × 190 input-output matrix, only 320 were identified as important by this criterion. Moreover, while all industries were affected by at least one coefficient, 134 industries were affected by fewer than 5 and 176 by fewer than 10.

Thus the assumption of constant input ratios can be placed in a more reasonable perspective. On the one hand, the results of input-output analyses are not sensitive to changes in a great many of the coefficients. On the other hand, the research task of examining the important coefficients for possible modifications of the assumption of constancy is a manageable one. The study described here has defects, it is true, notably in that it calculated the effects of separate variations in the individual coefficients, neglecting simultaneous variations.

Moreover, the calculations were made specifically for mobilization analyses, with a specific classification of industries. The indicated importance of a coefficient is affected by the size of the sectors to which it refers. Nonetheless the general conclusions reached are almost surely sound.

3. Time-Series of Selected Input Coefficients

Once the important coefficients were designated, an investigation of their actual past and prospective future variability was clearly in order. The U.S. government research program was unfortunately terminated before extensive work in this area could be completed, but a few indicative results may be cited.

TABLE 6.3. VARIATION OF INPUT COEFFICIENTS INTO THE STEEL INDUSTRY

Input From	Allowable Maximum Variation	No. Years Greater Variation	
Iron ore mining	82%	0 of 9	
Blast furnaces	6%	4 of 9	(Stated in value, ferroalloys dominant)
		0 of 9	(Stated in tons, pig iron dominant)
Primary zinc	13%	4 of 7	
Primary copper	52%	0 of 6	
Primary metals, n.e.c. (cobalt, nickel, tin)	6%	4 of 7	(Not corrected by separating alloy and stainless steels)

Five important coefficients for inputs into the steel industry were studied for actual variation over a nine-year period (Helzner, 1954). The results, as shown in Table 6.3, were that three of them had varied by more than the allowable maximum—"allowable" being a percentage which would not violate the conditions described above for selecting important coefficients. Only the coefficients with large allowable variations passed the test.

Special efforts were devoted, as one part of the interindustry research program, to the study of input requirements for the government's list of critical defense materials, and in many cases time-series of input coefficients could be assembled in physical units. Four examples may illustrate the types of variability encountered (Cumberland, 1952). Some coefficients showed definite stability; thus the manganese input per ton of steel ingots varied only from 12.1 to 13.0 pounds in the period 1945–1950, since there is an essentially fixed chemical requirement to desulfurize and deoxidize the molten steel. Other coefficients showed a distinct time-trend; tin was the outstanding example, the input per ton of tinplate falling quite steadily between 1939 and 1950 from 31.1 to 16.8 pounds, primarily because of the substitution of the more efficient electrolytic for the hot-dip process, and secondarily because of increased efficiency in both processes. Still other coefficients were much affected by wartime conditions; thus the platinum input per million 1947 dollars of electrical equipment, which ranged from 3.7 to 5.0 ounces in the peacetime periods 1937–1941 and 1946–1949, rose to a range of 12.5 to 23.2 ounces in the war years 1942–1945, because of the need for platinum electrodes in aircraft sparkplugs and magnetos. Finally, some coefficients were more stable than first observation of the data indicated; for example, the cobalt input per ton of high-speed steel appeared to be about twice as high in 1949 as in 1950, but investigation revealed that this was the result of inventory fluctuation, and that the actual coefficient ranged from 0.091 to 0.097 tons in the period 1946–1951, in accordance with indications in technical literature that the requirement is about 10%.

In still a third study (Phillips, 1953) the input coefficients for alloy steel, carbon steel, and copper and its alloys used by the ball and roller bearing industry were investigated, and a very interesting relationship between the coefficients of individual firms and the average coefficients of the industry was discovered. The variability of coefficients among the firms was two to five times the variability of the industry coefficients over time, indicating that the firms were not homogeneous. But the rank correlation over time of the outputs of the firms and of their input coefficients was very high—0.968 for output and 0.958, 0.951, and 0.860 for the input coefficients of alloy steel, carbon steel, and copper, respectively. In other words, the outputs of the firms tended to move together, despite the difference in their technologies. The industry coefficients were useful averages for dissimilar firms.

For Australia, Cameron (1953) has made somewhat similar analyses of time series of input coefficients over periods from five to ten years. His study covered inputs into 52 industries for which both input and output could be measured in homogeneous physical units. The published results give only the mean deviation from the mean of the 33 "major material coefficients" in 10 sectors.[2]   The distribution of these deviations in percentage terms was as follows:

Range	Number
0–2%	12
2–4%	13
4–6%	3
6–8%	3
8–10%	1
10–12%	1
	33

Cameron concluded that his results on the whole support the Leontief hypothesis of input proportionality in the short run for major material inputs in the sample of industries studied.

4. Implications of These Direct Tests

The main inference to be drawn from these direct tests of the input ratios is that the most important of them should be investigated independently, if at all possible, in an attempt to improve on the general assumption of constancy.   This assumption for the bulk of the coefficients in an input-output matrix is not likely to cause great difficulty, but for a relatively small number of coefficients it should be treated systematically as what it is—a first approximation.

C. Overall Tests of Input-Output Projections

The validity of the original Leontief assumption can also be tested in a second main way—by comparing output projections derived from an input-output analysis with actual outputs in some known period of time.   Several of these overall tests have been made; though they must be interpreted with care, they throw a good deal of light on the questions we are examining here.

Indeed, these overall tests of input-output projections are in principle more significant than the direct studies of coefficients described above.   We have already seen that a relatively small number of coefficients are the important ones in affecting the results of an input-output analysis.   Moreover, it is a notable feature of input-output matrices that errors in the coefficients do not lead to cumulative errors in the solutions, but on the contrary tend to compensate each other.

[2] Coke, brick making, tallow refining, iron and steel, cotton ginning, wool-scouring, flour milling, paper-making, gas works.

(See Chapter 5, and Evans, 1956.)   Thus we might find that input-output projections perform satisfactorily on these overall tests, even though individual coefficients prove to be variable on direct examination.   Most important of all, these projections provide the pragmatic test of an assumption which is originally conceived as only an approximate description of the productive structure.

The criterion to use on these overall tests, as in the direct study of coefficients, is not easy to establish.   Again a temptation to be avoided is that of simply presenting the reader with the observed errors for his own interpretation.   Again a conventional test of statistical significance applied to the hypothesis of no-error does not provide the desired indication of empirical usefulness.   Two kinds of comparisons do seem to throw light on the empirical question, however.   One is to compare the errors in an input-output projection with the errors in a "naive" projection, which uses some completely mechanical procedure.   The naive projection plays the role of a null hypothesis, and the input-output projection ought to prove "much better," perhaps measured by a conventional significance test.   The other illuminating comparison is with the errors in a projection based on a more serious alternative to the input-output technique, such as the method of multiple correlation of time-series.   Here the input-output projection ought to prove simply "better."   Existing instances of this sort of comparison have actually used multiple correlation rather mechanically, however.

A number of precautionary comments on the procedures in these tests are also in order.   First, in making an input-output projection two methodologically different steps are involved—estimating the final demands on all industries, and estimating the total production required in all industries to meet both these final demands and the intermediate demands from other industries.   Only the latter step is distinctive of input-output analysis, and therefore the overall tests should if possible be artificial projections based on actual final demands and actual total outputs in a past year.

Second, the input-output technique ought to be most useful in analyzing the effects of radical changes in the composition of final demands.   In the extreme case in which all final demands changed proportionately, it would project proportional changes in all outputs, and the technique is hardly necessary for such a simple projection.   In cases of radical change in final demands, on the other hand—as in war mobilization or in forced-draft economic development—alternative techniques based on continuation of the past run into difficulty, and the input-output technique ought to come into its own.   Unfortunately, the overall tests which have been made all refer to peacetime years which do not have such radical changes in the composition of final demands.

Third, the provision of reliable data on "actual" final demands and "actual" total outputs, consistent in form with input-output concepts, is a difficult task in its own right. Accurate information in considerable product detail on sales to final users is a weak spot in the statistical systems of all countries. Though output data on individual products are generally satisfactory, there are serious problems in deriving from these data measures of industry output consistent with input-output concepts. For example, conventional industrial production indexes refer to product classes wherever produced, and are weighted by value added; whereas indexes consistent with the concepts of the U.S. 1947 table should refer to product classes wherever produced plus secondary products of establishments in the industry, and should be weighted by total values.

1. Backward Projections with the U.S. 1939 Table

The most meaningful overall test made with the U.S. 1939 table[3] was the set of five 1929–1937 projections made by Hoffenberg (reported in Christ, 1955; also Arrow, 1951). He used a 38 × 38 matrix derived without any adjustments from the 1939 input-output table, estimated actual final demands from Department of Commerce data for the five odd (census) years 1929–1937, computed required total output of all industries in each year, and measured the errors from estimated actual total outputs based on Fabricant's indexes (available for 25 industries only). The results from the input-output technique were compared with results using two naive alternatives: projection of each industry's total output in the 1939 proportion to its own final demand, and projection of each industry's total output in the 1939 proportion to total final demand (essentially GNP).

The results in percentage terms indicated that the input-output projections were slightly better (if the difference is significant) than projections with the former "final-demand" technique, and much better than projections with the latter "GNP" technique. As shown in Table 6.4, the average percentage error for all 25 industries in all 5 years

---

[3] Earlier, Leontief made two test projections from 1939 to 1919 and 1929, using a 13 × 13 matrix (Leontief, 1949). This particular aggregation apparently led to a freakish result, however, since the 13 × 13 projections showed input-output markedly superior to two naive alternatives, whereas Leontief's alternative 9 × 9 projection and Hoffenberg's 38 × 38 projection for 1929 showed little difference.

was about 12% for input-output, 14% for final-demand, and 21% for GNP projections. The average absolute errors in 1939 dollars indicated that the input-output projections were slightly worse (again, if the difference is significant) than the final-demand projections, and again that both were superior to the GNP projections. These absolute errors, however, are not as significant as percentage errors when applied to all industries, since they give relatively large weight to later-stage industries selling mainly to final demand, and in particular to the large food and agriculture industries. Finally, an important result was that the errors became larger and larger for the earlier years, more distant from the 1939 base year, indicating that the assumption of constant input ratios became less and less reliable.

TABLE 6.4. AVERAGE ERRORS OF ALTERNATIVE PROJECTIONS, 1929–1937

	1929	1931	1933	1935	1937	All Years
A. Percentage Errors						
Input-output	18	17	13	7	5	12
Final-demand	19	24	14	8	5	14
GNP	23	26	35	10	10	21
B. Absolute Errors						
Input-output	438	374	212	166	181	274
Final-demand	371	293	243	162	148	243
GNP	583	459	335	213	204	359

For the purpose of evaluating the input-output technique, however, a useful distinction can be drawn between two main groups of industries—industries selling mainly to final demand and industries selling mainly to intermediate demand. Projections for the former depend primarily upon the final demand estimates, in these tests presumed to be "actual," whereas projections for the latter depend primarily upon the input-output matrix, which ought to show its superiority in this area if at all. Table 6.5 makes this distinction, even though roughly. It reveals substantial errors for the two sets of final demand industries (incidentally implying some inconsistency between the estimates of "actual" final demand and of "actual" total output). For these industries the input-output technique performed worse than the final-demand method. But for the three sets of intermediate demand industries, the input-output technique's margin of superiority is noticeably larger than when all industries are considered together.

TABLE 6.5. Average Percentage Errors by Industry Groups, All
Years

	Input- Output	Final- Demand
Consumption final demand	11	10
(food, ag., apparel, leather, motor veh., misc. mfg., printing)		
Investment final demand	17	12
(transport eq., ag. mach., mdsg. mach.)		
Consumption intermediate demand	11	16
(textiles, rubber, paper)		
Investment intermediate demand	12	16
(ferr. met., I & S foundries, I & S products, nonferr. met., nonmet. minerals)		
General intermediate demand	13	16
(petrol. prod., coal & coke, elec. & gas, chemicals, RR trans., other trans., communications)		

The results of this overall test[4] cannot be judged favorable to the
input-output technique when applied mechanically. Even though
we have no precise measure of the significance of the difference, to
perform only modestly better than the final-demand projections is a
low grade of performance, since the latter is a naive technique devised only as a standard of comparison. Yet the results, particularly
when we consider the intermediate demand industries, can reasonably
be called promising for subsequent improvements in the input-output
technique.

2. The 1950 Full Employment Projection

One of the most interesting published applications of input-output
analysis (which will be mentioned again in Chapter 10 as an illustration of a projection model) was that made by Cornfield, Evans, and
Hoffenberg (1947). This study investigated the industrial implica-

---

[4] These same input-output projections were also compared by S. Arrow (1951)
with projections derived from multiple regressions on GNP and time, but the
comparison had two rather serious shortcomings. The multiple regressions were
calculated over essentially the same period for which projections were made, and
in addition there were substantial discrepancies among the statistical series on
"actual" outputs. Barnett's analysis described below, despite its deficiencies, is
more relevant for evaluating multiple regression as an alternative technique.

tions of successful attainment of full employment in 1950. Its projections were subsequently evaluated by Barnett (1954), who estimated the actual 1950 results and compared the input-output projections with alternative projections using a multiple regression technique, and also using the naive final-demand and GNP techniques.

It should be made clear at the beginning that the BLS 1950 projections were not originally designed to provide an overall test of the input-output technique. They were presented not as forecasts but as two alternative hypothetical models—one in which full employment was attained solely by expanded investment and another in which it was attained solely by expanded consumption. The authors stated that if full employment were attained in fact, it would probably be by some combination of expanded consumption and investment. Any errors of these projections when confronted with 1950 actual outputs would be the combined effect of the hypothetical final demand assumptions and of the input coefficients. Barnett of course recognized this. He therefore used the same hypothetical final demand assumptions in constructing his alternative projections and made all comparisons with both the investment and the consumption models. And he presented his results as only the roughest test of the input-output technique, emphasizing the great need for more carefully designed tests.

Before considering Barnett's results, let us note a few details about the alternative projections. Cornfield, Evans, and Hoffenberg used a 38 × 38 input-output matrix based on the 1939 table, making adjustments for only four presumed changes in the 1939 input ratios—less coal and more diesel oil for railroads, less cotton and more synthetic fibers in tires and apparel. Their hypothetical final demands were developed by conventional methods. Barnett calculated linear multiple regression equations, with GNP and time for independent variables, for 28 industries, using mainly Federal Reserve Board indexes of industrial production for data and fitting for the period 1929–1941, 1946. In making projections he used the two slightly different hypothetical GNP estimates implied in the two models. Barnett also made final-demand and GNP projections in the familiar way. His estimates of actual 1950 outputs were again based mainly on FRB indexes, and the comparisons were limited to the 28 industries for which such data were available.

Barnett's results for all industries in terms of index points, as shown in the following table, indicated that the four methods were ranked in accuracy approximately as follows: input-output first by a small margin, then multiple regression and final-demand close together, then GNP last by a wide margin. His results in absolute value indicated a different ranking: multiple regression first by a wide margin, then input-output, then final demand, then GNP. As pointed out earlier, however, the absolute errors are less significant because of the implicit weighting of industries.

TABLE 6.6. AVERAGE ERRORS OF ALTERNATIVE PROJECTIONS, 1950

	Index Points		Absolute Value	
	Consumption Model	Investment Model	Consumption Model	Investment Model
Input-output	32	35	877	926
Multiple regression	42	30	662	424
Final-demand	34	39	975	1030
GNP	50	50	1115	1049

These results suffer, however, from the inherent ambiguity created by use of the hypothetical consumption and investment models. We may be able to extract more meaning from the test, therefore, by distinguishing among groups of industries. In this case it is particularly important to distinguish industries affected mainly by consumption from those affected mainly by investment. It is also useful to draw a distinction between final demand industries and intermediate demand industries, for reasons indicated earlier. When we do this for the input-output projections, we find that in the investment model the investment-affected industries have mainly positive errors and the consumption-affected industries mainly negative errors, and in the consumption model the opposite. The same is not true of the multiple regression projections.

Moreover, if we wish to get closer to the "actual" 1950 situation, we can correct very roughly for the diverging effects of the two extreme models by taking the midpoints between the projections for each individual industry. (Actual 1950 consumption was about 68% of total final demands, whereas the investment model assumed 62% and the consumption model 74%.) With these adjustments and classifications, the results of the 1950 projections for the input-output and multiple regression techniques appear as in the table on page 171.

This provides a more illuminating picture. First, a substantial part both of the total errors and of the *difference* between the two methods

—apparently showing the input-output projections superior in terms of index points but inferior in terms of absolute value—lay in the final demand industries, which are of minor importance for evaluation. Second, the input-output projections were better for the consumption intermediate-demand industries and worse for the investment intermediate-demand industries in terms of index points; about the same in

TABLE 6.7. Average Errors* by Industry Groups, 1950

| | Index Points | | Absolute Value | |
	Input-Output	Multiple Regression	Input-Output	Multiple Regression
Consumption final demand (food, ag., apparel, leather, motor veh., furn., misc. mfg., printing)	16	13	631	325
Investment final demand (machinery, ag. mach., ships, aircr., other trans. eq., construction)	54	107	1108	1143
Consumption intermediate demand (textiles, rubber, paper)	8	12	184	176
Investment intermediate demand (ferr. met., I & S products, nonferr. met., nonmet. minerals, lumber)	20	16	316	295
General intermediate demand (petrol. prod., coal & coke, elec. & gas, chemicals, RR trans., communications)	41	24	1204	605

* Errors computed at the midpoints of the investment and consumption models.

terms of absolute value. Finally, the input-output projections were distinctly inferior for the general intermediate-demand industries, the major discrepancies being large positive errors for the petroleum products and coal and coke industries, and a large negative error for the chemical industry. There was also a large negative error for the electricity and gas industry in both methods.

The initial inference to be drawn from these 1950 projections, ambiguous though they are, is that the input-output technique proved less reliable for post-war analysis than a set of independent multiple regressions. This is a challenging conclusion, considering the research resources devoted in this country to the input-output approach. Perhaps more important for the future, however, is the inference that the assumption of constant input ratios should be modified in at least two important areas. Fuel inputs, as indicated by the large positive errors for both petroleum and coal, typically vary less than proportionally with variations in output. Other inputs, illustrated here by the large negative errors for chemicals and electric power, are subject to a pronounced time trend. The path to improved input-output projections seems to run by way of such modifications as these in the simplifying input-output assumptions.

3. The 1951 Projection with the U.S. 1947 Table

A specifically designed overall test of the U.S. 1947 input-output table, in 190-industry detail, was made by Hoffenberg for the year 1951 (unpublished). This is interesting as the first test made with the 1947 table, which is much superior statistically, quite apart from its greater detail, to the 1939 table used in the tests described above. It is also the only test ever made in such great industrial detail.

The procedure followed in making the 1951 test is by now generally familiar. Estimates of the actual final demands in 1947 prices and in input-output detail were prepared by conventional methods. The 1947 matrix of input coefficients, 190×190, was used without adjustment. Estimates of actual 1951 outputs were made for 163 industries, based mainly on Federal Reserve Board industrial production indexes. Errors in the input-output projections were compared with those resulting from naive final-demand and GNP projections.

The input-output projections in this test proved to be markedly more accurate than those made in earlier tests using the 1939 table. For the complete detail of 163 industries, as shown in Table 6.8, between a fourth and a third had errors of less than 5%, nearly half had errors less than 10%, and over three-fourths had errors less than 20%. The mean error was 13.2%. When the results were aggregated to the two-digit level in the Standard Industrial Classification—which is a degree of aggregation more closely approximating that used in the other tests—the largest error was reduced to 17% and most were less than 5%. Thus the statistical improvements embodied in the 1947 table were reflected in improved accuracy of the projections.

The input-output technique also proved to be more accurate than the two naive alternatives used as standards of comparison. The standard error of the input-output projections in absolute value was $371 million, whereas the standard errors of the GNP and final-demand projections were $542 and $1596, respectively. Unfortunately the unweighted errors of the alternative techniques are not available, nor is a classification of the results by groups of industries. It is therefore difficult to evaluate the significance of the difference shown. Nonetheless it is clear that the results of this overall test with the U.S. 1947

TABLE 6.8. DISTRIBUTION OF PERCENTAGE ERRORS IN THE 1951
INPUT-OUTPUT PROJECTION

	Number of Industries	Per cent of Industries*
−50 to −40	2	1.2
−40 to −30	5	3.0
−30 to −20	8	4.9
−20 to −15	11	6.8
−15 to −10	17	10.4
−10 to − 5	11	6.8
− 5 to 0	24	14.7
0 to + 5	24	14.7
+ 5 to +10	15	9.2
+10 to +15	16	9.8
+15 to +20	8	4.9
+20 to +30	12	7.4
+30 to +40	7	4.3
+40 to +50	3	1.8
Total	163	100.0

*Percentages may not add exactly because of rounding.

table were more favorable to the input-output technique than the results of tests with earlier input-output tables.

4. Hatanaka's Tests of the U.S. 1947 Table

The best tests yet made involving overall input-output projections were those conducted by Michio Hatanaka (1957) of Princeton, using data provided by Hoffenberg. The test projections were based on the more advanced U.S. 1947 table, put into a special form to focus on those coefficients whose stability is most clearly implied in the input-output method. The input-output projections were compared both with the alternative multiple regression technique and with two kinds

of naive projections, and in both short-run (2–3 years) and long-run
(7–10 years) applications. Tests of statistical significance were applied to the difference observed. And finally, the observed errors in
projection were further tested for consistency, in particular for ran-
domness or trends. In short, the methodology used in these tests was
designed to make them considerably more informative than any previous trials of the original Leontief assumption.

For test purposes, the U.S. 1947 table was put into a rectangular
model, with 69 columns and 30 rows. There were 30 completely
endogenous sectors, including agriculture, all manufacturing, and the
energy industries. The base-year input coefficients of each of these
sectors from each other were assumed to be constant, and their 30
outputs were calculated in the test. Then there were 8 semi-exogenous sectors comprising the transportation, trade, and service industries, and 26 semi-exogenous construction sectors for different types
of new and maintenance construction. The base-year input coefficients of each of these sectors from the 30 endogenous sectors (except for the energy inputs into transportation, trade, and services)
were assumed to be constant, but the observed values of their outputs
rather than computed values were used in the projections. The energy inputs into transportation, trade, and services were likewise taken
at their observed values. Finally, there were 5 completely exogenous
sectors—the usual households, government, gross investment, net inventory change, and foreign—whose observed purchases from each of
the 30 endogenous sectors were specified. The test projections made
with this rectangular model started with the final demands of the
exogenous sectors, the outputs of the semi-exogenous sectors, and the
energy inputs into transportation, trade, and services, and derived
from the input coefficients in the rectangular matrix the projected
outputs of the 30 endogenous sectors. (Note that although agriculture was included as one of the endogenous industries in the projection, the results were presented either with or without it; here the results omitting agriculture are shown.)

The alternative multiple regression projections were based on 30
separate regression equations with GNP and time as independent
variables. For the short-run projections to 1949 and 1950, the basic
time-series data were taken from the years 1929–1940, 1946–1948.
Thus the multiple regressions were granted an additional year of information compared to the input-output projections, in keeping with
their greater simplicity. For the long-run projections to 1947, 1948,
1949, and 1950, the regressions were fitted only to 1929–40 time series.

The corresponding input-output projections in this case were *back-ward* projections to 1940, 1939, 1938, and 1937, respectively—obviously an imperfect method of comparison, though dictated by lack of comparable data for more recent years.

The principal results of the short-run and long-run input-output projections, in comparison with the multiple regression technique, are presented in Table 6.9. Inspection indicates that on the average the input-output projections proved to be superior. A test of the differences for individual industries further showed that they were

TABLE 6.9. ,COMPARISON OF AVERAGE WEIGHTED* PERCENTAGE ERRORS, INPUT-OUTPUT AND MULTIPLE REGRESSION PROJECTIONS

	Input-Output	Multiple Regression
Short-run:		
1949	4.4–4.8	6.9
1950	5.3–5.7	8.0
Long-run:		
7-year	10.1–10.4	15.2
8-year	10.8–10.9	14.7
9-year	13.0	16.5
10-year	12.1	14.1

* Weighted by observed outputs in year of projection. The range for certain years stems from uncertain weights for industries producing military goods.

statistically significant at the 25% level, though not at 10%, for both the short-run and the long-run projections. Thus Hatanaka's tests are the first to reveal a margin of superiority (though an uncertain one) for input-output over multiple regression projections.

The input-output projections were also compared with two different naive standards of comparison. Final-demand projections were prepared in the usual way, except that the calculated inputs into the semi-exogenous sectors as well as the observed purchases of the completely exogenous sectors were used as the base. A new kind of naive projection, which we may call an intermediate-demand projection, was also prepared, on the assumption that intermediate output of each endogenous sector would vary in the same proportion as total intermediate output of them all. This is not quite comparable to an input-output projection, because it requires advance information on total intermediate output.

The results, as shown in Table 6.10, were that the input-output projections performed better than the final-demand projections, but not better than the intermediate-demand projections. The margin of superiority over the final-demand projections appeared in both the short-run and long-run projections, though it proved to be significant at the 25% level only in the short-run. On the other hand, no difference could be observed in comparison with the intermediate-demand projections. Hatanaka himself concluded that the improvement over naive methods was not sufficient to warrant the great effort involved in input-output analysis. Surely it is a curious result that input-output

TABLE 6.10. COMPARISON OF AVERAGE WEIGHTED PERCENTAGE ERRORS, INPUT-OUTPUT, FINAL-DEMAND, AND INTERMEDIATE-DEMAND PROJECTIONS

	Input-Output	Final-Demand	Input-Output*	Inter-mediate-Demand*
Short-run:				
(1946, 48–50)	5.4–5.8	7.3	8.2–9.1	8.2
Long-run:				
(1937–40)	11.9	13.1	19.4	18.9

* Errors measured and weighted in terms of intermediate output rather than total output.

projections should perform better than multiple regressions, but not better than one of the naive projections made only as a standard of comparison.

Finally, Hatanaka made a number of interesting tests of the consistency of errors in input-output projections in the period 1929–1950. In particular, he found that for most industries the time-series of errors were significantly non-random, and further that significant trends could be identified in the underlying coefficients. Again these results underscore the need for direct study of at least the most important coefficients.

5. Tests in Other Countries

Overall tests have been made with the input-output tables of a number of other countries, but in general they have been simple tests without an adequate criterion for evaluation. In Italy (Chenery,

Clark, Cao-Pinna, 1953) a one-year projection, based on actual outputs of all industries rather than actual final demands, generated a median error in *intermediate* output (for 31 basic products) of 5%. In Japan (Shishido, 1957, based on Government of Japan, 1957) an identical test of one-year, two-year, and three-year projections (for 46 basic industries) produced median errors of 4%, 8%, and 9%. Also in Japan, a three-year projection based on actual final demands (i.e., using procedures as described previously in this section) revealed a median error in *total* output of 7% for a more aggregative 31-sector matrix, as against 6% for a 182-sector matrix with results consolidated into the same 31 categories. Finally, in Norway (Sevaldson, 1956) a one-year projection, compared to two kinds of naive projections, showed input-output best for 14 sectors, second-best for 12, and poorest for 2.

6. Time-Series Estimation of Interindustry Coefficients

An imaginative analysis by Arrow and others of the possible use of time series for indirect estimation of important input coefficients, although not designed specifically as a test, should be mentioned here (Arrow, Hoffenberg, Markowitz, Shephard, forthcoming). The analysis attempted to fit a model in which changes in important input coefficients from year to year were considered a function of one or more of the following factors: a time trend, the share of defense expenditures in GNP, real income per capita, and the excess of an industry's output over previous peak output. The data used were time series of industry outputs from 1929 through 1950, including the war years, plus the 1947 U.S. interindustry table, serving as a bench mark. Two methods of statistical fitting were studied—a limited-information variant of the simultaneous-equations approach, and a linear programming formulation. This was a unique instance of the use of sophisticated statistical techniques in empirical interindustry research (see Hurwicz, 1955, on this point). However, the simultaneous-equations experiment did not succeed in deriving plausible and reliable parameters relating changes in input coefficients to the four explanatory factors. And further investigation suggested that there are intrinsic difficulties in the use of time series in this way, because the number of independent predetermined variables generated by the economic system is small. The linear-programming experiment obtained closer fits over the entire time-period than projections with constant coefficients, but the improvement was hard to evaluate.

The analysis did provide additional evidence that input coefficients vary over time in response to economic influences. The time series of discrepancies between output projections based on the assumption of constant coefficients and actual outputs proved to be closely correlated with several sets of predetermined economic variables. Thus some kind of economic explanation of variations in input coefficients over time appeared to be possible, even though the models investigated did not provide it. To the present authors, separate study of important input coefficients, even with methods which are not mutually consistent, seems to be the most promising way to search for such explanations.

7. Implications of these Overall Tests

All of the test projections yet made involve a strict application of the original Leontief assumption of constant input coefficients. Although all of the tests have inadequacies, notably in that they are limited to relatively modest changes in final demands on the economy, the general tenor of their results is not favorable to such a strict application. At least with the improved U.S. 1947 table, input-output projections appear to be "better" than either multiple regression or naive projections, but not "much better." A larger margin of superiority would be needed to justify the additional cost and complexity of the input-output technique.

Yet it would be sensible to recognize that strict input-output analysis is only one kind of interindustry analysis, and that its theoretical structure is acknowledged to be only a first approximation to reality. The question we should like to have answered is this: can an interindustry system of analysis be *developed* which will make "much better" projections than similarly developed practical alternatives? Problems involving radical changes in the demands upon the economy, as in war mobilization or economic development, should be kept particularly in mind. The overall tests described here are of course not designed to answer this question, and indeed a satisfactory answer can come only with a great deal more experience. The overall tests do indicate, however, in conjunction with direct study of input coefficients, that in certain parts of the economic structure modifications of strict input-output assumptions are clearly desirable. As indicated in the last chapter, a variety of such modifications can be incorporated in the general framework of interindustry analysis. Improvements in the first-approximation theoretical structure based on empirical study should therefore be the first order of business in interindustry research.

BIBLIOGRAPHY

General

*Christ, C. F., "A Review of Input-Output Analysis," in *Input-Output Analysis: An Appraisal*, 1955.

*Dorfman, R., "The Nature and Significance of Input-Output," *Review of Economics and Statistics*, XXXVI, No. 2, 121–133 (May 1954).

*Hurwicz, L., "Input-Output Analysis and Economic Structure," *American Economic Review*, XLV, No. 4, 626–636 (September 1955).

*Koopmans, T. C., *Three Essays on the State of Economic Science*, McGraw-Hill Book Company, New York, 1957, 187–197.

Direct Study of Coefficients

Berman, E. B., "A Program for the Examination of Coefficient Variation in the Interindustry Context," Interindustry Item No. 47, U.S. Bureau of Mines, 1953. (The study and its results are also summarized in F. T. Moore, "A Survey of Current Interindustry Models," in *Input-Output Analysis: An Appraisal*, 1955.)

Cameron, B., "The Production Function in Leontief Models," *Review of Economic Studies*, XX, No. 1, 62–69 (1952–53).

Cumberland, J. H., "Examples of Variations in the Behavior of Critical Material Input Coefficients," Interindustry Item No. 17, U.S. Bureau of Mines, 1952.

Government of Japan, Ministry of International Trade and Industry, Research and Statistics Division, *Interindustry Analysis for the Japanese Economy*, 1957 (in Japanese).

Helzner, M. L., "A Study of Coefficient Variation of Selected Inputs into the Steel Industry," Interindustry Item No. 48, U.S. Bureau of Mines, 1954.

Leontief, W. (1953), "Structural Change," in *Studies in the Structure of the American Economy*, 1953.

Phillips, A., "Stability of Technical Coefficients," University of Pennsylvania, Philadelphia, Input-Output Project, 1953 (mineographed).

Overall Projection

Arrow, K., M. Hoffenberg, H. Markowitz, and R. Shephard, *A Time Series Analysis of Interindustry Demands*, North-Holland Publishing Company, Amsterdam (forthcoming).

Arrow, S., "Comparisons of Input-Output and Alternative Projections, 1929–39," Rand Corporation Paper P-239, 1951.

Barnett, H. J., "Specific Industry Output Projections," in National Bureau of Economic Research, *Long-Range Economic Projection*, Princeton University Press, Princeton, 1954. (An earlier version appeared as Rand Corporation Paper P-208, 1951.)

Chenery, H. B., P. G. Clark, and V. Cao-Pinna, *The Structure and Growth of the Italian Economy*, 1953, Chapter 3.

Cornfield, J., W. D. Evans, and M. Hoffenberg, "Full Employment Patterns, 1950," *Monthly Labor Review*, LXIV, No. 2, 163–190 (February 1947) and LXIV, No. 3, 420–432 (March 1947).

Hatanaka, M., *Testing the Workability of Input-Output Analysis*, Princeton, 1957 (mimeographed). (A few of the figures cited in Tables 6.9 and 6.10 are recalculations, kindly provided by the author.)

Hoffenberg, M. Unpublished 1951 projection with the U.S. 1947 table, kindly provided by the author. (The results by individual industries are classified, but the summaries given here are not. See also C. F. Christ, "A Review of Input-Output Analysis," cited above.)

Leontief, W. (1951), *The Structure of the American Economy, 1919–1939*, 1951, Part IV-D.

Sevaldson, P., "Norway," in *The Structural Interdependence of the Economy*, 1956.

Shishido, S., "Recent Input-Output Studies in Japan," Memorandum C-6 of Stanford Project for Quantitative Research in Economic Development, 1957 (mimeographed).

part II

Applications
of interindustry analysis

chapter 7

A survey of interindustry research

Statistical analyses of interindustry relations have now been undertaken in more than twenty countries.[1] In this chapter we present a short survey of the development of empirical work in this field and in so doing try to illustrate the variety of aims and the methods used. The technique is still considered experimental in most countries, since in none of them has it been pursued for a long enough period to establish a routine of data collection and analysis. In this respect, interindustry analysis is in a position comparable to that of national income analysis 10 or 15 years ago, before a measure of standardization had been attained.

The countries which have done some work on interindustry analysis include most of the more advanced countries (with a few notable exceptions) and a considerable number of less developed economies. Table 7.1 summarizes the work that has been completed, to the extent that we have been able to learn of it.[2] Substantial studies have been accomplished in the first nine countries, whereas more limited experiments have been completed in the other ten. In addition, input-out-

[1] Source materials are listed at the end of the chapter.
[2] Publication is exceptionally slow in the interindustry field because of the large volume of statistics involved, and there are undoubtedly studies in progress of which we have no knowledge.

TABLE 7.1. SUMMARY OF BASIC INPUT-OUTPUT TABLES

Country	Table	Date of Publication	Sectors: Industries	Sectors: Commodities	Prices Used	Prepared by‡
(1) United States	1919*	1941	41	41	Prod.	W. Leontief, Harvard University
	1929*	1941	41	41	Prod.	
	1939*	1951	96	96	Prod.	Bureau of Labor Statistics
	1947*	1951	450	450	Prod.	Bureau of Labor Statistics and Interagency Committee on Input-Output
(2) Norway	1948*	1952	27	27	Prod.	National Accounts Division, Central Bureau of Statistics
	1950	1954	27	27	Prod.	
	1950	†	122	122	Prod.	
(3) Denmark	1930–39	1947	14	14	Purch.	Statistical Department
	1947	1955	28	28	Prod.	
	1949*	1955	28	28	Prod.	
(4) Netherlands	1938		27	27	Prod.	Central Statistical Office and Central Planning Bureau
	1946–53		27	27	Prod.	
(5) Italy	1950	1952	56	200	Purch.	U.S. Mutual Security Agency
	1950*	1952	56	56	Purch.	
	1953	1955	25	300	Purch.	Istituto per la Congiuntura
(6) United Kingdom	1935*	1952	34	34	Prod.	T. Barna, London School and Oxford
	1948	†	400	400	Prod.	Department of Applied Economics, Cambridge, and Board of Trade

	Organization					
(7) Japan	Central Statistics Office	Prod.	1950*	1952	10	10
	Ministry of International Trade and Industry,	Prod.	1951*	1955	182	182
	Economic Planning Board, and other government agencies	Prod.	1954*	1957	36	36
		Prod.	1955	†	100	100
(8) Canada	Dominion Bureau of Statistics	Purch.	1949*	1956	42	42
(9) Australia	B. Cameron, Canberra University College	Prod.	1947	1957	79	150
		Prod.	1953	†	120	120
(10) Puerto Rico	A. Gosfield, University of Puerto Rico	Purch.	1948	1956	31	31
(11) Colombia	Economic Commission for Latin America	Purch.	1953*	1957	18	18
(12) Argentina	Economic Commission for Latin America	Purch.	1950	1958	23	23
(13) Peru	Economic Commission for Latin America	Purch.	1955	†	20	20
(14) France	Ministère des Affaires Economiques et Financières	Purch.	1951	1957	37	65
(15) India	Indian Institute of Public Opinion	Purch.	1952–53	1955	19	19
	Indian Statistical Institute	Purch.	1953–54	†	36	36
(16) New Zealand	New Zealand Government, Department of Statistics	Purch.	1952–53	1957	12	12
(17) Mexico	Banco de Mexico	Prod.	1950	†	32	32
(18) Yugoslavia	Federal Bureau of Statistics	Prod.	1955	1957	27	27
(19) Spain	Institute of Political Studies	Prod.	1954	1958	28	28

* Inverse matrix has been computed.
† In preparation.
‡ Publications are listed in the bibliography.

put research groups in other countries (including Israel, Poland, and Sweden) have not yet published their findings.[3]   We will confine our attention mainly to the countries for which a major study has been published.

A. Research in Selected Countries

1. The United States

Although Denmark and the Netherlands were the first governments to compile input-output statistics, techniques of interindustry analysis were first developed in the United States.   The early work of Leontief is well-known and has already been referred to in preceding chapters.   During World War II, it led to the first governmental research on interindustry analysis in the United States, undertaken by the Bureau of Labor Statistics with Leontief as an advisor.   This group produced the input-output table for 1939, which was considerably more detailed than Leontief's earlier studies, and the first exploratory applications to policy problems by Cornfield, Evans, and Hoffenberg.

The most important outcome of this early work was to arouse interest in the method in government circles, which led to the formation of an interagency research group in 1948.   The group undertook, from 1950 through 1954, the most extensive program of interindustry research so far attempted.   It is unfortunate, to say the least, that this research was cut off abruptly before its completion, and that no comprehensive report and evaluation of the experience has been or seems likely to be made.

For this brief survey, the U.S. government research program may be divided into three main parts.   The first was the construction of the basic 1947 input-output table by the Bureau of Labor Statistics.   The statistical data underlying the table were prepared in great detail, distinguishing some 450 industries and relying extensively on secondary sources to supplement official census returns.   (The statistical analysis was not closely integrated with the much more aggregative national income and product estimates.)   These underlying data were then aggregated and reconciled to form the 200-order general-purpose table used in the "emergency model" described in Chapter 10.   With the benefit of hindsight, one sees that it might have been wiser to focus the data collection more sharply on the information needed for subsequent applications.   Nevertheless, this general-purpose investigation

[3] We have no information on the interindustry studies which have been done in the U.S.S.R. and other Communist countries, apart from Yugoslavia.

provided a major advance in our statistical knowledge about the American economy.

The second part of the program consisted in a large number of research projects to develop supplementary statistics for use in making the table applicable to particular policy problems. The principal projects were undertaken by the Bureau of Labor Statistics, the Bureau of Mines, the Office of Business Economics, the Air Force, and Harvard University, with additional projects assigned to about a dozen agencies and universities. All work was coordinated by the Budget Bureau and by an interagency committee. This research produced detailed indices of price and production from the base year (1947), capital coefficients by separate types of equipment for each industry, input lead-times reflecting inventory requirements, and input structures for military industries and a few other sectors much changed from 1947. Notably missing were studies specifically aimed at discovering nonproportional input-output relations in particular parts of the table, though some significant improvements along this line were in fact noted in the course of the research. These supplementary projects, especially that on capital coefficients, were the most distinctive part of the American program.

The third phase involved applying these statistical results to the study of practical problems. Though a good deal of attention was given to model formulation, almost the only realistic application before the program was cut off was the "emergency model," which explored the economic implications of the post-Korean defense build-up. This was an elaborate analysis, distinguishing nearly 200 industries, time-phased by quarters over a three-year period, and with all the final demands including investment programmed in advance. Its evaluation was never satisfactorily completed, and its results continue to be classified as security information because of the military programs included. Time did not permit what would probably have been the most fruitful applications: experiments with a variety of smaller models designed for particular policy problems.

Despite the cessation of government work, a substantial program of interindustry research is carried out in the U.S., as it has been since 1947, by Leontief's Harvard Economic Research Project. This research is now aimed mainly at extending the analysis to the elements of final demand and the use of primary factors and thus toward more nearly closing the simple open model. One important phase of the work is concerned with household consumption, specifically the relation between demand and income, with allowance for such factors as city size. Studies of employment attempt to distinguish several categories of labor input and to relate factor compensation to the size distribution of income in the whole economy. Leontief himself has extended the analysis into the structure of U.S. foreign trade, which we shall discuss in Chapter 9. The Harvard work on technological change has already been referred to in Chapter 4. We shall discuss other main lines of research, natural resource use and regional studies, in Chapter 12.

Other research on different aspects of interindustry analysis has been done at Princeton by Morgenstern and his collaborators, at the Council for Economic and Industry Research in Washington, at the Rand Corporation in Santa Monica, and at Stanford University. It is clear, however, that more realistic experimentation with the application of interindustry analysis to policy problems must wait on a revival of interest by the U.S. government.

2. Norway

The Norwegian experience has been in some ways the opposite of that in the U.S. In the first place, input-output studies are closely integrated within the Central Bureau of Statistics with the entire body of governmental statistics. In fact, since national income is estimated largely from the output side, the smaller input-output tables for 1947 and 1948 were obtained almost as a by-product of this calculation. This close integration both improves the quality and reduces the cost of input-output work. In the second place, primary emphasis in research has been placed on improving the reliability of the simple open model, especially by varying the initial assumption of proportional input-output coefficients.

The analytical refinements are aimed at divorcing the input coefficients from the conditions of the base year. Changes in product-mix within an industry are considered likely, so every effort is made to detail significant inputs separately for each product. Changes in inputs for individual products are also anticipated, so an important objective is to obtain alternative input structures depending on such parameters as level of production, relative prices or availabilities, and technological trends. When some of these parameters are determined within the matrix (e.g., production levels), this variation can be conveniently taken into account using the iterative method of solution. Moreover, certain sectors of the economy are treated in special ways. Outputs in agriculture and printing, for example, are estimated autonomously —agriculture because supply conditions are dominant and printing because it is an overhead cost. The proportions between domestic production and competitive imports are studied commodity by commodity to assess the influence of production levels, relative prices, and government controls. All of these attempts to refine the simple open model appear promising, and the ultimate results of the Norwegian experiments should be illuminating for other countries.

No applications of the latest 122-sector Norwegian table have yet been published,[4] though in the immediate post-war years input-output studies were used for particular commodities subject to controls. Two suggested applications, however, bear on questions of concern to a number of European countries engaged in interindustry research. One focuses on international trade: If exports fall by a specified amount, and if construction is expanded sufficiently to restore full employment, what will be the net effect on the balance of payments? The other is a price problem: If wages are increased by a specified amount, what would be the justifiable price increases, under controls, in various industries?

3. Denmark

As in Norway, input-output research in Denmark grew out of the national accounts work of the Statistical Department and has remained an integral part of this work. Fourteen-sector input-output tables were compiled annually for the years 1930–1939 and 1946 in an effort to make more accurate estimates of the national income from the product side. This approach was facilitated by the availability of an annual census of manufacturing and by the high dependence of the economy on imports, since there are comprehensive statistics for the supply of imported products. These early tables included a detailed allocation of investment goods by sector as well as of inputs for current consumption.

In the postwar period, the input-output tables have been expanded to 28 sectors and the accounting conventions have been revised somewhat to make them more suitable for use in an econometric model. Experiments with such models have been made by Rasmussen at the Institute of Economics in Copenhagen, but so far his results have the mainly illustrative purpose of the early work of Leontief. The problems analyzed have included the effects of changes in factor costs and import prices; the terms of trade among industries; and the stability of interindustry relations between 1947 and 1949.

[4] This table is discussed in some detail in the next chapter.

4. Netherlands

Interindustry research in the Netherlands has been perhaps most notable for its close tie with policy formulation. The 27-order input-output table for 1938 was prepared by the Central Bureau of Statistics during the war; after the war, in an atmosphere of shortages and controls, the Central Planning Bureau used it in preparing detailed annual plans for the years 1946 to 1949. In view of the rather shaky statistics and the many post-war bottlenecks, however, the interindustry plan depended as much on judgment as on calculation. In principle each type of transaction was analyzed from two sides, by the specialist in the purchasing industry and by the specialist in the producing industry, and a consensus was reached by successive approximation. The constraints employed were that the volume index of raw materials used should change approximately in proportion to the volume index of output, that services used should vary nonproportionately because of fixed-cost elements, and that depreciation, indirect taxes, and income shares should be estimated from appropriate special circumstances. This use of the interindustry framework is about the most elementary possible, yet it retains the emphasis on mutual consistency of individual industry projections which is the principal asset of interindustry analysis for planning.

As more normal economic conditions returned and controls were relaxed, the need for an interindustry plan diminished. Since 1950, therefore, interindustry analysis has been used within the Central Planning Board only to supplement its aggregate plans, which focus on general tax, subsidy, and wage policies. A simple form of analysis (referred to again in Chapter 9) is to calculate the effects on employment, profits, and imports of the different kinds of final demand, and then to use the results as parameters in the aggregative model; to apportion the final demands among industries and calculate production levels from the interindustry model; to confront the two sets of results for employment, imports, and prices; and finally to evaluate reliability and adjust for sizeable discrepancies.

Interindustry statistical data have been progressively improved by the Central Bureau of Statistics. Annual tables have been prepared for most post-war years, and a promising experiment has been carried through in constructing quarterly tables for the years since 1950. Regrouping and subdividing industries for greater homogeneity and developing constant-price versions of the tables are other major improvements.

5. Italy

Interindustry studies in Italy also resulted from a need for analysis of post-war bottlenecks. Research was begun in 1950 in the U.S. Mission administering economic aid and was later taken over and further developed by the Italian government. Initially the work was under the direction of the present authors and was carried out by an Italian staff under Dr. Vera Cao-Pinna. The basic retabulation of the pre-war census data was done by the Central Institute of Statistics. The economic staffs of several Italian government agencies, private trade associations, and leading firms collaborated in preparing the table for 1950. In 1954, the Italian government established a new Institute for the Study of Economic Conditions, including as one section the former Mission input-output staff. The Institute has since integrated interindustry data into the body of governmental statistics and carried out a variety of applications, notably to foreign trade problems and to the long-term development program.

The construction of the original 56 × 200 sector input-output table for 1950 shows that useful results can be obtained, even though official statistical data at first appear deficient, by pulling together a wide range of unpublished and often unofficial information, and by exercising judgment on questionable points. The double-entry character of the input-output framework has considerable power in itself to integrate diverse sources of information. Improved current official data were available for the 25-industry 1953 table later prepared in the Institute, but the absence of an adequate post-war census prevented a more detailed industry breakdown.

Italian applications have emphasized the importance of improving the crude input-output assumptions in critical parts of the analysis. Refinement has been facilitated by the fact that in both input-output tables commodities were broken down in more detail than the basic industry classification. Nonproportional input functions have been applied particularly to imports, for which marginal requirements may differ from average requirements according to domestic production capacities; and to employment, for which marginal requirements are affected by widespread under-utilization of the labor force. The methodology used in making an overall projection in Italy is discussed in Chapter 10.

Finally, the program of promoting economic development in Southern Italy has suggested the use of interindustry analysis in regional models and models which minimize the use of capital, described in Chapters 11 and 12. An important step toward implementing this type of study has been accomplished by the Institute through a survey of marginal income-elasticities of demand for different consumer goods in different regions.

6. United Kingdom

British interindustry research to date has been centered in private universities. An experimental 34-industry table for 1935, prepared at London and Oxford after the war by Tibor Barna, showed that such research was statistically feasible. A 400-industry table for 1948 (to be consolidated later) is now under construction by a research group at Cambridge, in collaboration with the Board of Trade.

Actual applications have so far been limited to a summary ten-industry table for 1950 prepared in the Central Statistical Office from national accounts figures. It has been used modestly to provide rough answers to questions concerning the import content of different elements of final demand, the differential effects of general wage adjustments on prices, and the source in terms of elements of final demand of changes in the overall production index. What uses will be made of the very detailed 1948 table remain to be seen, but at least an adequate statistical foundation will be available.

7. Japan

Although interindustry research in Japan only began in 1953, the study which has been completed for 1951 is of high quality (see Chapter 8). The Japanese investigation was initiated by the Ministry of International Trade and Industry with the guidance of a university advisory group headed by Professors I. Yamada and S. Ichimura. A separate study of the agricultural sectors was later conducted by the Ministry of Agriculture, and a small table was compiled by the Economic Planning Board for purposes of long-term projection.

Materials for input-output analysis in Japan are exceptionally good in recent years because there is both an annual census of manufactures and a monthly sample survey of the use of some two thousand commodities. Both sources have been used to provide control totals for total production and total supply, whereas the monthly survey has proved to be the best source of estimates of input-output coefficients.

The original input-output tabulation for 1951 covers the use of 527 commodities in 182 using sectors. Of these, inputs of 345 commodities have also been measured in physical terms and their input coefficients published separately.   For analytical purposes, the table was aggregated to 182 × 182.

The statistical conventions used in the Japanese table follow closely those in the U.S. 1947 study.   One distinctive feature of the Japanese table is the extensive use that has been made of an activity basis for classification.   Instead of assigning an establishment entirely to one sector, it has been possible in many cases to disaggregate the inputs associated with secondary products and allocate them to the corresponding primary sector.

Another valuable feature of the Japanese work has been the emphasis on testing the stability of coefficients before analytical use is made of them.   Since it was known that changes are taking place in energy use and in import proportions, for example, a new 36 × 36 table was computed for 1954 and comparisons were made between it and the 1951 analysis.   The results of these comparisons have been summarized in Chapter 6.

Because a large staff was used in the preparation of the 1951 table —some fifty experts and their assistants—it was possible to publish the table in less than two years after work was started.   This experience demonstrates that long delays need not be characteristic of the publication of input-output tables.

As in most other countries, input-output analysis was started in Japan with various purposes in mind.   The principal applications to date have been structural analyses of the direct and indirect requirements of final demand elements for imports, for labor, and for capital. In particular, an analysis of trends in import and labor requirements from 1951 to 1954 was carried out.   Since most of the work has been done by the agency that compiles the industrial census, another purpose has been to improve the consistency of production data.   Application to long-term planning activities of the government was initially undertaken by the Economic Planning Board on a separate basis, but this work and that of the Ministry of International Trade and Industry and other agencies are being coordinated in further studies.

8. Canada

A 42-sector input-output study of Canada for the year 1949 was completed by the Dominion Bureau of Statistics in 1956.   It resembles the work in Denmark and Norway in that its initial purpose is to improve the national accounts and other governmental statistics.

The design of the table follows the lines established in other coun-

tries although little attempt was made to reconcile the industry outputs, which include all commodities produced in given establishments,
with a commodity classification by transferring secondary products.
Transactions are valued at purchasers' prices and imports are treated
as noncompetitive.

The study has been used to date solely to provide a detailed description of the economy rather than as the basis for an econometric
model. The work has apparently been done with the requirements
for such models in mind, however, and analytical applications may be
made in the future.

9. Australia

Input-output work in Australia has been done, as in England, by
a university research group with extensive collaboration from government statistical offices. The resulting study, directed by Professor
Burgess Cameron at Canberra University College, appears to be one
of the best so far produced with a modest research outlay, both as to
method and coverage.

The Australian analysis contains several novel features. Like the
Italian and Japanese tables, it includes many more commodities than
industries (150 against 79) which permits better use of the marketing
approach to constructing and checking the table. The data were
initially compiled for 266 commodities and 106 industries, using physical terms where possible, and secondary products were distinguished
in great detail. Another advance in the Australian study is the detailed breakdown of "value added" into labor income, taxes, depreciation, interest, and profit.

10. Latin America

In the past few years, there has been a considerable growth of interest in interindustry analysis in Latin America, and studies of varying
magnitude have been made in Puerto Rico, Argentina, Colombia,
Mexico, Chile, and Peru. The stimulus for this work has come mainly
from the Economic Commission for Latin America, which has initiated
or participated in all the studies except those of Puerto Rico and
Mexico.

Interindustry research in Latin America is focussed almost exclusively on determining the effects of economic development on the
structure of the economy. It has therefore concentrated on industry
and foreign trade, which are greatly affected by rapid development,
and which require some analysis of interdependent changes to foresee

the effects of growth in demand. Industrial production and imports are treated in considerable detail in these studies, while agriculture and services appear only in aggregate form.[5]

Of the six studies, those for Colombia, Argentina, and Peru have been used in an economic model.[6] These three are formally similar in design and use although the Argentine study covers all sectors of the economy and has been done in much more detail. The size of the matrix has been limited to about 20 sectors in each case in order to have a manageable number for projection and interpretation of the results. In the case of Argentina, an underlying table of some 200 sectors is virtually complete.[7] In Colombia, Peru, and other Latin American countries, on the other hand, the available census material is less adequate and has had to be supplemented from other sources.

The principal statistical novelty of the ECLA studies is the construction of a separate import matrix as a basis for detailed analysis of import requirements. All imports are initially treated as noncompetitive but they are classified by the same sectors as domestic production. Changes in coefficients are introduced at a later stage.

The general purpose of these studies, which will be discussed in more detail in Chapter 10, is to determine the demand for intermediate products, domestic and imported. Projections are made first with existing import proportions in each use, and import requirements are then compared with foreseeable earnings of foreign exchange to determine the overall need for import substitution.[8] The demand estimated for each commodity provides a basis for study of the desirability of domestic production of goods which are now imported.

B. Characteristic Features of Interindustry Research

Perhaps the most significant feature of the interindustry research projects that have been surveyed is the predominance of government

[5] This treatment is also due to the greater difficulty of obtaining data on the latter sectors.

[6] The Puerto Rican study was undertaken as an experiment by Professor Gosfield and the University of Puerto Rico and has not been applied. The Mexican study is being made by the Office of Industrial Planning of the Bank of Mexico, which has published some preliminary results.

[7] The initial tabulation was done by the Argentine Government as an extension of its work on national accounts, with benefits similar to those described in Norway and the Netherlands. The consolidation and application of the matrix has been carried out by ECLA as part of its study of Argentine development prospects.

[8] The methodology followed in this respect in the Colombia study is described in "The Input-Output Model," *Economic Bulletin for Latin America* (1956).

agencies in this activity. The principal reason is the cost of the detailed statistical analysis required. Although cost figures are hard to determine since the work is often done in conjunction with other studies, a minimum of ten man-years, say $50,000 at U.S. wage rates, may be estimated as the cost of assembling an input-output table of modest'size (40–50 industrial sectors), even when the basic census and other materials are in relatively good order.[9] Considerably more time has been spent on the much more detailed studies of the United States, Japan, and the United Kingdom. As in the case of national income analysis, moreover, realistic studies require extensive government collaboration and are more logically undertaken by the government itself. In fact, of the countries for which we have information, basic interindustry research has only been done by private agencies in the United States, the United Kingdom, Australia, and Puerto Rico, and in each case considerable help has been supplied by government agencies.

The large role which the government must play in interindustry research is desirable in most respects because one of the results of such research is to point up weaknesses in existing statistics which only the government is in a position to remedy. From the point of view of the scientific development of the field, however, the predominance of government activity raises some problems. The main emphasis of government research is likely to be on immediate applications rather than on sound methodological development and testing of hypotheses. Thus far it has been more difficult to work out a division of labor between the data-collecting and data-using agencies than it was for national accounts analysis because the specification of data requirements in interindustry analysis is more intimately related to the model to be used. It is also harder for outsiders to evaluate the statistical results, or to adjust them for specific uses, and hence applications tend to be limited to those of the agencies collecting the data. The principal exception is the Harvard Economic Research Project, which has continued to be a leader in both methodological development and applications.

Recent developments in Norway, Japan, and Australia appear quite promising because in each case the agency in charge of data collection is also testing the stability of the various parameters and considering a variety of models for practical applications. The main requirement for tests of stability is the compilation of basic data at sufficiently frequent intervals to make valid comparisons possible. The lack of

[9] A 20-sector table limited to industrial sectors, such as those used by ECLA, may cost only a fourth as much, however.

such data has been a notable weakness in research in the United States, where the tables are not really comparable in quality or coverage and have only been compiled at 8–10 year intervals.

In design, input-output tables fall into several fairly distinct categories. The smaller ones of less than 20 sectors can be based to a large extent on national income statistics and are often undertaken as an elaboration of existing national accounts work, as in Denmark, the Netherlands and the United Kingdom. The larger tables usually start from a much more detailed commodity breakdown than that finally used in the analysis in order to secure the most accurate distribution of each product. Two hundred or more commodities have been distinguished in the basic studies of the United States, United Kingdom, Japan, Norway, Australia, Italy, and Argentina, although for analytical purposes the tables are usually consolidated to a smaller size. The greater the detail of the unconsolidated tables the greater the use which can be made of physical units and hence the more practicable are control and revision of data when necessary. It is only at this level of refinement that it is feasible to study the variation in coefficients, the choice of alternative activities, and other topics leading to improvements in the basic model.

Interindustry analysis is not yet established as an integral part of government policy-making in any country. The applications that have been made so far constitute illustrations of its usefulness having varying degrees of realism, but the results must still be regarded as experimental. The closest approaches to policy and programming uses of the technique are probably those made in the United States and Italy, the results of which we shall evaluate in subsequent chapters. Applications to government planning have been made on a more limited scale in the Netherlands, Israel, Colombia, and Argentina; it may be expected that such applications will also result from current projects in Japan, Norway, Yugoslavia, Peru, and India, which have a specific policy orientation. Our discussion of the various uses of interindustry analysis in succeeding chapters will draw on all of these cases to the extent that we have been able to acquire and evaluate the results, many of which are as yet unpublished.

SUMMARY OF BASIC INTERINDUSTRY STUDIES

General Surveys

T. Barna (ed.), *The Structural Interdependence of the Economy*, 1956. (Part III contains chapters on research in Denmark, France, Italy, the Netherlands, Norway, and the United Kingdom.)

O. Aukrust, "Input-Output Tables: Recent Experience in Western Europe," *Economic Bulletin for Europe*, VIII, No. 1, 36–53 (May 1956). (Compares the accounting and statistical procedures followed in European countries.)

Country Studies

1. *The United States*
   (a) *1939 Study*

J. Cornfield, W. D. Evans, and M. Hoffenberg, "Full Employment Patterns, 1950," *Monthly Labor Review*, LXIV, No. 2, 163–190 (February 1947) and LXIV, No. 3, 420–432 (March 1947); the 1939 table is described in Appendix A (mimeographed).

   (b) *1947 Study*

Plans are described by E. Glaser, "Interindustry Research Program of the U.S. Government," in *Input-Output Relations* (Netherlands Economic Institute, ed.) H. E. Stenfert Kroese, Leiden, 1953.

The 1947 table is presented summarily in W. D. Evans and M. Hoffenberg, "The Interindustry Relations Study for 1947," *Review of Economics and Statistics*, XXXIV, No. 2, 97–142 (May, 1952). Also in detail in P. M. Ritz (ed.), *Input-Output Analysis: Technical Supplement*, 1954.

Individual agencies have a wide variety of limited-distribution reports, a notable one being R. N. Grosse, *Capital Requirements for the Expansion of Industrial Capacity*, 1953.

   (c) *Harvard Economic Research Project*

Principal sources for recent work are four limited-distribution annual reports, Harvard Economic Research Project, *Report on Research for 1953, 1954, 1955, and 1956–57*, Cambridge (mimeographed).

Published items include: E. W. Gilboy, "Elasticity, Consumption, and Economic Growth," *American Economic Review*, XLVI, No. 2, 119–133 (May 1956); A. H. Conrad, "The Multiplier Effects of Redistributive Public Budgets," *Review of Economics and Statistics*, XXXVII, No. 2, 160–173 (May 1955); W. Leontief, "Domestic Production and Foreign Trade: The American Capital Position Re-Examined," *Proceedings of the American Philosophical Society*, XCVII, No. 4, 332–349 (September 1953); and the studies of Henderson and Moses referred to in Chapter 12.

   (d) O. Morgenstern (ed.), *Economic Activity Analysis*, 1954.

2. *Norway*

   (a) P. Sevaldson, "Norway," in *The Structural Interdependence of the Economy*, 1956.

   (b) Central Bureau of Statistics, National Accounts Division, *Nasjonalregnskap. 1930–1939 og 1946–1951* (National Accounts, 1930–1939 and 1946–1951), by O. Aukrust, 1952.

   (c) ———, *National Accounts 1938 and 1948–1953*, 1954.

3. *Denmark*

   (a) K. Bjerke, "Denmark," in *The Structural Interdependence of the Economy*, 1956.

   (b) P. N. Rasmussen, *Studies in Intersectoral Relations*, North Holland Publishing Company, Amsterdam, 1956.

   (c) Statistical Department, *National produktet og Nationalindkomsten 1930–1946*, 1947, and *Nationalindkomsten 1938 og 1947–54*, 1955.

4. *Netherlands*

(*a*) J. Sandee, "Netherlands," in *The Structural Interdependence of the Economy*, 1956.

(*b*) Central Bureau of Statistics, Central Planning Bureau, *National Accounts of the Netherlands, 1948–1949.*

(*c*) O.E.E.C., *National Accounts Studies, Netherlands.*

5. *Italy*

(*a*) H. B. Chenery, P. G. Clark, and V. Cao-Pinna, *The Structure and Growth of the Italian Economy*, 1953.

(*b*) V. Cao-Pinna, "Italy," in *The Structural Interdependence of the Economy*, 1956.

(*c*) *Relazione generale sulla situazione economica del paese, presentata al Parlamento dal Ministro del Bilancio*, 1955, Appendix II.

6. *United Kingdom*

(*a*) T. Barna, "The Interdependence of the British Economy," *Journal of the Royal Statistical Society*, Series A (General), CXV, Part I, 52–53 (1952).

(*b*) Central Statistical Office, *National Income and Expenditure 1946–1951*, H.M.S.O., 1952.

(*c*) L. S. Berman, "United Kingdom," in *The Structural Interdependence of the Economy*, 1956.

(*d*) A monograph by I. G. Stewart describing the 1948 table is under preparation.

7. *Japan*

(*a*) Government of Japan, Ministry of International Trade and Industry, Research and Statistics Division, *Interindustry Analysis for the Japanese Economy*, 1957 (in Japanese).

(*b*) S. Shishido, "Recent Input-Output Studies in Japan," Memorandum C-6, Stanford Project for Quantitative Research in Economic Development, 1957 (mimeographed).

8. *Canada*

Dominion Bureau of Statistics, Research and Development Division, *The Inter-Industry Flow of Goods and Services, Canada, 1949*, Ottawa, 1956.

9. *Australia*

B. Cameron, "The 1946–7 Transactions Table," *Economic Record*, XXXIII, No. 66, 353–380 (December 1957); also "New Aspects of Australia's Industrial Structure," *The Economic Record*, XXXIV, No. 69, 362–374 (December 1958).

10. *Puerto Rico*

A. Gosfield, "Input-Output Analysis of the Puerto Rican Economy," in *Input-Output Analysis: An Appraisal*, 1955. Table published by the Council for Economic and Industry Research, Washington, D.C.

11. *Colombia*

United Nations, Economic Commission for Latin America, *Analysis and Projections of Economic Development, III, Economic Development of Colombia*, 1957.

12. *Argentina*

United Nations, Economic Commission for Latin America, *Analysis and Projections of Economic Development, IV, Economic Development of Argentina*, 1958 (mimeographed).

13. *Peru*
United Nations, Economic Commission for Latin America, *The Economic Development of Peru* (in preparation).

14. *France*
Ministère des Affaires Économiques et Financières, *Tableau Économique de l'Année 1951,* Paris, 1957.

15. *India*
Indian Statistical Institute, mimeographed working papers.

16. *New Zealand.*
Department of Statistics, "Report of the Interindustry Study of the New Zealand Economy in 1952–53," *Monthly Abstract of Statistics* (Supplement), February 1957.

17. *Mexico*
Banco de Mexico, Oficina de Planeación Industrial, *La Estructura Industrial de Mexico en 1950,* 1957.

18. *Yugoslavia*
Federal Bureau of Statistics, *Interindustry Relations Study of the Jugoslav Economy in 1955,* Belgrade, 1957.

19. *Spain*
A. Inchausti, G. Bequé, A. Santos-Blanco, *La estructura de la economía española,* Instituto de Estudios Políticos, Madrid, 1958.

20. *Israel*
L. Gaathon, *Four Year Development Plan of Israel, 1950–1953: Summary and Conclusions,* Central Bureau of Statistics and Economic Research, 1951.

21. *Belgium*
R. de Falleur and E. S. Kirschen, *Analyse Input-Output de l'Economie Belge en 1953,* Brussels, 1958.

22. *Europe*
E. S. Kirschen, *The Structure of European Economy in 1953,* Organization for European Economic Co-operation, Paris, 1958.

chapter 8

An international comparison
of the structure of production

The increasing availability of detailed input-output data enables us
to compare the structure of production in different countries in a way
that has not previously been possible.   Such a comparison might serve
a number of purposes, but for the present study the most important
is to reveal the nature of interdependence.[1]

The empirical form of interdependence determines the type of ap-
lication for which interindustry analysis will be useful.   If all production were "direct," in the sense that each plant produced a finished
product from primary inputs alone, there would be no need for interindustry analysis because all input coefficients for produced commodities would be zero.   Our first aim therefore will be to ascertain
the degree to which production is in fact indirect.   A measure of indirectness for each sector is provided by the extent to which it purchases inputs from other sectors, or alternatively by the extent to
which it sells its output for further use in production.   We shall, however, be interested not only in such over-all measures of indirectness

---

[1] Other aspects of this comparison are discussed in Chenery and Watanabe
(1958), of which the present chapter is a condensed version.

but also in discovering the extent to which there is a common pattern in the relations among different sectors.

There is a further aspect which it would be interesting to explore but which is not developed here: the similarity of individual input coefficients in different countries. To the extent that we observe similarities in the pattern of relations among sectors it must be due largely to the use of a common technology and to similarities in consumption patterns because other elements (varying factor prices, income levels, etc.) work against a constant input structure. Since our analysis will be conducted in terms of values rather than physical quantities, we will not pursue this topic beyond a few incidental observations.

Of the available input-output studies, those for the United States, Japan, Norway, and Italy lend themselves most readily to a comparative analysis.[2] We chose these countries primarily because their industry classifications could be reconciled without excessive aggregation. Fortunately, they cover a wide range of income levels and resource endowments, although all four are industrial economies by comparison to those of the less developed countries. As detailed studies for other countries are completed, it will be possible to extend the comparison to them.

A. Basis for the Comparison

The observed data in input-output tables are sales by one producing sector to another and to final users, measured at current prices. The magnitudes of these flows depend on the total amount and pattern of domestic demand, on the composition of imports and exports, on physical input-output proportions, and on relative prices. In order to compare interindustry flows, we shall eliminate the effects of variation in the first two factors, demand and trade, but shall make no attempt to separate the variations in physical inputs and in relative prices. The comparison in value rather than physical terms is largely determined by the data available, since a considerable amount of research would be needed to transform the input data into constant prices. In many respects, however, the comparison in value terms is the more meaningful one if we are interested in the overall pattern of interdependence rather than in its details, as will be shown in the course of the analysis.

[2] The studies for the United Kingdom, Australia, and India were not available when this work was done, but they appear to be suitable for this type of comparison.

The first step in the comparison was to consolidate the interindustry transactions data on a uniform basis. The basic tables used are those shown in Table 7.1 for Japan (1951, size 182 × 182); Italy (1950, size 200 × 56); Norway (1950, size 117 ×117) and the U.S. (1947, size 200 × 200). The industry classification given in Table 8.5, below, was devised as a basis for the comparison. It distinguishes manufacturing sectors (20 out of 29 sectors) in greater detail than others, since the former account for some eighty per cent of total intermediate use. At this level of aggregation, the classifications of the four basic tables can be made quite consistent. Since we have used gross rather than net value of production in each sector, aggregation of the original tables leaves the proportions of total intermediate use to total production unchanged. The effects of aggregation are shown in Table 8.1, in which our earlier example from Chapter 2 is consolidated from four sectors to two.

The concept of intermediate use will be used in the subsequent analysis for two purposes: (i) Individual elements, X_{ij}, represent the importance of the link between supplying sector i and using sector j. (ii) In the aggregate, all of the purchases by sector j, taken as a fraction of the total value of its production, represent the extent to which factors are used outside of the establishments in sector j in the production of commodity j.

The concepts of intermediate use in the four studies are not entirely comparable, either as among countries or as among sectors. The main differences are as follows:

(i) Although the establishment is usually taken as the basic accounting unit, transactions among establishments in the same sector are often not distinguished outside of manufacturing (particularly in Norway and Italy). In Japan, on the other hand, the *activity* is the basic unit in many manufacturing sectors, and the production of intermediate products consumed within the same plant is recorded as an intrasector transaction.

(ii) Investment is treated differently by Japan and the U.S., on the one hand, and Norway and Italy on the other. In the former, repairs and maintenance are classed as current inputs, whereas in the latter a substantial fraction is charged to final demand as part of gross investment. We have reduced this difference by treating all construction as part of final demand, but it persists in the use of machinery and equipment.

(iii) The extent to which artificial transactions are created by the transfer of secondary products to the sector of primary production varies considerably, being much greater in the U.S. than in other

TABLE 8.1. EFFECTS OF AGGREGATION

(a) Original Input-Output Table*

Producing Sector	Purchasing Sector 1	2	3	4	Total Inter-industry Use (W_i)	Final Demand (Y_i)	Total Demand (Z_i)	w_i
1	20	25	15	80	140	60	200	0.70
2	0	25	0	120	145	105	250	0.58
3	0	25	45	40	110	40	150	0.73
4	0	0	0	80	80	320	400	0.20
Total purchases (U_j)	20	75	60	320	475			0.475
Value added (V_j)	180	175	90	80		525		
Total output (X_j)	200	250	150	400			1000	
u_j	0.10	0.30	0.40	0.80	0.475			

(b) Consolidated Input-Output Table

Producing Sector	Purchasing Sector 1 + 2	3 + 4	W_i	Y_i	Z_i
1 + 2	70	215	285	165	450
3 + 4	25	165	190	360	550
U_j	95	380	475		
V_j	355	170		525	
X_j	450	550			1000

* Data taken from Table 2.2. The transaction for each cell in part (b) is equal to the total of the corresponding cells in part (a).

countries. After aggregation, most of these transfers become intra-sector transactions.[3]

Of these three sources of variation, the first and third impinge only on the diagonal elements (intrasector use), so that the pattern of in-

[3] These differences could be eliminated in more detailed comparisons by reference to the original worksheets.

terdependence among sectors remains the same although measures of the overall importance of indirect use will be affected. The different treatment of investment reduces the extent of interdependence in Norway and (to a lesser degree) in Italy.[4]

In section C, p. 212, we shall make some comparisons between columns of input coefficients for the same industries in different countries. To do this, we define input coefficients from Eq. (2.5), in which imports are treated as "competitive" and distributed to users along with the domestic supply of similar commodities. This treatment is necessary in order not to make an artificial distinction between, for example, inputs of domestic coal in one country and imported coal in another. The input coefficients computed on this basis are given for each of the four countries in Tables 8.6 to 8.9 of the Appendix of this chapter.[5]

B. The Nature of Interdependence in Production

The interdependence among productive sectors can be studied from several points of view. First, we can ask to what extent production involves the indirect use as compared to the direct use of capital and labor. In other words, what proportion of the factors of production is employed in the establishments which produce a given commodity? For each sector, the extent of indirect use of factors will be measured by the ratio of purchased inputs U_j to the value of total production X_j, which we call u_j. These values are shown in Table 8.1(a) for our example. The factors employed directly in establishments in sector 4, for example, account for only 20% of the value of production in that sector, the remainder being attributable to factors used in other establishments (including some in the same sector). We shall define a similar measure, $w_i = W_i/Z_i$, to denote the ratio of intermediate to total demand for a given product. These ratios are also shown in Table 8.1(a).

For the economy as a whole, the extent of indirect factor use and

---

[4] There are also significant differences in the statistical quality of the tables. One crude measure is the number of zero elements, which is as follows: U.S. (242), Japan (273), Italy (359), Norway (392), out of a total of 784 coefficients (omitting sector 29). The latter two tables were compiled in less detail and (at least in the case of Italy) from much less complete information, and hence omit data on some of the smaller flows.

[5] In order for the coefficients to be comparable, it was necessary to convert the Italian data from purchasers' prices to producers' prices, which are used in the other three tables.

the extent of indirect demand amount to the same thing if we make allowance for foreign trade. In Table 8.1 the ratio of interindustry use to total production of 0.475 constitutes a weighted average of either the w's or the u's. For any single sector, however, there is no necessary connection between the two measures. Since the study of interdependence among sectors involves their relation to other industries on both the demand side and the supply side, we can start such a study by classifying sectors according to these two measures.

We shall use a simple two-way classification for each measure, based on whether the values of u and w are above or below their mean values. These values are shown in Table 8.13 for each country:[6]

	Average u_j	Average w_i
Japan	48.7	46.1
Italy	43.8	41.1
U.S.A.	42.6	41.9
Norway	36.4	30.4

Since the first three countries' means are quite close, we have used an average value of w_i and u_j from these countries as a basis for classifying sectors. The results are shown in Table 8.2. In this arrangement, the word "final" describes sectors with low values of intermediate use (low w), and the word "primary" is used for sectors with low values of u (i.e., high value added). Since the value of w depends on the classification used, a greater degree of disaggregation would sharpen the distinction between intermediate and final use, and vertically consolidated sectors like "leather and products" would be separated. Even with the blurring due to aggregation, however, the second distinction between primary production and manufacturing is quite clear, and not many sectors are close to the mean value of u. With few exceptions, the same classification of sectors would be reached by considering the countries separately.[7]

There is a close relation between this classification and that of Colin Clark (1951). Clark's "primary" and "tertiary" categories are identified in Table 8.2 by low values of purchases from other producers (generally less than 0.30) whereas "secondary" production has higher values of u_j in all cases (generally 0.50 or above). Mining and elec-

---

[6] The average ratio to total demand w_i is lower than the ratio to total production u_j because imports have been excluded from the latter, whereas exports are included in final demand. The difference is important only in the case of Norway, however.

[7] The only exception on the u-axis is agriculture in the United States, which would appear in category II.

TABLE 8.2. Types of Productive Sector*

	By use of output					
By type of input	Final (Low w)	w	u	Intermediate (High w)	w	u
Manufacturing (high u)	**III Final manufacture**			**II Intermediate manufacture**		
	3 Apparel	0.12	0.69	13 Iron and Steel	0.78	0.66
	4 Shipbuilding	0.14	0.58	22 Paper and products	0.78	0.57
	8 Leather and products	0.37	0.66	28 Petroleum products	0.68	0.65
	1 Processed foods	0.15	0.61	19 Nonferrous metals	0.81	0.61
	2 Grain mill products	0.42	0.89	16 Chemicals	0.69	0.60
	5 Transport equipment	0.20	0.60	23 Coal products	0.67	0.63
	7 Machinery	0.28	0.51	11 Rubber products	0.48	0.51
	15 Lumber and wood products	0.38	0.61	12 Textiles	0.57	0.69
	14 Nonmetallic mineral prod.	0.30	0.47	9 Printing and publishing	0.46	0.49
	10 Industry n.e.c.	0.20	0.43			
Primary Production (Low u)	**IV Final primary production**			**I Intermediate primary production**		
	A Commodities			17 Agriculture and forestry	0.72	0.31
	6 Fishing	0.36	0.24	27 Coal mining	0.87	0.23
	B Services			20 Metal mining	0.93	0.21
	25 Transport	0.26	0.31	29 Petroleum and natural gas	0.97	0.15
	21 Trade	0.17	0.16	18 Nonmetallic minerals	0.52	0.17
	26 Services	0.34	0.19	24 Electric power	0.59	0.27

* The sectors are numbered in order of triangularity from Table 8.3. The values of w and u are averages for Italy, Japan, and the U.S. from Table 8.13.

tric power, which he classes as secondary, have the characteristics of primary production, however, and would be better considered as such for most purposes. The other variable, w, the proportion of intermediate purchases, serves to divide manufacturing between producer and consumer goods.[8] At this level of aggregation, w also distinguishes between Clark's primary and tertiary production although there is no reason why some services, for example, should not appear in category I. Conversely, some primary products may go to final use with little or no processing, as does the output of fishing, and therefore be in IV.

These categories bring out the quite different roles played by various sectors in the total process of production. Those in category IV are relatively independent of other producers and provide a direct link between final users and the owners of primary factors. Those in category II are at the other extreme; the cost of their use of primary factors is less than the value of their purchased inputs, and more than half of their output goes to other producers. Roughly speaking, categories I, II, and III may be thought of as successive stages of production, but the nature of the relations of the intermediate manufacturing industries to the other sectors complicates this pattern.

The distinctions which we have drawn so far neglect the fact that interindustry transactions may involve either one other sector or many and that the resulting patterns of interdependence might, at least *a priori*, take an infinite variety of forms. We now wish to see whether technological and other uniformities produce similar patterns of interdependence in the four countries studied.

The approach which we have adopted is to establish a hierarchy of sectors leading from primary to finished products and to see to what extent the resulting sequence is the same in each country. The pattern into which we have attempted to fit the interindustry flows of each country is that of one-way interdependence. Sequences like raw cotton→textiles→clothing fit nicely into such an arrangement, but circular relations like coal→steel→mining equipment→coal do not. If there were no circularity of this sort in the economy, it would be possible to arrange the input-output matrix in the triangular form used in Chapter 2.

The extent to which an actual economy departs from this one-way interdependence is indicated by the proportion of transactions which

---

[8] Some commodities, like flour and textiles, are mainly consumer goods in low-income countries but are processed further in higher-income countries. The extremes in the present case are Japan and the United States. In our classification, investment goods are part of final demand rather than producer goods.

TABLE 8.3. ORDERING OF SECTORS IN TRIANGULAR ARRANGEMENT

Per Cent of Transactions above Diagonal (t_i, t_j)†

Sector (Compromise Ranking)*	J	Country Ranking I	U	N	Japan Row	Col.	Italy Row	Col.	U.S.A. Row	Col.	Norway Row	Col.
1. Processed foods (4)	1	10	1	2	9.7	0	2.4	†††	4.0	0	1.4	0
2. Grain mill products (6)	3	11	2	3	4.6	0.2	9.6	†††	43.3	4.6	41.1	0.3
3. Apparel (1)	6	4	5	4	6.7	††	0.4	0	0.3	0.7	2.0	0
4. Shipbuilding (2)	4	3	7	5	5.0	0			18.3		2.1	0
5. Transport equipment (9)	7	2	4	6	12.9	††	0.4	16.2	11.8	0	0.3	1.4
6. Fishing (5)	2	12	6	18	10.5	3.2	0.6	0	10.4	0.3	0.3	0.9
7. Machinery (12)	11	5	8	9	10.5	1.1	0.5	††	5.0	0.2	0.5	0
8. Leather (3)	12	6	9	7	1.2	3.7			2.3	*	26.8	
9. Printing (17)	5	1	3	1	28.3	0.4	2.6	0.7	50.2	2.1	13.0	††
10. Industry, n.e.c. (8)	8	7	10	8	12.4		2.7	1.2	16.8	1.4	5.9	1.0
11. Rubber (10)	9	8	12	13	39.2	0.4	2.1	0.1	17.0	2.1	5.5	1.0
12. Textiles (11)	10	9	15	14	2.6	0.6	1.2	0.7	3.5	2.1	0.9	0.4
13. Iron and steel (13)	13	13	13	17	4.9	3.4	0.8	0.6	5.4	1.3	10.1	†††
14. Nonmetallic mineral prod. (14)	14	15	14	10	8.2	6.8	4.8	0.6	6.8	2.1	0.4	0.1
15. Lumber and wood products (15)	16	14	11	12	10.1	0.8	4.7	2.9	11.9	8.1	0.7	13.9
16. Chemicals (16)	18	18	16	16	8.1	13.1	3.6	7.6	14.9	9.5	6.0	7.0
17. Agriculture and forestry (18)	17	17	17	15	6.1	3.1	3.9	3.3	0.3	6.4	0.3	5.0
18. Nonmetallic minerals (19)	15	20	18	20	18.2	9.6	0.6	2.1	1.8	6.1	8.3	4.6
19. Nonferrous metals (21)	19	19	19	19	6.5	3.5	0	7.6	1.6	6.1	1.6	4.6
20. Metal mining (22)	21	21	20	21		22.3		1.5		9.1		1.9
21. Trade (24)	23	23	21	24	4.2	2.6	0.3	1.2	3.8	4.0	2.5	1.9
22. Paper products (25)	25	16	22	11	1.4	20.1	23.4	8.8	4.3	15.4	11.4	0.3
23. Coal products (23)	22	25	23	22	7.4	3.5	0.1	8.6	2.0	2.8	35.3	
24. Electric power (26)	20	26	24	27	19.6	9.6	0.5	1.9	17.7	2.8	2.9	5.1
25. Transport (7)	24	22	25	23	3.9	7.6	1.6	1.5	4.1	7.6	0	0.4
26. Services (28)	27	24	26	28	0.1	17.8	0.9	3.6	0.4	11.0	0.4	13.2
27. Coal mining (27)	26	27	27	25	1.9	20.4	1.9	15.0	0.1	10.5	0.2	31.2
28. Petroleum products (20)	28	28	28	26	0.1	8.7	0.1	6.4	0.1	13.6	7.7	26.9
29. Petroleum & natural gas (29)	29	29	29	§	0.1	22.4		8.9	5.0	3.1		4.2
Total					5.7	5.7	1.9	1.9	5.4	5.4	4.2	4.2

* Numbers in brackets are original code numbers.

† $t_i = \frac{1}{X_i} \sum\limits_{j > i} X_{ij}$ $(i = 1, 2, \ldots, 29)$, $t_j = \frac{1}{X_j} \sum\limits_{i < j} X_{ij}$ $(j = 1, 2, \ldots, 29)$.

‡ Indicates less than significant digit.
§ Not distinguished in Norwegian Table.

fall above the diagonal in the optimal arrangement of sectors. We have tried to minimize this proportion for each country by revising the order of rows and columns.[9] The results of this experiment for each of the four countries are given in Table 8.3. With few exceptions, the order of sectors in the optimal arrangement is much the same in all countries.[10]

This uniformity lends support to the idea of a natural hierarchy of sectors. Our categories I (primary production for intermediate use) and III (final manufacture) fit well into this scheme, since all of the latter group come before all of the former in the ranking. The intermediate manufactures (II) overlap both groups, however, and contribute a large fraction of the circular interrelations observed. This is particularly true of industries such as chemicals, paper, and fuels, which sell to many users. Textiles, on the other hand, fit the triangular pattern very well because there are relatively few users of their output.

The economic significance of the nearly triangular pattern of interdependence is that the effects of changes in final demand spread through the economy from higher to lower sectors, and that reactions in the opposite direction, resulting in a continuing series of repercussions, are quite limited. The degree of triangularity is affected to some extent by the nature and degree of aggregation, but other experiments with the U.S., Italian, and Argentine matrices have produced similar results.[11]

---

[9] This measurement of triangularity weights the input coefficients by total output in each sector. A trial and error method for finding the optimum is to arrange sectors initially in the order of increasing (w) or of decreasing (u). In Table 8.1, the first measure would give 4-2-1-3 and the second 4-3-2-1. The above-diagonal totals by row and column are then computed. An improvement results from moving a sector upward in the ranking if the reduction in its above-diagonal U component is greater than the increase in its W component, or in other words if the above-diagonal total of the two is reduced. There is no guarantee that making improvements one sector at a time will reach the optimum although it is unlikely that our results are far from it. (The reader can test this procedure for Table 8.1, for which the order 4-2-3-1 makes the flow matrix perfectly triangular.)

[10] Spearman rank correlations among pairs of countries are as follows:

Japan-United States	0.945
Italy-Norway	0.905
Italy-United States	0.902
United States-Norway	0.901
Japan-Italy	0.868
Japan-Norway	0.863

[11] The first experiment with triangular input-output matrices known to the authors is that of the Planning Research Division of the U.S. Air Force, reported

From a computational point of view, triangularity of the extent found here[12] may be a considerable advantage because an approximate solution to a triangular input-output system can be secured in two or three iterations by the Gauss–Seidel method discussed in Chapter 2.[13]

C. Similarities in Input Coefficients

The notable similarity just described in the observed patterns of interdependence is ascribable to uniformity in the basic raw materials provided by nature, in the technology which is used to process them, and in the products which have been grouped together as industries. To ascertain the extent to which these factors result in similar inputs per unit of output, it would be necessary to make a detailed study of individual industries, making allowance for price differentials, differences in product mix, and other factors. Since such studies have not been made, we shall give some of the results of a preliminary exploration in which there was no attempt to correct for price differences or the effects of aggregation.[14]

Because of the statistical discrepancies already referred to, we have compared the average differences in all the inputs into each industry (column) and in all the uses of a given commodity (row) rather than individual differences.[15] Since these calculations were carried out for the six possible two-country comparisons, they shed some light on the relative quality of the four tables and also permit some generalization

in a paper by Marshall Wood and H. Burke Horton to the American Statistical Association in December 1950, *An Experimental Dynamic Model of the U.S. Economy.* The model contained forty sectors with an (unweighted) average ratio of the elements above the diagonal to total demand in each sectors of 5%.

[12] The proportions of *intermediate use* which lie above the diagonal are as follows: Italy 4.3%, Norway 11.5%, Japan 11.6%, United States 12.7%. As a fraction of *total demand,* they vary from 2 to 6%. The lower figures for Italy result in part from allocating maintenance materials and office supplies to final demand.

[13] In linear programming models or in practical planning procedures the advantages of triangularization are likely to be even greater, as shown in Chenery and Kretschmer (1956). To reach a solution, numerous changes in the choice of activities are required and the inverse matrix, if used, has to be revised accordingly at each step. Input-output matrices are also more nearly triangular in the underdeveloped countries, since sectors in category II, which are responsible for much of the circular interdependence, are a smaller fraction of total production.

[14] Further results and details of the methodology are given in Chenery and Watanabe (1958). An interesting comparison of coefficients in Spain and Italy is given by Cao-Pinna (1958).

[15] A comparison of individual coefficients is hampered by the omission of minor flows in some tables.

as to the industries and commodities for which the coefficients are most similar.

For the comparison of industries, we have used the average difference between all the pairs of coefficients in a given column expressed as a ratio to their average sum and disregarding the sign of the difference.[16]   For each country, three such two-country comparisons are possible.   The combined results of all these comparisons are summarized in Table 8.4 by country and type of sector.

TABLE 8.4. Classification of Average Differences in Columns of Coefficients by Country and Type of Sector*

Range of Average Difference	Japan		Italy		Norway		United States		Totals		
	Manufacturing†	Other	Manufacturing	Other	Manufacturing	Other	Manufacturing	Other	Manufacturing	Other	Total
0–0.499	25	0	23	0	17	0	17	0	82	0	82
0.500–0.799	19	7	20	4	22	5	25	8	86	24	110
0.800–0.999	7	4	8	2	11	3	10	3	36	12	48
1.000–2.000	2	17	3	22	4	5	3	16	12	70	82
Total	54	28	54	28	54	23	55	27	216	106	322

* From Chenery and Watanabe (1958), Table 5.

† Manufacturing includes all sectors in categories II and III of Table 8.2.

The most marked differences are those between the 18 manufacturing sectors and the 9 others.   Nearly 80% of the comparisons in the former group had average differences[17] of less than 0.8, whereas only 23% of the differences for the nonmanufacturing sectors (agriculture, mining, services) are in this category.   The greater similarity in the first group can be attributed to the fact that a primary material is

[16] Algebraically, this measure is defined as:

$$\frac{\displaystyle\sum_i |a_{ij}{}^\alpha - a_{ij}{}^\beta|}{\tfrac{1}{2}\displaystyle\sum_i (a_{ij}{}^\alpha + a_{ij}{}^\beta)}$$

[17] If the inputs were completely uncorrelated, the value of the average difference would be 2.0.

being processed in manufacturing and perhaps to a greater similarity of technology.[18]

By comparing one country to the others in turn we also get an indication of the peculiarities of each table. At first sight, it is surprising that Japan and the United States show the smallest average differences in these paired comparisons.[19] The fact that the "most typical" tables are for the two countries which are at the extremes in per capita income, wage rates, resource endowments, and most other characteristics strongly suggests that statistical factors are the main source of the differences. Although we have only tested the effects of price corrections in a few sectors, it is unlikely that price variations account for a very large part of the observed differences.[20] The average difference between pairs of countries of about 0.7 is about twice the average difference found by Leontief in comparing the coefficients of the United States for 1929 and 1939 on a similar basis.[21]

The several types of comparisons made in this chapter indicate a general similarity in the relations among productive sectors in industrial countries, although there are substantial differences in individual input-output coefficients. The nature of interdependence is such, however, that we may expect conclusions from studies in one country to have some applicability to other industrial countries. No detailed comparisons have been made for the less industrial countries, but in general the lower proportion of production in the manufacturing sectors leads to a much smaller degree of interdependence in these countries.

APPENDIX

This appendix contains basic input-output data for Japan, Italy, Norway, and the United States aggregated in a comparable form.

[18] Since the nonmanufacturing sectors account for only about 20% of intermediate demand, a weighted average difference in coefficients for all sectors would be close to that for manufacturing.

[19] Based on the number of differences less than 0.8. Japan and Italy are the most similar pair of countries, despite the statistical shortcomings of the Italian table.

[20] Further evidence on this point is given in Chenery and Watanabe (1958), in which comparisons by type of input are also made.

[21] See Leontief (1953a), p. 30. Rasmussen (1956) gives similar measures for Denmark from 1947–1949, where the median difference by industry is about 0.10. A comparison of the ECLA tables for Argentina, Colombia, and Peru showed mean column differences of about 0.4 between pairs of countries, using 15 sectors. These several results are not comparable because of the varying degree of aggregation, which has the effect of reducing differences.

Apart from the comparisons made in the chapter, it should provide a basis for further input-output calculations by the reader. The inverses of three of the Leontief matrices have also been included to facilitate such calculations.

The several tables are as follows.

8.5 *Industry Classification.* The groupings are based on the International Standard Industrial Classification, which is used in most countries.

8.6 to 8.9. *Input-Output Tables.*

(*a*) The body of the tables consists of coefficients of the form $a_{ij} = X_{ij}/X_j$, computed from consolidations of the original transactions tables. Coefficients are given to four decimal places.

(*b*) Column totals are given for interindustry use, total production, imports, and total supply. Units are in the national currency with roughly the same number of significant figures.

(*c*) Row totals are given for total intermediate demand, exports, domestic demand, and total demand.

8.10 to 8.12. *Inverses to the Leontief Matrix.*[22]

Since the inverses are intended for general use, they are calculated with the import proportions of the original tables in each case. For computational convenience, the dependent variable is total supply Z_j rather than production X_j. The relation between the two is derived by substituting Z_j in the input-output equations of Chapter 2:

$$Z_i = X_i + M_i = (1 + m_i)X_i$$

$$(1 + m_i)X_i - \sum_j a_{ij}X_j = Y_i \tag{2.7}$$

$$Z_i - \sum_j \left(\frac{a_{ij}}{1 + m_j} \right) Z_j = Y_i$$

Substituting $\bar{a}_{ij} = a_{ij}/(1 + m_j)$,

$$Z_i - \sum_j \bar{a}_{ij}Z_j = Y_i \tag{2.7a}$$

or $$\mathbf{Z} = (\mathbf{I} - \bar{\mathbf{A}})^{-1}\mathbf{Y}$$

The inverse matrices in Tables 8.10 to 8.12 are therefore derived by first dividing each column j in the preceding table of input coeffi-

---

[22] The inverse for Norway is not included because the Norwegian data used here are being revised by the Central Statistical Office before publication.

cients by the corresponding $(1 + m_j)$ and then determining the general solution for the resulting Leontief matrix $(I - A)$. X_j and M_j are determined from the solution for Z_j as: $X_j = Z_j/(1 + m_j)$, $M_j = m_j X_j$.

8.13. *Ratios of Interindustry Use* to total production (u_j) and total demand (w_i) by country and sector.

TABLE 8.5. INDUSTRY CLASSIFICATION

Sector	International Standard Industrial Classification
1 Apparel	232, 243
2 Shipbuilding	381
3 Leather and products	291, 292, 241, 242
4 Processed foods	201, 202, 203, 204, 206, 207, 208, 209, 211, 212, 213, 214, 220
5 Fishing	04
6 Grain mill products	205
7 Transport	71
8 Industry n.e.c.	391, 392, 393, 394, 395, 396, 399
9 Transport equipment	382, 383, 385, 386, 389
10 Rubber products	300
11 Textiles	231, 233, 239, 244
12 Machinery	360, 370
13 Iron and steel	341, 350
14 Nonmetallic mineral products	33
15 Lumber and wood products	250, 260, 02 (except Forestry)
16 Chemicals	311, 312, 319
17 Printing and publishing	28
18 Agriculture and forestry	01, 02 (except Logging) 03
19 Nonmetallic minerals	14, 19
20 Petroleum products	321, 329
21 Nonferrous metals	342
22 Metal mining	121, 122
23 Coal products	322, 329, 512
24 Trade	611, 612
25 Paper and products	271, 272
26 Electric power	511
27 Coal mining	11
28 Services	513, 521, 522, 384
29 Petroleum and natural gas	13
30 Construction (included in final demand)	400

TABLE 8.6. INPUT-OUTPUT TABLE
$\begin{pmatrix} a_{ij} \times 10^4 \\ \text{Column and row totals} \end{pmatrix}$

Coefficients (a_{ij})

		1	2	3	4	5	6	7	8	9	10	11	12	13	14	15
1	Apparel	866			1		22	52								25
2	Shipbuilding					81		97								
3	Leather and products	1		3726			2	1	3	78		18	15			
4	Processed foods				774	315	18	3							4	
5	Fishing				96											
6	Grain mill products				963	57	9		11			28			1	
7	Transport	36	103	226	150	57	101	206	114	120	184	40	101	79	346	409
8	Industry n.e.c.	157	13	58	5			3	552	2			38	1		6
9	Transport equipment							111		1036						
10	Rubber products	65	60	148	7	147	1	152	14	578	201	6	30	9	48	1
11	Textiles	5868	144	158	13	811	20	119	443	28	2299	3740	36	7	77	2
12	Machinery	29	1998	2	1			55	35	547	1	40	1369	41	3	3
13	Iron and steel		2691		135	59		276	250	2366		6	2767	5511	204	7
14	Nonmetallic mineral products		62	10	95	5		23	67	130		1	91	81	775	33
15	Lumber and wood products	5	358	10	55	61		104	229	160	15	10	132	21	198	1239
16	Chemicals	137	140	36	268	15		53	1051	55	1476	863	107	8	372	120
17	Printing and publishing	1	1		12			22	23	1		1	2			
18	Agriculture and forestry	14		3261	1207	29	8768	28	324			2436		16	71	4443
19	Nonmetallic minerals				4			5	22		13		14	11	596	
20	Petroleum products	4	69	5	8	437		465	35	59	54	4	29	37	48	2
21	Nonferrous metals	1	75		10	7		80	536	492	1	1	834	133	45	19
22	Metal mining												3	255	11	
23	Coal products	1	5	4	6	5		11	15	14			17	410	80	2
24	Trade	328	302	338	190	165	347	136	267	460	359	166	294	93	235	117
25	Paper and products	74	14		138	14	20	36	383	26	32	15	76	4	507	18
26	Electric power	33	70	22	49		31	102	57	55	47	40	54	93	176	120
27	Coal mining	9	68	45	101	16	2	586	105	27	121	62	50	99	1235	22
28	Services	261	283	189	138	245	98	729	348	282	255	329	283	131	179	231
29	Petroleum and natural gas							10								6
30	Interindustry total (U_j)	916	646	327	2914	442	6641	1794	399	899	434	8877	2287	8044	776	1327
31	Total production (X_j)	1161	999	397	6583	1749	7035	5180	830	1380	857	11372	3575	11425	1485	1946
32	Imports (M_j)	12	91	10	198	15	445	0	19	60	1	33	61	34	5	8
33	Total supply (Z_j)	1173	1090	407	6781	1764	7480	5180	849	1440	858	11405	3636	11459	1490	1954

FOR THE JAPANESE ECONOMY

in 100 million yen)

					Coefficients (a_{ij})									Total Inter-mediate De-mand	Final Demand			Total De-mand	
															Ex-ports	Do-mestic	Total		
16	17	18	19	20	21	22	23	24	25	26	27	28	29	30	31	32	33	34	
1		23	3		8				14			11		194	141	837	979	1173	1
														64	61	965	1026	1090	2
1		1										2		192	7	208	215	407	3
167		4										338		1145	115	5521	5636	6781	4
226												34		242	60	1462	1522	1764	5
21	1	123							7			89		971	7	6503	6510	7481	6
172	88	54	114	37	120	89	498	98	297	302	183	71	61	1256	601	3324	3924	5180	7
								22				45		172	151	525	677	849	8
												87		319	48	1073	1121	1440	9
45	28	49	194	30	7	257	2	59	42	28	63	20		482	30	346	376	858	10
40	44	43	33	11	150	23	2		140	4	17	35		5649	1850	3906	5755	11404	11
5	53	23	6		3	16		2	3	84	156	165	6	1197	223	2216	2439	3636	12
63	4	18	697	100	32	828	180	85	68	189	495	22	970	8569	717	2172	2889	11458	13
73	1	13	24	12	44	17	36		6	27	21	16		457	184	849	1033	1490	14
19	1	9	102	16	11	20		42	47	197	102	15		678	78	1198	1276	1954	15
2361	307	683	124	237	93	357	83		266	59	171	215		4276	250	1581	1831	6107	16
		1	9	3	2			2	87	5	3	176	16	299	4	732	736	1035	17
581	13	285	176		3	207		33	635	41	344	105	106	11902	72	4213	4284	16186	18
53				8	1	1			63			2		164	2	150	152	316	19
14	28	14	198	395	48	57	13	4	9	33	34	16	84	516	1	134	134	650	20
199	22	4	134		2845	235	3		35	312	16	27		1444	184	530	714	2158	21
106					1030									571	2	10	12	583	22
234	20	1	95	2	68		1969	4	3		2	17		963	—	179	180	1143	23
268	329	183	161	47	166	171	151	59	193	198	94	211	100	2039	429	7713	8141	10179	24
452	3561	10		27	17		11	131	3665	9		17		1957	62	421	483	2440	25
198	50	17	88	30	117	259	40	10	146	119	372	45	266	728	0	509	509	1237	26
293	12		199	41	81	34	4552	5	258	2533	186	24		1959	1	54	55	2014	27
511	982	193	220	265	173	511	79	1054	255	610	296	708	625	4375	45	9250	9296	13671	28
				4995			7						1038	274	0	15	15	289	29
3584	568	2159	72	328	1046	98	871	1639	1457	589	469	3433	16	53054	5325	56596	61919	114973	
5853	1026	12347	281	524	2082	316	1142	10180	2319	1237	1838	13670	49						
254	9	3840	34	127	76	267	0	0	121	0	176	0	240						
6107	1035	16187	316	651	2158	582	1142	10180	2440	1237	2014	13670	289						

TABLE 8.7. INPUT-OUTPUT TABLE
$\begin{pmatrix} a_{ij} \times 10^4 \\ \text{Row and Column Totals} \end{pmatrix}$

Coefficients (a_{ij})

		1	2	3	4	5	6	7	8	9	10	11	12	13	14	15
1	Apparel	264										6				1
2	Shipbuilding															
3	Leather & products	7	6	3101					9	22	5		3			4
4	Processed foods			1250	393		2		1		11	10		3		26
5	Fishing				41											
6	Grain mill products			1	1430							2				
7	Transport	20	101	15	42	38	90	125	80	88	38	47	62	142	275	228
8	Industry n.e.c.	45	134	55		302			253	364	114	2	136	11		215
9	Transport equipment									504						
10	Rubber products	11	22	38				342	34	308	1171	6	37	1		1
11	Textiles	5504	43	199		1321			50	69	1184	4358	10		12	29
12	Machinery		2908						61	685		1491		2		5
13	Iron & steel	2	2439	38	45				2141	1803	101		1307	5251	51	24
14	Nonmetallic mineral products	2	160	8	4				120	133			138	101	699	180
15	Lumber & wood products	1	386	111	19				112	198	1		91	13		2499
16	Chemicals	243	91	483	74			3	329	174	1774	682	117	161	418	189
17	Printing & publishing															
18	Agriculture & forestry	65		12	3957		8723	109	29	1	22	1662	1	5	120	3087
19	Nonmetallic minerals		4	5	32				11	2	22	4	5	45	968	5
20	Petroleum products	26	88	16	53	404	8	1471	124	157	316	68	109	136	318	38
21	Nonferrous metals	2	579	3	4				877	524	9		618	195	12	10
22	Metal mining													67	3	
23	Coal products	4	45	6	6			12	39	14	133	4	43	303	175	5
24	Trade	275	171	265	350	101	408	240	82	181	239	255	136	52	223	294
25	Paper & products	2		33	9				13		82	7			358	14
26	Electric power	9	194	14	15		49	378	79	107	92	85	86	325	286	33
27	Coal mining	6	23	17	27		2	387	20	8	28	41	12	108	707	4
28	Services	115	90	171	278	160	241	263	163	90	129	114	68	77	222	270
29	Petroleum & natural gas				1			21	10	1	7	4	6	16	19	
30	Interindustry total (U_j)	1765	322	1028	13727	57	7043	1432	1741	2090	505	8692	1766	3563	816	1023
31	Total production (X_j)	2673	430	1761	20243	243	7395	4274	3755	3848	922	11816	3947	5080	1676	1428
32	Imports (M_j)	27	150	22	1104	1	36	0	298	75	133	296	538	518	82	107
33	Total supply (Z_j)	2700	580	1783	21347	244	7432	4274	4053	3922	1055	12113	4485	5597	1758	1535

FOR THE ITALIAN ECONOMY, 1950

in 100 Million Lire)

Coefficients (a_{ij}) — columns 16–29. Column 30 = Total Intermediate Demand. Columns 31–33 = Final Demand (31 = Exports, 32 = Domestic, 33 = Total). Column 34 = Total Demand.

16	17	18	19	20	21	22	23	24	25	26	27	28	29	30	31	32	33	34	
								2					2	80	354	2267	2620	2700	1
														0	163	417	580	580	2
	13							3					4	567	35	1182	1216	1783	3
289		73	17	97	1		2	47					62	1506	625	19216	19841	21347	4
												1		84	0	159	159	243	5
		258										7		3609	223	3600	3823	7432	6
112	39	19	7	35	235	14	470	3	80	46	62	6	5	748	113	3413	3526	4274	7
58	21		1		16	1			17					417	367	3269	3636	4053	8
														194	325	3403	3728	3922	9
1					2									419	79	557	637	1056	10
49	78						1	1	450			26		6961	1750	3402	5151	12112	11
					5									1003	601	2882	3482	4485	12
6	55				209				9					4938	157	503	660	5598	13
52	2	1			54			10	26			20		442	85	1232	1317	1759	14
8	7	1			27			12	327					662	69	804	873	1535	15
3534	491	237	178	197	431	914	55	14	1992		428	130	19	5196	551	1561	2112	7308	16
														0	10	934	944	944	17
235	1	1442	13	1	14	144	15		534	7	280	35		21150	1064	7944	9010	30160	18
182		4	26		30	1			47					410	172	229	401	811	19
135	141	28	99	157	181	86	62	20	169	117	186	21	157	1495	99	334	433	1928	20
152	58			2606					3					1292	77	6	83	1375	21
106				1276										239	41	0	41	280	22
128	19		26	2	80	17	756	15	28		22	40	12	489	8	389	397	886	23
216	257	120	24	44	42	87	368	10	171	44	91	26	10	2438	646	19031	19676	22114	24
62	3809							29	80	845			41	778	27	228	255	1033	25
401	114	8	68	6	977	224	77	48	419		535	60	578	1286	10	924	933	2219	26
85	6		11	7	27	28	3434		124	301	352			911	0	−15	−15	896	27
373	211	203		231	52		101	415	78	107	101	414	100	3365	0	4964	4964	8329	28
10				3439	17			39			9	22	152	643	0	0	0	643	29
4136	498	6524	33	728	655	38	469	1225	530	141	25	745	5	61322	7652	82835	90483	151805	
6678	936	27269	748	1716	1043	249	867	19414	985	2201	112	8329	58						
630	8	2890	64	213	331	30	18	0	48	19	785	0	586						
7308	944	30160	817	1929	1374	280	885	19441	1033	2220	897	8329	644						

TABLE 8.8. INPUT-OUTPUT TABLE FOR
$$\begin{pmatrix} a_{ij} \times 10^4 \\ \text{Row and Column Totals} \end{pmatrix}$$

Coefficients (a_{ij})

		1	2	3	4	5	6	7	8	9	10	11	12	13	14	15	16
1	Apparel	149					55					29					
2	Shipbuilding		1120										19	30			
3	Leather and products	143		3037					8	9				1		17	3
4	Processed foods				451		31					4			1		81
5	Fishing			102	723												2102
6	Grain mill products				403		65										
7	Transport	43	102	78	25	246	4	286	99	52	97	39	73	68	97	134	56
8	Industry n.e.c.	54	1	3					199	1		4	58	11			
9	Transport equipment		3							2087			7				
10	Rubber products			226						135	10		27	22	13	3	
11	Textiles	3881	12	337			31		31	75	1007	4296	44	25	20	298	12
12	Machinery		328					10		91		8	1158	24	2	1	
13	Iron and steel	54	1735	108	47	36			175	443	10		1232	2283	141	258	199
14	Nonmetallic mineral products		16	3	49	2				20			158	22	474	34	20
15	Lumber and wood products	6	244	13	65				214	104		1	141	102	173	1839	21
16	Chemicals	12	86	318	596	99		24	381	79	480	204	82	78	195	117	1972
17	Printing and publishing																1
18	Agriculture and forestry	80	1	1092	2918		9313			2	1556	1673		3	21	1999	830
19	Nonmetallic minerals		8		46					1			3	68	962	1	125
20	Petroleum products	20	45	28	36	352	10	228	46	74	98	53	56	54	361	46	177
21	Nonferrous metals		205	11	9				592	138			954	512	7	1	35
22	Metal mining												832				9
23	Coal products	4	10	5	3				8	11		1	9	173	30	2	27
24	Trade	226	357	406	136	155	20	254	518	271	509	205	380	314	507	231	296
25	Paper and products	36	2	79	91		134		122	13	118	53	94	61	300	57	423
26	Electric power	24	72	36	57			13	46	69	68	38	47	189	217	66	158
27	Coal mining	4	17	7	16	33	3	127		26	10	18	9	70	316	4	49
28	Services	161	97	298	94	229	37	388	778	209	597	265	86	114	103	43	84
29	Petroleum and natural gas																
30	Interindustry total (U_j)	246	190	241	1437	80	283	526	42	134	50	509	246	422	94	419	868
31	Total production (X_j)	502	427	390	2494	696	292	3948	131	343	102	739	531	835	238	813	1299
32	Imports (M_j)	2	888	80	94	7	36	0	62	128	37	567	474	461	68	37	258
33	Total supply (Z_j)	504	1315	470	2588	703	328	3948	193	471	139	1306	1005	1296	306	850	1557

THE NORWEGIAN ECONOMY, 1950

in Million Kroner)

				Coefficients (a_{ij})									Total Inter-mediate Demand	Final Demand			Total Demand	
														Exports	Do-mestic	Total		
17	18	19	20	21	22	23	24	25	26	27	28	29	30	31	32	33	34	
											21		19	0	485	485	504	1
				56							6		56	7	1252	1259	1315	2
40													130	1	339	340	470	3
	89							1			13		148	415	2025	2440	2588	4
	29										5		465	287	−49	238	703	5
	589												222	0	106	106	328	6
32	132	35	104	101	18			64	4	2600	273		349	2725	874	3599	3948	7
7				10							32		23	4	166	170	193	8
			54										72	1	398	399	471	9
											11		22	4	113	117	139	10
12	13		9	2			12	45			32		595	5	706	711	1306	11
				23							19		94	22	889	911	1005	12
5	33	67	284	86	206		14	44		126	159		504	228	564	79	1296	13
	10			189	5		6	26			24		57	14	235	249	306	14
	18	43		1			42	142			24		247	35	568	603	850	15
83	700	306	97	264	196		1	214		190	117		723	656	178	834	1557	16
2483								2			290		217	1	207	208	425	17
	148	22	3	1				1610			36		1687	55	1046	1101	2788	18
	21	7	78	116			1	50			12		77	4	32	36	113	19
19	35	60	89	91			75	246	40		31		261	0	60	60	321	20
14	19		3	4189			7	25			13		320	303	34	337	657	21
				1286				42					132	45	46	91	223	22
	15		2	181				1			14		38	0	44	44	82	23
167	190	184	539	338	97		244	204	25	53	161		544	134	1908	2042	2586	24
1038	6		1143	1			107	2466			78		506	638	46	684	1190	25
31	47	127	23	203	323	60		160			64		148	0	225	225	373	26
2	3	54	49	19	35	6228		91	75	316	3		110	4	15	19	129	27
777	112	12	39	115		239	535	140	446		1909		1262	12	2606	2618	3880	28
											—		—			—	—	29
199	448	6	16	311	8	11	268	644	22	11	1298	—	9028	5600	15118	20718	29746	
421	2031	60	26	439	87	17	2586	1156	373	32	3880	—						
4	757	53	295	218	136	65	0	34	0	97	0	—						
425	2788	113	321	657	223	82	2586	1190	373	129	3880	—						

TABLE 8.9. INPUT-OUTPUT TABLE

$$\begin{pmatrix} a_{ij} \times 10^4 \\ \text{Row and Column Totals} \end{pmatrix}$$

Coefficients (a_{ij})

		1	2	3	4	5	6	7	8	9	10	11	12	13	14	15	16
1	Apparel	1575		3	2						16		21			7	
2	Shipbuilding		155			322		75	10								
3	Leather & products	45	21	2770				1	22	9		2	7			15	3
4	Processed foods			1186	1502		458	14	24			28			5		486
5	Fishing				36	72	30		6						1		12
6	Grain mill products				258		634							2			28
7	Transport	67	126	152	213	79	570	536	110	170	154	177	131	344	547	456	279
8	Industry n.e.c.	160	120	42	8	336	2	46	587	47		25	61	42	17	18	39
9	Transport equipment		74		4		4	121	10	2128			19	20	4	22	1
10	Rubber products	16	3	135	2			60	56	319	157	12	64	3	18	20	13
11	Textiles	2752	192	250	5	729	345	8	402	150	1600	1894	26	5	86	150	64
12	Machinery	19	867		4		2	56	145	1069		32	1606	104	22	62	7
13	Iron & steel	3	914	37	154	50	24	91	337	1389	91	6	1221	3093	106	210	118
14	Nonmetallic mineral products		13	17	73			5	52	125	12	2	85	91	551	69	74
15	Lumber & wood products		178	64	30	21		5	104	50		26	103	33	46	2194	36
16	Chemicals	119	75	332	315	47	790	27	317	92	2178	742	172	88	252	98	2090
17	Printing & publishing				12			32	1			2	8	4			12
18	Agriculture & forestry	229		134	3880		4666	6	22			1830				260	901
19	Nonmetallic minerals				1		1	2	66		13		2	25	454		144
20	Petroleum products	4	37	7	16	243	7	356	14	22	46	30	19	100	223	74	157
21	Nonferrous metals		46	2	12			22	364	210		9	484	331	19	4	128
22	Metal mining												2	233	23		40
23	Coal products	1	4	1	10		4	4	8	10	6	2	17	393	187	48	86
24	Trade	279	200	159	136	118	112	159	229	70	225	302	203	519	171	139	225
25	Paper & products	41		151	148		46	6	212	31	72	54	50	37	661	11	260
26	Electric power	22	75	24	24		33	52	78	33	89	72	47	87	136	38	66
27	Coal mining	5	9	16	17		4	198	11	11	41	28	14	32	174	9	58
28	Services	216	291	243	282	333	219	506	412	147	204	146	201	147	236	310	417
29	Petroleum & natural gas						3										19
30	Interindustry total (U_j)	627	32	213	2390	7	423	522	240	971	136	594	1196	1097	161	312	778
31	Total production (X_j)	1126	93	372	3346	28	534	2186	670	1589	277	1097	2636	1914	408	740	1356
32	Imports (M_j)	8	1	4	154	3	1	26	23	2	0	16	6	4	4	20	66
33	Total supply (Z_j)	1134	94	376	3500	31	535	2212	693	1591	278	1113	2643	1918	412	760	1422

FOR THE AMERICAN ECONOMY, 1947

in 10 Million Dollars⟩

Coefficients (a_{ij})													Total Intermediate Demand	Final Demand			Total Demand	
														Exports	Domestic	Total		
17	18	19	20	21	22	23	24	25	26	27	28	29	30	31	32	33	34	
							3					2	184	26	924	950	1134	1
							2						21	10	63	73	94	2
8							3		1			5	121	7	248	255	376	3
1	12					1	8	41	2	2	33		681	124	2695	2819	3500	4
											1		15	0	16	16	31	5
	566			1							1		351	77	107	184	535	6
132	238	86	679	202	111	887	101	160	339	31	56	3	789	232	1191	1423	2212	7
49	4		7		2		37	10	2		88		203	33	457	490	693	8
1	25	97	1	5	16	8	92		21	6	130	8	528	136	927	1063	1591	9
5	31	15	1	1		2	16	13	1	1	13	1	132	17	128	145	277	10
38	22		1	1			12	88	5		7		707	103	302	405	1112	11
54	15	56		138	149	4	39	19	43	106	54	12	739	237	1766	1903	2642	12
1	23	207	111	255	202	25	56	32	36	109	5		1349	91	477	568	1917	13
	6	16	10	42	23	48	9	11	31		4		144	18	250	268	412	14
1	37	11	8	21	259		11	380	4	192	20		307	18	435	453	760	15
148	211	233	246	129	248	51	29	275	8	170	57	51	927	87	409	496	1423	16
1194			4			70	22				391		416	7	232	239	655	17
2656							13				15		2998	170	930	1100	4098	18
	10	136	9	9			25			5	1		54	4	44	48	102	19
5	110	168	952	62	89	270	48	92	208	31	21	9	332	55	323	378	710	20
22		14		3652	14		7	12	2	17	1		490	19	92	111	601	21
	31		1	1114									116	2	3	5	121	22
6		25	45	40		1702	7	13	97		59		177	3	114	117	294	23
48	347	142	9	1051	151	50	145	588	22	65	112	5	787	108	3461	3569	4356	24
1638		133	8	12		1	153	3571	8	1	16		618	16	146	162	780	25
37	14	209	31	101	358	76	91	71	887	183	79	24	265	0	181	182	447	26
3	1	42	8	19	50	1683	15	87	862	48	12		195	37	72	109	304	27
379	747	548	192	103	151	121	1472	141	163	160	1022	198	2279	18	5144	5162	7441	28
			5630			665						115	424	10	5	15	439	29
247	2030	19	557	394	16	163	1054	406	122	34	1598	18	16349	1665	21142	22708	39057	
654	4000	89	697	565	87	292	4348	717	446	304	7430	416						
1	98	13	12	36	34	1	8	64	1	0	10	23						
655	4097	102	709	601	121	294	4356	781	447	304	7440	439						

TABLE 8.10. The Inverse of the Leontief Matrix for the Japanese Economy, 1951

	1 Apparel	2 Ship-building	3 Leather	4 Proc. Foods	5 Fishing	6 Grain Mill Products	7 Transportation	8 Industry n.e.c.	9 Transport Equipment	10 Rubber	11 Textiles	12 Mach. & Elec. Equip.	13 Iron & Steel	14 Nonmet. Mineral Products
1 Apparel	1.0946	0.0005	0.0014	0.0010	0.0003	0.0040	0.0061	0.0005	0.0004	0.0006	0.0011	0.0004	0.0004	0.0006
2 Shipbuilding	0.0002	1.0003	0.0004	0.0003	0.0082	0.0002	0.0099	0.0003	0.0003	0.0003	0.0002	0.0003	0.0003	0.0005
3 Leather	0.0016	0.0006	1.5715	0.0001	0.0002	0.0005	0.0005	0.0007	0.0133	0.0006	0.0022	0.0027	0.0001	0.0001
4 Processed foods	0.0065	0.0030	0.0034	1.0841	0.0359	0.0046	0.0043	0.0055	0.0031	0.0072	0.0072	0.0029	0.0021	0.0036
5 Fishing	0.0039	0.0010	0.0015	0.0115	1.0011	0.0015	0.0009	0.0039	0.0010	0.0057	0.0050	0.0009	0.0005	0.0017
6 Grain mill products	0.0073	0.0014	0.0062	0.1041	0.0104	1.0099	0.0017	0.0038	0.0014	0.0040	0.0103	0.0012	0.0009	0.0016
7 Transportation	0.0169	0.0263	0.0422	0.0228	0.0104	0.0165	1.0279	0.0241	0.0289	0.0297	0.0162	0.0271	0.0299	0.0510
8 Industry n.e.c.	0.0187	0.0026	0.0098	0.0007	0.0004	0.0004	0.0010	1.0575	0.0011	0.0005	0.0006	0.0052	0.0005	0.0004
9 Transport equipment	0.0011	0.0010	0.0011	0.0006	0.0005	0.0006	0.0136	0.0049	1.1112	0.0010	0.0010	0.0066	0.0085	0.0011
10 Rubber	0.0167	0.0092	0.0274	0.0033	0.0169	0.0047	0.0185	0.0823	0.0663	1.0260	0.0137	0.0161	0.0049	0.0100
11 Textiles	1.0266	0.0302	0.0556	0.0093	0.1367	0.0145	0.0344	0.0076	0.0353	0.0047	1.6069	0.1617	0.0077	0.0230
12 Mach. & elec. equipment	0.0117	0.2176	0.0037	0.0022	0.0038	0.0029	0.0134	0.0766	0.0729	0.3813	0.0109	1.1617	0.0138	0.0055
13 Iron & steel	0.0204	0.6941	0.0131	0.0415	0.0264	0.0095	0.0960	0.0110	0.6188	0.0172	0.0208	0.7192	2.2549	0.0883
14 Nonmetallic mineral pro.	0.0027	0.0157	0.0033	0.0124	0.0063	0.0018	0.0047	0.0300	0.0226	0.0030	0.0031	0.0193	0.0213	1.0869
15 Lumber & wood	0.0046	0.0447	0.0043	0.0085	0.0086	0.0018	0.0151	0.0300	0.0247	0.0047	0.0042	0.0217	0.0086	0.0295
16 Chemicals	0.1633	0.0350	0.0595	0.0576	0.0291	0.0628	0.0240	0.1652	0.0356	0.2510	0.2153	0.0304	0.0143	0.0705
17 Printing	0.0025	0.0015	0.0014	0.0022	0.0010	0.0009	0.0042	0.0046	0.0016	0.0020	0.0023	0.0017	0.0011	0.0019
18 Agriculture	0.2799	0.0361	0.5384	0.2305	0.0570	0.8616	0.0263	0.0890	0.0326	0.1194	0.4269	0.0235	0.0164	0.0458
19 Nonmetallic minerals	0.0014	0.0024	0.0007	0.0017	0.0007	0.0006	0.0012	0.0045	0.0026	0.0030	0.0016	0.0040	0.0040	0.0657
20 Petroleum products	0.0066	0.0122	0.0043	0.0033	0.0465	0.0022	0.0509	0.0070	0.0122	0.0098	0.0084	0.0091	0.0115	0.0106
21 Nonferrous metal	0.0110	0.0501	0.0045	0.0054	0.0116	0.0033	0.0178	0.0854	0.0950	0.0100	0.0120	0.1481	0.0464	0.0150
22 Metal mining	0.0033	0.0231	0.0014	0.0022	0.0021	0.0012	0.0045	0.0121	0.0256	0.0040	0.0039	0.0337	0.1160	0.0057
23 Coal products	0.0064	0.0382	0.0035	0.0049	0.0031	0.0025	0.0075	0.0117	0.0681	0.0085	0.0077	0.0416	0.0292	0.0184
24 Trade	0.0670	0.0484	0.0666	0.0318	0.0246	0.0493	0.0231	0.0425	0.0132	0.0558	0.0435	0.0496	0.0621	0.0374
25 Paper	0.0305	0.0112	0.0083	0.0299	0.0073	0.0102	0.0116	0.0772	0.0179	0.0258	0.0216	0.0205	0.0061	0.0918
26 Electric light & power	0.0139	0.0192	0.0076	0.0095	0.0031	0.0065	0.0165	0.0151	0.0389	0.0143	0.0137	0.0192	0.0277	0.0307
27 Coal	0.0219	0.0430	0.0166	0.0216	0.0085	0.0068	0.0728	0.0323	0.0660	0.0332	0.0261	0.0445	0.0895	0.1626
28 Service	0.0940	0.0624	0.0592	0.0333	0.0416	0.0362	0.0958	0.0678	0.0660	0.0698	0.0858	0.0643	0.0487	0.0486
29 Crude petroleum	0.0027	0.0051	0.0018	0.0014	0.0190	0.0009	0.0220	0.0050	0.0050	0.0041	0.0035	0.0038	0.0048	0.0051
Import ratio (m_j)	0.010	0.091	0.025	0.030	0.009	0.063	0	0.022	0.044	0.001	0.003	0.017	0.003	0.003
Domestic production ratio $\left(\dfrac{1}{1+m_j}\right)$	0.990	0.917	0.976	0.971	0.992	0.941	1.000	0.978	0.958	0.999	0.997	0.983	0.997	0.997

TABLE 8.10. THE INVERSE OF THE LEONTIEF MATRIX FOR THE JAPANESE ECONOMY, 1951 (*Continued*)

	15 Lumber & Wood	16 Chemicals	17 Printing	18 Agric. & Forestry	19 Nonmet. Minerals	20 Petroleum Products	21 Nonferrous Metal	22 Metal Mining	23 Coal Products	24 Trade	25 Paper	26 Electric Light & Power	27 Coal	28 Service	29 Crude Petroleum
1 Apparel	0.0045	0.0007	0.0005	0.0020	0.0006	0.0001	0.0003	0.0006	0.0006	0.0003	0.0007	0.0020	0.0004	0.0015	0.0000
2 Shipbuilding	0.0005	0.0006	0.0003	0.0001	0.0002	0.0001	0.0002	0.0001	0.0008	0.0001	0.0005	0.0004	0.0002	0.0002	0.0000
3 Leather	0.0001	0.0002	0.0001	0.0002	0.0001	0.0000	0.0001	0.0000	0.0001	0.0001	0.0001	0.0001	0.0001	0.0005	0.0000
4 Processed foods	0.0031	0.0271	0.0064	0.0026	0.0017	0.0018	0.0020	0.0020	0.0023	0.0045	0.0037	0.0037	0.0021	0.0408	0.0005
5 Fishing	0.0015	0.0291	0.0021	0.0017	0.0007	0.0008	0.0008	0.0009	0.0009	0.0006	0.0018	0.0008	0.0008	0.0049	0.0001
6 Grain mill products	0.0059	0.0073	0.0030	0.0104	0.0008	0.0006	0.0009	0.0008	0.0010	0.0016	0.0033	0.0015	0.0011	0.0140	0.0002
7 Transportation	0.0534	0.0333	0.0305	0.0071	0.0161	0.0058	0.0213	0.0090	0.0785	0.0129	0.0513	0.0414	0.0227	0.0124	0.0020
8 Industry n.e.c.	0.0011	0.0006	0.0008	0.0002	0.0003	0.0002	0.0003	0.0003	0.0004	0.0029	0.0004	0.0006	0.0003	0.0054	0.0001
9 Transport equipment	0.0021	0.0013	0.0017	0.0003	0.0005	0.0004	0.0007	0.0005	0.0014	0.0013	0.0013	0.0014	0.0007	0.0107	0.0002
10 Rubber	0.0041	0.0093	0.0074	0.0049	0.0190	0.0032	0.0044	0.0152	0.0061	0.0069	0.0093	0.0063	0.0074	0.0042	0.0004
11 Textiles	0.0112	0.0211	0.0249	0.0104	0.0140	0.0037	0.0355	0.0098	0.0077	0.0047	0.0405	0.0089	0.0073	0.0119	0.0004
12 Mach. & elec. equipment	0.0036	0.0494	0.0104	0.0029	0.0030	0.0012	0.0026	0.0028	0.0125	0.0030	0.0042	0.0172	0.0192	0.0222	0.0007
13 Iron & steel	0.0133	0.0418	0.0262	0.0084	0.1487	0.0379	0.0330	0.1066	0.1274	0.0246	0.0410	0.0876	0.1214	0.0302	0.0388
14 Nonmetallic mineral pro.	0.0051	0.0124	0.0053	0.0020	0.0044	0.0018	0.0074	0.0026	0.0082	0.0009	0.0120	0.0054	0.0041	0.0037	0.0004
15 Lumber & wood	1.1432	0.0066	0.0052	0.0016	0.0121	0.0022	0.0036	0.0026	0.0091	0.0057	0.0110	0.0276	0.0132	0.0037	0.0003
16 Chemicals	0.0590	1.3148	0.0716	0.0738	0.0252	0.0288	0.0288	0.0330	0.0333	0.0079	0.0707	0.0231	0.0293	0.0398	0.0010
17 Printing	0.0012	0.0048	1.0072	0.0007	0.0009	0.0016	0.0013	0.0009	0.0013	0.0026	0.0141	0.0023	0.0012	0.0195	0.0005
18 Agriculture	0.5309	0.1026	0.0543	1.0400	0.0297	0.0063	0.0173	0.0194	0.0300	0.0126	0.1212	0.0327	0.0451	0.0375	0.0028
19 Nonmetallic minerals	0.0008	0.0082	0.0041	0.0006	1.0007	0.0010	0.0025	0.0006	0.0009	0.0003	0.0105	0.0007	0.0006	0.0008	0.0001
20 Petroleum products	0.0040	0.0062	0.0059	0.0019	0.0203	1.0342	0.0088	0.0046	0.0084	0.0015	0.0054	0.0074	0.0054	0.0034	0.0018
21 Nonferrous metal	0.0073	0.0396	0.0111	0.0033	0.0214	0.0022	1.3838	0.0220	0.0090	0.0022	0.0129	0.0500	0.0096	0.0101	0.0012
22 Metal mining	0.0017	0.0184	0.0025	0.0013	0.0062	0.0015	0.1387	1.0052	0.0045	0.0009	0.0031	0.0074	0.0043	0.0022	0.0011
23 Coal production	0.0030	0.0405	0.0065	0.0027	0.0191	0.0031	0.0140	0.0067	1.2531	0.0023	0.0052	0.0060	0.0075	0.0053	0.0021
24 Trade	0.0263	0.0454	0.0519	0.0186	0.0206	0.0075	0.0283	0.0145	0.0310	1.0108	0.0384	0.0299	0.0152	0.0297	0.0027
25 Paper	0.0101	0.0935	0.5530	0.0073	0.0037	0.0067	0.0077	0.0038	0.0073	0.0230	1.5496	0.0064	0.0041	0.0186	0.0006
26 Electric light & power	0.0176	0.0320	0.0171	0.0037	0.0124	0.0061	0.0207	0.0172	0.0292	0.0029	0.0274	1.0250	0.0385	0.0078	0.0053
27 Coal	0.0148	0.0722	0.0282	0.0055	0.0347	0.0086	0.0271	0.0130	0.5964	0.0048	0.0561	0.2727	1.0352	0.0111	0.0030
28 Service	0.0505	0.0913	0.1377	0.0249	0.0335	0.0335	0.0408	0.0393	0.0458	0.1188	0.0633	0.0886	0.0424	1.0903	0.0134
29 Crude petroleum	.0017	0.0027	0.0025	0.0008	0.0083	0.4235	0.0036	0.0019	0.0045	0.0006	0.0023	0.0031	0.0023	0.0014	1.0186
Import ratio (m_j)	0.004	0.043	0.009	0.311	0.121	0.241	0.036	0.844	0	0	0.052	0	0.096	0	4.902
Domestic production ratio $\left(\dfrac{1}{1+m_j}\right)$	0.996	0.958	0.992	0.763	0.892	0.806	0.965	0.542	1.000	1.000	0.951	1.000	0.913	1.000	0.169

TABLE 8.11. The Inverse of the Leontief Matrix for the Italian Economy, 1950

	1 Apparel	2 Ship Build-ing	3 Leather	4 Proc. Foods	5 Fishing	6 Grain Mill Prod-ucts	7 Trans-port	8 Indus-try n.e.c.	9 Trans-port Equip-ment	10 Rubber	11 Tex-tiles	12 Mach. & Elec. Equip.	13 Iron & Steel	14 Nonmet. Mineral Products
1 Apparel	1.0274	0.0000	0.0001	0.0000	0.0001	0.0000	0.0000	0.0000	0.0000	0.0007	0.0010	0.0000	0.0000	0.0000
2 Shipbuilding	0.0011	1.0000	0.0000	0.0000	0.0000	0.0000	0.0022	0.0013	0.0034	0.0029	0.0000	0.0004	0.0024	0.0000
3 Leather	0.0069	0.0008	1.4414	0.0007	0.0019	0.0000	0.0000	0.0028	0.0029	0.0103	0.0097	0.0314	0.0000	0.0034
4 Processed foods	0.0000	0.0017	0.1896	1.0442	0.0000	0.0000	0.0007	0.0000	0.0000	0.0000	0.0000	0.0000	0.0005	0.0000
5 Fishing	0.0059	0.0000	0.0007	0.0041	1.0000	0.0000	0.0000	0.0008	0.0009	0.0028	0.0019	0.0004	0.0300	0.0011
6 Grain mill products	0.0090	0.0007	0.0291	0.1559	0.0001	1.0252	0.0005	0.0176	0.0198	0.0097	0.0061	0.0135	0.0023	0.0314
7 Transportation	0.0057	0.0189	0.0061	0.0075	0.0000	0.0117	1.0139	0.0174	0.0413	0.0131	0.0000	0.0150	0.0014	0.0006
8 Industry n.e.c.		0.0148					0.0386	1.0254			0.0000			0.0013
9 Transport equipment		0.0035					0.0073	0.0044	1.0520		0.0001			0.0062
10 Rubber	0.0022	0.0075	0.0092	0.0004	0.0005	0.0002	0.0000	0.0102	0.0367	1.1145	0.0097	0.0048	0.0010	0.0000
11 Textiles	0.9758	0.2484	0.0064	0.0003	0.2299	0.0005	0.0009	0.0068	0.0205	0.2040	1.7425	0.0034	0.0005	0.0105
12 Mach. & elec. equipment	0.0000	0.0001	0.0525	0.0016	0.0002	0.0007	0.0002	0.3940	0.0818	0.0001	0.0000	1.1512		
13 Iron & steel	0.0028	0.4085	0.0001	0.0000	0.0120	0.0000	0.0001	0.0174	0.3927	0.0243	0.0001	0.2617	1.9130	
14 Nonmetallic mineral prod.	0.0013	0.0214	0.0159	0.0088	0.0007	0.0002	0.0159	0.0150	0.0213	0.0021	0.0009	0.0185	0.0193	1.0722
15 Lumber & wood	0.0008	0.0410	0.0028	0.0009	0.0006	0.0004	0.0167	0.0683	0.0299	0.0011	0.0012	0.0130	0.0032	0.0018
16 Chemicals	0.1424	0.0346	0.0216	0.0027	0.0281	0.0003	0.0007	0.0151	0.0592	0.2846	0.1856	0.0338	0.0500	0.0820
17 Printing		0.0186	0.1194	0.0326		0.0344	0.0004	0.0057	0.0186	0.0563	0.0008	0.0079	0.0064	0.0239
18 Agriculture	0.2026	0.0049	0.1334	0.6086	0.0463	1.0286	0.0002	0.0237	0.0352	0.0075	0.3441	0.0342	0.0106	0.1006
19 Nonmetallic minerals	0.0030	0.0206	0.0037	0.0041	0.0008	0.0011	0.0023	0.1142	0.0304	0.0393	0.0041	0.0198	0.0319	0.0415
20 Petroleum products	0.0137	0.0816	0.0076	0.0093	0.0445	0.0061	0.1535	0.0141	0.0869	0.0079	0.0174	0.0860	0.0433	0.0033
21 Nonferrous metal	0.0033	0.0107	0.0040	0.0013	0.0039	0.0006	0.0270	0.0179	0.0114	0.0031	0.0034	0.0103	0.0164	0.0015
22 Metal mining	0.0017	0.0184	0.0016	0.0005	0.0007	0.0004	0.0008	0.0144	0.0161	0.0188	0.0021	0.0140	0.0584	0.0214
23 Coal products	0.0032	0.0224	0.0035	0.0016	0.0011	0.0038	0.0403	0.0028	0.0278	0.0369	0.0035	0.0183	0.0145	0.0281
24 Trade	0.0586	0.0015	0.0519	0.0490	0.0178	0.0544	0.0418	0.0324	0.0020	0.0112	0.0524	0.0012	0.0014	0.0408
25 Paper	0.0026	0.0381	0.0069	0.0018	0.0007	0.0009	0.0344	0.0156	0.0350	0.0242	0.0031	0.0260	0.0647	0.0375
26 Electric light & power	0.0159	0.0161	0.0094	0.0053	0.0045	0.0082	0.0493	0.0255	0.0145	0.0138	0.0231	0.0117	0.0436	0.0835
27 Coal	0.0077	0.0180	0.0063	0.0042	0.0022	0.0015		0.0092	0.0216	0.0308	0.0109	0.0140	0.0202	0.0314
28 Service	0.0363	0.0074	0.0425	0.0483	0.0239	0.0497			0.0105	0.0132	0.0373	0.0074	0.0133	0.0151
29 Crude petroleum	0.0048		0.0026	0.0031	0.0138	0.0020					0.0063			
Import ratio (m_j)	0.010	0.349	0.013	0.055	0.003	0.005	0	0.079	0.019	0.443	0.025	0.136	0.102	0.049
Domestic production ratio $\left(\dfrac{1}{1+m_j}\right)$	0.990	0.741	0.988	0.948	0.997	0.995	1.000	0.927	0.981	0.693	0.976	0.880	0.908	0.953

TABLE 8.11. The Inverse of the Leontief Matrix for the Italian Economy, 1950 (*Continued*)

	15 Lumber & Wood	16 Chemicals	17 Printing	18 Agric. & Forestry	19 Non-met. Minerals	20 Petroleum Products	21 Non-ferrous Metal	22 Metal Mining	23 Coal Products	24 Trade	25 Paper	26 Electric Light & Power	27 Coal	28 Service	29 Crude Petroleum
1 Apparel	0.0001	0.0001	0.0001	0.0000	0.0000	0.0000	0.0000	0.0000	0.0000	0.0000	0.0003	0.0000	0.0000	0.0003	0.0000
2 Shipbuilding	0.0008	0.0001	0.0020	0.0000	0.0000	0.0100	0.0026	0.0036	0.0007	0.0008	0.0155	0.0002	0.0003	0.0076	0.0000
3 Leather	0.0085	0.0421	0.0086	0.0094	0.0025	0.0000	0.0000	0.0000	0.0000	0.0000	0.0000	0.0000	0.0000	0.0002	0.0000
4 Processed foods	0.0000	0.0002	0.0000	0.0290	0.0000	0.0015	0.0006	0.0010	0.0002	0.0002	0.0049	0.0001	0.0010	0.0020	0.0000
5 Fishing	0.0117	0.0076	0.0024	0.0029	0.0004	0.0036	0.0254	0.0030	0.0510	0.0007	0.0146	0.0047	0.0010	0.0014	0.0001
6 Grain mill products	0.0311	0.0182	0.0110	0.0002	0.0011	0.0002	0.0050	0.0022	0.0004	0.0003	0.0046	0.0001	0.0002	0.0002	0.0000
7 Transportation	0.0271	0.0083	0.0043		0.0002	0.0001	0.0108	0.0033	0.0001	0.0001		0.0002	0.0010	0.0014	0.0000
8 Industry n.e.c.															
9 Transport equipment															
10 Rubber	0.0014	0.0008	0.0005	0.0001	0.0000	0.0001	0.0012	0.0001	0.0019	0.0000	0.0007	0.0002	0.0000	0.0001	0.0000
11 Textiles	0.0078	0.0130	0.0463	0.0005	0.0002	0.0004	0.0010	0.0011	0.0010	0.0011	0.0846	0.0001	0.0001	0.0056	0.0000
12 Mach. & elec. equipment	0.0009	0.0001	0.0001	0.0000	0.0000	0.0000	0.0005	0.0000	0.0000	0.0000	0.0001	0.0000	0.0000	0.0000	0.0000
13 Iron & steel	0.0167	0.0059	0.0134	0.0002	0.0001	0.0002	0.0391	0.0005	0.0001	0.0001	0.0043	0.0000	0.0001	0.0000	0.0000
14 Nonmetallic mineral prod.	0.0244	0.0082	0.0030	0.0004	0.0001	0.0002	0.0064	0.0007	0.0002	0.0012	0.0056	0.0000	0.0001	0.0024	0.0000
15 Lumber & wood	1.3037	0.0022	0.0181	0.0003	0.0001	0.0001	0.0035	0.0002	0.0002	0.0020	0.0012	0.0000	0.0000	0.0003	0.0000
16 Chemicals	0.0553	1.4910	0.1980	0.0385	0.0248	0.0275	0.0786	0.1224	0.0141	0.0059	0.3224	0.0009	0.0083	0.0229	0.0003
17 Printing			1.0000									0.0002	0.0000		
18 Agriculture	0.4500	0.0674	0.0504	1.1842	0.0036	0.0070	0.0090	0.0208	0.0054	0.0023	0.1145	0.0012	0.0046	0.0115	0.0000
19 Nonmetallic minerals	0.0041	0.0260	0.0057	0.0012	1.0005	0.0028	0.0050	0.0050	0.0004	0.0003	0.0110	0.0001	0.0002	0.0007	0.0000
20 Petroleum products	0.0132	0.0243	0.0268	0.0042	0.0099	1.0157	0.0253	0.0103	0.0157	0.0026	0.0266	0.0126	0.0027	0.0031	0.0015
21 Nonferrous metal	0.0056	0.0269	0.0115	0.0007	0.0005	0.0005	1.2491	0.0022	0.0003	0.0001	0.0066	0.0000	0.0002	0.0004	0.0000
22 Metal mining	0.0012	0.0171	0.0031	0.0004	0.0003	0.0007	0.1220	1.0014	0.0002	0.0001	0.0038	0.0001	0.0004	0.0003	0.0000
23 Coal products	0.0029	0.0199	0.0066	0.0007	0.0030	0.0053	0.0108	0.0110	1.0806	0.0020	0.0078	0.0046	0.0015	0.0049	0.0001
24 Trade	0.0446	0.0347	0.0399	0.0153	0.0031	0.0003	0.0088	0.0009	0.0413	1.0017	0.0308	0.0046	0.0015	0.0042	0.0001
25 Paper	0.0038	0.0101	0.4126	0.0005	0.0002	0.0014	0.0120	0.0250	0.0136	0.0090	1.0904	0.0308	0.0071	0.0050	0.0001
26 Electric light & power	0.0102	0.0598	0.0380	0.0029	0.0074	0.0036	0.1007	0.0055	0.3677	0.0058	0.0584	1.0006	0.0302	0.0076	0.0052
27 Coal	0.0054	0.0219	0.0114	0.0008	0.0025	0.0014	0.0120	0.0060	0.0161	0.0011	0.0213	0.0001	1.0049	0.0024	0.0002
28 Service	0.0497	0.0598	0.0378	0.0259	0.0015	0.0239	0.0117	0.0033	0.0098	0.0440	0.0281	0.0118	0.0020	1.0451	0.0011
29 Crude petroleum	0.0043	0.0091	0.0089	0.0013	0.0031	0.3108	0.0098	0.0033	0.0098	0.0008	0.0096	0.0060	0.0028	0.0010	1.0005
Import ratio (m_j)	0.075	0.094	0.009	0.106	0.085	0.124	0.317	0.122	0.021	0	0.049	0.009	7.026		10.136
Domestic production ratio $\dfrac{1}{1+m_j}$	0.930	0.914	0.991	0.904	0.922	0.890	0.759	0.891	0.980	1.000	0.953	0.991	0.125		0.090

TABLE 8.12. THE INVERSE OF THE LEONTIEF MATRIX FOR THE AMERICAN ECONOMY, 1947

	1 Apparel	2 Ship Building	3 Leather	4 Proc. Foods	5 Fishing	6 Grain Mill Products	7 Transport	8 Industry n.e.c.	9 Transport Equipment	10 Rubber	11 Textiles	12 Mach. & Elec. Equip.	13 Iron & Steel	14 Nonmet Mineral Products
1 Apparel	1.1853	0.0001	0.0005	0.0003	0.0000	0.0001	0.0006	0.0001	0.0025	0.0000	0.0001	0.0001	0.0001	0.0000
2 Shipbuilding	0.0002	1.0158	0.0003	0.0005	0.0298	0.0008	0.0080	0.0002	0.0017	0.0003	0.0003	0.0003	0.0006	0.0006
3 Leather	0.0736	0.0033	1.3782	0.0002	0.0003	0.0002	0.0003	0.0033	0.0020	0.0003	0.0005	0.0013	0.0019	0.0001
4 Processed foods	0.0163	0.0020	0.1951	1.1770	0.0017	0.0692	0.0027	0.0071	0.0032	0.0180	0.0130	0.0026		0.0039
5 Fishing	0.0002	0.0001	0.0008	0.0042	1.0065	0.0008	0.0001	0.0007	0.0001	0.0004	0.0002	0.0001	0.0001	0.0001
6 Grain mill products	0.0100	0.0008	0.0145	0.0692	0.0016	1.1149	0.0004	0.0020	0.0012	0.0072	0.0205	0.0007	0.0007	0.0009
7 Transport	0.0271	0.0275	0.0390	0.0537	0.0147	0.0972	1.0628	0.0237	0.0464	0.0372	0.0402	0.0337	0.0683	0.0727
8 Industry n.e.c.	0.0229	0.0154	0.0080	0.0035	0.0337	0.0032	0.0064	1.0621	0.0100	0.0030	0.0052	0.0099	0.0081	0.0034
9 Transport equipment	0.0028	0.0121	0.0030	0.0060	0.0017	0.0071	0.0177	0.0037	1.2734	0.0027	0.0036	0.0056	0.0071	0.0037
10 Rubber	0.0047	0.0021	0.0201	0.0032	0.0007	0.0037	0.0073	0.0068	0.0432	1.0174	0.0034	0.0086	0.0016	0.0030
11 Textiles	0.4043	0.0268	0.0492	0.0081	0.0843	0.0521	0.0038	0.0540	0.0354	0.2037	1.2339	0.0075	0.0028	0.0138
12 Mach. & elec. equipment	0.0065	0.1097	0.0027	0.0047	0.0051	0.0052	0.0116	0.0216	0.1686	0.0033	0.0074	1.1974	0.0227	0.0059
13 Iron & steel	0.0076	0.1595	0.0172	0.0334	0.0149	0.0155	0.0229	0.0598	0.2924	0.0226	0.0088	0.2195	1.4600	0.0238
14 Nonmetallic mineral prod.	0.0015	0.0048	0.0053	0.0105	0.0008	0.0027	0.0015	0.0076	0.0223	0.0043	0.0020	0.0140	0.0094	1.0591
15 Lumber & wood	0.0047	0.0264	0.0157	0.0100	0.0046	0.0062	0.0024	0.0172	0.0139	0.0045	0.0077	0.0188	0.0238	0.0126
16 Chemicals	0.0674	0.0202	0.0829	0.0735	0.0176	0.1415	0.0101	0.0541	0.0417	0.3024	0.1276	0.0363	0.0040	0.0438
17 Printing	0.0038	0.0029	0.0041	0.0070	0.0023	0.0062	0.0070	0.0037	0.0030	0.0037	0.0041	0.0040	0.0054	0.0030
18 Agriculture	0.1587	0.0115	0.1540	0.6442	0.0248	0.7654	0.0048	0.0282	0.0166	0.0985	0.3350	0.0087	0.0049	0.0118
19 Nonmetallic minerals	0.0012	0.0010	0.0016	0.0022	0.0006	0.0028	0.0005	0.0081	0.0025	0.0052	0.0020	0.0021	0.0239	0.0491
20 Petroleum products	0.0072	0.0093	0.0079	0.0151	0.0266	0.0178	0.0427	0.0068	0.0122	0.0153	0.0131	0.0095	0.0769	0.0334
21 Nonferrous metal	0.0038	0.0250	0.0042	0.0062	0.0036	0.0048	0.0067	0.0629	0.0696	0.0077	0.0042	0.1008	0.0422	0.0065
22 Metal mining	0.0008	0.0065	0.0012	0.0017	0.0008	0.0014	0.0013	0.0082	0.0144	0.0025	0.0012	0.0161	0.0705	0.0040
23 Coal products	0.0018	0.0092	0.0026	0.0044	0.0013	0.0533	0.0022	0.0053	0.0173	0.0054	0.0025	0.0143	0.0900	0.0261
24 Trade	0.0578	0.0378	0.0396	0.0473	0.0184	0.0503	0.0215	0.0419	0.0419	0.0449	0.0558	0.0509	0.0145	0.0311
25 Paper	0.0183	0.0056	0.0417	0.0327	0.0038	0.0183	0.0046	0.0387	0.0157	0.0270	0.0181	0.0158	0.0197	0.1079
26 Electric light & power	0.0091	0.0129	0.0077	0.0077	0.0025	0.0096	0.0084	0.0133	0.0126	0.0162	0.0132	0.0122	0.0207	0.0205
27 Coal	0.0043	0.0053	0.0058	0.0057	0.0013	0.0054	0.0225	0.0051	0.0089	0.0101	0.0070	0.0073	0.0502	0.0275
28 Service	0.0670	0.0512	0.0721	0.1070	0.0459	0.1148	0.0679	0.0662	0.0478	0.0607	0.0673	0.0474	0.0183	0.0479
29 Crude petroleum	0.0043	0.0059	0.0048	0.0090	0.0151	0.0106	0.0246	0.0043	0.0082	0.0096	0.0078	0.0064		0.0207
Import ratio (m_j)	0.007	0.005	0.010	0.046	0.110	0.002	0.012	0.034	0.001	0.001	0.015	0.002	0.002	0.010
Domestic production ratio $\left(\dfrac{1}{1+m_j}\right)$	0.993	0.995	0.990	0.956	0.901	0.998	0.988	0.967	0.999	0.999	0.985	0.998	0.998	0.991

TABLE 8.12. THE INVERSE OF THE LEONTIEF MATRIX FOR THE AMERICAN ECONOMY, 1947 (*Continued*)

	15	16	17	18	19	20	21	22	23	24	25	26	27	28	29
	Lumber & Wood	Chemicals	Printing	Agric. & Forestry	Non-met. Minerals	Petroleum Products	Non-ferrous Metal	Metal Mining	Coal Products	Trade	Paper	Electric Light & Power	Coal	Services	Crude Petroleum
1 Apparel	0.0010	0.0001	0.0000	0.0001	0.0001	0.0000	0.0001	0.0000	0.0000	0.0004	0.0001	0.0001	0.0000	0.0003	0.0000
2 Shipbuilding	0.0005	0.0005	0.0002	0.0004	0.0001	0.0006	0.0004	0.0001	0.0009	0.0003	0.0003	0.0003	0.0001	0.0001	0.0000
3 Leather	0.0028	0.0006	0.0013	0.0002	0.0001	0.0001	0.0002	0.0001	0.0001	0.0006	0.0003	0.0002	0.0001	0.0010	0.0010
4 Processed foods	0.0025	0.0705	0.0037	0.0099	0.0020	0.0025	0.0023	0.0015	0.0015	0.0023	0.0101	0.0008	0.0017	0.0053	0.0005
5 Fishing	0.0001	0.0017	0.0001	0.0002	0.0001	0.0001	0.0001	0.0000	0.0000	0.0000	0.0001	0.0000	0.0000	0.0001	0.0000
6 Grain mill products	0.0035	0.0171	0.0008	0.0839	0.0005	0.0006	0.0006	0.0004	0.0003	0.0004	0.0017	0.0001	0.0004	0.0007	0.0001
7 Transport	0.0683	0.0522	0.0245	0.0463	0.0146	0.0822	0.0425	0.0007	0.1191	0.0156	0.0337	0.0445	0.0081	0.0107	0.0010
8 Industry n.e.c.	0.0040	0.0068	0.0073	0.0027	0.0012	0.0012	0.0032	0.0007	0.0015	0.0061	0.0029	0.0009	0.0007	0.0112	0.0003
9 Transport equipment	0.0062	0.0040	0.0020	0.0082	0.0125	0.0029	0.0050	0.0025	0.0041	0.0151	0.0028	0.0043	0.0016	0.0190	0.0014
10 Rubber	0.0037	0.0030	0.0014	0.0053	0.0021	0.0009	0.0012	0.0005	0.0013	0.0026	0.0176	0.0007	0.0005	0.0024	0.0003
11 Textiles	0.0252	0.0131	0.0096	0.0096	0.0015	0.0010	0.0018	0.0011	0.0010	0.0035	0.0057	0.0012	0.0010	0.0032	0.0002
12 Mach. & elec. equipment	0.0121	0.0048	0.0060	0.0055	0.0090	0.0026	0.0290	0.0142	0.0054	0.0085	0.0135	0.0082	0.0139	0.0106	0.0017
13 Iron & steel	0.0439	0.0290	0.0010	0.0107	0.0326	0.0210	0.0664	0.0262	0.0127	0.0144	0.0031	0.0112	0.0205	0.0083	0.0008
14 Nonmetallic mineral prod.	0.0101	0.0111	0.0010	0.0019	0.0025	0.0019	0.0084	0.0027	0.0067	0.0018	0.0677	0.0041	0.0009	0.0012	0.0001
15 Lumber & wood	1.2734	0.0105	0.0134	0.0079	0.0032	0.0021	0.0098	0.0246	0.0057	0.0037	0.0539	0.0035	0.0252	0.0043	0.0002
16 Chemicals	0.0237	1.2666	0.0334	0.0505	0.0298	0.0394	0.0320	0.0247	0.0160	0.0087	0.0065	0.0057	0.0233	0.0123	0.0066
17 Printing	0.0032	0.0064	1.1391	0.0066	0.0031	0.0024	0.0046	0.0011	0.0021	0.0159	0.0215	0.0015	0.0012	0.0500	0.0010
18 Agriculture	0.0561	0.1968	0.0097	1.4165	0.0054	0.0067	0.0062	0.0050	0.0034	0.0038	0.0044	0.0017	0.0050	0.0078	0.0012
19 Nonmetallic minerals	0.0010	0.0150	0.0012	0.0022	1.1126	0.0016	0.0023	0.0005	0.0007	0.0004	0.0184	0.0004	0.0009	0.0004	0.0013
20 Petroleum products	0.0156	0.0285	0.0057	0.0208	0.0191	1.1088	0.0164	0.0096	0.0423	0.0075	0.0052	0.0282	0.0054	0.0042	0.0004
21 Nonferrous metal	0.0050	0.0264	0.0065	0.0026	0.0053	0.0025	1.5301	0.0046	0.0096	0.0037	0.0011	0.0022	0.0011	0.0030	0.0002
22 Metal mining	0.0017	0.0084	0.0010	0.0007	0.0041	0.0010	0.1012	1.0012	0.0007	0.0008	0.0042	0.0005	0.0017	0.0006	0.0012
23 Coal products	0.0101	0.0150	0.0021	0.0015	0.0051	0.0075	0.0113	0.0022	1.2055	0.0021	0.0882	0.0138	0.0103	0.0017	0.0006
24 Trade	0.0266	0.0460	0.0250	0.0552	0.0186	0.0062	0.1628	0.0151	0.0119	1.0208	0.0138	0.0058	0.0020	0.0163	0.0012
25 Paper	0.0064	0.0533	0.2799	0.0066	0.0206	0.0041	0.0104	0.0023	0.0027	0.0285	1.4945	0.0027	0.0213	0.0166	0.0012
26 Electric light & power	0.0079	0.0133	0.0083	0.0054	0.0223	0.0070	0.0245	0.0296	0.0161	0.0127	0.0027	1.1004	0.0075	0.0110	0.0006
27 Coal	0.0056	0.0131	0.0046	0.0026	0.0074	0.0049	0.0092	0.0072	0.2071	0.0040	0.0154	0.0987	1.0075	0.0032	0.0028
28 Service	0.0601	0.0909	0.0618	0.1337	0.0624	0.0456	0.0539	0.0098	0.0339	0.1717	0.0473	0.0276	0.0239	1.1226	0.0004
29 Crude petroleum	0.0095	0.0195	0.0034	0.0119	0.0112	0.6264	0.0101	0.0056	0.1046	0.0044	0.0108	0.0169	0.0032	0.0025	1.0118
Import ratio (m_j)	0.027	0.049	0.001	0.024	0.150	0.017	0.064	0.392	0.004	0.002	0.089	0.001	0.001	0.001	0.056
Domestic production ratio $\left(\dfrac{1}{1+m_j}\right)$	0.974	0.954	0.999	0.976	0.870	0.983	0.940	0.718	0.996	0.998	0.918	0.999	1.000	0.999	0.947

TABLE 8.13. RATIOS OF INTERINDUSTRY USE

	A Ratio to Total Production (u_j)				B Ratio to Total Demand (w_i)			
Sector	Japan	Italy	U.S.A.	Norway	Japan	Italy	U.S.A.	Norway
1	78.9	66.0	55.5	49.0	16.5	3.0	16.2	3.8
2	64.6	74.8	34.0	44.6	5.9	0	22.4	4.3
3	82.4	58.4	57.3	61.9	47.1	31.8	32.1	27.7
4	44.3	67.8	71.4	57.6	16.9	7.1	19.4	5.7
5	25.3	23.3	23.5	11.5	13.7	34.6	48.8	66.2
6	94.4	95.2	79.2	97.0	13.0	48.6	65.6	67.7
7	34.6	33.5	23.9	3.9	24.2	17.5	35.7	8.8
8	48.1	46.4	35.9	32.2	20.3	10.3	29.3	11.9
9	65.2	54.3	61.1	39.1	22.1	4.9	33.2	15.3
10	50.6	54.8	48.9	49.3	56.2	39.7	47.6	15.8
11	78.1	73.6	54.1	68.9	49.5	57.5	63.6	45.6
12	63.4	44.8	45.4	46.4	32.9	22.4	28.0	9.4
13	70.4	70.1	57.3	50.6	74.8	88.2	70.4	38.9
14	52.2	48.7	39.4	39.4	30.7	25.1	35.0	18.6
15	68.2	71.6	42.1	51.5	29.6	43.1	40.4	29.1
16	61.2	61.9	57.3	66.8	70.0	71.1	65.2	46.4
17	55.4	53.2	37.7	47.2	28.8	0	63.6	51.1
18	17.5	23.9	50.8	22.1	73.5	70.1	73.2	60.5
19	25.7	4.4	21.7	9.2	51.8	50.6	52.7	68.1
20	62.6	42.4	79.9	60.1	79.3	77.5	46.8	81.3
21	50.2	62.8	69.7	70.9	66.9	94.0	81.5	48.7
22	30.9	15.1	18.2	7.6	98.0	85.4	95.9	59.2
23	76.3	54.1	55.9	11.1	84.3	55.2	60.3	46.3
24	16.1	6.3	24.3	10.4	20.0	12.6	18.1	21.0
25	62.8	53.8	56.6	55.7	80.2	75.3	79.2	42.5
26	47.6	6.4	27.4	5.9	58.9	58.0	59.4	39.7
27	25.5	22.1	11.3	10.5	97.3	101.6	64.3	85.3
28	25.1	9.0	21.5	33.5	32.0	40.4	30.6	32.5
29	32.7	8.8	4.3		94.9	99.9	96.5	
Average*	48.7	43.8	42.6	36.4	46.1	41.1	41.9	30.4

* The average is based on the total intermediate transactions and hence represents a weighted average of the sector measures.

BASIC DATA

United States
U.S. Department of Labor, Bureau of Labor Statistics, *The Interindustry Flow of Goods and Services, 1947,* and *Industry Classification Manual, 1950.*
Italy
Chenery, H. B., P. G. Clark, and V. Cao-Pinna, *The Structure and Growth of the Italian Economy,* 1953.
Japan
Government of Japan, Ministry of International Trade and Industry, Research and Statistics Division, *Interindustry Analysis for the Japanese Economy,* 1957 (in Japanese).
Norway
Government of Norway, Central Bureau of Statistics, *Input-Output Table for 1951* (unpublished).

BIBLIOGRAPHY

Cao-Pinna, V. "Principali Caratteristiche Structurali di Due Economie Mediterranee: Spagna e Italia," *Economia Internazionale,* XI, No. 2, 3–55, (May 1958).

Chenery, H. B., and K. S. Kretschmer, "Resource Allocation for Economic Development," *Econometrica,* XXIV, No. 4, 365–399 (October 1956).

Chenery, H. B., and T. Watanabe, "International Comparisons of the Structure of Production," *Econometrica,* XXVI, No. 4, 487–521 (October 1958).

Clark, C., *The Conditions of Economic Progress,* Macmillan and Company, London, second edition, 1951.

Leontief, W. (1953a), "Structural Change," in *Studies in the Structure of the American Economy,* 1953.

Rasmussen, P. N., *Studies in Inter-Sectoral Relations,* 1956, Chapter 8.

chapter 9

Structural analysis

A. Nature of Structural Analysis

Many of the existing applications of the interindustry approach come under the heading of "structural analysis," which may be defined as the study of the properties of an economic model, in contrast to its use in making projections and predictions. Since an interindustry model involves a large number of empirically estimated structural relations whose individual significance is not intuitively obvious, there is considerable interest in working out the effects of changes in one or more of its parameters on the outputs of all sectors of the economy. Most commonly the initial change affects some of the elements of final demand, with the other elements and the structural parameters held constant, but the effects of changes in input coefficients, in import proportions, or in the prices of primary factors can be analyzed in a similar way. In comparison with other fields of econometrics, this sort of application is analogous to calculating the *ceteris paribus* price elasticity of demand for cotton, or the *ceteris paribus* income elasticity of U.S. imports, or the *ceteris paribus* consumption multiplier. What structural analysis within the interindustry framework should provide is greater detail in the results of such calculations, and the

232

ability to take into account changes in the composition of the aggregates used in other methods.

From the standpoint of interindustry method, this sort of application consists logically in various ways of studying the inverse matrix. It is true that some interesting structural insights can be obtained simply by examination of the basic input-output table, as illustrated in the last chapter, but straightforward study of the basic table cannot trace out more than one or two links in the chain of indirect demands connecting various industries. A satisfactory structural analysis must therefore be based on an interindustry solution. In practice the solution may be partial and iterative, but its logic is that of the inverse matrix.

The inverse matrix[1] sets forth in each cell the total direct and indirect demand on industry i generated by a unit of final demand for industry j. If you wish to study the ultimate impact of demand for a commodity on all industries, you read down the appropriate column. If you are interested in a composite structural analysis, involving a particular cluster of final demands, you can do this by multiplying the columns by appropriate weights. If you wish to examine the effects of all final demands upon the sales of industry i (a "marketing analysis"), you read across the appropriate row. Each of the illustrative applications of structural analysis described in this chapter can be readily interpreted as a study of the inverse matrix along one of these lines.

It should be noted that in the nature of structural analysis there is not likely to be any direct test of accuracy. Just as for other econometric calculations using a *ceteris paribus* assumption, it is impossible to experiment with the economy to reproduce the assumed initial changes in parameters under study. The credibility of structural analyses must therefore depend in part on subjective judgment that interindustry exchanges are important for the question under study (or even that there is no practicable alternative approach), and in part on extension from general tests involving actual changes in all parts of the economy, of the kind discussed in Chapter 6.

B. Individual Industries

Studies of the role of individual industries in a national economy are the most common kind of structural analysis. In the U.S., Leon-

---

[1] See the Appendix to Chapter 2 for an exposition of the nature of the inverse. Three actual inverses are found in the Appendix to Chapter 8.

tief's first application of his open model was a calculation of the different amounts of employment throughout the economy supported by final demands on individual industries (Leontief, 1951). In Italy, Cao-Pinna has calculated the repercussions on all other industries of declining textile exports from 1950 to 1952 (Cao-Pinna, 1956). In Norway, Sevaldson has suggested a comparison of the interindustry effects of export industries and of domestic construction in supporting equal amounts of employment. (Sevaldson, 1956.) The UN Economic Commission for Europe has carried out a structural analysis which traces the major components of final demand in seven countries back to factor costs in individual sectors of their economies (United Nations, 1958). Analyses of individual industries, singly or in groups, seem to be one of the natural applications of interindustry research in all countries.

1. Offshore Procurement in Italy

The nature of structural analysis of individual industries can perhaps best be illustrated by examining a concrete case in some detail. The U.S. defense establishment in the fiscal years 1951–52 and 1952–53 placed contracts with Italian firms for production of specified military equipment amounting to $385 million. These contracts were of course concentrated in a small number of mechanical industries capable of producing finished military equipment. What would be the effects throughout the economy of OSP (offshore procurement) production in these individual industries? Specifically, these contracts would be paid in dollars, thus alleviating part of the deficit in the balance of payments; but production under these contracts would also require dollar imports, both extraordinary imports like components and ordinary imports of raw materials. To what extent would dollar receipts for each type of contract be offset by these necessary dollar expenditures? What particular imports should the Italian exchange authorities expect to be demanded to support the entire $385 million program? Production in the OSP industries would also call forth supporting production throughout the economy. What amounts of employment in the various Italian industries would be supported by each type of contract? These and other similar questions are questions which might be asked of an interindustry analysis —and which actually were asked in this particular case (Clark, 1953).

The analysis started with a classification of OSP contracts by industry. This was readily done for all contract types except ammunition, but here the need arose (as it so often does in interindustry applications) for a supplementary study. Ammunition had not been produced in Italy in the base year of the table, so a special tabulation of direct inputs into ammunition production had to be prepared—in this case based on cost estimates included in OSP bids. These direct inputs could then be added to the basic table to provide, in effect, a new industry column.

The next major step was to calculate the total production throughout the economy resulting from final output of each of the five OSP industries—ships, aircraft, vehicles, electronics, and ammunition. Conceptually, as indicated above, this involves studying the appropriate columns in the inverse matrix. Actually a separate iterative solution was calculated for one billion lire of domestic production in each of the five industries. (The matrix, consisting of 25 industries and 75 products, was specially aggregated on the principle of retaining detail for all the main import materials and their major uses.)

The import coefficients, used in each iteration to divide the demand for each material between imports and domestic production, were particularly important. These import coefficients, as well as the dollar area and employment coefficients mentioned below, were all average ratios prevailing in the most recent year available. The OSP contracts, though highly important to the economy, still constituted only a small fraction of the normal annual increase in final demands, so any deviations of marginal requirements from recent average requirements would depend primarily on these other final demands. (Chapter 10 gives an analysis embracing all final demands and hence requiring explicit recognition of possible divergence between marginal and average import requirements.)

The main features of the five iterative solutions are summarized in the following two tables. Table 9.1 sets forth the ordinary import requirements stemming from a unit of each type of OSP production. Ships have the heaviest requirements, in the order of 11%; followed by aircraft and ammunition, about 9%; and then by vehicles and electronics, about 7%. Ships, using much steel both directly and indirectly, generate relatively large import demands for scrap, iron ore, finished steel, and coal; and because of the large amount of complex machinery which they contain, also for mechanical products. Aircraft present notable import requirements for copper and for crude petroleum (because of petroleum products used in testing), but the large direct input of aluminum has little effect on imports. Ammunition production depends on significant imports of toluene and cotton linters for embodiment in propellants and explosives, of copper for shells, and of

TABLE 9.1. ORDINARY IMPORTS REQUIRED THROUGHOUT THE ITALIAN ECONOMY PER BILLION LIRE OF OSP PRODUCTION OF DIFFERENT KINDS*

Imports Required	Ships Quantity (tons)	Ships Value (mil lire)	Aircraft Quantity (tons)	Aircraft Value (mil lire)	Vehicles Quantity (tons)	Vehicles Value (mil lire)	Electronics Quantity (tons)	Electronics Value (mil lire)	Ammunition Quantity (tons)	Ammunition Value (mil lire)
Iron ore	872.7	3.7	452.0	1.9	522.7	2.2	274.7	1.1	432.9	1.8
Ferrous scrap	517.7	8.5	268.1	4.4	310.1	5.1	164.2	2.7	255.2	4.2
Ferroalloys		0.5		0.3		0.3		0.2		0.5
Finished steel prod.		4.1		2.1		2.3		1.2		2.0
Copper	66.3	18.5	64.3	17.9	36.9	10.3	72.3	20.2	50.5	14.1
Lead	2.1	0.3	1.3	0.2	1.2	0.2	14.2	2.1	0.8	0.1
Tin	62.0	7.5	41.7	4.8	40.6	4.7	29.5	3.4	37.8	4.3
Nickel	5.1	3.1	1.5	0.9	1.9	1.2	4.5	2.7	1.2	0.7
Other nonferrous		0.4		1.8		0.9		2.1		0.9
Petroleum derivatives		2.8		2.8		2.5		1.8		2.8
Crude petroleum	680.2	8.7	1,289.1	16.6	715.5	9.2	543.0	7.0	657.8	7.4
Coke and coal deriv.		1.3		0.2		0.2		0.1		0.2
Coal	1,665.1	19.2	1,196.8	13.8	1,086.3	12.5	925.9	10.6	1,065.3	14.7
Other minerals		1.7		1.8		1.3		2.4		1.4
Mechanical products		16.1		6.4		6.6		6.6		2.9
Chemicals		1.7		1.8		1.9		2.3		4.4
Toluene		—		—		—		—		5.7
Cotton linters		—		—		—		—		9.0
Building materials		1.6		0.7		1.2		2.6		0.3
Timber	431.5†	4.1	522.1†	4.9	210.7†	2.0	179.8†	1.7	566.0†	5.4
Cotton, wool, & other agric. products		1.3		2.7		2.5		0.8		1.5
Other industrial products		1.6		1.9		5.8		2.7		3.4
Total		107.0		88.1		72.9		74.3		88.7

* Value of imports and production at 1950 prices, imports CIF. A billion lire is $1,600,000.
† Thousand cubic meters.

TABLE 9.2. VALUED ADDED AND INDUSTRIAL EMPLOYMENT GENERATED THROUGHOUT THE ITALIAN ECONOMY PER BILLION LIRE OF OSP PRODUCTION OF DIFFERENT KINDS*

Employing Industry	Ships Value Added (mil lire)	Ships Employment (man-yrs.)	Aircraft Value Added (mil lire)	Aircraft Employment (man-yrs.)	Vehicles Value Added (mil lire)	Vehicles Employment (man-yrs.)	Electronics Value Added (mil lire)	Electronics Employment (man-yrs.)	Ammunition Value Added (mil lire)	Ammunition Employment (man-yrs.)
Mechanical	247.3	619		774		707		884		849
Ships										
Aircraft			442.2							
Vehicles					420.3					
Electrical	15.3		1.5		12.7		552.0		0.5	
Ammunition									522.7	
Other	137.7		57.0		24.2		20.2		25.7	
Metallurgy		213		140		133		102		116
Ferrous	174.0		90.2		104.5		54.2		86.4	
Nonferrous	28.0		42.2		21.9		42.5		23.6	
Energy		25		27		19		15		18
Electric power	60.5		52.8		39.6		36.4		35.9	
Petroleum	27.5		51.6		29.8		20.7		26.3	
Coal derivatives	13.4		8.1		7.8		5.7		9.3	
Mining	24.9	22	24.0	21	17.9	15	24.0	20	19.7	17
Chemicals	14.4	12	14.5	12	13.7	12	18.3	15	37.1	33
Other industry		52		48		79		64		50
Bldg. materials	13.5		6.4		9.6		20.5		2.9	
Lumber	11.5		13.9		5.3		4.5		14.7	
Textiles	3.1		6.3		8.2		2.7		3.3	
Other	7.3		6.2		18.6		16.9		13.1	
Agriculture	12.0	n.a.	13.9	n.a.	8.3	n.a.	7.3	n.a.	16.4	n.a.
Services	104.6	n.a.	82.3	n.a.	171.8	n.a.	99.7	n.a.	76.8	n.a.
Total	895.2	943	913.3	1,022	927.0	965	925.7	1,100	914.8	1,083

* Value added and production at 1950 prices. A billion lire is $1,600,000.

timber for wooden packaging. The import requirements for vehicles and electronic equipment are similar in several respects, but those for vehicles include relatively more ferrous materials, whereas those for electronics include relatively more nonferrous, in keeping with the difference in direct inputs into these two industries.

Table 9.2 gives the value added in domestic production and the industrial employment supported by a unit of each type of OSP production. The value added results are in part the obverse of the import results, since the higher the imports from abroad, the lower the value added in domestic production. (Except for rounding errors in the iterative solutions, the sum of imports and of domestic value added should equal the one billion lire of final demand.) The industrial breakdown of value added, however, brings out a number of distinctive structural characteristics already suggested—the importance of machinery and ferrous metals for ships, of nonferrous metals and petroleum products for aircraft, of chemicals and lumber products for ammunition, of ferrous metals for vehicles and nonferrous metals for electronics.

The employment results presented in the table depend both on the input-output solution itself and on a separate study of employment per million lire of value added. Thus the relatively low employment supported by ship contracts is due both to large import requirements and to the fact that a substantial part of domestic production is in the less labor-intensive metallurgical industries. On the other hand, ammunition contracts support relatively more employment than vehicles contracts, despite larger import requirements, because a greater share of domestic production is in the more labor-intensive mechanical industries.

The next step was to study the combined effects of the entire $385 million program. This was essentially a weighting process; the results in Tables 9.1 and 9.2 were multiplied by the appropriate value for each type of contract. For the combined import requirements there were also two important calculations to make—one to estimate the proportion of each ordinary import normally purchased in the dollar area, and the other to tabulate the extraordinary imports, which were not structurally determined but derived from the terms of particular OSP contracts.

Table 9.3 indicates that the principal ordinary imports from all currency areas (with their estimated values) would be copper, coal, scrap and other ferrous materials, crude oil, cotton linters and toluene,

TABLE 9.3. TOTAL IMPORTS REQUIRED FOR OSP PRODUCTION
OF $385 MILLION

	All Currency Areas (mil lire)	Dollar Area (thousand $)
Ordinary Imports:		
Iron ore	505.7	—
Ferrous scrap	1,175.5	808.8
Ferroalloys	107.7	29.3
Finished steel products	559.7	215.0
Copper	3,750.6	4,380.7
Lead	70.9	—
Tin	1,167.4	—
Nickel	314.6	115.8
Other nonferrous	238.7	38.3
Petroleum derivatives	650.8	978.9
Crude petroleum	2,224.9	2,491.9
Coke and coal derivatives	93.4	31.5
Coal	3,613.4	867.2
Other minerals	375.4	60.0
Mechanical products	1,444.6	624.1
Chemicals	814.6	417.0
Toluene	829.9	1,128.6
Cotton linters	1,310.4	2,012.8
Building materials	184.8	29.6
Timber	1,135.6	36.3
Cotton, wool, other agric. prod.	376.9	180.9
Other industrial products	700.8	112.0
Total Ordinary Imports	21,646.3	14,558.7
Extraordinary Imports*	11,513.8	12,274.7
Total Imports	33,160.1	26,833.4

* Incomplete tabulation, provided by the Italian government.

mechanical products, tin, and timber. Of this list, copper, cotton
linters, toluene, and crude oil would come significantly from the dollar
area. In addition, the extraordinary imports—special components,
certain materials, and invisible items like royalties and license fees—
would constitute about a third of total imports and about a half of
dollar imports. The sum of ordinary and extraordinary imports would
be about 14% of the value of the contracts, with dollar imports about
7%. Total industrial employment supported by the OSP program was

estimated, in a similar fashion, at about 225,000 man-years (170,000 in the mechanical industries, 30,000 in metallurgy, 4000 to 5000 each in energy, mining, and chemicals, and 10,000 in other industries).

So much for this analysis of offshore procurement in Italy. It illustrates the nature of a common kind of structural analysis—tracing the direct and indirect repercussions, through the interindustry matrix, of final demand on one or more individual industries, while other final demands are taken as given. Incidentally, it also points out a general feature of interindustry applications: that in order to answer particular questions the basic matrix must often be supplemented with side calculations like the estimates of dollar imports.

It is difficult to see how a structural analysis with this richness of commodity and industry detail could be accomplished without using some variant of the interindustry approach. In what other way could we estimate satisfactorily the commodity composition of import requirements, the differential import requirements of the five types of contracts, and the industrial pattern of employment? This point was emphasized in this particular case because the Italian government did attempt to obtain much the same results by a direct survey of OSP contractors. The survey was of course essential for extraordinary imports and proved to be fairly satisfactory for major embodied materials, but was unsatisfactory for energy sources and other materials. Only the inclusive framework of the interindustry approach could provide the desired detail.

2. Marketing Analyses

A rather different kind of study of individual industries is a marketing analysis. This is a study of the elements of final demand upon which sales of an industry ultimately depend. Conceptually, as already indicated, it involves examination and manipulation of the cells in a *row* of the inverse matrix (rather than a column as in the OSP example). An example is given in a monograph prepared by the Italian Steel Industry Association soon after the Italian input-output table was published, which among other things traced the ultimate use of steel both to major final demands—consumption, investment, etc.—and to individual industries supplying these final demands (Assider, 1953). A somewhat similar analysis of American agriculture is given by Heady and Schnittker (1957).

A marketing analysis is a type of application which ought to be useful for private businesses, particularly in basic industries which sell directly to other industries but of course ultimately depend on final demands. Evans (1952) has discussed possibilities along this line, and further research seems clearly called for.

C. International Trade

A country's foreign trade presents another important field for structural analysis using the interindustry approach. Imports typically consist in substantial part of raw materials, which are used directly by the various producing sectors of the economy, but which are related indirectly to consumption and other final demands via the interindustry structure. Exports can be studied as external stimuli to the industries of the domestic economy, and, in conjunction with an interindustry import analysis, as differential net contributors to a country's foreign exchange earnings. Accordingly European countries engaged in interindustry research have had a major interest in structural analyses of their international trade relationships. A fine example is the work in the Netherlands on "import quotas"—total direct and indirect import requirements of various elements of final demand, calculated with an interindustry model and then used in an aggregative model oriented toward policy decisions. (See Sandee and Schouten, 1953, and Verdoorn, 1956.)

A rather different application to an international trade question is Leontief's comparison of capital and labor requirements of U.S. exports and of domestic replacements for U.S. imports. This is a particularly interesting case because the quantitative results of the interindustry analysis contradict a common presumption about our comparative advantage in international trade. The presumption is that since the U.S. has much more capital per worker than foreign economies, our exports are dominated by relatively capital-intensive commodities, and our imports by commodities whose domestic production would be relatively labor-intensive.[2] Leontief's results indicate that this pre-

[2] The Heckscher-Ohlin theorem on factor proportions, from which this presumption is derived, states that a country in which capital is cheap relative to labor (as compared to its trading partners) will export commodities that are more capital-intensive than its imports as produced abroad. The proposition which Leontief tested (that U.S. exports should be more capital-intensive than the production in the U.S. of the commodities imported) requires an additional assumption, though a mild one, about production functions here and abroad. The assumption is that potential factor substitution in both countries is sufficiently constrained to make the *ranking* of industries by capital-intensity similar even with different capital-labor price ratios. It is not necessary to assume that factor proportions in each industry are the same here and abroad. (See Robinson, 1956, and Jones, 1957.)

sumption is false, and he himself has suggested that the opposite is true. Since the results conflict with theoretical expectations, it is not surprising that considerable controversy has been stirred up by this analysis.

From the standpoint of interindustry methods, Leontief's study involved a comparison of two structural analyses: one for the cluster of final demands making up (proportionally) $1 million of U.S. exports, and one for the cluster of domestic outputs necessary to replace (proportionally) $1 million of U.S. competitive imports. Noncompetitive imports like coffee and jute (but not rubber, which can be produced synthetically) were not considered. In order to calculate total capital and labor requirements, the 1947 input-output matrix was supplemented by separately derived employment coefficients (in man-years per dollar of output) and capital coefficients (in 1947 dollars per dollar of output).

The results of Leontief's original calculation, applying to 1947 exports and imports, are stated in Table 9.4. (See Leontief, 1953.)

TABLE 9.4. CAPITAL AND LABOR REQUIREMENTS PER MILLION DOLLARS OF U.S. EXPORTS AND IMPORT REPLACEMENTS: 1947 TRADE

	Exports	Imports
Capital (in 1947 dollars)	2,550,780	3,091,339
Labor (in man-years)	182,313	170,004

The presumption of capital-intensive exports and labor-intensive imports is clearly not supported by these data. In fact, it appears that 1947 exports embodied both less capital and more labor than import replacements. The ratio of capital per man-year in imports to capital per man-year in exports proved to be 1.30, instead of less than one. This overall analysis was supplemented by further examination of individual commodities within smaller "internally competitive" groups, leading to the same result.

Leontief himself proceeded, on the basis of these quantitative results, to suggest a rather startling hypothesis. The U.S. resorts to trade, he surmised, "to economize its capital and dispose of its surplus labor, rather than vice-versa." Economists should not assume that the relative productivity of capital and labor is the same here is abroad, but rather that with given capital a unit of American labor is equivalent to several units of foreign labor. Viewed in this way, there would be *less* capital per equivalent worker here than abroad, and the empirical results would be consistent with orthodox theory. The enhanced labor productivity in the U.S. might be due to a variety of circumstances—stronger entrepreneurship, superior organization, wider education, a production-oriented society, richer natural resources—but whatever the causes they must have raised the productivity of labor more than that of capital.

This analysis of U.S. comparative advantage was promptly attacked on two planes. (Ellsworth, 1954; Swerling, 1954; and Valavanis-Vail, 1954.) On the theoretical plane, critics asserted that given our factor supplies the capital–labor ratios in domestic industries competing with imports could be expected to be higher than in foreign industries producing the imports. Furthermore, the capital-labor ratios in import industries might even be raised above those in export industries to offset the relatively low productivity of high-wage labor there, given the existence of transport costs and artificial protection which permits these industries to survive in the U.S. (As Robinson (1956) has shown, however, this would require particular shapes of production functions in the export and import industries, such that their least-cost capital-labor input ratios would change their relative *ranking* at different capital–labor price ratios.) Critics also suggested that a more satisfactory explanation of the observed facts would be to recognize explicitly the factors other than capital and labor which affect costs, notably natural resource endowment and entrepreneurship.

On the statistical plane, critics argued that 1947 was an unsuitable year, with exports nearly three times competitive imports, and with many disorganized markets; that two of the seven leading export industries were wholesale trade and railroad transport, which do not appear at all among imports for definitional reasons;[3] that agriculture, which dominated the import side, had a suspiciously high capital coefficient and an unreliable labor coefficient; and that all of the seven leading import industries were natural resource industries.

Leontief (1956) subsequently undertook twelve additional comparative-advantage calculations along the same lines. He did not contest the theoretical points (and indeed expanded on some of them, e.g., the fact that his data were limited to the U.S. economy), but rather kept his emphasis on the empirical calculation, the surprising results,

---

[3] In the U.S. table commodities are stated at producer's value, so transportation and trade margins on commodities which are exported are listed as separate exports. Imports, however, are valued c.i.f.

and the need for further work to provide adequate means of testing unsettled issues. He did attempt to meet the statistical points, however, by using 1951 trade as well as 1947 (though 1951 would hardly qualify as "normal"!), and by preparing alternate calculations omitting services, agriculture, or natural resource industries. A new methodological feature was that in four of the calculations the input coefficients included replacement of capital stock according to depreciation, to approximate more closely a long-run equilibrium situation.

TABLE 9.5. Capital and Labor Requirements per Million Dollars of U.S. Exports and Import Replacements: Additional Calculations for 1951 Trade*

Nature of Calculation		Capital (10^4 1947 \$)	Labor (10^3 Man-yrs)	Ratio, C/L imports ÷ C/L exports
A. All 192 sectors Capital replacement included	Exports Imports	225.68 230.34	173.91 167.81	1.0577
C1. 164 non-service sectors (aggreg. to 50 for indirect demands)	Exports Imports	214.10 230.59	167.61 160.46	1.1112
C4. 154 non-service, non-ag. sectors (aggreg. to 50 for indirect demands)	Exports Imports	156.22 186.82	168.77 150.51	1.3410
D. 173 nonresource sectors. Capital replacement included	Exports Imports	257.71 209.27	224.23 206.61	0.8813

* All calculations use the 1947 matrix, however.

The most revealing of these additional calculations are indicated along with their results in Table 9.5. Calculation A shows that when 1951 trade is studied, and allowance is made for capital replacement, the relatively higher capital–labor ratio for import replacements is still observed, but in much smaller degree than for 1947 trade. Calculations C1 and C4 show that neither omitting services nor omitting services and agricultural products alters the qualitative character of the result. On the other hand, calculation D reveals that omitting resource industries *does* alter the results, giving the remaining import replacements a relatively lower capital–labor ratio than the remaining exports.

The present authors feel that these additional analyses of U.S. comparative advantage still leave us with a rather surprising result: that the presumption of capital-intensive exports and labor-intensive imports is not empirically sustained. The data might be interpreted cautiously as showing no significant difference between exports and imports taken as a whole. The results are more orthodox when resource industries are omitted. But the net effect of this empirical study is still striking. Our main inference would be that the common explanation of comparative advantage in terms of only the two factors, capital and labor, is oversimplified, and that theory should place considerable emphasis on the limitational role of natural resources, and possibly on economies of scale and the importance of rapid innovation.[4]

This case also illustrates two points about interpreting interindustry analyses. In the first place, the inference should be kept logically distinct from the quantitative calculations. Some inferences may be wholly based on the calculations, while other often broader inferences may depend on additional observations or guesses as well. In this case Leontief's proposed explanation of the observed phenomena is a good deal broader than the interindustry results standing alone, and the calculations retain their validity even if this interpretation does not. The calculations have already stimulated considerable clarification of the theoretical issues they raise. In the second place, interindustry analyses from which specific inferences are to be derived should be designed *in detail* to provide an appropriate basis. It is important, before "turning the crank" in an involved interindustry calculation, to check directly the appropriateness of the most critical coefficients for the problem at hand. In this case, because of the possible unreliability of agriculture and services coefficients, the alternate calculations omitting these sectors were particularly desirable.

Finally, it may be suggested that some version of the interindustry approach is peculiarly useful for empirical analysis of a country's comparative advantage—a field previously explored largely via hypo-

---

[4] Shishido and Komiya (1957) have applied Leontief's methodology to a comparison of factor proportions in exports and other components of final demand in Japan, with the finding that exports are the least labor-intensive component of final demand. They conclude that natural resources and technological differences must be considered explicitly to explain the pattern of Japanese trade.

thetical models and casual illustrations.[5] Traded commodities enter
the structure of a national economy in many different ways, and their
ultimate drafts on primary factors of production involve many interdependent industries. The point is further dramatized in this case by
the fact that the interindustry approach contradicted the common
presumption about U.S. comparative advantage.

D. Final Demands, Primary Factors, and Prices

Structural analysis can also be extended beyond the basic interindustry matrix to the structure of final demands, or of primary factors,
or of prices. Research in these areas is currently in an exploratory
stage, however, so that realistic applications cannot be cited. We can
only sketch briefly the nature of the analysis in each case, and refer
to essentially methodological discussions.

Analysis of the structure of prices has the longest history, since one
of Leontief's early illustrations was a price study (Leontief, 1951). If
we assume that wages rise uniformly throughout the economy, and
that each industry raises its price by just the amount of the rise in its
labor costs plus the rise in its input costs from other industries, then
the strict input-output model provides a determinate price increase
in every industry. Merely stating the necessary assumptions of this
kind of price analysis suggests that the results are not likely to be
realistic. Nonetheless, there has been considerable interest in price
applications of the interindustry approach in a number of European
countries. Recently Rasmussen (1956) has developed an interesting
methodological extension of price analysis to the terms of trade among
sectors of a national economy. Still the pressing need is for more
empirically realistic assumptions about price adjustments in individual
industries, which can only come from explicit research in price
formation.

Structural analyses of final demands and of primary factors both
involve a partial closing of the basic open model by including in the
matrix additional structural coefficients describing, e.g., marginal
propensities to consume or marginal requirements for different grades

[5] It may also be suggested that a fruitful approach would be to determine first
the relation between relative prices within a country and factor proportions. If
factor proportions explain a substantial part of variations in relative prices among
countries, then a firmer foundation will be provided for an attempt to isolate the
effects of other factors affecting trade. A promising beginning on this type of
analysis has been made by Tarshis (1959).

of labor. As discussed in Chapter 3, the expanded matrix can then be solved and studied in much the same way as the basic matrix of current input coefficients. Conrad's study (1955) of the multiplier effects of income redistribution due to government taxes and expenditures is an illustration of a possible extension of interindustry analysis to the structure of final demands. Conrad has also done research, as yet unpublished, on the occupational structure of labor within the interindustry framework. Finally, explicit consideration of the use of primary factors is an important part of studies related to economic development programs, which are taken up in the next two chapters.

BIBLIOGRAPHY

Associazione Industrie Siderurgiche Italiane (Assider), "Interdipendenza Strutturale della Siderurgia con gli Altri Settori dell'Economia Nazionale," Milan, 1953 (mimeographed).

Cao-Pinna, V., "Italy," in *The Structural Interdependence of the Economy,* 1956.

Clark, P. G., "Economic Consequences of Offshore Procurement in Italy" (unpublished analysis undertaken in the U.S. Mission to Italy), 1953.

Conrad, A. H., "The Multiplier Effects of Redistributive Public Budgets," *Review of Economics and Statistics,* XXXVII, No. 2, 160–173 (May 1955).

Ellsworth, P. T., "The Structure of American Foreign Trade: A New View Examined," *Review of Economics and Statistics,* XXXVI, No. 3, 279–289 (Aug. 1954).

Evans, W. D., "Marketing Uses of Input-Output Data," *Journal of Marketing,* XVII, No. 1, 11–21 (July 1952).

Heady, E. O., and J. A. Schnittker, "Application of Input-Output Models to Agriculture," *Journal of Farm Economics,* XXXIX, No. 3, 745–758 (August 1957).

Jones, R. W., "Factor Proportions and the Heckscher-Ohlin Theorem," *Review of Economic Studies,* XXIV, No. 1, 1–10 (1956–1957).

Leontief, W. (1951), *The Structure of the American Economy, 1919–1939,* 1951, Parts IV-A and IV-C.

————— (1953), "Domestic Production and Foreign Trade: The American Capital Position Re-Examined," *Proceedings of the American Philosophical Society,* XCVII, No. 4, 332–349 (September 1953).

————— (1956), "Factor Proportions and the Structure of American Trade: Further Theoretical and Empirical Analysis," *Review of Economics and Statistics,* XXXVIII, No. 4, 386–407 (November 1956).

Rasmussen, P. N., *Studies in Intersectoral Relations,* 1956.

Robinson, R., "Factor Proportions and Comparative Advantage," *Quarterly Journal of Economics,* LXX, No. 2, 169–192 (May 1956) and LXX, No. 3 346–363 (August 1956).

Sandee, J., and D. B. J. Schouten, "A Combination of a Macro-Economic Model and a Detailed Input-Output System," in *Input-Output Relations,* 1953.

Sevaldson, P., "Norway," in *The Structural Interdependence of the Economy,* 1956.

Shishido, S., and R. Komiya, "Applications of Input-Output Analysis in Japan," unpublished paper.

Swerling, B. C., "Capital Shortage and Labor Surplus in the United States?" *Review of Economics and Statistics,* XXXVI, No. 3, 286–289 (August 1954).

Tarshis, L., "Factor Inputs and International Price Comparisons," in *The Allocation of Economic Resources,* Stanford University Press, 1959.

United Nations, *Economic Survey of Europe in 1957,* Geneva, 1958.

Verdoorn, P. J., "Complementarity and Long-Range Projections," *Econometrica,* XXIV, No. 4, 429–450 (October 1956).

Valavanis-Vail, S., "Leontief's Scarce Factor Paradox," *Journal of Political Economy,* LXII, No. 6, 523–528 (December 1954).

chapter **10**

Projection of the economic

structure

A. Nature of Interindustry Projection

Another important type of interindustry analysis is an overall economic projection. Going beyond structural analysis, with its inherent
ceteris paribus assumption, an overall projection aims at the more ambitious goal of explicitly considering developments in all parts of the
economy. Typically such a projection is concerned with analyzing
the repercussions of major government policies or programs, such as
investment in public works and basic industries for economic development. The new final demands stemming from the government policy
provide the initial stimulus to change, but they are considered along
with all other final demands arising from the private economy.

An interindustry projection might be undertaken simply to examine the implied demands on all individual industries. More charac-
teristically, however, the feasibility of the overall projection, and thus
of the government program around which it is built, can be tested.
In the light of known limitations on certain natural resources, on
capital stock in individual industries, on labor force in particular
occupations, and on foreign exchange resources for financing imports,

can the economy support both the governmental program and the likely private demands? If the overall projection is not feasible under present conditions, where are the principal bottlenecks, which might be evaded either by altering the program or by other policies designed to expand the underlying constraints? In this chapter, we shall examine this kind of use of interindustry projections as a guide to sensible government policies.

An interindustry projection designed to test feasibility has three main parts: (a) a projection of all elements of final demand in appropriate industry detail; (b) a matrix of input coefficients and other parameters of the model; and (c) a set of constraints on the availability of particular primary factors required in production. The procedure is to take the detailed final demands, to multiply them by the matrix, thus obtaining estimates of all outputs and requirements for primary factors, and then to check these projections against the constraints. (Variations are possible, however. As indicated in Chapter 2, for some sectors it may be preferable to fix a maximum level of production and determine the availability of products for final demand from the solution.)

As already suggested, it is the final demand part which primarily distinguishes an overall projection from the structural analyses discussed in Chapter 9. The need to study all elements of final demand, in the industry detail of the basic interindustry matrix, is a considerable extension of the research. It involves, for example, study of marginal consumption demands for as many separate commodity groups as are distinguished in the matrix.

On the other hand, it is primarily the treatment of constraints which distinguishes an overall projection from the linear-programming analysis discussed in Chapter 11. In linear programming the solution itself specifies choices among alternative economic activities which take account of the resource limitations considered. Here the calculation is permitted to violate the constraints if necessary, and then the policy choices which might correct the violations are raised as a separate question. For example, if the projected demand for steel is greater than steel capacity, alternative methods of construction using more lumber and less steel are not specified in the calculation proper, but can be considered later as one means of eliminating the excess steel demand. Any large adjustments resulting from such separate policy choices can be tested in a second-approximation solution, if their feasibility remains doubtful.

National accounts analysis is of course also frequently used for testing feasibility of overall economic projections. The more elaborate interindustry approach ought to provide two significant improvements in the results. First, it should make the feasibility test more reliable by taking account of differing factor requirements of different elements in final demand, and by recognizing a larger number of specialized factor limitations. Conventional national accounts analysis, considering only the limitation of full-employment GNP, overstates the substitutability of final demand elements and of specialized resources (particularly capital equipment) in a modern economy. An interindustry analysis, it is true, can be made so detailed as to understate substitutability, but its emphasis on industrial specialization is a movement in the right direction.

Second, interindustry analysis should make the results more operational for policy purposes. Analysts of economic development programs, for example, quickly become aware of the difficulties in relating an aggregative national accounts analysis to the detailed questions which must be answered in allocating foreign exchange or distributing investment funds. Industry and product detail can help greatly in making studies meaningful in the narrower decision areas of individual government agencies and business firms.

There are a number of instances of overall economic projections in the published interindustry literature. The first major study was that of Cornfield, Evans, and Hoffenberg (1947), which examined the implications of post-war full employment in the United States. We have already discussed this projection briefly in Chapter 6. Later, Berman (1953) prepared a set of projections to 1975, illustrating various patterns of expansion of consumption, investment, or defense expenditures. In the Netherlands, Van den Beld (1954) has studied prospective long-run developments in the Dutch economy with an interindustry model. Finally, the UN Economic Commission for Latin America has made interindustry projections for Colombia (1957) and Argentina (1958), with emphasis on the import repercussions of industrial development.

For the purpose of this chapter, we shall discuss in some detail three sets of projections with which the authors have had some personal contact—in Italy, in Latin America, and in the United States.

B. The Italian Five-Year Expansion Goals

A convenient illustration of an interindustry projection is a study undertaken by the authors some years ago in Italy. This study attempted to predict the repercussions in the Italian economy of a 25% expansion of GNP over the five years from 1951 to 1956, a goal adopted at that time by the member countries of the Organization for European Economic Cooperation.   (See Chenery, Clark, and Cao-Pinna, 1953, Chapter IV. The projections used data up to the middle of 1952 in some cases.)   In addition to illustrating the detailed methodology of an interindustry projection, this example indicates concretely some of its possible substantive applications.   Since the time-period of the projection has now passed, we can also carry out in the next section an evaluation of the results.

The study listed six principal substantive questions for investigation. Let us quote them verbatim:

1. What expansion of investment and government expenditures would be required to generate adequate final demand for the OEEC goal?
2. What individual industries may be expected to have the most favorable development prospects?   [For consideration in planning investment allocations, development of the South, and productivity programs with least adverse effect on employment.]
3. What capacity limits, if any, is the economy likely to encounter?
4. What are the increases in imports which are likely to be required? [Both the total increase and its composition.]
5. What is the probable fuel balance of the Italian economy in 1956? [Primarily the consequences of substituting natural gas for imported coal.]
6. What are the probable effects upon the volume of industrial employment and the number of man-hours worked?

This group of questions was designed to test the feasibility of the OEEC goal and to derive some leading policy implications.   The variety of economic repercussions in this list is worth noting.   The interindustry approach tends to make the analyst consider many aspects of an economic process and above all to consider them in a mutually consistent way.   As compared to other methods of applied economic analysis, this tendency to ask different questions is as significant as any difference in the answers which it suggests.

The methodology of the study can be conveniently discussed in terms of the three main parts of a feasibility analysis: (a) the final demand projection, (b) the matrix of input coefficients and other parameters, (c) the constraints on availability of primary factors.

The final demand projection started with a conventional national accounts analysis.   The probable expansion of exports was estimated independently, considering recent trends and such special circumstances as the British and French import restrictions then in force. Consumption was projected on the basis of a roughly calculated marginal propensity to consume, and imports on the basis of a marginal import coefficient. (Actually, there were two approximations here; in the second approximation the marginal import coefficient was raised to check with the total detailed commodity imports indicated in the interindustry solution.) The increase in investment and government expenditures needed to provide sufficient aggregate demand for the desired GNP was then derived as a residual.

The next step was to break down these aggregated final demands among the 200 product classes distinguished in the Italian interindustry table. The considerations affecting these detailed estimates of course differed for different elements of final demand. For exports, trends for various groups of products could be studied separately. For consumption, the increases in food demands were estimated to be lower than the increases in non-food demands. For investment and government, separate projections were prepared for the defense program (assuming completion of the NATO build-up then in progress), government civil expenditures, public investment, private investment, and inventories. Within these eight major categories of final demand, however, the base-year proportions among detailed product classes were to a large extent carried forward into the projection.

Turning now to the interindustry matrix, the study followed usual input-output practice in deriving most of the input coefficients directly from the base-year table (in this case for 1950), using an unmodified proportionality assumption. A few adjustments were made, however, for technological changes already under way. For example, as a result of blast furnace expansion under the Marshall Plan, the steel industry was using more pig iron relative to scrap, and appropriate adjustments were made in these coefficients, as well as in the related input coefficients for iron ore and pyrite ashes.

A more important variation from the proportionality assumption was attempted for the major fuels. Here it was clear that a significant technological change was in progress, centered around widespread substitution of domestic natural gas for imported coal. The situation was complicated further by interrelations with fuel oil and domestic low-grade coal (lignite and Sulcis), as well as by differences in the ability of different consuming industries to make fuel substitutions. These potential fuel substitutions were treated in an auxiliary fuel balance, made consistent with the input-output projection proper by successive approximations. The input-output calculation estimated the relative expansion of fuel-consuming industries, and hence their total fuel demands in standard units of heat (bituminous coal equivalents). The auxiliary fuel analysis then estimated the economic feasibility of meeting these demands with alternative fuels, taking into account the technology of each consuming industry and any special circumstances affecting fuel supplies (e.g., the fact that natural gas pipelines would only serve the North). The resulting increases in production of the various fuels were then fed back into the input-output calculations, so that their repercussions in the remainder of the economy could be considered. Whatever the merits of this treatment of fuels in the Italian study, this general method of tying an auxiliary analysis of substitution possibilities into a central input-output model appears to offer considerable promise for making the interindustry approach more flexible.

Imports were also handled in a special way. For each of the 200 product classes in the table, a marginal import parameter, measuring the fraction of additional requirements expected to come from imports rather than domestic production, was estimated. Some of these import parameters were in fact based on the average import proportions of the base year, others on a more recent year, still others on marginal trends in imports from year to year, but in principle each was an independent estimate of import substitution possibilities for a particular product class. In addition, as explained below, for some of the product classes the import results were affected by domestic capacity constraints. (Imports of coal were also estimated separately in the auxiliary fuel balance.)

Turning now to the constraints used to check the results of the interindustry projection, a serious continuing problem for the Italian economy is limited domestic capacity in agriculture, the main sector depending on natural resources. Accordingly, 1956 capacities were estimated for eight important groups of agricultural products, based largely on trends in yields per hectare. (1956 capacities were also estimated for ferrous metals, because of the expected effect of the European Coal and Steel Community then coming into operation, and for domestic fuels, in the fuel analysis.) If demand for these products rose above domestic capacity, however, it was assumed that they could be imported. At that point in the calculation the marginal import parameter was therefore raised to 100%. In other words, this treatment implied that the ultimate agricultural constraint on achievement of the OEEC goal was the foreign exchange needed to finance supplementary imports of food and agricultural raw materials.

A second set of constraints considered was existing domestic capacities in basic industries producing materials widely used in further processing. These capacities, however, were limited primarily by existing capital equipment rather than by natural resource scarcity, and could be expanded by investment during the time-period under study. Accordingly, expected 1953 capacities were estimated for some twenty basic materials—various nonferrous metals, the pulp-paper-cellulose complex, sulphur, cement, electrical power, petroleum products, and coke and gas. These 1953 capacities were not incorporated in the input-output calculation proper. Rather they were used, after the calculation, to consider whether investment during the rest of the time-period seemed likely to be adequate.

A third type of constraint in most overall economic projections is the availability of labor. To study this limitation, two elements are needed: a set of parameters relating changes in production in the various sectors of the economy to changes in their employment demands and a separate estimate of the expansion of the labor force. In the Italian study such employment parameters were developed for the industrial sectors of the economy, taking into account both trends in productivity per man-hour and the tendency to extend hours per worker. The implied expansion of industrial employment was then checked against official estimates of prospective growth in the labor force. In Italy, however, with large continuing unemployment, there was no possibility that economic expansion would soon be constrained by availability of labor. The point of the employment analysis was rather to judge whether attainment of the OEEC goal would be sufficient to reduce significantly the long-run unemployment which already existed.

So much for the methodology of this Italian study. For our present purposes, it illustrates the steps involved in carrying through an overall interindustry projection designed to test feasibility. It also suggests a range of questions to which such an analysis may be addressed, and the possibility of treating particular parts of the economy in a flexible way. We shall now attempt to evaluate the results of this study.

C. Evaluation of the Italian Projection

Let us make clear at the beginning the nature of the evaluation we wish to undertake here. We are not attempting a test of the stability of the Italian matrix of input-output coefficients, of the kind discussed in Chapter 6. For one thing, such a test ought to be based on a re-construction of actual final demands in full interindustry detail, and we have not had the statistical resources to do so. But more important, since we have stressed the application of interindustry analysis in policy-making, a different kind of evaluation seems called for.

Accordingly, in this section we are attempting to judge the value of the complete projection as a quantitative guide for economic policy. In practical applications the input-output matrix is supplemented with other pieces of quantitative analysis—at least a final demand projection and estimates of specific resource constraints, and possibly some auxiliary analyses of nonproportional relationships (e.g., for imports) or substitution possibilities (e.g., for fuels). A policy-oriented evaluation ought to take account of the reliability of these elements as well as the matrix itself.

The criterion of evaluation is not easy to establish. Ideally we should like to compare the accuracy of results of the interindustry study with the accuracy of results from an equivalent alternative study using conventional techniques of analysis. But typically there is no equivalent alternative study. An obvious characteristic of the inter-industry approach is that it generates a wide range of results for many parts of the economy, all derived simultaneously from the same calculation. Studies based on conventional techniques are not likely to cover such a wide range, at least in part because their results are often derived from separate and independent calculations. So it is in this case. For only a few of the interindustry results do alternative conventional projections exist which might serve as a standard for comparison.[1] For most of the results, therefore, we are limited to evaluating their reliability by comparing the projections directly to the actual developments.

[1] Some alternative projections were prepared within the Italian government at about the same time, based on a combination of trend extrapolation and the judgment of industry experts. These were not published, however, and an attempt by the authors to make a relative evaluation proved inconclusive. With respect to expansion of individual industries, comparison was possible for only four of the nineteen industries in Table 10.2, below. For two industries the projections were almost identical; for a third, the conventional projection was moderately better; while for the fourth it was somewhat worse. With respect to the fuel balance, discussed in connection with Table 10.5 below, there was some indication that the conventional projection hadn't allowed sufficiently for fuel substitutions. With a similar assumption about expansion of the economy, it indicated a larger increase in *both* natural gas and coal consumption than the interindustry projection—and also more than actually occurred. But the material is too scanty to be of help for our present purpose.

Moreover, several measures of accuracy seem to be appropriate. Errors are of course to be expected, and one of our measures surely ought to be an average percentage error for each group of results. Since the projection covers several years, we should not be surprised if the average errors were large. But for effective policy guidance, it is often more important that a study provide a reliable forecast of the relative pattern of change in a group of variables than that it give an accurate forecast of the absolute change in each variable within the group. For example, in allocating limited government investment funds among industries, what is needed is a listing of industries in order of their prospective demand expansions. Accordingly, we shall also stress as another measure of reliability the rank correlation between the projections and the actual developments. Finally, large individual errors are significant as indicators of major flaws in some element of the model which was applied. We shall attempt to investigate these, at least cursorily, to indicate those features of the model most in need of improvement through future research.

Unfortunately, throughout the evaluation we are limited to summary data on the Italian economy readily available to us. Most of these data are only approximately consistent with categories in the interindustry projection. In particular, it has not been possible to reconstruct even a rough 1956 input-output table, which would be the best kind of statistical check.

It is convenient to present the results of this Italian study, and to evaluate their reliability for policy guidance, in terms of the six substantive questions to which the study was addressed, as listed earlier. The first concerned the expansion of investment and government expenditures necessary to generate adequate final demand. The conclusion on this point was that:

> Attaining the OEEC five-year expansion goal in 1956 will require an expansion of total investment and government expenditures (in relation to 1950) in the order of 41% (i.e., higher than the expansion of GNP), in addition to favorable and perhaps optimistic export developments.

The study also drew the inference that the Italian government should envision continued growth of its budget for defense and investment purposes, offsetting these expenditures by rising tax revenues resulting from economic expansion.

The projected and actual changes in Italian national accounts from 1950 to 1956 are set forth in Table 10.1. (Note that all projections in the study were from a 1950 base, the year of the input-output table.

TABLE 10.1. NATIONAL ACCOUNTS
(1956 Indexes, 1950 = 100)

	Projected Index	Actual Index
Total Final Demand		
Exports	140	157
Investments	$\Big\}$141	174$\Big\}$165
Government		150
Consumption	129	126
Total Supply		
Imports	140	181
GNP	132	134

Source: Actual indexes are derived from official national accounts and trade data, deflated with price indexes for exports, imports, cost of living, government wages, machinery, and construction. Original sources are *Relazione Generale sulla Situazione Economica del Paese* (for national accounts), bulletin of Centro per la Statistica Aziendale (for construction costs), and ISTAT, *Bolletino Mensile di Statistica* (for summary trade data and other price indexes). Resulting index of 134 for GNP checks approximately with index of 135 derived by linking official estimates of year-to-year real increases in *reddito nazionale*, as reported in successive annual editions of the *Relazione Generale*.

The OEEC goal was redefined as a 32% expansion of GNP, to take account of the increase actually accomplished in 1951.) It is clear that the OEEC goal for expansion of GNP was attained, with a small margin to spare. This was accomplished, however, by a substantially larger growth of investment, government expenditures, and exports than had been anticipated, offset by a smaller growth of consumption and an even sharper rise in imports. Although the qualitative picture of national accounts developments was valid, and the inference for the government budget appropriate, the study underestimated the extent to which the various elements of the national accounts would diverge in the course of economic expansion.

The fact that the national accounts analysis was "too proportional" of course affected the detailed final demand projection. When we come to examine results for individual industries, we should expect that growth of investment goods and export industries would tend to be understated, and that growth of consumption goods industries would tend to be overstated. (Note the signs of the errors in Table

10.2, below.) Moreover, within these broad elements of final demand, the procedure for projecting demand by detailed product
classes was almost surely "too proportional" as well. This is a concrete illustration of one of the points stressed in Chapter 5. To take
advantage of the detail in an interindustry classification, improved
methods of final demand analysis are seriously needed.

The second objective of the study, and the one to which the interindustry approach might be expected to contribute most, was to
project the expansion of demands on individual industries and thus to
indicate those industries with most favorable development prospects.
The conclusion was that:

> The industries deserving particular attention in Italian develop-
> ment programs are methane [natural gas], mechanical products,
> building materials, nonferrous metals, electric power, and chemicals.

This statement was backed with an industry-by-industry discussion of
the main considerations affecting development prospects in all sectors of the economy. The quantitative results which contributed to
this conclusion are set forth in Table 10.2, along with the actual expansions which have now taken place. (The nineteen sectors listed
in the table are those for which reasonably comparable official indexes
of industrial production are published.)

The industries selected as good development prospects all were in
the top half of the list in the projection, and all ended up in the top
half of the list in actuality. Moreover, in the list as a whole the projected and actual rankings proved to be in reasonable agreement.
Kendall's coefficient of rank correlation is 0.60, and this is significant
at the 0.001 level.

On the other hand, there were substantial percentage errors in the
individual results, the average being 16%. For nine industries the
error was less than 10%, and for five industries between 10% and 20%,
but there were four errors between 30% and 40%, and one greater than
50%.

The five large errors are especially significant in indicating major
weaknesses in the analysis. In the case of petroleum refining, the
error seems to arise primarily from an underestimate of the export
market for finished products refined from temporarily imported crude
oil, and secondarily from an underestimate of the rise in domestic
demand with improving standards of living. The reason the study
had not listed petroleum refining among the good development prospects was that very large margins of spare capacity already existed,

TABLE 10.2. PRODUCTION IN INDIVIDUAL INDUSTRIES
(1956 Indexes, 1950 = 100)

	Projected Index	Actual Index	Percentage Error	Projected Ranking	Actual Ranking
Nonferrous metals	166	158	+ 5%	1	9
Ferrous metals	165	251	−34%	2	2
Coke	164	159	+ 3%	3	8
Electric power	163	164	− 1%	4	7
Metallic minerals	157	187	−16%	5	4
Petroleum refining	154	353	−56%	6	1
Mechanical products	151	172	−14%	7	6
Nonmetallic mineral products	148	182	−19%	8	5
Chemicals	145	234	−38%	9	3
Nonmetallic minerals	144	149	− 3%	10	11
Pulp and paper	140	153	− 8%	11	10
Lumber and products	138	140	− 1%	12	12
Leather	137	102	+34%	13	18
Rubber	135	138	− 2%	14	13
Wool textiles	132	130	+ 2%	15	14
Clothing and knitwear	130	114	+14%	16	17
Cotton textiles	122	90	+36%	17	19
Food	122	126	− 3%	18	16
Cellulose and artificial fibers	112	128	−12%	19	15

Source: Actual indexes derived by shifting base of official industrial production indexes, published in ISTAT, *Bolletino Mensile di Statistica*. Percentage error is the difference between the indexes divided by the actual index.

but in fact these margins were more than absorbed by the demand increase which occurred. In the case of ferrous metals, the underestimate stemmed in part from misjudging the strength of the investment boom, but apparently also in part from too low input coefficients for steel-using industries. The reason this industry (as well as coke) was omitted from the list of good development prospects was concern about competition from within the European Coal and Steel Community then coming into operation. Actually, favorable transitional arrangements with the CSC softened this competition considerably. In the case of chemicals, the error seems to be due to neglecting the pronounced time trend, both in the development of new finished products and in the use of chemicals in other industries, characteristic of this industry. In the case of cotton textiles, the major cause of error was that exports did not recover as anticipated, but rather continued to decline. For leather, no explanation is readily discernible; it may well be that the actual production index for this industry is not sufficiently representative, since it does not seem to check with the apparent use of hides and skins.

To sum up, the interindustry study provided a reasonably reliable ranking of industries according to their demand prospects, which could be helpful as a quantitative guide for government development policies. A number of large absolute errors were made, however, stemming in general from "too proportional" final demand projections and from insufficient attention to the special circumstances of individual industries. Some of the largest errors resulted from inaccurate export forecasts.

The third substantive question to which the study was directed was that of capacity limits on economic expansion. The conclusion here was that:

> Capacity limits in agriculture are the principal bottleneck for the economy, and a major effort should be made to extend them. Capacity limits in industry are not likely to curb expansion of domestic production, so the danger of general inflationary pressure arising from supply shortages is small and need not present an obstacle to an expansionary program.

Domestic production of all but two of the agricultural products for which 1956 capacities had been estimated was expected to be held back by these limits. For all the basic industries, on the other hand, the estimated 1953 capacities were close enough to projected 1956 production so that the necessary expansion could be accomplished by investment in the remaining years.

Actual developments in agricultural production are set forth in Table 10.3. The projected capacities appear reasonably accurate, except for a substantial underestimate of the amount of land which might be transferred from other field crops to cotton. Actual production was of course affected by the year's weather conditions, most notably in that it was a bad year for wheat (after a bumper crop in 1955) and a very bad year for oil seeds. But production in every case but one was so constrained by capacity that increases in demand had to be met by even sharper increases in imports. (See the discussion of imports below.) The exception was wheat, for which the 1955 crop had been so bounteous that 1956 imports could be sharply reduced; since imports normally provide only a small fraction of the

TABLE 10.3. PRODUCTION AND CAPACITIES OF AGRICULTURAL PRODUCTS
(1956 Indexes, 1950 = 100)

	Projected Production	Projected Capacity	Actual Production	Maximum Production 1950–1956
Wheat	113	113	109	119
Corn	121	148	136	136
Oil seeds	122	138	96	122
Cotton	151	151	326	326
Wool	86	86	84	84
Timber	108	108	101	109
Meat	114	114	115	115

Source: Actual indexes derived from official production estimates, published in ISTAT, *Bolletino Mensile di Statistica*.

supply, a small error in the capacity estimate led to a large error in the import projection.

Price developments in the Italian economy throw further light on the significance of agricultural and industrial capacities. The relevant time-period is from 1952 to 1956, after international prices had first risen and then receded as a result of the Korean war. The general index of wholesale prices rose only 2% over these four years, and seven of the ten major component indexes actually fell. But wholesale food prices rose 13%. At the same time, the cost of living index, in which retail food prices have a heavy weight, also rose 13%.

The fourth question raised in the study was that of the imports required for an economic expansion of this magnitude. The inference drawn from the calculations was that:

> Inports must increase more rapidly than GNP because of agricultural capacity limits, and because industry with large raw material requirements is likely to expand more than agriculture and services. Thus, the trade deficit will probably increase . . .

Large increases (in value terms) were projected for wheat, meat, cotton and wool, metallic minerals and copper, timber, and crude petroleum. On the other hand, it was expected that fuel substitutions would permit an actual reduction in imports of coal. The increase in the trade deficit would have to be covered by a substantial rise in net invisible receipts.

The actual expansion of total imports, as already mentioned in connection with the national accounts, was significantly greater than expected. In part the explanation is that with investment and exports booming, production in the industrial sectors of the economy also rose more than expected. But in part the explanation is also that the

TABLE 10.4. MAJOR IMPORTS
(1956 Indexes, 1950 = 100)

	Projected Index	Actual Index	Percentage Error	Projected Ranking	Actual Ranking
Meat	382	384	− 1%	1	2
Hides and skins	225	185	+22%	2	6
Wheat	211	62	+402%	3	15
Timber	192	201	− 4%	4	4
Copper	153	198	−23%	5	5
Wool	147	123	+20%	6	12
Crude petroleum	144	396	−64%	7	1
Oils and fats	144	236	−39%	8	3
Cellulose and pulp for paper	137	172	−20%	9	7
Rubber	136	169	−20%	10	8
Coffee	125	159	−21%	11	9
Cotton	122	90	+36%	12	14
Fish	118	128	− 8%	13	11
Steel	107	118	− 9%	14	13
Coal	92	137	−49%	15	10

Source: Actual indexes 1950–1952 derived from study of production, imports, exports, and availability of each interindustry product class, prepared within the U.S. Mutual Security Agency mission to Italy, and multilithed under the title *Valutazione della Produzione e Disponibilita Totale di Beni e Servizi in Italia 1950–1951–1952*. Actual indexes 1952–1956 derived from official quantity data for similar product classes, published in ISTAT, *Statistica Mensile del Commercio con l'Estero*, Table 8. Percentage error is the difference between the indexes divided by the actual index.

import parameters, embodying assumptions about substitutability of domestic production for imports in individual commodity groups, were unduly optimistic. This sharp rise in imports was permissible, of course, only because of the concurrent rise in exports (though the trade deficit still expanded) and in net invisible receipts.

The actual results for major imports are set forth in Table 10.4.

(For data reasons, the table is limited to large-valued imports for which reasonably homogeneous quantity measures are published. These fifteen groups comprise about three-fifths of the total value of imports, however.)   The errors proved to be much larger than in the projections of industrial production, averaging 31% even excluding wheat.   The largest errors appeared in wheat and in oils and fats, largely because of weather effects discussed above; in crude petroleum and cotton, largely because of corresponding errors in the export forecasts; and in coal, to be discussed below.

It is true that the ranking of imports with respect to their indexes of expansion was reasonably reliable.   Kendall's coefficient of rank correlation is .37, which is significant at the .06 level.   Thus, the qualitative picture of the composition of rising total imports might have been of some use for policy guidance.   On balance, however, the reliability of the import projection in this study does not appear satisfactory.   Considerable improvement in the methods of import analyses used here is needed in order to obtain more reliable interindustry import projections.   What specific changes in method to introduce is a subject for research, but in general more attention to the particular supply and demand forces affecting individual imports seems to be indicated.[2]

The fifth objective of the study was to examine the probable fuel balance of the economy in 1956.   The central judgment was that:

> Methane (natural gas) use can increase from 5% to 30% of total fuel requirements, while coal can fall from 60% to 35%.

This extensive substitution involved an eightfold expansion of natural gas to the limit of its projected capacity, and a small absolute decrease

---

[2] Some progress in this direction has been made by the Interindustry Relations group of the Italian government's Istituto Nazionale per lo Studio della Congiuntura.   (See Cao-Pinna et al., 1955.)   In preparing a new input-output table for 1953, the group distinguished between imports and domestic products in each individual cell of the table, obtaining a matrix with 30 sector columns, 300 domestic-product rows, and 300 import rows.   Thus separate import parameters could be developed for each cell of the matrix, rather than for each row as in the earlier 1956 projection.   Then, with import parameters calculated by the simple proportionality assumption, the import matrix was tested by forecasting 1954 imports from the known final demands of that year.   The results for thirteen major raw material imports (more or less the same as in Table 10.4, omitting the foods) left an unweighted mean error of 4.8 per cent.   Of course, this was a one-year projection from known final demands.   But preparing a separate import matrix, especially if supplemented by refining the simple proportionality assumption, seems to be a promising approach.

in consumption of coal. The analysis also indicated the principal industries which should be able to increase consumption of natural gas in substitution for coal.

A summary of developments in the country's fuel balance is presented in Table 10.5. The extensive substitution of natural gas for

TABLE 10.5. CONSUMPTION OF FUELS
(1956 Indexes, 1950 = 100)

	Projected Index	Actual Index	Projected Percentage of Total	Actual Percentage of Total
Coal	92 ⎫ 107	129 ⎫ 124	35 ⎫ 47	41 ⎫ 45
Lignite and Sulcis	215 ⎭	90 ⎭	12 ⎭	4 ⎭
Natural Gas	887	875	30	24
Fuel Oil	145	238	23	31
Total (in BCE)	159	193		

Source: Actual indexes derived from estimates of consumption of all energy products in bituminous coal equivalents, published in the *Quarterly Statistical Bulletin* of the American Embassy, Rome.

coal was projected with reasonable reliability. Consumption of natural gas rose to the maximum considered feasible, and its share increased to about a quarter of the total fuel supply. The share of coal plus lignite and Sulcis (a domestic low-grade coal) declined as indicated. On the other hand, the consumption of coal itself actually increased nearly 30%. One reason was that total fuel consumption rose more than expected, in line with the expansion (similarly underestimated) of industries like steel and chemicals which are heavy consumers of fuel. A second reason was that an Italian government program for expanding production of Sulcis was abandoned just about the time the study was published.

The last substantive objective of the study was to examine the employment implications of attaining the OEEC goal. The conclusion here was that:

Increased employment in industry (excluding construction), estimated perhaps conservatively, should absorb in the order of a third of the prospective increase in the labor force, which is more than in recent years . . . Thus some improvement in the employment picture is in sight, but less than the desired objective of absorbing most of the increased labor force in industry . . .

The likely effect on average hours per worker and the industrial composition of the increase in employment were also analyzed.

This picture of the overall effect on the labor market appears to have been borne out in the actual development. Registered unemployment continued to rise gradually from about 1.9 million in 1950 to about 2.2 million in 1953, but then it leveled off for the next three years. During the latter half of 1956 unemployment finally began to fall below the levels of the previous year, and this modest improvement continued into 1957. (Unfortunately, it has not been possible to prepare data on industry-by-industry employment to check that aspect of the projection.)

All in all, what does this Italian study suggest about the strengths and weaknesses of the interindustry approach in making overall economic projections? Of course this is only a single study; its results depend on the judgments embodied in it and on the statistical data used to implement it, as well as on the interindustry technique. But an attempt to generalize may still be illuminating.

One major strength of the interindustry approach is that its comprehensiveness forces the analyst to take conscious account of many interdependent parts of a modern economy. His judgments on the quantitative relationships among these parts may prove wrong, but he is not likely to overlook the necessity of considering them. A second strong point is that an interindustry projection can be made to embrace a variety of flexible treatments of particular parts of the economy. The real limitations here are the analyst's understanding of what deviations from the Leontief proportionality assumption are appropriate and his willingness to take pains to incorporate them quantitatively into the model. Third, even without major research advances, an interindustry projection seems to be sufficiently reliable in projecting the relative expansion of individual industries to provide a useful quantitative guide for economic policies affecting industrial expansion. The richness of detail with respect to individual industries, individual imports, individual basic materials like fuels, and individual groups of employees is helpful in making such studies operational.

On the other hand, the principal weakness of the interindustry approach in making overall projections is that the supplementary quantitative analyses needed for this kind of application are often done rather mechanically. Methods of treating final demands and imports especially need to be improved. Yet there is a temptation for the analyst to concentrate too much attention on a meticulously constructed interindustry matrix and to neglect devices for making the model more flexible and for treating special circumstances. A second weakness, in part a consequence of the first, is that an interindustry projection at present may yield large errors in some of its individual results. In particular, it tends to underestimate the extent to which developments in different sectors diverge over time. Thus the interindustry approach is certainly not a substitute for other methods of making economic projections, or for the exercise of judgment in interpreting the results of any quantitative study.

D. Projections for Colombia and Argentina

Since interindustry analysis is most relevant in situations where the composition of output is expected to change rapidly, particular interest attaches to its possible application in countries undergoing industrialization. The most detailed analyses that have been made of such cases are the studies by the Economic Commission for Latin America of the development prospects of Colombia (1957) and Argentina (1958). These studies are valuable in showing what can be done with the statistics of less developed countries in analyzing growth patterns. For interindustry analysis the most interesting feature of industrial development is its irregularity. Individual sectors do not grow proportionally, nor do they follow the same course in all countries, so that an explicit analysis of the pattern of growth is desirable in order to formulate development policy.[3]

Industrialization in Argentina has already reached a fairly advanced stage, with about 30% of national product derived from manufacturing and construction. Colombia is at an earlier stage but is developing very rapidly. Since 1925 industry has grown at nearly 8% per year, whereas the national product has grown at 4.5%, so that manufacturing now accounts for about a fifth of the national product.

The input-output data compiled for the ECLA studies have already been discussed in Chapter 7. In both countries, the analysis was concentrated on the industrial sectors, which were broken down into about 15 industries, with the remainder of the economy treated in very aggregated fashion. In addition to the interindustry flow matrix,

---

[3] Kuznets' study of the "Industrial Distribution of National Product and Labor Force" (*Economic Development and Cultural Change,* 1957) has shown a substantial correlation between the proportion of national income originating in industry and the level of per capita income, but the growth patterns of individual industries show much less uniformity.

estimates were made of income elasticities of consumption by commodity, of the use of imported inputs by each industry, and of productive capacity and marginal capital-output ratios for each sector.

The methodology used by ECLA was broadly the same as that already described for Italy, but included some significant adaptations to the particular problems of the countries studied. The primary aims of the studies were to estimate what overall growth rate could be sustained and to determine which sectors would require substantial amounts of investment in order to avoid bottlenecks. Even more than in Italy, however, emphasis was placed on the limitation imposed by the balance of payments. In both Argentina and Colombia (as in all underdeveloped countries) a high proportion of capital goods is im-

TABLE 10.6. DATA FOR PROJECTIONS

	Colombia	Argentina	Italy
Period of analysis	1953–1960	1955–1962	1950–1956
Per capita income*	$250	$460	$310
Increase in GNP			
(a) Index	156	140	134
(b) Annual rate	6.5%	4.9%	5.0%
Increase in exports	144	164	157
Proportion of national product derived from manufacturing and construction†	19.0%	29.0%	39.0%

* U.N. Statistical Office, *Per Capita National Product of Fifty-five Countries, 1952–1954* (1957).

† Kuznets, *op. cit.*

ported, and a miscalculation of import requirements is likely to result in a shortage of capital goods.

A range of demand and import possibilities was explored by making several alternative assumptions. Two rates of growth in GNP were assumed, and projections were made first with existing import proportions. In each case, the initial projection showed a substantial deficit in the balance of payments, which was eliminated by successively increasing the production of domestic substitutes. This process was necessarily one of trial and error, because each substitution changed the import proportions of the original matrix and generated additional indirect effects of increased domestic production.

Some of the data underlying these projections for Colombia and Argentina are given in Table 10.6, with corresponding figures from the

Italian experience for purposes of comparison.   The higher hypotheses as to growth rates are shown for Colombia and Argentina and the actual data for Italy.

Since it is too early to compare these projections with the actual course of development, we shall limit our observations to two features of particular interest to countries that are industrializing: the increase in import requirements and the relative growth rates of the major sectors.

Although in both Argentina and Colombia a substantial increase in exports was anticipated, the calculated increase in imports in the absence of import substitution was considerably higher.   In a revised calculation, therefore, the increase in imports was held down by expanding domestic production of substitutes.   (Actually the rise in imports was held below the rise in exports to allow for the existing balance of payments deficit and to permit payments on capital account.) In the case of Argentina, the effects of import substitution on production in each sector are shown by the differences between the two sets of production indices in Table 10.7.

The Argentine study is of further interest because the input-output analysis was used as a basis for detailed projections of investment requirements by sector and type of capital goods.   This calculation was important in estimating the demands for imported capital goods, which are a large element in the balance of payments, and the feasibility of financing the indicated total investment.

Despite the diversity among countries in industrial development, resulting from differences in natural resources and other factors affecting the pattern of international trade, there are some elements of similarity, which are also discernible in these three cases.   An idea of the nature of such similarities can be obtained by grouping industrial sectors according to whether they typically grow faster or slower than industry as a whole.   The typically slow-growing industries are shown in group A of Table 10.7.[4]   In general, they are industries

---

[4] This classification is based on a comparison, for 19 countries classified according to income per capita, of the average proportion of value added in manufacturing derived from the two groups of industries.

Income Per Capita	$50–200	$200–750	Over $750
No. of Countries	7	6	6
Group A	75%	60%	37%
Group B	25%	40%	63%

Group A includes sectors 20–26, 29, and 33 of the international standard industrial classification (see Chapter 8).   A more detailed breakdown would include in group A elements of other industries, such as chemicals.

TABLE 10.7. COMPARISON OF PROJECTIONS

	COLOMBIA			ARGENTINA Projected Index			ITALY	
	Actual Index 1946–1953	Projected Index	Rank	Without Import Substitution	With Import Substitution	Rank	Actual Index	Rank
Production: Group A								
Food and tobacco	180	143	8	128	128	8	126	7
Textiles and clothing	150	162	7	137	138	7	108	8
Wood products, building materials	190	188	6	143	153	6	161	5
Production: Group B								
Paper and printing	250	227	5	148	166	3	153	6
Chemicals, rubber	260	257	3	147	163	4	220	3
Fuel and power	200	250	4	147	162	5	240	1
Metals	270	457	1,2	141	192	2	235	2
Mechanical industry				177	211	1	172	4
Production: All industries	179	181		144	159		170	
Imports								
Without substitution		192			180		181	
With substitution		127			127			

producing the basic necessities of life—food, clothing, and shelter—
which exist in economies at all levels of development. To the extent
that a typical pattern of industrialization can be identified, it consists
of industry as a whole increasing from less than 10% to more than 30%
of national product, and the sectors in Group A declining in importance from 70–80% of all industry to 30–40%.

The past and prospective developments of all three of the economies
under discussion fit this broad generalization. The group A sectors
show the lowest growth rates in all three countries (with one exception). Group A sectors accounted for 80% of value added in manufacturing in Colombia in 1953, but at the projected growth rates the
proportion will decline to 65% by 1960. A continuing decline in the
relative importance of Group A sectors is also in progress in Argentina
and Italy, which started from 55% and 50%, respectively.

Since most of the more rapidly growing sectors are producers of intermediate goods, the input-output projections have formed a basic
element of the analysis of development prospects in both Argentina
and Colombia. In Argentina, some 85% of all industrial investment
is expected to fall in group B, though partly because of excess present
capacity in some of the group A sectors.

Perhaps the main omission in the methodology of the studies discussed here is an explicit analysis of alternative uses of resources.
Possible extensions of the analysis, using some elements of linear programming with supplementary statistical data, are considered in
Chapter 11.

E. The U.S. Emergency Model

The most elaborate feasibility analysis using the interindustry approach made to date was an overall projection made within the U.S.
government in 1952. This analysis, usually referred to as the emergency model, dealt with the rearmament program stemming from the
Korean War, and was the principal application of the interindustry research program being carried on at that time by the Federal government. The rearmament program presented a problem for which the
interindustry approach should have been particularly useful. It is
most unfortunate for progress in this field, therefore, that the results
of the emergency model remain classified as security information, so
that an adequate public evaluation is still impossible. At least the
nature of the analysis, however, can be made clear.

The emergency model embodied significant elaborations of all three parts of an overall projection. (*a*) The final demand projections were specified in 200-industry detail, and separately by quarters, from 1951 through 1954, with the military demands analyzed initially in a special matrix. (*b*) The basic 1947 input-output matrix was adjusted substantially in certain critical areas, notably energy requirements and imports, and input lead-times were added to link the successive quarters. (*c*) Feasibility was tested against a variety of constraints, including industry capacities and investment programs, employment and occupational requirements, and availability of critical materials from production and stockpiles.

Turning first to final demand, the model necessarily put considerable strain on existing analytical techniques, since it specified quarter-by-quarter projections in 200-industry detail. Great efforts were made to meet these specifications, however, largely by dividing final demand (within a GNP control projection) into elements susceptible of conventional analysis by appropriate government agencies. The elements were: private consumption; monmilitary federal, state, and local government expenditures; farm equipment and farm construction; net change in agricultural inventories held by government; residential construction and maintenance construction; investment programs in nine priority industries and four others; investment in equipment and investment in construction by the remainder of the economy; exports and imports; and military procurement. The projection of each element was made in the maximum detail possible with conventional data sources, with further breakdown to the 200-industry level based largely on 1947 or 1950 interindustry tabulations. The timing of demand by quarters had to be based in practice on relatively simple patterns of change.

Making the final demand projections conceptually consistent with the basic interindustry matrix was a difficult technical problem. A great deal of research effort had to be put into the construction of special price indexes for deflating the final outputs of each industry; as a control these indexes were checked against similar price indexes for all of each industry's inputs. Purchasers' values had to be reduced to producers' values by estimating and eliminating transportation charges, excise taxes, and trade margins. And adjustment had to be made for numerous small definitional points, e.g., the fact that the input-output matrix combined both force account work and contract work in maintenance construction.

Perhaps the most imaginative projection procedure was followed in the case of military procurement. The items in the delivery schedules were classified into three groups: (*a*) major items produced only for the military; (*b*) major items similar to civilian products, which were simply classified by input-output industry; and (*c*) minor items, which were estimated from a scientific sample blown up to the necessary total value. Each item in the first group, such as a particular model of military airplane, was treated as a fictitious industry, with its input requirements determined from technical data provided by the manufacturer. The matrix of these fictitious industries thus translated a military projection in terms of major items into an economic projection in terms of demands on input-output industries. Of course there were many difficulties in empirical implementation, such as how to classify complex purchased parts, but this structural approach to final demand appears to be a promising development.

The investment projection should also be mentioned here, because although methodological improvements were limited in the emergency model itself, the whole research program on individual industries' capital requirements (see Chapter 5) was aimed at a major advance. The big gap in statistics on investment is a cross-classification of investment by investing industry with investment by type of capital equipment. In the model this gap was bridged in the projection for the nine priority industries, but the balance of investment could be projected only by type of capital equipment. Adequate studies of capital requirements for all industries, however, would permit the investment projection to be built up from anticipated expansions by investing industries. These could later be checked against required expansions as calculated in the model, and the comparison would be an important feasibility test.

Turning now to the input-output matrix itself, several significant adjustments were made in parts of the matrix to refine the original assumption of proportional input relationships. Many energy coefficients were adjusted for trends in efficiency of utilization, trends in substitution among fuels, and abnormal 1947 influences (such as a shortage of coal-washing equipment). Other energy coefficients were replaced by autonomous demands, after special side analyses (e.g., relating diesel oil requirements of railroads to outstanding orders for diesel locomotives).

Imports were also treated nonproportionally by defining each industry to consist of domestic production only, and entering imports as a negative final demand. Imports were then estimated autonomously on the basis of such considerations as world supplies and trends in import substitution. Note the difference between this treatment of imports and that used in the Italian study. Both methods recognized that import demands are likely to be nonproportional, but here domestic production was derived after allowing for available imports, whereas there imports were derived after allowing for domestic capacities. The difference in analysis of course reflects differences in the size and character of the two economies.

A notable extension of the basic interindustry matrix in the emergency model was the addition of coefficients for input lead-times. These lead-times, which amount to the assumption that raw-material and goods-in-process inventories must be kept proportional to output, tied together the successive quarters of the model into a dynamic whole. Statistical estimation of lead-times was inevitably rough, however, because of the statistical weaknesses of inventory data and the inherent difficulty of distinguishing speculative and technically necessary holdings. In the subsequent evaluation it appeared that the rough coefficients, in conjunction with relatively smooth time-patterns for final demands, contributed little to the solution. It may be that lead-times are only worth while for a relatively few industries with long production periods and hence large goods-in-process inventories.

Perhaps the most illuminating modifications of the interindustry matrix were those introduced after the emergency model had been run, in preparation for other possible applications. Quite a number of important products were reclassified, in an attempt to get more reliable estimates of demands for individual products previously combined in an industry's output. For example, the steel industry was subdivided into carbon steel, alloys, stainless, and forgings. Steel-reinforced aluminum cable was transferred from the wire products industry to the aluminum industry, so that increased use would be reflected directly in requirements for aluminum rods. Another innovation was to prepare an auxiliary matrix of coefficients in physical units for 28 key industrial products, so that requirements estimates for those products would be independent of price differences among sales to different sectors. All of these modifications represent the kind of structural improvements which might be expected as the fruit of accumulating experience.

Turning now to the third part of the emergency model—the constraints—quite a variety of checks was attempted. Of course, the central results were the calculated activity levels of each industry quarter by quarter, and these could be examined qualitatively by the appropriate government agencies. Discrepancies from prior anticipations could then be further investigated. Capacity estimates for a substantial number of industries with meaningful capacity limitations provided a more explicit quantitative test. For these industries capacities were projected independently over the time-period of the model —sometimes on the basis of government programs, sometimes on the basis of private expansion trends—and these capacity projections were then checked against the calculated production levels.

Employment requirements were also estimated in considerable detail, allowing for trends in output per production worker in individual industries (another important subsidiary research problem). The calculated employment demands were then evaluated in the light of probable labor supply, both in total and to some extent in particular occupations. Finally, requirements for selected critical materials were determined from a variety of side-calculations (including both structural analyses and time-series regressions) tied into the inter-industry solution proper. The computed requirements were then tested against availability of these critical materials from production, imports, and stockpiles.

So much for the methodology of the U.S. emergency model. Unfortunately, as already indicated, the substantive results of the study remain under security classification, so that their reliability and significance for policy guidance cannot be assessed. In the context of this chapter, however, we are interested in the study as a further illustration—more complex than the Italian or Argentine examples— of the scope and detail which are possible in an interindustry projection. In particular, more possibilities for flexible treatment of individual parts of the model were explored.

The emergency model is also of interest because it represents one kind of application of interindustry analysis in the field of war economics. Even in the era of nuclear weapons, so long as limited local wars of the Korean type are likely, this kind of study of partial economic mobilization for an abrupt expansion of defense production may continue to be relevant. In such a mobilization the economy would be faced with a substantial change in the composition of final demand in a short period of time, and in trying to adjust to the change would run into constraints of industry capacity, manpower, and natural resources. Of course, some changes in input structures would also be likely as adjustments to these constraints, but nonetheless the existing technology would be a more stable element in the short-run economic problem than the final demands. Moreover, a national emergency almost surely would call forth government policies to guide and accelerate the desired reallocation of resources. Under these circumstances an interindustry analysis along the lines of the Emergency Model ought to be useful in formulating mobilization policies.

On the other hand, for planning government policies which might cushion the disaster of an all-out nuclear war, if it occurred, a different kind of interindustry analysis may be useful. In such a case what happened in the economy would be almost completely irrelevant for the military outcome, but measures to reactivate and recuperate surviving resources of the economy after the military decision had been reached could be important in saving lives and restoring national institutions. The post-war situation would be one of quite unbalanced destruction, so that the pattern of final demands which could be satisfied would be constrained by the uneven availability of specialized industrial capital and manpower. Here a form of interindustry analysis of the linear-programming type discussed in the next chapter—with primary attention to conversion and substitution possibilities—seems to be indicated. Research in designing and implementing such a model might throw a good deal of light on appropriate government policies to take as partial insurance against the emergency.

BIBLIOGRAPHY

Berman, E. B., "The 1955 and 1975 Interindustry Final Bills of Goods and Generated Activity Levels," Interindustry Item No. 16, U.S. Bureau of Mines, 1953.

Cao-Pinna, V., and others, "Relazioni di Interdipendenza tra la Domanda di Beni e Servizi Finali e le Importazioni di Beni Strumentali," Appendix 2 in *Relazione Generale sulla Situazione Economica del Paese*, 1955. A mimeographed version in English has been prepared by Dr. Cao-Pinna.

Chenery, H. B., P. G. Clark, and V. Cao-Pinna, *The Structure and Growth of the Italian Economy*, U.S. Mutual Security Agency, Rome, 1953. An Italian version covering the 1956 projections appeared as P. G. Clark, "Analisi delle Prospettive di Espansione per l'Economia Italiana nel Caso di Realizzazione del Programma O.E.C.E. per 1956," *L'Industria*, No. 2 (1953).

Cornfield, J., W. D. Evans, and M. Hoffenberg, "Full Employment Patterns, 1950," *Monthly Labor Review*, LXIV, No. 2, 163–190 (February 1947), and LXIV, No. 3, 420–432 (March 1947).

National Bureau of Economic Research, *Input-Output Analysis: An Appraisal*, 1955. Chapters by W. D. Evans and M. Hoffenberg, J. D. Norton, and F. T. Moore discuss certain aspects of the government research program and the emergency model.

United Nations, Economic Commission for Latin America, *Analyses and Projections of Economic Development, III, Economic Development of Colombia*, 1957.

United Nations, Economic Commission for Latin America, *Analyses and Projections of Economic Development, IV, Economic Development of Argentina,* 1958 (mimeographed).

Van den Beld, C. A., "Input-Output Analysis as a Tool for Long-Term Projections," paper presented to the Varenna Input-Output Conference, 1954. The paper is summarized in P. J. Verdoorn, "Complementarity and Long-Range Projections," *Econometrica,* XXIV, No. 4, 429–450 (October 1956).

chapter **11**

Resource allocation

in development programs

This chapter investigates further the usefulness of interindustry analysis for underdeveloped economies. In the postwar period almost all of the countries of Asia, Africa, and Latin America have adopted some form of development program in an effort to accelerate economic growth. Government action under these programs takes a variety of forms, from tax incentives for private investors in Puerto Rico to state investment in steel mills in India. Whatever the instruments of public policy selected, some kind of analysis of present and future use of resources is needed to make them effective.

The functions of a development program depend to a considerable extent upon the existing economic structure. In a very poor agricultural economy, the most important problem may be to bring about an initial increase in agricultural production and income and to provide some of the institutional requirements for further growth. A policy to carry out these objectives does not need to be based on elaborate economic analysis. As the economy grows and becomes more complex, however, a greater choice of alternatives has to be considered, and the consistency of development plans for different sectors becomes more important.

278

In the last chapter we were concerned with projections of the effects of an increase in national income on various sectors of the economy. Although the making of such projections on a consistent basis is an important aspect of a development program, its main purpose is more ambitious. In principle, a development program aims at finding the combination of investments, technological and institutional changes, and other measures which will produce the greatest increase in future income. The analytical techniques used must therefore incorporate a mechanism for choosing among alternatives as well as a way of achieving consistent results.

In practice the criteria for choice of investments have been separated from the techniques for projection of demand and production to a large extent. When the development problem is formulated in programming terms, it is apparent that this procedure at best provides only a first approximation to the desired result. We can think of the choice of investments as a choice among activities to reach an optimum solution. If existing prices are used to guide this choice, they ignore differences between market prices and opportunity costs of inputs. On theoretical grounds, then, we should use linear programming techniques instead of input-output in order to combine the making of consistent projections with the making of efficient choices among alternative uses of resources.

Since linear programming is a more recent theoretical development and requires more data for its use than input-output, its application to the analysis of whole economies is still in an exploratory stage. For practical applications, some combination of the two techniques is the best that can be hoped for in the near future. To indicate the aspects of linear programming that are needed most, we shall first outline the typical features of the resource allocation problem in underdeveloped economies and the programming methods actually used. We then discuss the results of experiments that have been made in using a linear programming model to explore development possibilities for Southern Italy. These experiments help to clarify the conceptual basis for choice among investment projects, and they also suggest ways of improving the analytical techniques now in use.

A. Structural Disequilibrium in Underdeveloped Economies

One of the most significant characteristics of the economies that are loosely described as "underdeveloped" is the inefficient use that is made of available resources. The causes of this situation are very complex and cannot be analyzed here,[1] but in sum they result in an economic structure for which some of the crucial assumptions of general equilibrium theory are invalid. The price system does not function so as to produce full employment of labor and natural resources even with a high level of demand, and the tendency to equate the marginal returns to factors in different uses is limited. This result can be attributed to small markets, ignorance of technological possibilities, lack of complementary public investment, an aversion to risk taking by the propertied classes, a shortage of industrial entrepreneurs, the low level of savings, and a variety of other factors. Although they may not all be encountered in any single instance, these features are sufficiently important to make the assumption of structural *disequilibrium* a more probable starting point for our analysis than that of full-employment equilibrium.

The term "structural disequilibrium" is used here to denote a condition in which the existing distribution of the stock of capital and other complementary factors does not permit the best use to be made of the available labor and natural resources. The resulting underemployment of labor is thus in contrast to cyclical unemployment of the Keynesian type and frequently persists during periods of chronic inflation. In more general terms, structural disequilibrium reflects an inequality between the proportions in which factors are available and the proportions in which they are used in production.[2] The disproportion is often aggravated by a distribution of capacity by sector which does not correspond to the present pattern of foreign and domestic demand. An increase in domestic demand will therefore produce either inflation or increased imports before there is full use of capacity in all sectors and long before labor is fully employed.

The fact that capital and foreign exchange are typically scarce in underdeveloped countries makes their allocation the central feature of most development programs. The existence of underemployed labor and scarce foreign exchange distorts the price system and often results in a wide divergence between the social and private benefits of investment. For this reason, among others, government intervention in economic activity tends to be more widespread than in more advanced countries. It focusses on the investment process because

[1] See Lewis (1955), Buchanan and Ellis (1955), and Meier and Baldwin (1957) for surveys of causes of underdevelopment.

[2] Conceivably, this condition may exist even with optimal resource allocation if there are limits to factor movements or technological alternatives.

a change in the pattern of investment is needed to change the structure of production.[3]

B. Development Programs in Practice

Although the widespread use of development programs as a part of government policy-making is a recent phenomenon, these programs have quite similar functions in most of the noncommunist countries.[4] In countries where effective use has been made of development programs, a Planning Board or other special agency has been set up to prepare general economic analyses and to coordinate plans in various sectors. The discussion of this chapter is particularly relevant to the work of such a central agency.

The more complete development programs include the following features:

(i) A statement of objectives of national policy, the most common of which are increasing national income, reducing unemployment, maintaining or achieving balance in international trade, and improving the distribution of income.

(ii) Projections of the growth of national income, consumption, investment, and the balance of payments.

(iii) Estimation of the supply of domestic savings, foreign investment, various categories of labor, and other resources.[5]

(iv) A statement of criteria for the allocation of investment funds and foreign exchange subject to government influence in the light of their aggregate supply and demand and of the national objectives.

(v) Projection of the growth of various sectors of the economy and the needs of each sector for investment funds and other resources.

(vi) A balancing of resource needs from (v) against availabilities from (iii), and a reconciliation of sector and aggregate projections.

Since the techniques of projection have been discussed in the last chapter, we shall be mainly concerned here with methods of allocation

---

[3] Arguments for government intervention based on the existence of structural disequilibrium are given in Rosenstein-Rodan (1943), United Nations (1951), Nurkse (1953), Tinbergen (1957), and Chenery (1953, 1958).

[4] A selected list of development analyses and programs for countries in Europe, Asia, Africa, and Latin America is given at the end of the chapter.

[5] Throughout this discussion, "investment resources" refer to the total of domestic saving plus foreign investment.

and revision.[6] The first step in the allocation procedure is the determination of priorities among sectors and projects for the use of investment funds, foreign exchange, and other scarce factors. We can distinguish three general approaches to this problem.

(i) The first approach, which is derived from classical principles of economics, is to try to maximize the national product by equating the marginal productivity of investment or other resources in different uses. Although this test is commonly referred to, it is not widely used because of the difficulty of measuring the marginal product attributable to a given factor in a given use.

(ii) The second and commonest method, which may be called the scarce-factor approach, is derived from the existence of structural disequilibrium. It tries to allow for the defects in the price system by giving priority to projects which economize on scarce factors, such as foreign exchange or investment funds, or alternatively to those which use large amounts of the abundant factors, labor and local resources. The weakness of this method lies in the difficulty of combining these often conflicting criteria and the consequent danger that a partial rule, such as foreign exchange saving, will be used as an excuse for a project (e.g., a steel plant) which uses excessive amounts of capital or other scarce inputs.[7]

(iii) A third approach to the selection of priority sectors ignores short-run calculations based on increases in production and cost and concentrates on the selection of "key sectors" which will contribute to a balanced pattern of growth in the long run. The sectors chosen are typically "social overhead" facilities, such as transportation and electric power, and "basic" or heavy industries such as steel, chemicals, and machinery. The selection of these sectors is usually based more on the structure of advanced countries than on a detailed estimate of the effects on the country concerned of development of these sectors. This approach is popular in many underdeveloped countries because the creation of heavy industry serves national pride and reduces dependence on external sources for some important industrial materials. The main difficulties with this method of determining

---

[6] This procedure has the effect of separating the allocation of resources from the estimate of the rate of growth. In actuality, the aggregate projections will have to be revised and the process repeated to take account of the interrelations between the two.

[7] The difficulties in using such rules are discussed in Kahn (1951) and Chenery (1953).

priorities lie in the choice of a valid analogy from the experience of other countries and the lack of any quantitative basis for comparing alternatives.

Each of these approaches is likely to conflict with some of the objectives of social policy because each is based on only a partial analysis of the effects of investment. The tests of increasing employment, reducing a balance of payments deficit, and maximizing national income can only be applied consistently in the framework of an overall analysis in which the relative importance of each objective can be evaluated.

C. The Use of Linear Programming Concepts

The use of a linear programming framework may contribute to development programs in several ways. In the first place, the more complete model that is used in linear programming reveals clearly the relation between projections of production levels and use of resources on the one hand and the criteria for choice of investments on the other. Even when data are not available to utilize such a model in its entirety, the rationale of programming solutions may serve as a guide to better methods of approximation. Secondly, the setting up and solution of linear programming models on a trial basis provides insight into the quantitative significance of the interrelations among decisions in each sector that are ignored by simpler techniques. Such testing of the method is needed before a full-scale application is attempted.

We must first consider the extent to which development programs fit into the conceptual framework of linear programming. The formal programming problem is to maximize (or minimize) a function of the activity levels subject to a set of linear constraints on these variables. In planning development, the function to be maximized is almost always taken to be the national product.[8] The other objectives listed above—employment, balance of payments equilibrium, income distribution, etc.—can be considered as constraints which qualify the main objective. Other restrictions include the desired commodity composition of consumption, the availability of labor and

---

[8] An alternative formulation uses *per capita* product, but the result will only differ if population growth is a function of the allocation chosen, c.f. Galenson and Leibenstein (1955). There is also the problem of weighing the near against the more distant future.

natural resources, and the supply of capital, i.e., domestic saving plus foreign borrowing.[9]

The nature of these constraints determines the activities which must be included in the model. In the examples of Chapter 4 the only variables were the levels of production by different techniques. Now we must allow for a variable composition of foreign trade by treating importing and exporting as activities. Other possible activities include capital building, labor training, and the consumption of individual commodities. Whether choices affecting a given economic function should be included within the model or decided in advance depends on whether the result influences the remainder of the solution in a way which cannot be adequately allowed for otherwise. For example, labor training might be included as an activity, but its effect on the solution may be allowed for satisfactorily by assigning a price to skilled labor determined by the resources needed to train it. This procedure cannot be applied to foreign exchange, however, because its equilibrium price depends on the working out of comparative advantages for the whole economy, which can only be determined in the course of the solution.

The most important allocation problem for an underdeveloped country is to choose the sectors in which it should try to increase its exports and those in which it should expand production for the domestic market, usually as a substitute for imports. A selection of techniques of production in each sector is also required, but here the choice is more limited. We shall defer consideration of this question to simplify the analysis.

We can illustrate the nature of the linear programming solution by starting from aggregate projections of income, consumption, and total investment resources similar to those discussed in the last chapter. The essential difference between the programming model and the input-output analysis in this case is that the levels of imports and exports in each sector are to be determined from the solution.[10] Since in

[9] The stock of particular kinds of capital goods—i.e., the productive capacity in each sector—is also an effective restriction in some instances, but in a long-term analysis the supply of capital as a whole is the more important limitation, since most capital goods are imported. In order to differentiate among capital goods having different lives, it would be desirable in a more realistic model to represent the capital required by two input coefficients, one for the capital stock (as in this chapter) and a second for the annual depreciation. The total cost of using capital would then be made up of interest plus depreciation, in variable proportions.

[10] In the input-output model, imports have a specified relation to production in each sector, which is not true in programming models.

the first approximation domestic demands for each commodity are taken as fixed by the forecast level of income, a given investment decision implies that the difference between production and domestic demand for each commodity will be imported (or exported).

An example embodying these assumptions is shown as model VIII in Table 11.1. The final demands (B_1 to B_4) and production activities (X_j) are taken from model I of Chapter 2.[11] In addition, Equation (5) has been added to indicate the balance of payments limitation. The negative coefficients in row 5 indicate the amount of foreign exchange required to buy a unit of imports, the positive ones the amount to be received from the sale of a unit of exports. Importing activities M_j therefore show a positive entry for the commodity imported and an input of foreign exchange, whereas exporting activities E_j have a commodity input and an output of foreign exchange. The effects of transportation are taken care of by the fact that import prices (c.i.f.) include transport costs and export prices (f.o.b.) do not. For example, activity M_2 shows that it takes 1.1 units of foreign exchange to purchase 1 unit of commodity 2, but E_2 shows that only 1.0 unit of foreign exchange is received if this commodity is exported. The exchange rate used in this calculation is immaterial, since it merely multiplies all entries in the foreign exchange equation by a constant.

This programming formulation with the addition of importing and exporting activities affects the original input-output model in three ways:

(i) In model VIII the balance equations of the Leontief model (1-4) are changed so that imports and exports appear as separate variables and the constant term includes only domestic demand. For example, the third equation in model VIII reads:

$$-0.1X_1 - 0.1X_2 - 1.0E_3 + 0.7X_3 + 1.0M_3 = 40$$

(ii) Equations for foreign exchange and labor use become part of the model. Equation (5) of model VIII states that foreign exchange uses for imports (negative) less exchange earnings from exports (positive) plus non-use of foreign exchange equal the given supply of foreign exchange from other sources such as loans or gifts (-20). The disposal activity D_5 represents any accumulation (non-use) of foreign

---

[11] For convenience in the solution, production, importing, and exporting activities for the same commodity are grouped together as an "industry." Within each industry, each type of activity is identified by the symbol for its activity level.

TABLE 11.1. MODEL VIII: DEVELOPMENT PROGRAMMING

Commodity	a_{ij}	Basis*	1 Finished Goods E_1	X_1	M_1	2 Agriculture E_2	X_2	M_2	3 Basic Industry E_3	X_3	M_3	4 Services X_4	Resource Disposal D_5	D_6	B_i	P_i	$P_i B_i$
I. Price Analysis	a_{1j}		-1.0	0.8	1.0												
(1) Commodity 1 (finished goods)		a	-2.33	1.86	2.33										320	2.33	746
		b	-2.33	1.86	2.33											2.33	746
		c	-2.27	1.81	2.27											2.27	726
		d	-2.26	1.81	2.26											2.26	724
	a_{2j}		-0.3			-1.0	0.9	1.0									
(2) Commodity 2 (agricultural products)		a	-0.78			-2.59	2.33	2.59							105	2.59	272
		b	-0.78			-2.59	2.33	2.59								2.59	272
		c	-0.76			-2.54	2.29	2.54								2.54	267
		d	-0.76			-2.54	2.29	2.54								2.54	267
	a_{3j}		-0.1			-0.1			-1.0	0.7	1.0						
(3) Commodity 3 (basic materials)		a	-0.27			-0.27			-2.66	1.86	2.66				40	2.66	106
		b	-0.27			-0.27			-2.66	1.86	2.66					2.66	106
		c	-0.23			-0.23			-2.29	1.60	2.29					2.29	92
		d	-0.23			-0.23			-2.26	1.58	2.26					2.26	91
	a_{4j}		-0.2			-0.1			-0.1			0.9					
(4) Commodity 4 (services)		a	-0.12			-0.06			-0.06			0.55			60	0.61	37
		b	-0.12			-0.06			-0.06			0.55				0.61	37
		c	-0.12			-0.06			-0.06			0.55				0.61	37
		d	-0.12			-0.06			-0.06			0.55				0.61	37

		E_1	X_1	M_1	E_2	X_2	M_2	E_3	X_3	M_3	X_4	D_5	D_6	B_i	P_i	P_iB_i
		0.9	**-1.0**	**-1.0**	**1.0**	**-0.20**	**-1.1**	**0.8**	**-0.14**	**-0.9**	**-0.79**	**-1**	**-1**	**-20**		**Capital Used**
f_{5i} (5) Foreign exchange	a	0	0	0	0	0	0	0	0	0		0	0		0	0
	b	2.66	-2.95	-2.95	2.95	-3.25	-3.25	2.13	-2.66	-2.66		-2.95	-2.95		2.95	-59
	c	2.29	-2.54	-2.54	2.54	-2.79	-2.79	2.03	-2.29	-2.29		-2.54	-2.54		2.54	-51
	d	2.26	-2.51	-2.51	2.51	-2.76	-2.76	2.01	-2.26	-2.26		-2.51	-2.51		2.51	-50
l_{6i}			-0.06			-0.20			-0.14		-0.79		-1	-300		
(6) Labor	a														0	0
	b														0	0
	c														0	0
	d														0	0
(7) Criterion Function (capital) c_j		0	0.7	0	0	2.0	0	0	1.80	0	0.55	0	0	*Minimum*		
II. Profit (π_j)	a	-2.33	0	2.33	-2.59	0	2.59	-3.66	0	2.66	0	0	0			
	b	0.33	0	-0.62	0.37	0	-0.66	-0.53	0	0	0	-2.95	0			
	c	0.2	0	-0.28	0	0	-0.20	-0.26	-0.26	0	0	-2.54	0			
	d	0	0	-0.25	-0.03	0	-0.17	-0.25	-0.28	0	0	-2.51	0			
III. Activity level (x_j)	a	0	400	0	0	250	0	0	150	0	200	20	47			
	b	0	400	0	0	250	0	0	118	22	196	0	58			
	c	0	400	0	83	392	0	0	0	115	194	0	55			
	d	99	524	0	0	290	0	0	0	122	215	0	40			
IV. Total capital (c_jx_j)	a	280			500			270			110					1160
	b	280			500			213			108					1101
	c	280			684			0			106					1070
	d	367			583			0			118					1068

* The six activities in each basis are indicated by positive activity levels and zero profits.

† The total capital used is equal to both the row and column totals, which are identical (except for differences due to rounding).

exchange, but drawing down reserves below the amount included in the restriction is not permitted because the level of this activity cannot be negative.

Equation (6) states that the demand for labor plus the labor not used (activity D_6) must equal its supply. If we wanted to distinguish skilled and unskilled labor, we could insert an activity to convert the latter into the former at a given cost. The skilled labor equation would then be completely analogous to the foreign exchange equation.

(iii) A criterion function, Eq. (7), which consists of minimizing the use of capital, has been added.[12] As we showed in Chapter 4, solving a minimizing problem is easier than solving the corresponding maximizing problem, and the maximum output for a given amount of capital can be determined in successive approximations. This procedure corresponds to the approximate methods actually used in development planning and permits a programming interpretation to be made of them.

We have already solved the input-output model corresponding to model VIII with no imports. The solution to model I from Chapter 3 therefore provides an initial basis for the programming problem. Since it leaves some foreign exchange and some labor unused, the disposal activities D_5 and D_6 are added to the basis to satisfy Eqs. (5) and (6). The mechanics of solving this type of problem by the simplex method have already been explained in Chapter 4, so we shall only comment on the economic significance of the steps in the solution. The computational procedure followed is identical to that illustrated in Tables 4.6 and 4.7.[13]

Basis a $(X_1\,X_2\,X_3\,X_4\,D_5\,D_6)$

Calculations for basis a are shown in the first line of each section. The activities in the basis can be identified by the fact that they have zero profits and positive activity levels. The shadow prices of the two primary factors, labor and foreign exchange, are both zero because they are in excess supply. All imports are therefore profitable and exports unprofitable. The most profitable importing activity M_3 is

---

[12] Another scarce primary factor—such as foreign exchange—could have been chosen as the criterion without affecting the final outcome, but capital is the most logical choice since it provides the most critical limitation to increased national income.

[13] An alternative solution to this example using a version of the gradient method, which more closely approximates empirical trial-and-error procedures, is given in Chenery (1958).

added to form a new basis and the disposal activity for foreign exchange D_5 drops out.

Basis b $(X_1 X_2 X_3 M_3 X_4 D_6)$

Since the supply of foreign exchange is not sufficient to entirely replace domestic production of commodity 3 by imports, commodity prices in basis b are unchanged from a. The available supply of foreign exchange has a value equal to the amount of capital which it replaces—its opportunity cost. Since an import of one unit of commodity 3, worth 2.66, can be had for 0.9 units of foreign exchange, the shadow price of foreign exchange is $2.66/0.9 = 2.95$. The total capital required is lowered by $20 \times 2.95 = 59.0$, or from 1160 to 1101.

An evaluation of the excluded activities shows that exports of either commodity 1 or commodity 2 would now be profitable and E_2 (the most profitable) is added to form a new basis. Domestic production of 3 can now be replaced entirely, and X_3 drops out.

Basis c $(X_1 E_2 X_2 M_3 X_4 D_6)$

In basis c, foreign exchange derives its price from the cost of producing exports rather than from the alternative cost of domestic production of imports. Its price now falls to 2.54, and the price of commodity 3, which is entirely imported, falls from 2.66 to 2.29. This drop has repercussions on P_1 and P_2, which also fall somewhat. A recalculation of the profitability of the excluded activities shows that it would now be slightly more profitable to export commodity 1, and E_1 replaces E_2 in the next basis.

Basis d $(E_1 X_1 X_2 M_3 X_4 D_6)$

The price solution for basis d shows that all of the excluded activities are now unprofitable, which indicates that this is the optimum solution.[14] The total capital required in basis d is 1068, computed as either $\sum_j c_j X_j$ or $\sum_i P_i B_i$.

[14] It is of interest to compare the autarchic solution in which there are no exports, represented by basis b, to the optimum. . The total saving in capital between the two, resulting from exporting commodity 1 and importing all of 3, is 33 units. This saving can be allocated to the cost of various items of final use and payment to primary factors by multiplying each constraint B_i by the fall in its price between basis b and basis d.

$$\Delta C = 320(-0.067) + 105(-0.045) + 40(-0.396) + 60(0) - 20(-0.440)$$
$$= -21.4 - 4.7 - 15.8 + 8.8 = -33.1$$

Since the imported commodity (3) is mainly used by other industries, the fall in its price affects the final consumer primarily through the reduced cost of other commodities.

D. A Pilot Study of Southern Italy

In order to have a more realistic test of the workability of the programming technique outlined in the previous section, one of the
present authors has performed several experiments with a model for
Southern Italy based on these principles. The work was done in
collaboration with two Italian research organizations, and most of the
results of these experiments have been published in Chenery (1955)
and Chenery and Kretschmer (1956). The present section makes use
of these results to discuss three aspects of development programming:
the relation of factor prices to the choice of activities, the substitutability of capital and labor, and the productivity of investment. Only
a very brief outline of the model and the method of solution will be
given, since they have been discussed elsewhere.

1. Methodology and Data

The general form of the pilot model constructed for Southern Italy
follows closely that of model VIII, p. 286. To reduce the amount of
computation required, the input-output table discussed in the previous
chapter was consolidated to fourteen sectors, using production levels
for Southern Italy as weights. An increase in final demand for each
commodity corresponding to a 75% increase in regional income over
10 years was estimated from budget studies and projections of population growth. The remaining parameters in the model—capital and
labor coefficients, export demands, and import prices—were estimated
or assumed from much less adequate information, which makes the
results more an illustration of the potentialities of the method than
a serious attempt to outline an investment program. In setting up the
model, however, only the type of data obtainable by a planning au-
thority was used, and the calculations were shown to be quite feasible
in practice. The data are summarized in Tables 11.2 and 11.3 in the
Appendix.

Activities. The activities of domestic production, imports, and
exports are essentially the same as those used in model VIII. The
additional assumption is made that the production activity in each
sector is an aggregate of separate activities which have the same inputs
of purchased materials but differing capital coefficients.[15] The capital
coefficient for the entire sector is therefore assumed to increase as

[15] The justifications for this assumption and its effect on the solution are given
in Chenery and Kretschmer (1956).

the proportion of domestic production increases and the more capital intensive products are produced. Because of this assumption, the solutions to this model result in both importing and producing some commodities in most sectors. This is a more realistic outcome than that of model VIII in which each commodity group was generally either entirely imported or produced entirely at home.

Constraints. The final demand constraints represent increases in domestic demand above that producible in the base year, as in the projections discussed in Chapter 10. The restrictions on exports are made a function of their price, however, which introduces a nonlinear element into the model. With the technique of solution used, this complication causes no difficulty.[16]

The primary factors considered are labor, capital, and foreign exchange. The amount of foreign exchange (i.e., nonlocal resources) available from external borrowing and grants from the central government is taken as given. Labor is divided into two categories, agricultural and nonagricultural. Agricultural labor is omitted from the model because it appears to be in excess supply in Southern Italy for the period under consideration. Nonagricultural labor has a real cost determined by the capital requirements for urbanization and labor training, if demand for labor in nonagricultural employments exceeds the existing level of unemployment. Since these capital costs are not known with any accuracy, solutions are given for several alternative assumptions as to the incremental capital cost of urban labor in order to illustrate their effect on the solution.

The Objective Function. As in model VIII, the objective adopted is to minimize the use of capital rather than to maximize the output from a given amount of capital. This version corresponds more closely to political reality in Southern Italy, where local saving can be augmented by investment funds from the central government and from foreign sources. If the requirement for external capital turned out to be excessive, the period to which the targets apply could be extended or they could be scaled down.

2. The Value of Foreign Exchange and the Choice of Activities

As we have seen in the previous section, there are only two types of choice to be made in finding the optimum solution to an interindustry

---

[16] It would be possible to secure the same effect in a linear model by placing limits on the amount of exports that could be made at each price. This would result in a series of export activities for each commodity, each with a different foreign exchange (output) coefficient and a limit to its maximum level.

model in which the composition of demand is fixed and alternative technology is not considered. One is the choice between imports and domestic production in each sector, and the other is the choice of export activities to earn the foreign exchange required by imports. The only significant difference between the Italian pilot model and model VIII is that the demands for exports in the Italian model are assumed to depend on their prices. As a result, exports should take place in each sector up to the point at which marginal revenue from exports equals marginal cost in that sector.[17]

As will be shown below, both these choices depend only on the relative prices of the primary factors: labor, capital, and foreign exchange. Since capital provides the unit of measurement (criterion function) in our model, the prices of the other two factors are stated in terms of the effect of a marginal variation in their supply on the capital required—their opportunity cost. It is useful to analyze the effects of these two prices separately since they provide a link between partial analysis and over-all programming. It also turns out that this procedure provides a convenient way of solving the nonlinear programming model with which we are concerned.

Consider first the case in which labor is in excess supply and its price is therefore zero. The choice between imports and domestic production in a given sector is determined by a comparison of the total capital required for production in that sector to the opportunity cost of the foreign exchange required for imports. For very low prices of foreign exchange, all possible commodities will be imported, whereas at a high enough price of foreign exchange everything will be produced domestically. Between these extremes there will be a progressive substitution of domestic production for imports as the price of foreign exchange is increased.

When the shadow price of labor is given, the choice of import and export activities can be shown to depend only on the price of foreign exchange and not on the final demands. This results from an application of the substitution theorem. With given prices of all the primary factors, they can be treated as a single combined input, as we showed in Chapter 4; the choice of activities in each sector is determined by the total amount of this input used. Once these choices have been made, a basic solution for the programming model is reduced to an input-output system because we have in effect specified the proportions between imports and domestic production in each sector and

[17] This rule follows from the Kuhn–Tucker theorem, as indicated in the Appendix to Chapter 4.

the level of exports. The relation between the levels of imports and exports and the price of foreign exchange can therefore be determined by solving the input-output system corresponding to each price of labor and foreign exchange.[18] This has been done in Table 11.4 and Fig. 11.1.

This analysis leads to a solution of the programming problem by a method different from the simplex approach and resembling somewhat the successive approximations used in practice. Instead of solving

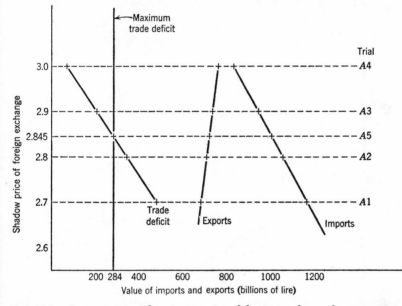

Fig. 11.1. Determination of optimum price of foreign exchange for zero price of labor.

the full nonlinear system directly, we have computed a number of solutions to the smaller linear model in which the foreign exchange and labor restrictions are eliminated and their prices are included instead. The optimum solution is found at the price which equates supply and demand for foreign exchange. In this case, supply from external sources is assumed to be 284 billion lire. The corresponding price of foreign exchange is determined by interpolation to be 2.845 units of capital per unit of foreign exchange. The activity levels in the corresponding basis (trial $A5$ in Table 11.4 below) represent the

[18] The method of solution is indicated in Chapter 4, Appendix.

solution to the given problem. If the amount of labor required by this solution should exceed its availability, however, it would be necessary to repeat the calculation using a higher labor cost. The effect of assuming a labor cost of 0.3 units of capital is shown (trial B2 in Table 11.4) to be an increase in the price of a unit of foreign exchange from 2.845 to 3.3 units of capital. This change also produces a shift away from labor-intensive activities, and the total nonagricultural labor employed is reduced from 3,145,000 to 2,929,000.

3. Labor Costs and the Substitution between Capital and Labor

By making solutions at varying relative prices of labor and capital for the same level of GNP we can trace out an isoquant for the whole

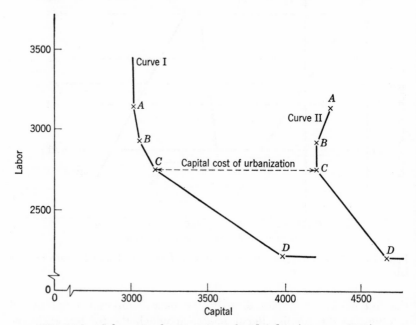

Fig. 11.2. Substitution between Capital and Labor (constant GNP).

economy, just as we did in Fig. 4.7.[19] The result is shown graphically as curve I in Fig. 11.2. The variation shown in factor use, which

[19] Since final demand is held constant, a constant GNP is indicated by the trials in which the excess of imports over exports is the same as in the first solution (284). This occurs in trials A5, B2, and C3 of Table 11.4, which are plotted as points A, B, and C. (The slight variation in GNP at these points in Table 11.4 is due to the measurement of exports in constant domestic prices.)

amounts to about one-third of the minimum for capital and nearly one-half for labor, is due entirely to a change in the composition of exports and imports, since final demands and the trade deficit are fixed and no alternative techniques of production were included in the model. The initial solution is point A on curve I with zero cost of labor.

It is generally recognized that although underemployment is widespread in many underdeveloped countries, there may be a considerable cost involved in making use of this labor, which is usually concentrated in rural areas. For simplicity, we shall call the resources needed for this purpose the "cost of urbanization." We now wish to see what effect the inclusion of these costs will have on the optimum investment program.

The problem is complicated conceptually by the fact that part of the capital invested to convert rural into urban labor produces an increase in welfare (e.g., better housing) and should be counted as part of national income. The relevant investment cost would therefore seem to be the cost of an urban labor force (e.g., for public utilities, housing, training) above that needed to produce a comparable increase in the value of consumption without the movement of population. Available studies indicate only the total cost of urban facilities,[20] but we can use them to get an idea of the magnitudes involved. Assuming a marginal capital cost of urbanization of 600,000 lire (about $1000) per worker, we can compute the additional capital required by each solution.[21] The total capital is shown by curve II,

[20] A. Molinari ("Industrialization and Decentralization," paper presented to the Tokyo Conference on Problems of Economic Growth, April 1957) gives the following estimates of the average overhead investment per capita in cities of different sizes in Southern Italy (in thousands of lire):

	City Size		
	Under 30,000	30,000–200,000	Over 200,000
Public services and utilities	123	189	350
Dwellings	400	500	650
Total per person	523	689	1,000
Total per worker (assuming two people)	1,046	1,378	2,000

There is no way of telling from this study how the quality of service varies with increase in size, but it may be assumed that the improvement does not compensate for the increase in cost. A figure of 600,000 lire per worker has been used in the text to illustrate the possible incremental capital cost, which corresponds to about half of the total cost in towns of moderate size.

[21] We assume facilities for a million urban workers available to start with.

which gives the optimum program at point C.[22] The addition of a capital cost for labor therefore leads us away from point A, which maximizes the use of labor, but it is unlikely to go to the other extreme, as some have suggested, of leading to the solution which minimizes its use.

4. The Productivity of Investment

Perhaps the most interesting outcome of this set of calculations is the evidence which it provides of the difference between a partial

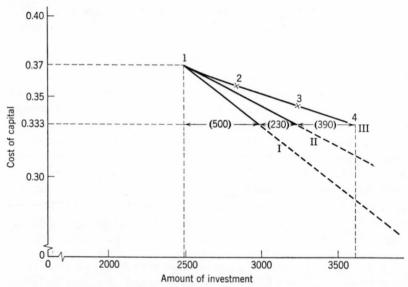

Fig. 11.3. Partial and Total Estimates of the Productivity of Investment. (I) Direct demand for investment, (II) Direct plus indirect demand at constant prices, (III) Total demand at equilibrium prices.

analysis of investment and a general equilibrium analysis. We can use these results to illustrate the difference in the total demand for investment under various assumptions and also the effects of interdependence on the profitability of investment in individual sectors.

To study the total demand for investment we construct a curve (Fig. 11.3), similar to Fig. 11.1 for foreign exchange, in which the

---

[22] The same result can be gotten from curve I by taking an isocost line with a slope of 0.6 and finding the point at which it touches the isoquant. This merely confirms the programming solution, which assumes P_l equal to 0.6 billion lire per thousand workers at point C.

demand for investment is calculated as a function of its cost. Heretofore we have used the cost of capital as the numeraire for the price system, but now the price of foreign exchange will serve this purpose. The price (opportunity cost) of capital is therefore given in Table 11.4 as the reciprocal of the previously assumed price of foreign exchange. Curve III in Fig. 11.3 shows the increase in demand for investment that would occur if the cost of capital were successively lowered from 0.37 to 0.333, assuming that the economy made the optimal adjustments indicated by the programming solutions (A1 to A4) and final demand remained constant.

For purposes of comparison, we consider two partial analyses of investment possibilities. The first assumes that both commodity prices and demands remain constant. Investment will take place in sectors where exports or substitutes for imports are profitable until the return on capital falls to the lower cost of 0.333. The result, as shown in curve I, is an increase in investment of 500 (from about 2500 to 3000) for a 10% fall in the cost of capital. As a second assumption, we take only prices as fixed and calculate (by an input-output solution) the additional amount of investment that would take place to satisfy the indirect demands resulting from case I. The result (curve II) is a further increase of 230, but this still falls short by 390 of the optimum amount already calculated. This last difference is attributable to the lowering of prices of domestic materials which would take place (with competition) as a result of the fall in capital cost.

A further measure of the difference between these partial and total estimates of the productivity of investment is provided by the elasticities of the three demand curves: 1.7 for curve I, 2.4 for curve II, and 3.5 for curve III. These results illustrate the point made by Rosenstein-Rodan (1943) and Nurkse (1953) that the total returns on a balanced program of investment will be significantly greater than the sum of those calculated for its components by individual investors.

The difference between over-all and partial analysis is reflected in the composition of the optimum program as well as in its total yield. Investment in one sector will provide cheaper materials for processing by another, and further investment in both will be justified.[23] Partial criteria therefore tend to understate the profitability of projects which depend on investment in other sectors, and they correspondingly overstate the relative attractiveness of projects lacking these interconnections. In the present example, textiles and agricultural products

[23] The nature of this type of external economy has been shown very clearly by Scitovsky (1954).

would be lowered in price as a result of the investment program, and hence investments in clothing and food processing would be more profitable than would be indicated by a partial analysis. The quantitative significance of these external economies is likely to be much greater when there are economies of scale, which are excluded from the present model.[24]

If the prices of the optimum solution can be determined, they can be used to test further investment possibilities or alternative production techniques in the same way as excluded activities are examined to see whether an optimal solution has been reached. For this purpose the simplex criterion can be restated in terms of the marginal productivity of capital as: "expand any type of production in which the social marginal productivity (SMP) of investment is greater than its opportunity cost."[25] The use of a programming model to determine the equilibrium prices of some of the most important inputs (e.g., labor, foreign exchange, electric power, steel, etc.) may therefore make it possible to use the classical marginal tests of the efficiency of resource allocation, which are otherwise not very operational concepts.

E. Practical Use of Programming Methods

It is too soon to say how much formal programming methods can contribute to the work of economists and government policy makers concerned with economic development. Practical work so far has been limited to the use of input-output analysis to test the consistency of programs along the lines indicated in Chapter 10. The only tests

---

[24] The effects of interdependence on investment decisions when there are economies of scale are discussed in Chenery (1959).

[25] An expression for the SMP can be derived from Eq. (4.8) as follows:

$$\pi_j = \sum_i a_{ij} P_i - c_j = Z_j - c_j \tag{4.8}$$

$$(\text{SMP})_j = \frac{\sum_i a_{ij} P_i}{c_j} = \frac{Z_j}{c_j}$$

When $\pi_j > 0$, Z_j/c_j will be greater than the opportunity cost of capital (1.0). The social marginal product can be used in a gradient method for solving the investment programming problem by revising the prices at each stage, as shown in Chenery (1958), part II.

of linear programming for a whole economy of which we are aware,[26] other than those just discussed, are those reported by Frisch (1954) for Norway. The problems analyzed by him, however, are even more hypothetical than those we have considered.

Linear programming is being employed increasingly to study the allocation problems of single industries. Notable examples are given by Massé and Gibrat (1957) in their analysis of investment alternatives in the French electric power industry and by Henderson in the study of the coal industry discussed in Chapter 12. In these cases, the interrelations among investment decisions in a single industry are sufficiently complicated to warrant the use of linear programming techniques. In both studies, the results achieved represent a considerable improvement over alternative methods of analysis.

The main obstacle to the ready adoption of linear programming for national planning is the heavy demand that it makes for data. The construction of an input-output table of 40–50 sectors, with a corresponding breakdown of final demand, is a strain on the statistical resources of most countries, and the adoption of activity analysis in a very detailed form is not a feasible task at the present time. The more likely evolution of programming techniques is therefore first to develop models which only include alternative activities in sectors where they are critical to the solution.

The criterion for determining whether alternative activities should be included within the model should be the extent to which the choice among them depends on the solution to the system. In addition to imports and exports, alternative production techniques using different inputs may in some cases have to be analyzed within a general equilibrium framework. For example, the decisions as to the extent to which agriculture should be mechanized may depend on the effect of fuel imports on the balance of payments as well as on the relative prices of capital and labor. Here the alternative production methods should be included in the model.

In most cases (such as the example just given), the choice of technique can be made without regard to the decisions in other sectors if equilibrium prices of primary factors and foreign exchange are known. An important contribution of linear programming is to provide a better understanding of the nature of the factor costs which

---

[26] Some experiments are also being made with programming models for the whole economy at the Indian Statistical Institute, but the results have not yet been published.

should be used in making investment decisions and also a technique for calculating their magnitude in the form of shadow prices. The most serious mistakes of resource allocation could probably be avoided if planners had a better idea of the relative worth to the economy of capital, labor, and foreign exchange.

As it has been presented in this book, linear programming, when applied to a whole economy, is an extension and generalization of input-output analysis in which alternative activities and resource limitations are explicitly taken into account. Input-output, in turn, gives a way of calculating the effects on the economy of a proposed economic program. The results of such a calculation, even if they do not satisfy all the resource limitations, can be used as a basis for improving the trial program. Formal programming methods provide a systematic way of carrying out these revisions, whatever the method initially used to draw up the program.

The analysis required for a development program takes place on at least three levels: the projection of national income and its major components, the study of sectors of the economy, and the evaluation of individual projects. Each of these types of analysis encounters its main difficulties at the points where it must be consistent with the results of the others. The necessary connections can be made either in the form of quantities (for example, targets for each sector) or prices (for example, a minimum social return required on invest-ment). In general, prices provide a more desirable means of coordi-nation than quantities, particularly for relating project evaluation to the over-all analysis, since they allow more scope for the working of market forces and for detailed analysis of individual proposals. Pri-mary reliance on targets and on quantitative adjustments to plans tends to obscure the possible alternative uses of resources and increases the need for government intervention.

Linear programming concepts provide the needed connections among the three levels of analysis in an ideal form. In contrast to other methods of obtaining consistent programs, they produce tests of efficiency in the form of prices as part of the solution. The use of these shadow or accounting prices[27] would make it easier to decentral-ize investment decisions and to guide private initiative through indi-rect measures. Furthermore, the correct price solution may be more important than consistent targets because the choice of the wrong

---

[27] The use of accounting prices to evaluate investment projects is also suggested in Tinbergen (1958).

type of investment is usually more serious in the long run than the construction of the wrong *amount* of capacity. The latter error is likely to be rectified in time by the growth of demand, but an inefficient type of production may be perpetuated through tariff protection and subsidies for a long period. It can be argued, therefore, that the correct evaluation of the real contribution to national income of alternative investment projects is at least as important as the balancing of demand and supply for various commodities.

In the field of resource allocation, there has been relatively little study of the relation between various instruments of government policy and the analysis needed to utilize them. It is by no means clear, for example, that a government which relies primarily on tax incentives to private industry to bring about development needs a less detailed analysis of investment alternatives than does a government which invests directly in industrial sectors. In either case, the main function of a long-term development program is to establish guides for public and private agencies whose actions have an influence on resource use. The type of analysis needed is likely to be determined more by the structure of the economy than by the form of government influence on economic growth.

A P P E N D I X : Data for the Programming Model of Southern Italy

The principal data for the model of Southern Italy are reproduced here from Chenery (1955) and Chenery and Kretschmer (1956) with minor changes in form in order to fit the programming framework used in this chapter.

Table 11.2 gives the activities and restrictions in a form similar to model VIII. The range of capital coefficients in sectors where imports are possible is due to the aggregation from a more detailed commodity breakdown. Since it is assumed that the commodities requiring less capital will be produced first, the average coefficient for each sector is taken to be an increasing function of the proportion produced domestically, d_j: $c_j = \alpha_j + \beta_j d_j$. The values given correspond to $d_j = 0$ and $d_j = 1.0$ (except in sector 12). Production for export is considered as a separate activity.

Table 11.3 gives the assumed demand functions for exports. The coefficients for foreign exchange earned by the corresponding export activities are determined by inserting the export levels in these equations.

TABLE 11.2. BASIC DATA FOR MODEL OF SOUTHERN ITALY

Activities

Commodity	E_1	X_1	M_1	E_2	X_2	M_2	X_3	E_4	X_4	M_4	X_5	M_5	E_6	X_6	M_6
1 Clothing	−0.08	0.92	1.0												
2 Textiles	−0.25	−0.25		−0.38	0.62	1.0									
3 Construction	···*						0.82								
4 Mechanical	−0.01	−0.01					−0.06				−0.86	1.0			
5 Other Industries	−0.03	−0.03					−0.03	−0.10	0.90	1.0					
6 Food								−0.04	−0.04		−0.02		−0.13	0.87	1.0
7 Metallurgy				−0.14	−0.14		−0.08	−0.22	−0.22		−0.15		−0.43	−0.43	
8 Agriculture				−0.01	−0.01		−0.01	−0.01	−0.01		−0.05		−0.02	−0.02	
9 Transport				−0.01	−0.01		−0.03	−0.01	−0.01		−0.01		−0.01	−0.01	
10 Petroleum				−0.06	−0.06		−0.04	−0.02	−0.02		−0.09		−0.01	−0.01	
11 Chemicals	−0.02	−0.02		−0.01	−0.01		−0.06	−0.02	−0.02				−0.01	−0.01	
12 Mining				−0.01	−0.01		−0.04	−0.14	−0.14				−0.19		
13 Services	−0.36	−0.36		−0.17	−0.17						−0.19		−0.19	−0.19	
14 Power				−0.01	−0.01		−0.01	−0.01	−0.01						
15 Foreign Exchange	†		−1.0	†		−1.0		†		−1.0		−1.0	†		−1.0
16 Labor	−1.00	−1.00	−1.0	−0.50	−0.50	−1.0	−1.80	−0.65	−0.65	−1.0	−0.90	−1.0	−0.15	−0.15	−1.0
17 Capital§	0.50	0.20−0.30		0.65	0.50−0.78		0.45	0.87	0.50−1.25		0.20−1.10		0.58	0.33−0.58	

TABLE 11.2. Basic Data for Model of Southern Italy (Continued)

Activities

Commodity	X_7	M_7	X_8	M_8	X_9	X_{10}	E_{11}	X_{11}	M_{11}	X_{12}	M_{12}	X_{13}	X_{14}	Restrictions B_i‡
1 Clothing							1.1							162
2 Textiles							−0.01	−0.01						191
3 Construction	−0.01													280
4 Mechanical							−0.01	−0.01						383
5 Other Industries					−0.04	−0.01	−0.02	−0.02						144
6 Food			−0.02				−0.02	−0.01						443
7 Metallurgy	0.52	1.0					−0.01	−0.01						31
8 Agriculture			0.90	1.0	−0.01		−0.02	−0.02		−0.01				98
9 Transport			−0.02		0.97	−0.03	−0.01	−0.02		−0.15				24
10 Petroleum					−0.25	0.99	−0.02	−0.02					−0.02	168
11 Chemicals			−0.02			−0.01	−0.31	0.69	1.0	−0.03				149
12 Mining					−0.05	−0.21	−0.07	−0.07		1.00	1.0		−0.04	68
13 Services			−0.17		−0.03	−0.08	−0.13	−0.13		−0.07		0.96	−0.01	40
14 Power					−0.04		−0.04	−0.04		−0.01		−0.01	1.00	22
15 Foreign Exchange		−1.0		−1.25			*		−1.0		−1.0			−284
16 Labor	−0.50				−0.50	−0.15	−0.35	−0.35		−0.45		−3.00	−0.20	−3200
17 Capital§	0.60–1.50		2.00–2.83		3.86	0.72	0.75	0.38–1.38		1.00–1.50		0.58	3.00	Minimum

* ... denotes a coefficient of less than .005.

† See Table 11.3.

‡ B_1 to B_{15} in billions of lire; B_{16} in thousands of nonagricultural workers. Restrictions 1–14 represent the excess of final demand over the amount that could be supplied from existing capacity.

§ Capital coefficients are assumed to vary between the given limits in proportion to the fraction of demand produced domestically.

TABLE 11.3. Foreign Exchange Earnings per Unit of Exports as a Function of Quantity Exported*

	Sector	Coefficient
1	Clothing	$1.00-0.005E_1$
2	Textiles	$1.00-0.0033E_2$
4	Mechanical	$1.00-0.0017E_4$
6	Food	$1.10-0.0005E_6$
11	Chemicals	$1.00-0.005E_{11}$

* All demand functions are hypothetical.

Table 11.4 gives selected solutions to the model, which have been used to construct Figs. 11.1, 11.2, and 11.3. Further details are given in the original publications.

TABLE 11.4. RESULTS OF TRIAL SOLUTIONS*

Solution Number	A1	A2	A3	A4	A5	B1	B2	B3	C1	C2	C3
Price of foreign exchange (capital units)	2.7	2.8	2.9	3.0	2.84	3.0	3.3	3.5	3.5	3.8	3.719
Price of labor (capital units)	0	0	0	0	0	0.3	0.3	0.3	0.6	0.6	0.6
Price of capital (foreign exchange units)	0.370	0.357	0.345	0.333	0.352						
Exports†	686	714	739	766	725	597	680	737	582	666	643
Imports	1163	1062	944	832	1009	1278	964	739	1208	823	927
Trade deficit	477	348	205	66	284	681	284	2	626	158	284
Increase in GNP	1391	1524	1672	1812	1590	1150	1553	1834	1187	1652	1527
Investment in:											
Industry	1436	1600	1789	1959	1685	1063	1494	1824	1023	1468	1348
Agriculture	389	519	676	838	589	376	840	1231	625	1289	1110
Services	669	717	772	818	742	579	720	818	592	746	704
Total‡	2494	2836	3238	3615	3016	2019	3054	3874	2240	3503	3162
Total labor§	2839	3042	3270	3473	3145	2346	2929	3347	2298	2923	2755

* All values are in billions of lire; labor in thousands of workers. Quantity and price solutions for the A trials are given in Chenery and Kretschmer (1956), tables 4 and 5.
† Exports are valued here at foreign prices but at domestic prices in computing GNP.
‡ Excluding investment not directly related to production (housing, public works, roads, etc.).
§ Excluding labor in agriculture.

BIBLIOGRAPHY

Buchanan, N. S., and H. S. Ellis, *Approaches to Economic Development*, Twentieth Century Fund, New York, 1955.

Chenery, H., "The Application of Investment Criteria," *Quarterly Journal of Economics*, LXVII, No. 1, 76–96 (February 1953).

————, "The Role of Industrialization in Development Programs," *American Economic Review*, XLV, No. 2, 40–57 (May 1955).

————, "Development Policies and Programmes," *Economic Bulletin for Latin America*, III, No. 1 (March 1958).

————, The "Interdependence of Investment Decisions," in M. Abramovitz and others, *The Allocation of Economic Resources*, Stanford University Press, 1959.

Chenery, H., and K. Kretschmer, "Resource Allocation for Economic Development," *Econometrica*, XXIV, No. 4, 365–399 (October 1956).

Frisch, R., *Principles of Linear Programming*, Universitetets Socialøkonomiske Institutt, Oslo, 1954.

Galenson, W., and H. Leibenstein, "Investment Criteria, Productivity, and Economic Development," *Quarterly Journal of Economics*, LXIX, No. 3, 343–370 (August 1955).

Kahn, A., "Investment Criteria in Development Programs," *Quarterly Journal of Economics*, LXV, No. 1, 38–61 (February 1951).

Lewis, W. A., *The Theory of Economic Growth*, George Allen and Unwin, London, 1955.

Massé, P., and R. Gibrat, "Applications of Linear Programming to Investments in the Electric Power Industry," *Management Science*, III, No. 2, 149–166 (January 1957).

Meier, G. M., and R. E. Baldwin, *Economic Development*, John Wiley and Sons, New York, 1957.

Nurkse, R., *Problems of Capital Formation in Underdeveloped Countries*, Oxford University Press, New York, 1953.

Rosenstein-Rodan, P., "Problems of Industrialization of Eastern and South-Eastern Europe," *Economic Journal*, LIII, No. 210, 202–211 (June-September 1943).

Scitovsky, T., "Two Concepts of External Economies," *Journal of Political Economy*, LXII, No. 2, 142–151 (April 1954).

Tinbergen, J., *The Design of Development*, Johns Hopkins Press, Baltimore, 1958.

United Nations, Department of Economic Affairs, *Measures for the Economic Development of Under-Developed Countries* (E/1986-ST/ECA/10 3 May 1951).

————, Economic Commission for Asia and the Far East, "Economic Development and Planning in Asia and the Far East," *Economic Bulletin for Asia and the Far East*, VI, No. 3 (November 1955).

————, Economic Commission for Latin America, *Analyses and Projections of Economic Development*, I, *Introduction to the Technique of Programming* (E/CN.12/363, June 1955).

Selected Examples of Development Programs

Burma, Economic Planning Board, *Two-Year Plan of Economic Development for Burma*, Rangoon, 1948.

Government of India, Planning Commission, *Second Five Year Plan*, 1955.

Government of Pakistan, National Planning Board, *The First Five Year Plan, 1955–60*, Karachi, 1957.

International Bank for Reconstruction and Development (Analyses of development prospects in British Guiana, Chile, Colombia, Cuba, Guatemala, Iraq, Jamaica, Malaya, Mexico, Nicaragua, Nigeria, Syria, Turkey), Johns Hopkins Press, Baltimore.

Japanese Government, Economic Planning Agency, *New Long-Range Economic Plan of Japan* (*FY 1958–FY 1962*), Tokyo, 1957.

Lewis, W. A., "Report on Industrialisation and the Gold Coast," Government Printing Department, Accra, 1953.

Netherlands, Central Planning Bureau, *Central Economic Plan*, 's-Gravenhage, 1956.

Organisation for European Economic Co-operation, Council, *Outline of Development of Income and Employment in Italy in the Ten-Year Period 1955–64*, Paris, 1955 (mimeographed).

Puerto Rico Planning Board, *Economic Development of Puerto Rico: 1940–1950, 1951–1960*, San Juan, 1951.

Republic of the Philippines, National Economic Council, *The Five-Year Economic and Social Development Program for FY 1957–1961*, Manila, 1957.

Royal Norwegian Ministry of Finance, *The National Budget of Norway*, Oslo, 1954.

United Nations, Economic Commission for Asia and the Far East, "Salient Features of Economic Development Plans," Chapter 2 in *Economic Survey of Asia and the Far East, 1956.*

United Nations, Economic Commission for Latin America, *Analyses and Projections of Economic Development, II, Economic Development of Brazil* (E/CN.12/364/Rev.1 April 1956).

——, *Analyses and Projections of Economic Development, III, Economic Development of Colombia* (E/CN.12/365/Add.2 6 August 1955).

——, *Analyses and Projections of Economic Development, IV, Economic Development of Argentina* (E/CN.12/429 30 June 1958).

chapter 12

Interregional analysis

All of the three types of model discussed earlier—national income, input-output, and linear programming—have been applied in empirical studies of economic relations among regions. Although our main interest is in the two interindustry techniques, it will be useful to start by comparing the formulations used in all three methods.

A. Comparison of Interregional Studies

Just as interindustry analysis breaks down aggregate production and consumption by commodity, so interregional analysis decomposes these aggregates by region. Although formally there is little difficulty in combining the two types of disaggregation, the empirical problems are multiplied. The various types of data required are rarely broken down both by region and by commodity, and even when they are the cost of manipulating the system goes up very rapidly when a regional breakdown is introduced. For these reasons, empirical studies have been designed to take advantage of particular types of data, and each is useful only for limited purposes.

The few studies made so far can be classified into three types on the basis of their purpose and analytical technique:[1]

[1] A fourth type of regional study may be mentioned although it will not be dis-

(1) *International trade models*, whose main purpose is to explain the level of trade among countries. In order to include a number of countries, commodity detail has been sacrificed. The variables are national aggregates with the internal structure of production in each country not introduced explicitly.

(2) *Interregional input-output models*, whose purpose is to analyze the interrelations among trade and production in two or more regions. In these studies, a compromise has been made between the number of regions and the number of commodities included.

(3) *Interregional programming models*, whose purpose is to determine the optimum allocation of resources among regions. So far such models have been constructed only for single industries.

Leading examples of each of these types of study are given in Table 12.1 together with some of their structural characteristics. All of the models have in common the feature that exports from one region become imports into another. Export levels in each region are explained by the demand for imports in other regions, given an assumption as to how this demand will be divided among alternative sources of supply.

In the Neisser–Modigliani study, imports are assumed to be a function of income (or industrial output) and in some cases of other variables such as price. Exports from each of the six regions are taken as a function of total import demand for a given class of commodity. The structural parameters are determined by multiple regression analysis of time series for several inter-war periods.

The other four studies use a model in which interindustry relations are made explicit. In these cases, the structural parameters are estimated from observations of only one or two sets of cross-section data. The two input-output models (of Moses and the authors of this book) differ in the greater amount of regional detail in the first and greater commodity detail in the second. Each explains exports from one region as a constant fraction of the total demand for a given commodity in each of the other regions. Production levels as well

---

cussed: the use of a national input-output table to construct a model for a single region. Such studies have been made for Maryland (University of Maryland, 1954), Utah (Moore and Petersen, 1955), and the Eighth Federal Reserve District (Freutel, 1952). Similar regional breakdowns have been made in Japan. Unless they are combined with other analyses, however, these single-region models present no features different from the national models already discussed, aside from the empirical problems of securing data on a regional basis.

as levels of trade are therefore determined from this analysis. Henderson's programming analysis of the coal industry also determines production levels, but he takes total consumption levels as given in each region. Fox's programming model for livestock feed makes demand in each region a function of price, while production is given. Both programming models determine the optimum supply pattern from the assumption of minimum aggregate cost.

TABLE 12.1. Characteristics of Interregional Models

	Commodities	Regions	Principal Variables		Equations*
			Endogenous	Exogenous	
1. Neisser–Modigliani (1953) (world trade model)	3	6	(1) Exports (2) Imports	(1) National income (2) Industrial production (3) Prices	36
2. Moses (1955) (input-output model of U.S.)	10	3	(1) Production levels (2) Interregional shipments	(1) Final demands	33
3. Chenery–Clark (1953) (input-output model of Italy)	22	2	(1) Production levels (2) Interregional shipments	(1) Final demands	46
4. Henderson (1958) (programming model of U.S. coal industry)	2†	14	(1) Interregional shipments (2) Production levels (3) Prices	(1) Total demand by regions (2) Regional capacity	36
5. Fox (1953) (model of U.S. livestock-feed economy)	1	10	(1) Interregional shipments (2) Regional demand (3) Prices	(1) Regional production	20

* In the reduced form used in solving the system.
† Two types of coal production, which are substitutes in use.

Since the size of the equation systems in the five models is much the same, they indicate a variation in emphasis on regional *versus* commodity disaggregation. In going from the first to the third model, the number of regions is reduced from six to two while the number of commodity groups increases from three to twenty-two. Since no attempts have been made to apply alternative models to the same set of data, one can only speculate as to the advantages of one or the other type of disaggregation for different problems. Some suggestions on this point will be given below.

Of the questions that can be studied with the help of interregional models, we are mainly concerned with those to which interindustry analysis can make a unique contribution: the interrelations between production and trade in various sectors. Since national income analysis sheds little light on this problem, we shall not discuss the Neisser–Modigliani study further but shall compare the other four cases. As national income and interindustry studies are developed further, however, it is to be expected that they will be integrated in various ways to produce systems that are more widely applicable than the models that have been tested up to now.

B. Regional Input-Output Studies

The interregional input-output studies which have been published so far all stem from the work of the Harvard Economic Research Project. Before discussing the two completed models for Italy and the United States, therefore, we shall outline some of the earlier results of this project.

1. The First Explorations

The first years' work of the Harvard Project on interregional analysis is reported on by Leontief (1953a) and Isard (1951, 1953). Leontief first proposed a "balanced regional model" which could be used to disaggregate the solution of a national model into regional components. He made the assumption that, to a first approximation, industries could be characterized as "national" or "local." For local industries, it was assumed that regional demand would be supplied entirely from local sources; such industries were said to be regionally balanced. For national industries, on the other hand, it was assumed that each producing region would supply a constant proportion of the demand in *each* consuming region. This assumption about national industries was recognized to be only a rough approximation, but it offers the great practical advantage that the model can be tested empirically by the use of production and consumption data alone. (See Leontief, 1953a.)

Tests of the balanced regional model, as reported by Isard (1953), showed that although a considerable number of sectors could be accurately described as local, the concept of a national industry in which the pattern of supply was unaffected by the location of demand needed further refinement. A large proportion of nonlocal industries fall into an intermediate category in which the location of demand as well as the distribution of production capacity determine interregional flows.

Isard (1951) proposed an alternative input-output model which made quite a different assumption about the nonlocalized industries. He suggested that a commodity supplied from one region should be considered as a different input from a similar commodity supplied from another source and that separate input coefficients should apply to each. This amounts to saying that automobile production in Michigan requires steel in fixed proportions from Pennsylvania and Illinois, and that other steel users in Michigan may purchase steel from these sources in different proportions. Leontief's assumption about national commodities would appear in this model as a special case in which the proportions among steel supplied from different sources are the same for all uses in all regions.

Isard's model has not been applied in empirical work because it would require information on the source of supply for each commodity and each sector of use. The model discussed in Chapter 3, which has been used by Moses and by the present authors, differs from it in assuming that sources of supply are fixed for *all* uses of a given commodity in a given region rather than depending on the type of use.[2]

Isard and Leontief at first attempted to account for the variation in supply of nonlocalized commodities by introducing regions of different order. It was assumed that for some commodities supply and demand would be balanced within quite small regions and for others they would balance within areas of different sizes. Experiments with different groupings of states, however, did not reveal any satisfactory two-region breakdown within the United States. The basic problem seems to be that market areas for different commodities are overlapping and that a number of different breakdowns would be needed in order to produce regional balance.

These experiments provided useful guides for further research. One result was the ranking of industries according to the ratio of interregional trade to total national use, which is reproduced in Table

[2] This assumption is convenient because it requires data only on total interregional flows of each commodity. Its theoretical justification is that all uses in a region constitute a single market and that the supply patterns are determined more by total demand than by the nature of the intended use. This type of aggregation may assume more similarity than actually exists, but the separation of supply according to type of use errs in the other direction by eliminating offsetting variations in demand.

TABLE 12.2. RATIO OF NET INTERREGIONAL TRADE TO NATIONAL
CONSUMPTION IN THE U.S. (1939)*

Sector†	Based on States (%)	Based on Census Regions (%)
Construction	4	2
Households	7	3
Trade	9	4
Gas and electric power	12	6
Steam railroads	26	11
Business and personal services	17	13
Communications	15	13
Nonmetallic minerals	42	13
Eating & drinking places	24	18
Miscellaneous transportation	31	20
Printing & publishing	33	23
Iron & steel foundry products	57	26
Chemicals	45	29
Food processing	43	30
Wood pulp and paper	51	30
Furniture	40	31
Nonferrous metals	78	38
Iron & steel n.e.c.	55	38
Ferrous metals	102	42
Transportation equipment n.e.c.	84	43
All other manufacturing	57	45
Agriculture & fishing	56	48
Industrial & heating equipment n.e.c.	60	49
Leather and leather goods	78	49
Rubber	86	55
Coal & coke	102	55
Apparel	72	64
Electric equipment n.e.c.	82	66
Merchandise and service machines	91	69
Engines & turbines	104	71
Shipbuilding	101	75
Aircraft	122	78
Petroleum	110	82
Textile mill products	99	87
Lumber & timber products	95	87
Motor vehicles	122	111
Machine tools	112	112
Agricultural machinery	136	117

* Based on Charts 17 and 19, pp. 144 and 146, in Isard (1953). Net trade
is defined as the sum of net regional surpluses and deficits without regard
to sign.
  † In order of figures in second column.

12.2. This table shows the effect of two different regional break-downs, one using the 48 states and the other using the nine census regions. The median ratio of trade to total demand is only reduced from 60 to 43% by the use of larger regions, but a few commodity groups come much closer to balancing in the latter case. Interregional trade in non-metallic minerals is reduced from 42 to 13%, for example, and in ferrous metals from 102 to 42%. With few exceptions, however, the ranking of sectors is not greatly affected by the choice of region.

Although the data in Table 12.2 are suggestive, they do not constitute an adequate basis for classifying industries because they conceal compensating flows into and out of regions. Direct measurement of these flows and supplementary locational analyses are needed to construct even a first approximation to a regional model. The first ten sectors, most of which are services which must be rendered locally, do qualify on further examination as local industries. These localized sectors, which typically account for at least half of regional income,[3] are the most stable elements in interregional models.

2. A Two-Region Model of the Italian Economy

The interregional model of the Italian economy was designed to bridge the gap between a purely regional analysis, such as that given in section D of Chapter 11, and the national projections discussed in Chapter 10. It had the same purpose as those two studies: to analyze the effects of programs of economic development. Since large investment programs were being carried out in Southern Italy, it was important to know their effect on the rest of the country as well as on the South itself.

The specific use for which the analysis was intended determined to a large extent the choice of sectors and the method of estimating the structural coefficients. Like Leontief and Isard, the present authors had to rely mainly on regional production figures for each sector and to derive trade patterns indirectly from the application of national input coefficients. The drawbacks to this procedure are less serious when only two regions are distinguished because the commodity destinations are not in doubt.

The logic of separating the Italian economy into two regions is more apparent than it would be for most countries. The North and South have been politically united for less than a century, and structural differences in the economies of the two regions have, if anything,

[3] Excluding the "household" or consumption sector.

tended to increase since unification. Industry is heavily concentrated in the North, which makes the problem of estimating regional supply coefficients easier than it is in an economy like the United States, where industry is widely dispersed.

The input coefficients were obtained by aggregating the original Italian matrix into 22 sectors. The coefficients for the household sector, which must be included in a regional model because of the effect of the location of consumption on the location of production, were determined from preliminary budget studies. Somewhat different coefficients were estimated for each region.

Since our analysis was intended to measure the effects of a combined program of public and private investment, we assumed that an increase in regional self-sufficiency would result in sectors where investment appeared likely, particularly in market-oriented industries. Otherwise, we derived the supply coefficients from the existing capacity and production in each region.

The model used has been given in Eqs. (3.7) to (3.11). The supply coefficients for both regions are shown in Table 12.3. They indicate the proportions in which a commodity is expected to be supplied from each region or from imports. The total of the supply coefficients is 1.0 in each case except for rounding. The first ten sectors were assumed to be "national" in Leontief's sense of having identical supply patterns determined by the distribution of capacity. This assumption is strengthened by the very small capacity in the South in most of these sectors. The last eight sectors can be identified as local, since their supply coefficients are approximately 1.0 from the region concerned and zero from other sources. Except for clothing and lumber, these are the same sectors as those which were shown to be regionally balanced in Table 12.2 for the United States.

The remaining "mixed" sectors include agriculture, food processing, and petroleum refining, which comprise 85 per cent of all commodity production in the South. In each case the South is a net exporter to the North, but the location of demand has a substantial effect in determining the source of supply. For these sectors, the supply coefficients were inferred from the existing net balance of trade, assuming that local demand is met from local supply to the extent possible.

The inputs going to public and private investment, totalling 150 billion lire, constitute the final demands whose effects are to be determined. No change in exports or in current government expenditure is assumed. The breakdown of this demand by source of supply and the final solution are shown in Table 12.4.

TABLE 12.3. Italian Regional Supply Coefficients*

Demand in:	North			South		
Supply from:	North	South	Imports	North	South	Imports
National Sectors						
1 Textiles	0.93	0.05	0.02	0.93	0.05	0.02
2 Artificial fibers	0.86	0.01	0.13	0.86	0.01	0.13
3 Ferrous metals	0.82	0.09	0.09	0.82	0.09	0.09
4 Nonferrous metals	0.55	0.21	0.24	0.55	0.21	0.24
5 Metal products	0.88	0.05	0.08	0.88	0.05	0.08
6 Mining	0.59	0.33	0.08	0.59	0.33	0.08
7 Paper	0.92	0.04	0.04	0.92	0.04	0.04
8 Rubber	0.85	0.04	0.11	0.85	0.04	0.11
9 Other industries	0.82	0.17	0.01	0.82	0.17	0.01
10 Chemicals	0.85	0.08	0.07	0.85	0.08	0.07
Mixed Sectors						
11 Agriculture	0.84	0.07	0.08	—	0.92	0.08
12 Food processing	0.86	0.11	0.03	—	0.97	0.03
13 Fuel extraction	0.34	0.04	0.62	—	0.20	0.80
14 Petroleum refining	0.75	0.18	0.07	—	0.93	0.07
Local Sectors						
15 Clothing	0.99	—	0.01	—	0.99	0.01
16 Lumber	0.99	—	0.01	—	0.99	0.01
17 Nonmetallic minerals	0.96	—	0.04	—	0.96	0.04
18 Construction	1.00	—	—	—	1.00	—
19 Gas and coke	0.98	—	0.02	—	0.98	0.02
20 Electric power	0.99	—	0.01	—	1.00	—
21 Services	1.00	—	—	—	1.00	—
22 Transportation	1.00	—	—	—	1.00	—
23 Household	1.00	—	—	—	1.00	—

Source: *The Structure and Growth of the Italian Economy*, p. 111.

Three general features of these results are of particular interest: the distribution of incomes between regions; the effects of the investment program on the regional balance of payments; and the differing roles of the localized and non-localized sectors. Although more accurate data would change the details of the analysis, it seems unlikely that they would affect the broad conclusions on these points.

The initial investment of 150 billion lire is shown to generate income

TABLE 12.4. SOLUTION TO ITALIAN REGIONAL MODEL*

	Increase in Shipments for Final Demand†				Increase in Production			
	North	South	Imports	Total	North	South	Imports	Total
National Sectors:								
1–2 Textiles	...	...	...	...	44	2	1	48
3–5 Metals and metal products	41	3	1	45	83	8	6	97
6–10 Other industries	2	...	...	3	36	5	3	44
Mixed Sectors:								
11 Agriculture	...	...	...	...	60	58	9	127
12 Food processing	...	...	...	...	41	59	3	104
13–14 Fuels	...	3	...	3	6	9	8	22
Local Sectors:								
15 Clothing	...	...	...	...	8	10	...	18
16 Lumber	...	4	...	4	3	8	...	11
17 Nonmetallic minerals	...	18	1	19	1	20	1	22
19–20 Gas and electricity	...	3	...	3	9	7	...	16
21 Services	9	2	...	11	61	41	...	102
22 Transportation	...	...	...	...	11	10	...	21
23 Households‡ (value added)	...	63	...	63	160	194	...	354
Totals	52	96	2	150	524	431	31	985

* *Structure of the Italian Economy*, pp. 115–116. Figures in billions of lire.

† Inputs into construction have been allocated directly to the producing sector.

‡ The total production by households includes taxes and is approximately equal to the income generated in the region.

of 354 billion lire (total of sector 23) in all Italy plus 31 billion lire of imports. Of the total resources of 385 billion required to support the program, only about half represent value added within the South itself. Since 63 billion of value added in the South occurs in the investment process, the induced effects of investment on incomes in the North (160 billion) outweigh those in the South (131 billion). These results have some political significance, since they suggest that a public investment program in the South will be of almost as much benefit to the North as to the South in terms of incomes generated.

From an analytical point of view, it is of interest to compare this result to a solution to a model for the South alone. This was done by Chenery (1956). When the effects of Northern demand for imports from the South are not taken into account, income in the South is increased by 165 instead of by 194 billion lire. This difference of 18 per cent illustrates the importance of the "foreign trade repercussion" within a single country. Expressed in multiplier terms, the more complete system raises the investment multiplier in the South (taking 96 as the multiplicand) from 1.7 to 2.0.

The structure of interregional trade between the South and the North is typical of that between underdeveloped and advanced areas. Since the South imports a large fraction of its manufactured goods, an increase in investment has a large impact on the regional balance of payments. Of the 150 billion lire invested, 54 billion go directly for commodities not produced locally, most of which come from the North. The total imports into the region—from the North and abroad —required by the increase in regional income of 194 billion amount to 82 billion (not shown) giving a net[4] marginal propensity to import of 0.42.

Finally, it is instructive to consider the way in which income is divided between localized and nonlocalized sectors in the two regions. For the country as a whole, it can be calculated that 55% of income resulting from the investment program is generated in local sectors as we have classified them. In the South, however, 68% of the income is produced in local sectors, while in the North the proportion is only 42%. In large part this difference is due to the fact that the initial investment took place in the South, but the disparity is augmented by the predominant location of the national sectors in the North. In Table 12.7 we shall compare these results to those found in Moses' study of the United States.

3. A Three-Region Model of the American Economy

Although an increase in the number of regions beyond two has no effect on the conceptual scheme, the empirical problems become much more difficult. It is no longer possible to assume that an export from one region becomes an import of the other, and direct measures of interregional trade are essential.

[4] That is, making allowances for the induced exports to the North. The marginal propensity to import when the South is analyzed alone is 0.56.

Moses' three-region model of the United States represents a major advance in the empirical development of interregional models. It is the first study to make systematic use of direct estimates of inter-regional trade and to test the stability of trade coefficients over several years. Although it is too aggregated to give a detailed picture of interregional trade, it suggests the direction that further work in this field may take.

Moses' analysis utilizes the large 1947 input-output study that has already been described. The earlier work of Isard and Leontief with 1939 data provided a basis for dividing the United States into three regions: the East, Middle West and West. The West (Pacific Coast and mountain states) constitutes a natural region, much as the South does in Italy, although it produces only about 15% of the total income of the country. The division of the remainder into two parts is more arbitrary. The East is defined to include the New England, Middle Atlantic and South Atlantic census regions, and the Middle West the remainder.

The analytical model for Moses' study is also given by Eqs. (3.7) to (3.11). The regional supply coefficients—or trade coefficients, as Moses calls them—for these three regions are shown in Table 12.5. For commodities, they are estimated from the gross interregional trade in 1947, derived mainly from a sample of railroad carloadings. For the localized sectors, which in this more aggregated model are only utilities and services, the coefficients are derived from production and consumption data, using locational considerations as in earlier studies.

At this level of aggregation, none of the six nonlocalized sectors conforms very closely to Leontief's concept of a national industry. The consolidation of all manufacturing into one sector prevents a more detailed analysis of the industries to which this assumption is likely to apply. Since the regions in this model are large diversified economic units, they tend to supply more than half of their own requirements for all the major commodity groups listed. The only exception to this generalization is provided by the imports of animal products and petroleum and natural gas into the East. Conversely, only 7 of the 99 coefficients representing interregional trade are as large as 0.20. This contrasts with 16 out of 92 in the Italian model. The difference is due, in the first instance, to the aggregation of all manufactures in the American case and secondly to the lack of industry in Southern Italy.

The problem to which Moses has applied his model is a hypothetical one, but it is conceptually similar to the Italian example. He as-

TABLE 12.5.   AMERICAN REGIONAL SUPPLY COEFFICIENTS*

Demand in:	I. East				II. Middle West				III. West			
Supply from:	I	II	III	Imports	I	II	III	Imports	I	II	III	Imports
Nonlocal Sectors:												
1 Agriculture	0.47	0.32	0.07	0.14	0.04	0.85	0.10	0.02	0.00	0.10	0.85	0.04
2 Animals and products	0.37	0.57	0.03	0.04	0.08	0.84	0.08	0.00	0.02	0.36	0.60	0.02
3 Mining	0.79	0.13	0.00	0.08	0.20	0.68	0.02	0.10	0.00	0.01	0.99	0.00
4 Lumber and products	0.71	0.10	0.11	0.08	0.05	0.69	0.20	0.06	0.00	0.02	0.98	0.01
5 Manufactures	0.74	0.21	0.02	0.04	0.20	0.75	0.03	0.01	0.00	0.24	0.65	0.02
6 Petroleum and natural gas	0.17	0.64	0.00	0.19	0.01	0.97	0.02	0.00	0.00	0.01	0.56	0.42
Local Sectors:												
7 Electric power	1.00	0.00	0.00	0.00	0.00	1.00	0.00	0.00	0.00	0.00	1.00	0.00
8 Transport and comm.	0.99	0.00	0.02	0.00	0.00	1.00	0.01	0.00	0.00	0.00	1.00	0.00
9 Trade, finance	0.98	0.02	0.00	0.00	0.00	1.00	0.00	0.00	0.00	0.02	0.98	0.00
10 Other services	1.00	0.00	0.00	0.00	0.04	0.95	0.02	0.00	0.00	0.00	1.00	0.00
11 Households	1.00	0.00	0.00	0.00	0.00	1.00	0.00	0.00	0.00	0.00	1.00	0.00

* Source: Moses (1955), p. 818.   Data have been rounded.

sumes a 10% increase in all nonconsumption items of final use—investment, government expenditure, and exports—in the Eastern region alone. The increases in production levels in each region resulting from this assumption are shown in Table 12.6.

Despite the structural differences between Italy and the United States, and the different composition of final demand, there is a considerable similarity in the pattern of income generation in the two analyses. A comparison between them is given in Table 12.7, in

TABLE 12.6. SOLUTION TO AMERICAN REGIONAL MODEL*

	Increase in Production by Region		
	I	II	III
Nonlocal Sectors:			
1 Agriculture	27	70	17
2 Animals and products	55	146	17
3 Mining	13	7	2
4 Lumber and products	7	4	3
5 Manufactures	414	264	33
6 Petroleum and gas	4	25	1
Local Sectors:			
7 Electric power	13	6	0
8 Transport and comm.	72	30	6
9 Trade, finance	174	72	11
10 Other services	243	96	19
11 Households	698	310	50

*Source: Moses (1955), p. 821. The data published do not permit a calculation of the increase in shipments for final demand.

which the Middle West has been combined with the West to form a single region. In the originating region (Southern Italy and Eastern U.S.), the increase in income occurs mainly in the local sectors (68% in Italy and 73% in the U.S.). In the other region, the opposite is true; 58% of the increase in Northern Italy and 61% of the increase in the Middle and Western U.S. comes in nonlocalized sectors. Since the Eastern United States is more self-sufficient than is Southern Italy, however, a larger proportion of the total increase in income occurs in the Eastern United States (66%) than in Southern Italy (55%).

The empirical validity of interregional analyses of this type hinges on the stability of the regional supply coefficients. The theoretical case is best for the two extremes of complete market orientation and complete regional specialization. Since the service sectors, which produce from 30 to 50% of national income, fall into the first category, they provide a strong argument for distinguishing regional effects. The extent of specialization depends on resource endowments, on the degree of economic development, and on the size of the regions distinguished. Specialization and stable supply coefficients may result from the absence of natural resources, as for oil and gas in the Eastern United States; from the concentration of production due to economies

TABLE 12.7. COMPARISON OF REGIONAL ANALYSES, IN PER CENT

		Italy		United States	
		South	North	East	West
1	Initial division of income	25	75	42	58
2	Division of increase in shipments for final demand	63	37		
3	Division of total income produced	55	45	66	34
4	Distribution of income by sectors:				
	(a) local	68	42	73	39
	(b) nonlocal	32	58	27	61
5	Regional propensity to import	0.42	...	0.30	...

of scale, as for automobiles in Northern Italy; or from product differentiation related to the source of supply. In each of these cases there will be substantial differences in the cost of supply from different sources and the existing supply patterns will tend to persist.

The only empirical test of the stability of regional supply coefficients is that reported by Moses. He calculated such coefficients for his first five commodity groups for the years 1947, 1948, and 1949. The average change from year to year was 0.013. When 1949 coefficients were used with 1947 data, the average error in predicting the 15 total regional shipments was 4%, and it was 12% for the individual interregional flows.[5] Although no tests over longer periods have been

[5] Details of this test are given in Moses (1955), pp. 824–826. Omission of the Western region reduces the average error for individual flows from 12 to 6%.

made, these results are certainly sufficiently encouraging to warrant further experiments on a less aggregated basis.

It is not necessary for regional supply coefficients to be constant to use the type of model which we have discussed, but only that they should be predictable. Supply coefficients are least predictable when there are only small differences in the cost of supply from different sources or when capacity limitations are effective. In the former case, small changes in price may produce large variations in the pattern of trade, as in the international markets for relatively homogeneous commodities like wheat, cotton, petroleum, etc. When capacity limitations are important, the amount imported depends to some extent on the level of demand in each region and the supply coefficients may vary considerably. Models permitting choice among alternative sources of supply, which are described in the next section, can shed some light on the quantitative significance of these factors in actual cases.

C. Interregional Programming Models

Linear programming may be suggested as one way to overcome the difficulties of interregional analysis when there are alternative sources of supply of substitute commodities. As in the previous chapter, we can introduce alternative activities for parts of the model while maintaining the input-output structure for the rest. The analyses that have been made so far, however, have taken total regional demands as already determined and have studied only the optimum supply pattern for a single industry in isolation. It would not be difficult to combine this approach with an over-all interindustry solution by an iterative procedure if there were not too many industries requiring such special studies.

The application of programming models to the allocation of basic industrial commodities among regions has been suggested by several authors, such as Manne (1956) for petroleum, but the only detailed studies available are those of Henderson (1958) and Fox (1953). These results are particularly interesting for comparison with input-output studies because they show the advantages as well as the difficulties of the programming approach.

1. A Model for the Coal Industry

In Henderson's study, the United States is divided into 14 regions, of which 11 produce coal. Two types of production, underground and surface mining, are distinguished in each region because their production costs are different. The data for the model consist of the following:

(1) Capacity for each type of production in each region;
(2) Total regional demand for coal;
(3) Unit cost of production of each type in each region;
(4) Unit cost of transport to each destination.

In this form, the model contains only the results of interindustry analysis in the form of total demands and total production and transport costs rather than an explicit interindustry structure. So long as demands and costs are not much affected by the solution, however, such a division of the analysis is valid.

These data can be put in the form of the classical Hitchcock-Koopmans transportation model by combining production and transport costs into a single delivery cost for each combination of sources and destinations. There are 22 sources and 14 destinations or 308 theoretically possible deliveries, but data were only collected for the 168 which might conceivably be used. The programming problem is to allocate sources of supply in such a way as to satisfy the given regional demands at minimum total cost.[6]

There are two types of equation in the quantity solution for this model, as in the more general interindustry programming model. First, the total of the flows to a given region must equal total demand in that region. In contrast to the input-output model, however, each of these flows is treated as a separate variable rather than as a constant fraction of regional demand. Second, the total supply from a given region must not exceed its capacity for each type of production. This type of equation is absent from the input-output model. Linear programming thus provides the same kind of generalization of the multi-regional input-output system as it did for exports and imports in a single region in the preceding chapter.

Since each shipment in the model enters into both a supply and a demand equation and there are no interindustry demands, the quantity equations of the transport model can be represented in the simple form shown in Table 12.8, which corresponds to Table 3.5. (The price equations can be analyzed in the same way.) Here the demand equations are given by columns and the supply equations by rows. Input

[6] Good discussions of this type of model and its solution are given in Manne (1956), and in Dorfman, Samuelson, and Solow (1958), Chapter 5.

TABLE 12.8. MINIMUM-COST SOLUTION TO HENDERSON MODEL FOR COAL DELIVERIES (1947)*

Region of Supply†	1	2	3	4	5	6	7	8	9	10	11	12	13	14	Excess Capacity	Total Supply (Capacity)
1 U	78				48									47	52	226
S	143															143
2 U		66	99				35					29	123		104	382
S			40									31				97
3 U				99		43		12							17	271
S																41
4 U															50	50
S				8												8
5 U					65											65
S					52											52
6 U						165										165
S						75										75
7 U															13	13
S							28									28
8 U								1								1
S								3								3
9 U									21		9				7	37
S									7							7
10 U										17					3	20
S										1						1
11 U											1					1
S											1					1
Total Demand	221	66	140	107	165	283	63	16	29	18	11	60	123	47	336	1686

* Source: Henderson (1958), Table 19. Units are 10^{13} Btu equivalent.

† Regions (U denotes underground mining, S surface): 1. Pa., Md. 2. W.Va. 3. Va., Ky., D.C. 4. Ala., Tenn., Ga., N.C., S.C., Fla., Miss., La. 5. Ohio. 6. Ill., Ind., Mich. 7. Ia., Mo., Kan., Ark., Okla., Tex. 8. N.D., S.D., Neb. 9. Mont., Wyo., Utah, Idaho. 10. Colo., N.M., Ariz., Calif., Nev. 11. Wash., Ore. 12. Me., Vt., N.H., Mass., Conn., R.I. 13. N.Y., N.J., Del. 14. Minn., Wis.

coefficients are not included since they are all unity. The optimum quantity solution to the model for 1947 is shown. The fourth demand equation in the solution, for example, states that total demand of 107 in region 4 is supplied by 99 units of underground output from region 3 and 8 units of surface output from region 4. The first supply equation states that underground capacity of 226 in region 1 delivers 78 to region 1, 48 to region 5, 47 to region 14, and has unused capacity of 52 remaining. Since excess capacity is included, total supply equals total demand.

There are 36 equations in this model,[1] and the basic theorem of linear programming assures us that there will be only 36 positive variables in the solution. Of these, 7 represent non-use of capacity in the present case, so there are only 29 positive shipments out of the 308 *a priori* possibilities. Twenty are shipments for use within the producing region and nine are interregional movements. Exports come almost entirely from the first three surplus regions, but they are spread among eight deficit regions. No region both imports and exports, an inherent feature of linear programming models. The corresponding unit prices and royalties in the optimum solution are determined by a similar calculation.

Henderson has calculated solutions for the years 1947, 1949, and 1951 and has compared them to actual shipments in those years. If his cost assumptions are correct, the difference in total cost between the optimum and observed patterns amounts to about 10%, or $200 million. The difference is greater in 1949, when there was a large fall in demand, than in 1947 because the industry and the labor union acted to spread the reduction among all districts rather than having the high-cost producers bear the full effect.

2. A Model for Feed Grain

A more general interregional model of trade in a single commodity, in which both supply and demand are functions of price, has been analyzed by Samuelson (1952). He shows that the solution to this nonlinear model includes the solution to the simpler Hitchcock-Koopmans transportation model and that successive approximations in an iterative solution will converge. Although the demand and supply functions needed to implement this type of model are not likely to be ascertainable in many cases, Fox (1953) has applied a simplified version of the model to a study of interregional trade in feed grain.

The model used by Fox differs from that of Henderson in two re-

[1] Twenty-two supply equations and fourteen demand equations.

TABLE 12.9. QUANTITY AND PRICE SOLUTIONS FOR FEED GRAIN SHIPMENTS, 1949–1950*

Producing Region	Consuming Region										Total Output	Price†
	1	2	3	4	5	6	7	8	9	10		
1. Northeast	7.4 *0*										7.4	1.52
2. Corn Belt	1.7 *0.22*	47.7 *0*				1.9 *0.16*	2.3 *0.22*	1.6 *0.15*			55.1	1.31
3. Lake	2.8 *0.31*		15.6 *0*								18.4	1.21
4. Northern Plains	1.8‡ *0.36*			13.3 *0*				1.4 *0.26*		1.9 *0.41*	18.4	1.17
5. Appalachian					8.6 *0*						8.6	1.46
6. Southeast						4.6 *0*					4.6	1.52
7. Delta							3.2 *0*				3.2	1.45
8. Southern Plains								5.7 *0*			5.7	1.43
9. Mountain									2.9 *0*	0.4 *0.30*	3.3	1.27
10. Pacific										2.7 *0*	2.7	1.57
Total Demand	13.8	47.7	15.6	13.3	10.6	6.8	4.7	7.2	2.9	5.0	127.6	
Price	1.52	1.31	1.21	1.17	1.46	1.52	1.45	1.43	1.27	1.57		

* Source: Fox (1953) p. 558. Output in millions of tons and price in dollars per bushel.

† Price in each exporting region is equal to the price in the importing region less transportation costs (with allowance for rounding). Transport costs are shown in italics.

‡ Reassigned arbitrarily from re-export via Corn Belt.

spects: (i) Demand for feed grain in each region is assumed to be a linear function of its price.[8] (ii) Production rather than capacity in each region is taken as given. Aside from these features, the model is similar to Henderson's. The United States is divided into ten regions according to the location of production and use. Transport costs are given as before, but prices are assumed to adjust in each region so as to equate demand and supply. Because the same demand function was used for all regions (with appropriate values of the predetermined variables inserted), the solution to the system turned out to be surprisingly simple despite the complicating factor of a nonlinear model. Apart from adjustments in the level of demand, the logic of the solution is the same as in Henderson's model and involves minimizing transportation costs. The result is shown in Table 12.9, which is similar in form to Table 12.8 but includes prices as well as quantities shipped.

We can compare these results to the optimum solution for coal movements. Even though transportation costs are a smaller fraction of total price in the present case, interregional shipments account for only 12% of total production as compared to 35% for coal. The difference is explainable largely by the fact that land for feed grain production is more universally available than coal resources (also somewhat fewer regions are used). Delivered prices of feed grain vary only from $1.17 per bushel to $1.57, which is much less than the range of 15¢ to 35¢ per million btu for coal. (In both cases, the highest price is on the Pacific Coast and depends on the cost of importing.)

An important factor, absent in nonagricultural commodities, which leads to short-run instability in supply patterns for feed is the variability of supplies due to weather. Fox shows that drought conditions such as those that have actually occurred would cause a very large change in production and in the optimum pattern of trade even though normal production patterns are quite stable.

3. Comparison of Linear Programming to Input-Output Results

These several results allow us to compare the input-output and programming approaches to regional analysis. Input-output assumes the persistence of both existing technical coefficients and existing supply patterns, while linear programming assumes that the most efficient adjustment will be made to changing conditions. Although we

[8] Demand also depends on the number of animals and their price in each region, but these are taken as given.

have not made an analysis of the last two cases using an input-output model for comparison, two features of the programming solutions are relevant to the design of such a model. First, in almost all cases it was shown to be efficient to utilize domestic resources fully before importing.[9] The use of this assumption in input-output analysis would therefore be justified in these two cases. Secondly, the stability of the flow patterns in the optimum solution is quite pronounced for coal. Although there was a marked drop in demand over the period analyzed, 29 of the 36 positive deliveries and unused capacitites were the same in all three years.

For making policy recommendations, the programming model is clearly to be preferred where data are available, but for analyzing the actual working of the economic system the choice is not so clear and may vary from sector to sector. Although Henderson did not make such a comparison, it is quite likely that a prediction of 1949 outputs based on 1947 supply patterns would have been closer to the actual result than the programming solution. Henderson tried to take account of the effects of labor union policy in a second calculation by lowering productive capacity in order to conform to the shorter work week imposed by the union. He thereby reduced the absolute net deviations between the calculated and actual results from 42 to 10% of the total demand. It may be that by introducing such qualifications to socially efficient behavior it will be possible to develop models that are superior, for predictive purposes, to either input-output or linear programming in their present forms.[10]

D. Uses of Interregional Analysis

As with all econometric models, the applicability of the various types of interregional analyses must be determined from their structure and from the stability of the parameters which can be estimated for them. Although supply coefficients on the whole are probably more variable than technical input-output coefficients, one can better ascertain in advance which supply coefficients are likely to be stable and which are not. There is no question of the stability of the co-

[9] Exceptions are shipments from regions 3 to 4 and from 2 to 7 in the coal analysis. These would be intraregional shipments in a more aggregated model.

[10] As Henderson points out, his solutions cannot be interpreted as being socially optimal because they do not take account of the varying social cost of unemployment in different regions.

efficients for noncommodity inputs which must be provided locally, and the mere division between local and nonlocal commodities, as suggested by Leontief, adds considerably to the realism of some applications of input-output models. For most manufactured goods, however, further studies of supply patterns over time are needed before we will know much about the extent of their variation.

The addition of a regional dimension to interindustry models makes the aggregation problem more acute because the data required increase with the square of the number of regions and the work of solution with the cube. Interregional models are therefore likely to be designed for special purposes, as in the examples we have discussed, rather than for general use. One way of reducing the costs of interregional models is to use a greater degree of aggregation for the multiregion analysis and a more detailed commodity breakdown within the single region which is of principal interest. For some studies, in which the given region is a small part of the total economy, the interregional repercussions may be ignored entirely without much loss of accuracy. The study of Utah by Moore and Peterson (1955), the study of the impact of steel development on a single region by Isard and Kuenne (1953), and the National Planning Association study of *Local Impacts of Foreign Trade* are examples of this sort.

With these considerations in mind, we can suggest four types of problem for which interregional interindustry analysis may be expected to be useful:

(1) *In determining the employment effects* on different regions of government expenditures or of other policies.

(2) *As a guide to regional development policy.* For this purpose, the model of the region concerned can be somewhat more detailed than the model for the rest of the economy. Where feasible, choice among sources of supply should be included for the more important sectors.

(3) *In the analysis of interregional and international trade.* Here the stability of supply coefficients is quite important and supplementary locational analyses will be needed if formal programming methods are not used. Where import controls are an instrument of government policy, however, supply patterns are more predictable and such models can be used to work out the implications of alternative policies.

(4) *In studying the efficiency of resource allocation among regions.* Although the studies of Henderson and Fox are the only ones of this

type known to us, it should be possible to make programming analyses of other homogeneous commodities having capacity limitations, such as steel or petroleum refining, and of resources which have alternative uses, such as agricultural land.

In all of these potential applications, the greatest initial benefit is likely to come from a better understanding of the phenomena involved and of the defects of simpler models rather than from the direct use of the numerical results in prediction or planning. In the long run, however, this type of study may succeed in integrating location theory[11] and regional planning into the main body of economic analysis in a way which has not yet been possible.

BIBLIOGRAPHY

Chenery, H., "Inter-regional and International Input-Output Analysis," in *The Structural Interdependence of the Economy*, 1956.

———, "Regional Analysis," in *The Structure and Growth of the Italian Economy*, 1953. (Published in Italian in *L'Industria*, No. 1, 3–26 (1953).)

Fox, K. A., "A Spatial Equilibrium Model of the Livestock-Feed Economy in the United States," *Econometrica*, XXI, No. 4, 547–566 (October 1953).

Freutel, G., "The Eighth District Balance of Trade," *Monthly Review*, Federal Reserve Board of St. Louis, June 1952.

Henderson, J. M., *The Efficiency of the Coal Industry*, Harvard University Press, Cambridge, 1958.

Isard, W., "Some Empirical Results and Problems of Regional Input-Output Analysis," in *Studies in the Structure of the American Economy*, 1953.

———, "Interregional and Regional Input-Output Analysis," *Review of Economics and Statistics*, XXXIII, No. 4, 318–328 (November 1951).

Isard, W., and R. Kuenne, "The Impact of Steel on the New York-Philadelphia Region," *Review of Economics and Statistics*, XXXV, No. 4, 289–301 (November 1953).

Lefeber, L., *Allocation in Space*, North-Holland Publishing Company, Amsterdam, 1958.

Leontief, W. (1953a), "Interregional Theory," in *Studies in the Structure of the American Economy*, 1953.

Manne, A. S., "A Crude Oil Allocation Problem," in *Scheduling Petroleum Refinery Operations*, Harvard University Press, Cambridge, 1956.

Moore, F. T., and J. W. Petersen, "Regional Analysis: An Interindustry Model of Utah," *Review of Economics and Statistics*, XXXVII, No. 4, 368–383 (November 1955).

[11] A restatement and extension of location theory using activity analysis has been given by Lefeber (1958) in a form suggesting possibilities for empirical applications.

Moses, L. N., "The Stability of Interregional Trading Patterns and Input-Output Analysis," *American Economic Review*, XLV, No. 5, 803–832 (December 1955).

National Planning Association, *Local Impacts of Foreign Trade* (forthcoming).

Neisser, H., and F. Modigliani, *National Incomes and International Trade*, University of Illinois Press, Urbana, 1953.

Samuelson, P. A., "Spatial Price Equilibrium and Linear Programming," *American Economic Review*, XLII, No. 3, 283–303 (June 1952).

University of Maryland, Bureau of Business and Economic Research, *A Regional Interindustry Study of Maryland*, September, 1954.

chapter 13

The future of interindustry analysis

Both the methods and the empirical bases of interindustry analysis have been considerably improved in recent years. The concepts of activity analysis permit a more rigorous statement of its theoretical foundations, and the increasing power of electronic computers makes it possible to think of solving systems containing hundreds of variables. On the empirical side, detailed input-output statistics have been collected for a considerable number of countries, and experiments have been made with activity analysis in individual sectors.

In contrast to these developments, relatively little attention has been given to practical applications of interindustry analysis. In the last several chapters, we have illustrated the types of application for which it promises to be most helpful. We suggest that further development of interindustry methods should concentrate on the uses for which this approach shows a real advantage over alternative techniques. These are problems which involve a pronounced departure from previous trends in one or more parts of the economy. Causes of such changes include an accelerated rise in income, industrialization, changes in world markets for imports and exports, introduction of new technology, and mobilization for defense. The design of an inter-industry analysis with a particular set of problems in mind has the advantage of providing criteria for defining the model and for select-ing the most important interindustry relations for empirical study.

The detailed model which characterizes the original form of input-output analysis has been both its strength and its weakness in em-pirical work. It has provided a comprehensive and internally consist-ent set of relationships which could actually be fitted with available statistical data, largely from census sources. On the other hand, the necessity of estimating a large number of input-output parameters has so far implied basing these estimates on one or two observations, with the result that it has been impossible to determine the stability of these parameters over time, or to introduce more complex relationships between inputs and outputs. The direct study of production func-tions for separate industries would probably make the greatest single improvement in the reliability of the interindustry approach. The several empirical studies reported in Chapters 6 and 8 suggest that the simple assumption of proportionality between input and output is likely to be acceptable for some industries and some commodities but not for others. Many ways of recognizing more complex relationships between inputs and outputs are available once an empirical basis for more realistic assumptions has been established.

The issue between input-output models and linear programming models loses much of its sharpness when we descend from the level of abstract theory to that of application. Input-output has several advantages for a descriptive analysis. Not only does linear program-ming require much more information than will be available for many sectors in the near future, but its assumption of optimization as a way of describing the complex effects of actual market forces is as yet un-tested. In choosing among alternative government policies, on the other hand, linear programming is clearly the better formulation be-cause it provides a systematic method for reaching an optimum solu-tion. The essential point, however, is that there is no inherent contra-diction between the two approaches, and that they can be combined whenever it seems both desirable and practicable. A given set of parameters in an input-output model represents one of many possible solutions to a more general linear programming model. The choice of activities can be either predetermined or based on a criterion function, or these alternatives can be used for different sectors in the same model. Such combined models seem promising for future applica-tions.

The main virtue of an interindustry formulation—whether input-output, linear programming, or a combination—is that it ensures consistent estimates of the effects of complicated structural changes. This result is achieved at the cost of considerable simplification of individual relations, necessitated by the handling of large amounts of data. In order to reduce the loss of information concerning variables other than the ones included in the interindustry model, it is important to analyze separately those aspects of production and final use which can be considered independently of the over-all solution. By methods of partial analysis, it is possible to take account of many of the effects of technological change, regional variation, changes in product-mix, and other factors not related to production levels. Even when there is some feedback from the overall solution to the choice of activities in a given sector, this repercussion can often be incorporated through a process of successive approximation. In short, the use of an interindustry model does not preclude separate analyses of important sectors, but rather serves to make the sector results consistent with each other.

The diversity of possible uses of the interindustry approach will probably require construction of special purpose models. Basic data should therefore be collected in considerable detail and aggregated with specific applications in mind. The size of the model used is likely to be limited in the future more by the difficulties of analyzing final demands for a large number of commodities than by the availability of interindustry data or computational facilities. This consideration suggests the use of models of fifty sectors or less for most purposes, but the type of aggregation needed for one purpose is likely to be somewhat different from that required by another. Aggregation is guided by similarities in the most important coefficients—for capital, labor, imports, interindustry flows, or elasticities of demand—and the relative importance of each of these varies with the problem in hand. Studies of individual sectors may require even greater variety in model design.

The diversity of interindustry applications also has implications for the task of organizing interindustry research. Government agencies must continue to play a leading role in the collection of basic data, as they do in all types of national accounting, and in developing applications that are primarily of use for government policy. These facts need not inhibit other workers in their use of the results, however. Before the U.S. government program was suspended, an extensive system of collaboration with universities had been established, and this has also been the case in other countries where a serious research program has been undertaken. Once the basic information has become generally available, a variety of new uses is likely to be found for interindustry techniques by workers in particular fields.

Interindustry analysis is one of the areas of economics in which formal models are being confronted with statistical measurements on an increasingly wide scale. The underlying general equilibrium theory is much more complex than the available data, and rather heroic assumptions are being made to bring the two together in exploratory models. Judging by recent work in a number of countries, however, the prospect of further progress in adapting models and empirical data to each other is good. Exploitation of the potentialities of the interindustry approach depends ultimately on experimentation with a variety of theoretical formulations and sources of data. For this reason, the introduction of competing models and the increasing diversity of applications should be regarded as signs of progress.

Index

Acceleration principle, in dynamic
    models, 71, 78, 79
  tests of, 71–72
Activity, axes, 89–90
  combined, 112–113
  concept of, 83–84, 97–98
  definition, 76, 84
  derived, 104
  determination of levels, 134
  disposal, 87
  in development program, 283–284
  level, 84, 119, 130
  mathematical representation, 84
  to be replaced, 119, 132
Activity analysis, 82–83, 126
Aggregation, and relative errors, 37–38
  conditions for, 30, 34
  in regional study, 330
Air Force, U.S., 72–73, 187
Algorithms, capacity of, 128
  features of, 116
  for nonlinear programming, 134
Allocation among regions, 330
America, see United States
Argentina, 185, 194–197, 210, 213,
    251, 267–271
Arrow, K. J., 86, 107, 134, 166, 177

Arrow, S., 168
Assider, 240
Assumption, of additivity, 34, 35, 88,
    103
  of complementarity, 40
  of linearity, 34, 85
  of no excess capacity, 77
  of no joint products, 17, 33
  of nonnegativity, 88
  of nonsubstitutability, 35
  of price stability, 41
  of proportionality, 88, 143–144
  of supply source, 67
Australia, 140, 153, 163, 185, 196,
    197, 202
Axes, activity, 89–90, 92
  choice of, 92
  input, 90, 92
  output, 90–92

Balance equation, 18–19
Balance in development, 281
Balance of payments, 268
Balderston, J. B., 2
Baldwin, R. E., 280
Barna, T., 34, 192
Barnett, H. J., 168–169

Basic theorem, 97
Basis, 97, 98, 119
Berman, E. B., 161, 251
Boundary, 95, 96
Buchanan, N. S., 280
Budgetary data, 148
Bureau of the Budget, 187
Bureau of Mines, 187
Business Economics, Office of, 187

Cameron, B., 163, 164, 194
Cao-Pinna, V., 177, 191, 211, 234, 252, 264, 310, 312
Capacity, 71, 72, 152, 252, 254, 255, 261, 274, 275
Capital, as constraint in Southern Italy, 291
  coefficient, 72, 79, 100, 149–150, 151
  formation in dynamic models, 71–73
  requirements in U.S. for exports and imports, 242, 244
  requirements for interindustry model, 147
  scarcity in underdeveloped regions, 280
  structure, 149
  U.S. emergency model, 272
Capital-use models, Italy, 191
Japan, 193
Capital-building activity, 72–73
Carter, A., 127, 159
Cassel, G., 2
Charnes, A., 116, 117, 130, 133
Chenery, H. B., 70, 72, 134, 155, 201, 211–213, 281–282, 288, 290, 298, 301, 318
Chile, 194
Chipman, J., 64, 105
Christ, C. F., 157, 166
Clark, C., 206, 208
Clark, P. G., 177, 252, 310, 312
Classification, problem of, 138
  see Aggregation
Coal industry, regional study, 310, 324
Coefficients, as physical or value ratios, 41
  capital, 72, 79, 100, 149–150, 151
  import, 23

Coefficients, input, 22, 100, 143–145, 157, 159–164
  regional supply, 67, 100
  stability of, 163, 177–178, 189, 193
Colombia, 7, 185, 194–197, 213, 251, 267–269, 271
Commodity, in activity analysis, 83
  quality as constraint, 85
Comparative advantage, 241, 245–246
Competitive imports, 142
Complementarity, 40
Conrad, A. H., 247
Constraint, definition for activity analysis, 85
  in development programs, 291
  in emergency model, 274
  in feasibility analysis, 252, 272
  use in input-output and linear programming, 250
  see Capacity
Consumption function, 147
Consumption in regional model, 68
Control total, 140, 145
Convexity, 98
Cooper, W. W., 116, 117, 130, 133
Cornfield, J., 168–169, 186, 251
Cost, of input-output studies, 196
  of inverse matrix, 33
  opportunity, 63, 125
Council for Economic and Industry Research, 188
Criterion, for allocation in development, 281, 288
  in activity analysis, 86
  simplex, see Simplex criterion
Critical materials, 162
Crosson, P., 152
Cumberland, J. H., 163

Dantzig, G., 3, 87, 116, 118, 130, 133
Demand, estimates of total, 29
  export elasticities, 147
  factor, 57–59
  final, 15–20, 24, 29
  government, 148, 272
  import elasticities, 147
  in regional model, 68
Denmark, 3, 7, 184, 189, 197, 213, 246

Development programs and planning, 281, 300
Disposal activities, 87, 92, 124
Dorfman, R., 2, 31, 34, 39, 46, 60, 74, 82, 88, 112, 116, 124, 130, 135, 157, 324
Dual theorem, 124
Dwyer, P. S., 50–51

Economic Commission for Europe, 234
Economic Commission for Latin America, 194, 195, 196, 251, 268
Efficiency, of economy, 106
single-factor measures, 110
Efficient combination, 107, 110
Ellis, H. S., 280
Ellsworth, P. T., 243
Emergency model, see United States, emergency model
Employment, effects of policy on, 330
Italy, 238, 239, 252
Japan, 193
requirement, see Labor, requirement
U.S. emergency model, 275
Energy requirements, 172, 265, 273
Equivalent combination, 116–117, 132
Errors, in Italian study, 257, 259
in Japanese study, 176
of alternative projections in U.S., 166–168, 170–173
Estimation of parameters, 143, 154
Evans, W. D., 22, 23, 26, 30, 31, 33, 43, 44, 46, 58, 143, 165, 168–169, 186, 241, 251
Expansion, balanced, 150
in powers, 150
Exports, choice in activity analysis, 284–285, 292
estimation of, 153, 154
in open model, 152

Fabricant, S., 166
Factor, intensity, 58–60
price, 61, 124
total use of, 59–60
Feasibility, analysis, 252, 271
of dynamic program, 77
tested by projection, 250
Feasible area, 95, 96

Feasible basic set of activities, 130
Final demand, see Demand
Final output, price of, 124–125
Final use, see Demand
Fisher, W. D., 34, 38
Foreign exchange, and optimum solution, 293
as primary factor, 291
as scarce factor, 280, 288
equation, 285
Fox, K. A., 310, 323, 326–328, 330
France, 185
Freutel, G., 309
Frisch, R., 299
Fuel, projections in Italy, 252–254, 264–265

Galenson, W., 283
Gauss-Seidel method of iteration, 44–46, 211
Georgescu-Roegen, N., 105, 107
Gibrat, R., 299
Gilboy, E. W., 148
Goldstein, H., 152
Goodwin, R. M., 64
Gosfield, A., 195
Government expenditure, 252, 257
Government policies, 334–335
Grosse, R. N., 150

Harvard Economic Research Project, 127, 148, 187, 188, 241 ff., 247, 311
Hatanaka, M., 173, 175, 176
Hawkins, D., 71
Heady, E. O., 240
Heckscher-Ohlin theorem, 241
Helzner, M. L., 162
Henderson, A., 116, 117, 130, 133
Henderson, J. M., 299, 310, 323–326, 328–330
Hitchcock-Koopmans transportation model, 326
Hoffenberg, M., 166–169, 172–173, 177, 186, 251
Holley, J., 71–72, 79
Holzman, M., 34
Horton, H. R., 211
Hurwicz, L., 157, 177

Ichimura, S., 192
Import content of final demand, 192–193
Import function, 23–24
Import matrix, 195
Imports, 18, 100, 142, 154, 235, 238–240, 241, 252, 254, 262–264, 268, 273, 284–285, 292, 293
Import substitution, 284
Income, distribution between regions in Italy, 316
  generated in regional model, 70
  generation in dynamic models, 71
  generation in U.S. and Italy, 321
India, 8, 185, 197, 202, 278
Industry, census of, 140
  classification, 138, 214
  concept of, 16, 22, 35, 83
  fictitious, 273
  local: nonlocal, 311, 315–316, 318, 320
  see Sector
Input function, aggregation, 33
  form of, 22
  stability, 33
Input-lead times, 73, 274
Input-output accounts, relation to national income accounts, 19
Input-output tables, design of, 138, 140, 197
Inputs, primary, 15–19
  produced, 15, 17
  time trend, 172
  unallocated, 144
  see Coefficients
Interindustry use, ratio of, 15
Intermediate points, 104
Intermediate use, 15–19, 29, 203
Internal Revenue, Bureau of, 152
International trade, analysis, 241
  models, 309, 330
Interregional models, 65–70, 309, 330
Inventory, depletion, 100
  in dynamic model, 72
Inverse matrix, applications, 233, 240
  as general solution, 31
  calculation of factor intensities, 58
  cost, 33
  disadvantages, 32
  to Leontief matrix, 214

Investment, 26
  allocation over time, 77
  and relative prices, 297
  as final demand, 315
  feasibility, 77
  projection, 273
  replacement, 152
  see Capital
Investment programs, 149
Isard, W., 66, 311–314, 319, 330
Isocost lines, 116
Isoquant, 90–92, 114–116
Israel, 186, 197
Italy, basic data, 213
  classification of industries, 206
  comparison of structure of production, 202
  data for projections, 268
  design of table, 197
  five-year expansion goals, 251–266
  industry studies, 234, 240
  input-output tables, 184, 218
  inverse matrix, 226
  offshore procurement in, 204, 235, 238
  policy uses of table, 197
  ratios of interindustry use, 230
  test of table, 176
  treatment of imports, 154, 274
  triangularity of matrix, 46, 210
Italy, Southern, development possibilities, 279
Iterative procedure, 46

Japan, classification of industry, 206
  comparative analysis, 138, 202
  description of 1951, 1954, 1955 tables, 185, 196–197
  factor proportions and final demand, 245
  import coefficients, 155
  inverse matrix, 224
  labor inputs, 153
  ratios of interindustry use, 230
  recent development, 196
  similarity to U.S., 213
  statistical conventions, 193
  statistical quality, 205, 261
  table for 1951, 192, 216–217
  testing of coefficients, 160, 193

Japan, test of input-output projections, 177
  test of stability of coefficients, 260
  trade analysis, 153
  treatment of investment, 203
  triangularity of matrix, 46
  use of activity basis, 193
  use of production classification, 139
Jones, R. W., 241

Kahn, A., 281
Kemeny, J. G., 46
Keynesian system, 5, 25–32, 52
Klein, L. R., 41–42, 46
Komiya, R., 245
Koopmans, T., 3, 83, 85, 87, 107, 116, 123, 130, 157
Kretschmer, K., 211, 290, 301, 305
Kuenne, R., 2, 330
Kuh, E., 72
Kuhn, H., 135
Kuhn-Tucker theorem, 292
Kuznets, S., 267–268

Labor, effect of cost on solution, 294
  equation, 285, 288
  requirement, estimation of, 153
  requirement for expansion of U.S. trade, 242, 244
  requirement in Italy, 238, 255, 266
  treatment of, 291
  underemployment and distortion, 280
  use shown graphically, 89–90
Labor Statistics, Bureau of, projection for 1950, 169
  relation to U.S. studies, 186–187
  table for 1939, 159
Latin America, 8, 194–195
Lead time, 274
Leakage, 31
Lefeber, L., 331
Leibenstein, H., 283
Leontief, W., 2–3, 22, 33–34, 39, 60–62, 66, 188, 213, 233–234, 314, 330
  assumption on national commodities, 312, 315
  assumptions, 33–34, 40, 42, 71, 74, 100, 157, 164, 174

Leontief, W., comparative advantage study, 241–246
  interregional analysis, 311
  matrix, 49, 51–52, 56–57, 84, 88, 214
  model, 4–6, 16, 22–25, 33–34, 41–42, 72, 74, 77, 81–84, 86–87, 89, 93, 100, 105, 107, 110, 112, 117, 125, 129, 146, 155, 285
  model, solution of, 31
  prices, 117
  tables for 1919 and 1929, 159
  test of coefficients, 159
Lewis, W. A., 280
Liebling, H. I., 20–21
Linear programming, and allocation in Southern Italy, 279
  and capital requirements, 71
  and data requirements, 299
  and investment, 74
  definition, 85
  disadvantages, 334
  general problem, 86
  in application to whole economy, 300
  uses of, 83
Livestock feed, regional study, 310

Manne, A. S., 127–128, 323–324
Marketing analyses, 240
Markowitz, H., 127–128, 177
Marshall, representative firm, 35
  system, 45
Massé, P., 299
Matrix, addition of, 48
  definition, 46
  diagonal, 47
  form of solution, 50
  identity, 47
  imports, 48
  inversion, 49, 51
  iterative solutions, 52
  Leontief, square, 47, 49, 51
  multiplication, 48
  of dynamic model, 77, 79
  technological, 47, 84
  triangularity, 44
Meier, G. M., 280
Metzler, L. A., 66

Mexico, 7, 185, 194
Meyer, J., 72
Military procurement, treatment of, 272
Mobilization and labor requirements, 152
Models, illustrative:
 Model I, 27–32
 Model II, Income generation, 63–64
 Model III, Regional, 68–70
 Model IV, Capacity building, 74–77
 Model V, Choice among final uses, 93–94
 Model VI, Choice of technology, 101–102
 Model VII, Choice of technology, 119–123, 131
 Model VIII, Development programming, 285–288
Modigliani, F., 209–211
Molinari, A., 295
Moore, F. T., 146, 309
Morgenstern, O., 188
Moses, L. N., 309–310, 312, 319–322
Multiple regression projection, 174–175
Multiplier, 64, 245

National accounts, and feasibility, 250–251
 relation to input-output, 19–21
National Accounts Review Committee, report, 141
National Planning Association, 330
Neisser, H., 309–311
Netherlands, government planning, 190, 197
 import quotas, 241
 input-output analysis, 3, 7, 184, 197
 projections, 145, 251
New Zealand, 185
Noncompetitive imports, 142
Nonproportionality, in fuel analysis, 253
 in treatment of imports, 273
 input functions in Italy, 191
 of consumption function, 148
Norway, agriculture, 187
 comparative analysis, 202, 238

Norway, current research, 7, 184, 196–197, 202–206, 213, 214
 exports, 234
 industry studies, 234
 input structure, 188
 linear programming for whole economy, 299
 trade analysis, 153, 189
 triangularity of matrix, 46
 wage-price relationship, 189
Notation in linear programming, 130
Nurkse, R., 281, 297

Objective function, 86, 93, 97, 99, 125, 291
 see Criterion
Offshore procurement in Italy, 234, 235, 238
Optimal point, 96
Outputs, unallocated, 142

Pareto, W., 1–2
Peru, interindustry study, 185, 194–195, 197
 international comparison, 213
Petersen, J. W., 309
Petroleum refining study (Manne), 127
Phillips, A., 142, 163
Planning, Italy, 191
 Netherlands, 190
 use in countries, 197
Poland, 186
Policy use, see Planning
Predictions, 6–7
Prices, accounting, see Prices, shadow
 and input functions, 42
 changes in Denmark, 189
 changes in Italy, 262
 changes in Norway, 188
 commodity, 62
 determination in input-output, 60, 62
 effects of profits on, 62
 effect of wages on, 62
 equations, 61
 implicit, see Prices, shadow
 imputed, see Prices, shadow
 Leontief computation, 61

Prices, producers' system, 141–142
  purchasers' system, 141–142
  shadow, 117–119, 124, 126, 130
  solution, 124
Princeton University, 188
Process analysis, 128–129
Production, alternative techniques, 100
  in dynamic system, 78
  stages of, 38
  techniques in dynamic models, 71
Production function, 24, 39, 40, 41–
  42, 91, 102, 147, 155
Production possibility curve, 91
Product mix, and input coefficients, 42
  changes, 145
  changes in Norway, 188
Products, by-products, 145
  primary, 138, 206–208
    multiple, 139–140
  secondary, 139, 206–208
  tertiary, 206–208
Profitability, 118, 119, 122, 132
Program, definition, 85, 86
Programming, nonlinear, 135
Programs of action, 6–7, 197
Projections, final demand, 251, 252,
  271
  for Colombia and Argentina, 267–
    271
  for development, 281, 300
  for Italy, 255–267
  for Japan, 192
  for U.S., 271–276
Projects, evaluation of, 300
Proportionality, assumption, 88, 266
Puerto Rico, 185, 194, 196, 278

Rand Corporation, 188
Rasmussen, P. N., 189, 213, 246
Rectangularity, advantages, 139–140
  in Australian table, 194
  in Italian table, 191, 194
  in Japanese table, 194
Regional balance of payments, 316
Regional development policy, 330
Regional model, coal, 323–326
  evaluation of, 328, 331
  feed grain, 326–328
  formation of, 65
  Italy, 191, 317–318

Regional model, stability of coefficients,
  66, 322–323
  United States, 318–323
Replacement investment, estimation
  of, 152
Requirements, 15–20, 24, 29
Resources, price of, 124
  supply in development, 281
  unused, 94
Restriction, *see* Constraint
Robinson, R., 241, 243
Rosentein-Rodan, P., 281, 297
Russia, information, 186

Samuelson, P. A., 2, 31, 34, 39, 44,
  46, 60, 74, 82, 107, 112, 116,
  124, 135, 324, 326
Sandee, J., 241
Scarce factor approach, 282
Schnittker, J. A., 240
Schouten, D. B. J., 241
Scitovsky, T., 297
Secondary products, 139, 206–208
Sector, 16, 22
  categories of, 208
  classification, 138
  criteria for, 33
  government, 148
  hierarchy of, 210
  household, 148
  part of transactions matrix, 14
  producing, 29
  projections in development, 281,
    300
  relation between, 213
  using, 29
Sevaldson, P., 177, 234
Shephard, R., 177
Shishido, S., 177, 245
Side analyses, 146, 253, 265, 272, 274,
  275
Simplex criterion, 98, 117, 118, 119,
  123, 134, 298
Slack vector, 87
Snell, J. L., 46
Solow, R., 2, 31, 34, 39, 46, 60, 74,
  82, 112, 116, 124, 235, 324
Solution, accuracy, 28, 30, 31, 46
  basic, 97, 99, 116, 130
  disadvantages of general, 32

Solution, elementary, 112, 114
  existence of, 31
  extrapolation formula for, 30
  feasible, 86, 116
  feasible basic, 119
  general, 25, 31–32, see also Inverse
    matrix
  incremental, 46
  iterative methods, 25–33
  method of substitution, 43
  nonbasic, 99
  nonlinear programming, 135, 293–
    294
  of dynamic system, 77–78
  optimum, 96–99, 115, 116, 124
  particular, 26
  price, 118, 120–121, 124, 131
  prices at optimum, 298
  quantity, 119, 123–124, 131
  regional, 68, 70
  simplex, 116–124, 130–134
Sonenblum, S., 152
Spain, 185, 186
Stability of coefficients, 163, 177–178,
    189, 193
Stanford University, 188
Structural analysis, 6–7, 232–233
Sub-analyses, use of, 146, 242
Substitution, and aggregation, 34
  in manufacturing, 42
Substitution theorem, 107–108
Supply in interregional model, 70, 100
Sweden, 186
Swerling, B. C., 243

Tarshis, L., 246
Taxes, 17
Technological change, 42, 111, 127,
    188
Technological efficiency, 104
Technology matrix, 84
Teitelbaum, P., 152
Terms of trade between industries,
    189
Tests of input coefficients, 159–164
Tests of input-output projections, 165–
    167, 169–170, 172–178
Theil, H., 34
Thompson, G. L., 461
Tinbergen, J., 281, 300

Trade, in Italy, 191
  in Latin America, 194
  in the United States, 188
  sector, 141
Transactions, artificial, 203
Transactions matrix, 14
Transformation curve, 91
Transportation sector, 141
Tucker, A. W., 135

Unallocated inputs and outputs, 142
Unit, choice of, 18
United Kingdom, 8, 196, 197, 184–185
United States, application of input-
    output, 187, 197, 233–234
  capital requirements, 149–153
  comparative advantage, 241–245
  comparative analysis, 138, 178, 202,
    210
  emergency model, 153–154, 186–
    187, 271–275
  foreign trade study, 188
  government research program, 149,
    161–162, 186–187
  import coefficients, 154
  industry studies, 234, 240
  input-output tables, 159, 184, 203–
    208, 222
  interindustry projections, 251, 271 ff.
  Interindustry Research Program,
    149 ff., 161, 162, 251, 271 ff.
  interregional study, 311–312
  inverse matrix, 229
  price analysis, 246
  study of full employment, 251
  test of stability of coefficients, 159–
    161
  tests of input-output projections,
    166, 169, 172, 173 ff., 177
United States Mission to Italy, 191
University of Maryland, 309
Urbanization, cost, 295
Utah, regional study, 330
Uzawa, H., 134

Vajda, S., 88
Valavanis-Vail, S., 243
Valuation of resources, see Prices
Value, gross, of activity, 118
  of a program, 94

Value, one-factor theory of, 61
Value added, breakdown in Australia,
    194
  concept of, 17, 19, 29
Van den Beld, C. A., 251
Vector, as activity, 76
  column, 47
  row, 47
Verdoorn, P. J., 241

Wages, effect on prices in United
    Kingdom, 192

Wagner, H., 74
Wald, A., 2
Walrasian system (model), 1–3, 22,
    35, 143
War economics, 275–276
Watanabe, T., 201, 211–213
Whitin, T. M., 34
Wood, M., 211

Yamada, I., 192
Yugoslavia, 7, 185, 197